EXPLORING HUMAN NATURE

Sidestone Press

EXPLORING HUMAN NATURE

A REFLEXIVE MIXED METHODS ENQUIRY
INTO SOLO TIME IN THE WILDERNESS

© 2018 Jana Lemke

Published by Sidestone Press, Leiden
   www.sidestone.com

Imprint: Sidestone Press Dissertations

Lay-out & cover design: Sidestone Press
Photograph cover: © mooshny - stock.adobe.com

ISBN 978-90-8890-558-2 (softcover)
ISBN 978-90-8890-559-9 (hardcover)
ISBN 978-90-8890-560-5 (PDF e-book)

> There are many ways one can go on a solo journey
>
> to the wilderniss beyond and the wilderniss within.
>
> If one understands the complex circles of life
>
> and the connectedness of all things,
>
> then going outside and going inside
>
> is really the same journey.
>
> (Smith, 2005)

Contents

1 Introduction   **19**

    1.1 Current situation and problem statement   *19*

    1.2 Outlook for the present work   *21*

    1.3 Self-reflective preface   *22*

2 The human-nature relationship through the lens of contemporary science   **25**

    2.1 The emotional and social dimension of human care for nature   *25*

       2.1.1 The influence of emotions   25
       2.1.2 Coping mechanisms and the role of hope   28
       2.1.3 The human disposition to imitate   32
       2.1.4 The influence of social norms   35
       2.1.5 Environmental identity and the social environment   36

    2.2 The relational and experiential dimension of human care for nature   *38*

       2.2.1 Environmental identity and the experience of nature   38
       2.2.2 Nature connectedness   39
       2.2.3 Formative experiences in the course of life   43
       2.2.4 Transcendence and the human experience of nature   45

3 The human-nature relationship through the lens of an expanded worldview   **51**

    3.1 A brief history of the human-nature relationship   *52*

    3.2 Expanding the contemporary worldview   *54*

       3.2.1 A critical examination of the contemporary worldview   54
       3.2.2 A brief introduction to deep ecology   56

    3.3 An ancient practice revisited – Solos in nature   *58*

       3.3.1 Introduction   58
       3.3.2 The structure of the Solo as a rite of passage   59
       3.3.3 Research findings   61

4 Mixed methods enquiry of immersive experiences in wild nature — 65

4.1 Overarching aims and objectives — 65

4.2 Extracted hypotheses and research questions — 67
    4.2.1 Quantitative research questions and hypotheses — 67
    4.2.2 Qualitative research questions — 68
    4.2.3 Mixed methods research question — 68

4.3 Method — 69
    4.3.1 Introduction to the mixed methods approach — 69
    4.3.2 The applied mixed methods approach — 70
    4.3.3 Evaluated programmes — 75
    4.3.4 Sample description and data collection — 79
    4.3.5 Quantitative research strand — 83
    4.3.6 Qualitative research strand — 100
    4.3.7 Expanding the view of validity — 106
    4.3.8 Self-reflection on different ways of knowing in the research process — 109

4.4 Results — 112
    4.4.1 Phenomenology and underlying processes of immersive experiences in wild nature — 112
    4.4.2 Further emergent contributing features and processes of the Butterfly Effect programme — 131
    4.4.3 Qualitative evaluation of the long-term effects of the Butterfly Effect programme — 138
    4.4.4 Quantitative immediate effects — 152
    4.4.5 Quantitative long-term changes — 161
    4.4.6 Exploring quantitative patterns of change — 166
    4.4.7 The influence of the control variables — 176

5 Intuitive dream enquiry — 179

5.1 Introduction — 179

5.2 Distilling the objective of the dream study — 183

5.3 Method — 184
    5.3.1 Outline of the intersubjective-heuristic method — 184
    5.3.2 Sample — 186
    5.3.3 Dream data — 187
    5.3.4 Applied elements and stages of the intersubjective-heuristic method — 187

5.4 Results	*188*
5.4.1 Results of the intersubjective-heuristic enquiry	188
5.4.2 Results of the applied thematic analysis	199
5.5 Discussion	*202*
5.5.1 The interface between results	202
5.5.2 Dreams as data and methodological considerations	204

6 Overall discussion   209

6.1 Summary and integration of survey, interview and dream data   *209*
    6.1.1 Phenomenology of immersive experiences in wild nature   209
    6.1.2 Short- and long-term programme evaluation outcomes   213
    6.1.3 Activism as part of the long-term results   218
    6.1.4 Interconnectedness and separateness as meta-level outcomes   220

6.2 Further elaborations of selected outcomes   *222*
    6.2.1 Nature experience   222
    6.2.2 The social dimension of nature experiences   228
    6.2.3 Meaning-making   229

6.3 Methodological considerations   *231*

6.4 Self-reflection on the research process   *236*

7 Conclusion   241

7.1 Practical implications   *242*

7.2 Closing words   *243*

References   245

Appendices   263

Appendix A   *263*

Appendix B   *264*

Appendix C   *265*

Acknowledgements   271

List of tables

Table 1.	Emotions and associated thought-action tendencies	27
Table 2.	Distribution of age and gender in the Butterfly interview sample	80
Table 3.	Distribution of age and gender in the Butterfly survey sample	81
Table 4.	Distribution of nationalities and residential areas in the survey sample	81
Table 5.	Past contact with nature during childhood in the Butterfly survey sample	82
Table 6.	Distribution of age and gender in the Solo-only interview sample	83
Table 7.	Distribution of age, gender and original residential area in the Solo-only PCI sample	83
Table 8.	Subscales of the Coping with Global Environmental Problems (GEP) Scale by Homburg et al. (2007)	85
Table 9.	Subscales of the Emotional Affinity toward Nature (EAN) measure by Kals et al. (1999)	87
Table 10.	Sample items of the Connectedness to Nature Scale (CNS) by Mayer and Frantz (2004)	87
Table 11.	Subscales of the Life Values Inventory (LVI) by Brown and Crace (1996)	88
Table 12.	Subscale sample items of Miller's Hope Scale (MHS)	89
Table 13.	Sample items for Trust, Gratitude (GRA) and Capacity for Love (CAP) from the International Personality Item Pool (IPIP)	90
Table 14.	Sample items for each of the applied subscales of the Civic Attitudes and Skills Questionnaire (CASQ)	91
Table 15.	Sample items for the applied subscales of the Individual Community-Related Empowerment (ICRE) scale	92
Table 16.	Sample items of the Proenvironmental Behaviour (PEB) Scale	93
Table 17.	Sample items of the Social Desirability Scale-17 (SDS-17)	93
Table 18.	Subscales and sample items of the Sense of Community Index II (SCI-2)	94

Table 19.	The 26 Dimensions of the Phenomenology of Consciousness Inventory (PCI), Clustered into 12 Major Dimensions	95
Table 20.	Personal guidelines for the process of data collection	100
Table 21.	Main areas of focus according to the interview samples	102
Table 22.	Sample size, interview length and interview setting categorised by interview sample	103
Table 23.	Roles and effects of the Solo intention on the participants' Solo time	119
Table 24.	Means (standard deviations) of the PCI dimensions for the Solo, religious, happy and ordinary experience	122
Table 25.	Effect sizes (Cohen's d) for the differences of mean between the Solo experience versus the religious, happy and ordinary experience	123
Table 26.	Two-sided non-parametric Spearman correlations between the major dimensions of the PCI	129
Table 27.	Summary of statistical parameters for the implemented scales assessing the participants' relationship with nature	154
Table 28.	Statistical parameters for each value	156
Table 29.	Statistical parameters of the (sub-) scales assessing the participants' attitude towards others and life	158
Table 30.	Statistical parameters of the test results for each subscale of the Civic Attitudes and Skills Questionnaire (CASQ)	160
Table 31.	Overview of constructs, sample size, p-values and effect sizes	164
Table 32.	Mean, standard deviation and median of overall programme evaluation items	166
Table 33.	Significant correlations of community participation	167
Table 34.	Significant correlations with proenvironmental behaviour	168
Table 35.	Multiple regression model for the participants' proenvironmental behaviour one and a half years after the Butterfly programme	169
Table 36.	Significant correlations for activism, concern for the environment and nature connectedness	170
Table 37.	Significant correlations with two styles of coping with environmental problems	171
Table 38.	Multiple regression model for the coping style Problem Solving	171
Table 39.	Significant correlations with the participants' gain of responsibility	173

Table 40.	Significant correlations with participants' increase of self-efficacy	173
Table 41.	Significant correlations with the participants' increase of hope	174
Table 42.	Significant correlations with the participants' sense of community	175
Table 43.	Significant correlations between control variables and relevant differential values	177
Table 44.	Composition of the dream sample	187
Table 45.	Stages of application of the intersubjective-heuristic enquiry	188
Table 46.	Emergent pairs of opposites in the dream contents	200

List of figures

Figure 1. The global-local visual processing task in Fredrickson and Branigan's (2005) study. Harré (2011) after Fredrickson and Branigan (2005). — 26
Figure 2. Overall research process and design. — 71
Figure 3. Applied evaluation model and design. — 73
Figure 4. The Inclusion of Nature in Self (INS) scale by Schultz (2001). — 84
Figure 5. Overview of the assessed constructs at the various points of measurement. — 98
Figure 6. Scribble while daydreaming about, "What is real?" — 112
Figure 7. Dimensions of interconnectedness with nature according to their frequency of occurrence and setting. — 117
Figure 8. The participants' process in nature leading to self-access and insights based on within-code relationships. — 120
Figure 9. Intergroup comparison of means for the subdimensions of Altered Experience. — 124
Figure 10. Intergroup comparison of means for the subdimensions of Attention. — 125
Figure 11. Intergroup comparison of means for the subdimensions of Imagery. — 126
Figure 12. Intergroup comparison of means for the subdimensions of Negative Affect. — 127
Figure 13. Intergroup comparison of means for the subdimensions of Positive Affect. — 127
Figure 14. Intergroup comparison of means for the dimensions Altered State of Awareness, Self-Awareness, Arousal and Internal Dialogue. — 128
Figure 15. Intergroup comparison of means for the dimensions Memory, Rationality and Volitional Control. — 128
Figure 16. The initiated process and context of sharing stories according to code co-occurrence and code frequency. — 135
Figure 17. Comparison of code occurrences in the area of "community experience" across samples. — 137
Figure 18. Butterfly participants' perceived triggers of the implemented actions. — 149

Figure 19.	Comparison of code occurrences in the areas of assessed changes across samples.	151
Figure 20.	Boxplots of pre- and posttest scores for the eight subscales of the Coping with Global Environmental Problems (GEP) Scale.	153
Figure 21.	Effect size r for detected increases of value activation.	155
Figure 22.	Effect size r for detected decreases of value activation.	156
Figure 23.	Boxplots of pre- and posttest scores for overall hope.	157
Figure 24.	Boxplots of pre- and posttest scores for the subscale Satisfaction with Self, Others and Life (SSOL).	157
Figure 25.	Boxplots of pre- and posttest scores for the subscale Avoidance of Hope Threats (AHT).	158
Figure 26.	Boxplots depicting the changes in the distribution for gratitude, capacity for love and trust.	158
Figure 27.	Effect size r for changes on the empowerment subscales.	160
Figure 28.	Boxplots depicting the development of Inclusion of Nature in Self (INS) across time.	161
Figure 29.	Boxplots depicting the development of proenvironmental behaviour (PEB scale) across time.	162
Figure 30.	Boxplots depicting the development of community participation (ICRE scale) across time.	163
Figure 31.	Boxplots depicting contact with nature across time.	164
Figure 32.	Boxplots for the rating of the overall programme evaluation items.	165
Figure 33.	Boxplots for change of hope over time split by gender.	177
Figure 34.	Boxplots for change of gratitude over time split by gender.	177
Figure 35.	Kerr and Key's adaptation (2011) of Jahn and Dunne's (2001) model of mind-matter interactions. Kerr & Key (2011) after Jahn & Dunne (2001).	180
Figure 36.	Sketch of my experiences in the focusing session (left) and of the figure used as an evaluation tool for participants at the end of the Butterfly programme (right).	190
Figure 37.	Illustrations of the phases immanent in rites of passage (left) and Kerr and Key's (2011) adaptation of Jahn and Dunne's (2001) model of mind-matter interactions (right).	191
Figure 38.	Dreams assigned to the different phases of the Hero's Journey.	195

Figure 39.	Illustrations depicting Kerr and Key's (2011) adaptation of Jahn and Dunne's (2001) model of mind-matter interactions (left), the phases of rites of passage (middle) and the Ouroboros snake (right).	198
Figure 40.	Emergent pattern of dream themes.	201
Figure 41.	Summary of the phenomenology of immersive experiences in wild nature across data sources.	211
Figure 42.	Summary of the short- and long-term evaluation outcomes across data sources.	214
Figure 43.	Summary of reported activism across data sources.	219
Figure 44.	Interconnectedness and separateness as emergent throughout the thesis.	221
Figure 45.	My epistemological understanding derived from my experience of the present research process.	238

1

Introduction

1.1 Current situation and problem statement

It is now a well-known fact that numerous of the environmental problems that we observe such as global warming, the extinction of species, deforestation and desertification, are caused by our contemporary lifestyle.

The Intergovernmental Panel on Climate Change (2014) confirmed that

> *human influence on the climate system is clear, and recent anthropogenic emissions of greenhouse gases are the highest in history. […] Their effects, together with other anthropogenic drivers, have been detected throughout the climate system and are extremely likely to have been the dominant cause of the observed warming since the mid-20th century.* (p.1)

However, strictly speaking, the problems that we face go way beyond "environmental problems". After all, global environmental change unavoidably entails a great number of implications for human well-being, too. The environmental pollution of air, soil and water, for instance, is found to increase the risk of cancer (Fajersztaijn, Veras, Barrozo, & Saldiva, 2013) as well as to harm cognitive functioning (Gatto *et al.*, 2014). Reversely, humans seem to highly benefit from the mere exposure to nature (e.g. see review by Bratman, Hamilton & Daily, 2012) as a study with more than 10,000 participants showed. Urban residents who lived in areas with more green spaces reported lower levels of mental distress and higher life satisfaction. This was the case even after controlling for various alternative explanations such as, for instance, income, age and marriage (White, Alcock, Wheeler, & Depledge, 2013). Indeed, in times of stress, nature represents an essential health resource as it helps humans to restore attention (Kaplan & Kaplan, 1989). This has been demonstrated in a famous hospital study, which revealed that the recovery process after surgery went more favourably when patients were able to view elements of nature from their hospital room (Ulrich, 1984). Notably, direct interactions with the natural world, such as socialising and living within nature, have been shown to not only contribute to a sense of connection to nature (Howell, Passmore, & Buro, 2012) but also to a sense of connection to community (Helliwell & Putnam, 2004).

While these benefits and implications of global environmental change are rather anthropocentrically oriented, public surveys additionally reveal that people also value the natural world and feel that the extinction of species and biodiversity diminishes human experience (Oskamp, 2000). Studies have shown that many young people experience concern, worry, sadness, anger, helplessness and pessimism with regard to environmental problems and the global future (e.g. see Threadgold, 2012).

These are only a few of the facts that demonstrate that environmentally harmful lifestyles are, in the long run, quite literally synonymous with self-abusive behaviour. The discrepancy between acknowledging the problem, on the one hand, and applying a lifestyle and worldview that persistently contributes to it, on the other hand, reveals the psychological dimension of the problem we are facing. The exploitation of the natural resources is driven by short-term self-interest instead of enforcing the long-term interest of the world (Oskamp, 2000). Clearly, we are not only dealing with environmental issues but over and above with a societal one that prevents us from connecting the dots and from perceiving the bigger picture.

Therefore, it appears to be thoughts, values, beliefs and worldviews that are crucial and need to be tackled in order to change course (Winter & Koger, 2004). As Winter and Koger (2004) put it, "we will also have to make psychological changes: changes in the way we behave, see ourselves, see our relationship to nature, and even, perhaps, the way we see the meaning of our lives (p. 3)." Hence, the artificial separation between humans and the rest of the world not only brings about natural destruction but also psychological consequences, as Hillman and Ventura (1999) summarise in the question "How can we be healthy in an unhealthy world?" (p. 33). It is in this context that biologist and cultural scientist Weber (2013) calls the global situation a "crisis in global sense making" which he sees expressed in the rapidly rising prevalence rate of unipolar depression (World Health Organization, 2012).

Nevertheless, even though, by nature, we are deeply embedded in the world through countless physical and psychological interdependencies, the notion of separateness from nature[1] appears to dominate the human mind and behaviour. This is not surprising as people nowadays spend approximately 90 percent of their lives in buildings (Evans & McCoy, 1998) and with regard to the additionally rapidly progressing urbanisation of the world (United Nations Department of Economic and Social Affairs, 2014) this situation seems to be worsening.

Consequently, the increasing need for action not only calls for technical solutions but also for a new consideration and experiential exploration of the human-nature relationship as a prerequisite for change, not to say survival (Schultz, 2002). Insofar, it will be critical to identify approaches that are capable of equally facilitating external as well as creating space for internal change. For, as many scholars believe, it is our understanding of self, which needs to be tackled and which would, once extended to the scope of the world, prevent environmentally destructive behaviour (e.g. see Roszak, 1992).

It is in this context that I chose to explore immersive experiences in wild nature. The so-called Solo time in nature serves as a catalyst for such experiences, and, in

---

1   For better readability I have separated non-human nature and humans, respectively human nature, artificially. As Russell (2013) aptly stated, "ultimately, nature and humanity are truly inseparable; nature cannot be defined in a way such that it does not also include humanity or some of its work" (p. 475).

the case of this study, was facilitated as the core element of two experiential outdoor programmes for young adults.

The Solo comes from a long tradition that spans various cultures and in the investigated programmes involved spending 24 hours alone in nature. The alone time in nature creates space for deep questioning, insight, inspiration and connection both to self and the wider community of life (Knapp & Smith, 2005).

In that sense, the Solo presents a novel, unconventional and uniquely experiential response to the earlier outlined problematic lack of connection and sense-making in the world. The goal of this research project is therefore firstly to explore the phenomenology of such an experience and secondly to evaluate its impact in relation to internal and external individual change in a longitudinal study such as changes in the participants' approach to nature or in their proenvironmental behaviour. Furthermore, deeply embedded in this research endeavour are the often-neglected questions of "what is the human place in nature, and what is nature's place in the human being?" (Clayton & Myers, 2011, p.4).

1.2 Outlook for the present work

As the complex connections between humans and nature are subject to countless psychological, evolutionary, cultural and ecological perspectives I chose to highlight only those facets in the literature review, which are relevant for contextualising my research. Thus, the following literature section does not represent an exhaustive overview of all the variables that influence human behaviour or reflect the human-nature relationship.

The literature section is divided into two main parts:

In the first main part I address the fact that we are emotional and deeply socially-wired beings. I further relate these aspects of human nature to the question of how they might influence our behaviour in the context of dealing with environmental problems. I then investigate what is known about the human-nature relationship, in particular about the human experience of nature. This journey highlights the human gift of meaning-making which constitutes the lens through which we perceive and experience.

This leads to the second main part in which I give voice to an expanded worldview. I start by providing a brief summary of how changing worldviews affected the human-nature relationship over time. As the worldview-lens turns out to be inseparable from meaning-making and the experience of our relationship with nature I explore how an expanded worldview, as suggested by numerous scholars, might affect the human-nature relationship, in particular our sense of self. Following this approach, I then turn to explore a particular practice model, namely the wilderness Solo, which is frequently promoted as a way to extend our sense of self and assist the process of self-realisation.

The literature section frames the methods and results section, which is again divided into two parts.

The first part encompasses the mixed methods enquiry of immersive experiences in wild nature that is the mixed methods research process and design, programme and sample description, an outline of the qualitative (interview) and quantitative (survey) research strand as well as a presentation of the results along with a first rudimentary integration of the quantitative with the qualitative results. In the process, it becomes evident that the endeavour of mixing methods, bears an important analogy to the notion of separateness immanent in our contemporary worldview, as outlined in the literature section. While in the latter we dealt with the contemporary human habit to perceive and understand the world in isolated pieces and the associated struggle of relating this to our subjective experience of being part of the web of life, in the methodological realm we face the divide between quantitative and qualitative research, thus the objective and subjective perspective on life.

Even though naturally a part of the mixed methods enquiry, I assigned a separate chapter to the applied method, results and discussion of the dream enquiry of immersive experiences in wild nature. As dreams are an unconventional data source, in this chapter I additionally contextualise this enquiry by giving a brief overview of dream research and depicting the applied method and results in their own right. It turns out that my own, the researcher's, process to some degree mirrors the participants' programme experience and that the dreams only start to tell a larger story once put together across dreamers. This again seems to highlight the two seemingly opposing realities of separateness and interconnectedness and thereby pinpoints an important aspect of the topic of enquiry.

This leads to the overall discussion of the mixed methods enquiry, including the dream enquiry, where I relate the result to the literature but also regard them from a meta-perspective integrating qualitative, quantitative and intuitive results with my own research process and the patterns that emerged from each section of the present work.

Notably, in the process of engaging with the data and writing this dissertation I encountered several areas of friction. This, in turn, led me to the integration of three self-reflective sections as part of this dissertation, which will be marked for the reader by their presentation in a special font as evident in the following section.

1.3 Self-reflective preface

In the process of engaging with the data I encountered more and more areas of friction. An area of friction emerged when I discovered that common methods could not fully capture the content of my data and it emerged again when I encountered the boundaries of the culturally biased language available to me. However, over and above, I experienced friction when I attempted to transfer my research process and results to the imposed format, that is, structure and chronology of a standard academic thesis. This is a format, which, I assume, was initially introduced by virtue of depicting most simply and logically the research process of scientific discovery.

However, the more I unravelled the content of my data the more I understood which subject areas needed to be covered in order to contextualise the data appropriately. More specifically, the data redefined the problem statement and associated literature review, a section, which is commonly found in the very beginning of a dissertation. Thus, there was a part of my research process, which appeared opposed to the commonly proposed research process and structure of an academic paper. As I dug deeper I found that the incompatibility I encountered was based on two circumstances immanent in the conventional way of illustrating research.

Firstly, the process of the researcher is generally almost completely neglected as a relevant part of the knowledge acquired throughout the research process and thus owns no official section in the structure of a standard thesis or paper. This in turn brought about some difficulty when writing the present work, as it was this very process that periodically helped to illuminate different aspects of the data and naturally and undeniably influenced the way I worked with the data.

Secondly, the predetermined sections of a thesis and their order imply linearity in the research process, a case, I would argue, that hardly ever occurs as such. Nevertheless, the implied chronology of the process and therefore chronology of sections is claimed as the best fit, the most logical order and associated with thorough research. This undeniably impedes leaving the well-trodden paths even if another format appears more appropriate.

However, the more I tried to make my research process fit the more incomplete and misleading the depiction of my research felt and the more it seemed as though I was engaging in acrobatics instead of thorough research. In fact, I felt it in my body as a knot in the pit of my stomach, which refused to dissolve, an event that will be addressed as "bodily wisdom" (see chapter 4.3.7).

Therefore, I needed to change something.

So instead of concealing my research process in order to be able to follow the given format, I will try and depict it for the reader as it took place in order to maintain transparency, completeness and truthfulness but also in order to achieve coherence and logic when reading this work.

This, by no means, implies the complete abandonment of the commonly used format, as I will retain the overall sections. Nevertheless, in contrast to the conventional format, hereby and recurrently later on I disclose and integrate an authorial narrative on my research. These narratives are deliberately free to take different shapes such as dreams, intuitions or meta-perspectives like this one and are associated with various aspects of my research process. Therefore they cannot be assorted to one specific formal section but appear occasionally throughout the whole thesis wherever they emerged[2]

By depicting my research process I aim to formally acknowledge that this work includes a meta-perspective or that of a weaver who knows the robe already.

As psychologist and scholar Romanyshyn (2007) appropriately formulated in his book on a novel approach to research which aims "to keep soul in mind"

> *Maybe we miss the weave when we see only the end results […] and maybe we miss all the threads that compose the weave when we move too far away from the multiple threads that compose the pattern […] and slip into the singularity […]. (p.24)*

---

2   You will recognise the self-reflexive sections by the font utilised in this passage, which differs from the one used in the other conventional sections.

2

The human-nature relationship through the lens of contemporary science

2.1 The emotional and social dimension of human care for nature

As briefly touched upon in the problem statement, natural environments have an extensive impact on various aspects of human well-being (Bratman *et al.*, 2012). Moreover, survey studies revealed that most people appreciate nature and assign its preservation great importance (European Commission, 2009). Furthermore, in an extensive European survey study 75 percent of the Europeans indicated that they buy environmentally friendly products. However, when asked to specify how often they have bought environmentally friendly products in the past month only 17 percent of the same sample indicated that they have actually done so (European Commission, 2009). This raises the question as to why these opinions and the knowledge we carry only marginally translates into concrete environmentally responsible behaviour[3].

In the following section, I will describe relevant underlying factors of human care for nature that may be categorised as the emotional and social dimension. Not all of the selected aspects presented have been researched directly with regard to proenvironmental behaviour, yet. However, the presented aspects all represent factors which are known to impact human behaviour considerably and which have been recognised as important influences to consider in the context of proenvironmental engagement by experts in the field (e.g. see Harré, 2011).

2.1.1 The influence of emotions

Emotions are short-lived experiences that play a decisive role in how we perceive the world as well as in the decisions we make. Therefore, they are essential to understand when examining the conditions for sustainable behaviour.

For instance, emotion researchers Fredrickson and Branigan (2005) found that positive emotions rather broaden our sense of what we can achieve while negative emotions narrow this sense in. This was demonstrated in a study with 105 college students who were divided into groups and watched films that either elicited positive, neutral or negative emotions (Fredrickson & Branigan, 2005). Then, the participants' scope of atten-

---

[3] For a brief summary on the gap between attitudes and action see Csutora (2012).

Figure 1. The global-local visual processing task in Fredrickson and Branigan's (2005) study. Harré (2011) after Fredrickson and Branigan (2005).

tion was assessed using a global-local visual processing task. Here, participants were presented with three clusters of squares and triangles (see Figure 1).

Their task was to rate which of the bottom clusters was more similar to the top one. Of course, there was no right or wrong answer but participants were nevertheless forced to pick one. Thus, they had to choose between concentrating on the overall, global pattern of the clusters or on their local features. Those participants who chose to go with the overall pattern were considered to have a global bias whereas those who chose the individual patterns were considered to have a local bias. Afterwards participants were asked to relive the emotion in the film and then to list all the things that they could imagine to do. As it turned out participants who watched a movie that made them happy rather saw the shapes with a holistic gaze and were able to think of a large variety of things to do. However, those who were presented with films that elicited anger and anxiety rather concentrated on the local features of the clusters and revealed a restricted sense of options.

In a review Fredrickson (2013) summarised research on a range of emotions drawing on her own but also on other laboratories' findings. Fredrickson suggests that different emotions trigger different thought-action tendencies[4] and create specific additional resources. A selection of those is depicted in Table 1.

As shown, inspiration, for instance, occurs when people observe others doing a good deed. This in turn sparks the urge to strive for one's own higher ground and thus, the resource it establishes is the motivation for personal growth (Algoe & Haidt, 2009).

The reason why these considerations are relevant to sustainable behaviour is that emotions, as in the case of the above mentioned positive emotions, not only generate beneficial social relationships and potentially needed resources to realise global change but also because they determine considerably how we respond to threats.

This has been shown in a study by Reed and Aspinwall (1998). Female high and low level caffeine users were presented with risk-confirming and risk-disconfirming information about the link between caffeine and fibrocystic breast disease. Participants were randomly assigned to two groups. One was encouraged to think of a past act of

---

4   Fredrickson uses the term "thought-action tendencies" as a replacement for "action tendencies" because positive emotions primarily spark changes in cognitive activity which only potentially entail physical activity.

kindness, thus they were brought to think positively about themselves, whereas the other was not. Those of the frequent caffeine drinkers who were encouraged to think of a past act of kindness were shown to be more open and less-biased processors of the risk-confirming information than the high caffeine drinkers in the control group. Furthermore, the group who previously thought of their acts of kindness perceived more control over reducing their caffeine consumption than the control group. This implies that, in the face of threat, people who feel positive are more likely to examine the situation, take in uncomfortable information and re-examine their personal practice than those feeling less positive.

That being said, positive emotions can have problematic side effects, too. Studies show that people who are in a good mood display a lack of concentration in boring situations and are motivated to quickly move on from a boring task (Carver, 2003). In order to do so people in a good mood are more ready to make use of stereotypes (Bodenhausen, Kramer, & Süsser, 1994) or latch onto weak arguments (Bless, Bohner, Schwarz, & Strack, 1990; Mackie & Worth, 1991).

As shown in Fredrickson's study (2005) negative emotions can narrow down one's attention. However, this is not necessarily a disadvantage as high attention and concentration on a matter can be of value for inspiring action. Fear, for instance, is an effective emotion to attract attention and, in the context of sustainability issues, to involve people. Nevertheless, fearful messages can go both ways as we will see later on: people either lapse into avoidance or start to work on the problem depending how capable they feel of tackling the source of the fear.

In a study on water consumption, recycling and energy conservation, Seattle businessmen were asked to rate the importance of the issues under two conditions (Obermiller, 1995). Two groups were created: one received information on the issue which emphasised the severity of the problem, in advertisement called the "sick baby appeal", while the other groups' messages highlighted the problem yet stressed the participants capability of tackling the problem, called the "well baby appeal". Even though, concerning the topics water and energy, the "sick baby appeal" group rated the matter as more important compared to the "well baby appeal" group the latter felt more capable of dealing with the problem. However, with regard to recycling the "well baby" group rated both the importance as well as their capability of addressing the

Table 1

Emotions and associated thought-action tendencies

Emotion label	Thought-action tendency	Expanded resource
Joy	Play, get involved	Skills gained via experiential learning
Gratitude	Creative urge to be prosocial	Skills for showing care, loyalty, social bonds
Contentment	Savor and integrate	New priorities, new views of self
Interest	Explore, learn	Knowledge
Hope	Plan for a better future	Resilience, optimism
Pride	Dream big	Achievement motivation
Inspiration	Strive toward own higher ground	Motivation for personal growth
Awe	Absorb and accommodate	New worldviews
Love	All of the above, with mutual care	All of the above, especially social bonds

issue more highly. Obermiller (1995) assumes that the people's concern and awareness regarding recycling is high to start with as opposed to concern and awareness regarding water and energy issues. Thus, the author suggests that a sick baby appeal might be efficient regarding low awareness issues but may cause a rebound effect, that is a sense of helplessness, when the attention is directed to the severity of a problem that is already in people's awareness and highly concerns them.

Summarised, negative emotions are important as they can serve as a reality check and can have beneficial effects under particular circumstances when experienced in small doses while positive emotions seem to be advantageous in large portions in a greater variety of circumstances (Harré, 2011)[5].

2.1.2 Coping mechanisms and the role of hope

The way environmental problems present themselves and are presented in media today, it seems as though we are soon facing catastrophic consequences and a rather hopeless future. Consequently, the situation can feel overwhelming, and as a single individual, one can quickly start to feel paralysed and disempowered when confronted with it (Clayton & Myers, 2011). This is supported by studies focusing on the next generations, namely young people from middle childhood to late adolescence. The research confirms that many members of this age group experience negative emotions such as helplessness, pessimism, worry and sadness regarding environmental problems and the global future (e.g. Hicks & Holden, 2007; Naval & Repáraz, 2008; Threadgold, 2012).

Especially with respect to the often-mentioned puzzling gap between knowledge and action this challenging circumstance demands further attention. It is in this context that it seems worthwhile turning to a phenomenon known as "learned helplessness" (Seligman, 1975).

Learned helplessness has been found in a wide variety of contexts as well as in human and non-human organisms and describes the expectation of an individual that situations or circumstances are unchangeable and uncontrollable. Characteristically, this expectation arises from prior experiences of loss of control in which the individual perceived her or his actions and their consequences as independent from one another. As a result, based on the experience of helplessness and powerlessness individuals slip into inaction even if the situation is unpleasant to endure and regardless of the actual possibilities for action or change. This ingrained expectation further influences the way the individual experiences and behaves in the future and holds the potential to manifest in motivational, cognitive and emotional deficits such as depression (Seligman, 1975).

Generally, performance deficits as an outcome of learned helplessness have been confirmed in experimental (e.g. Jones, Nation, & Massad, 1977) as well as field studies (e.g. Metalsky, Abramson, Seligman, Semmel, & Peterson, 1982). Furthermore, the theory has now been extended and refined. For example Abramson, Seligman and Teasdale (1978) found out that it is vital to integrate how an individual explains (negative) events. Evidently, individual explanatory styles vary in terms of internal versus external, stable versus unstable and global versus specific attributions. For instance, in the event of a negative experience an unfavourable explanatory style would be internal,

---

5   Based on their research Fredrickson and Losada (2005) even identified an optimal minimum ratio of positive to negative emotions, namely 2.9 : 1, for human flourishing.

stable and global as exemplified in the attitude "It happened because I am a useless person." A more positive way to make sense of a negative event, on the other hand, would be to attribute the event to external factors that are perceived as unstable and specific as illustrated in the belief "It happened just because someone misinformed me."

Against this backdrop it becomes apparent that explanatory styles may play a crucial role in the matter of environmental problems. As environmental problems are often attributed to global and stable factors such as the generally greedy nature of humans or the overpowering influence of multinational corporations they may easily lead to symptoms of helplessness (Clayton & Myers, 2011).

However, psychologist and researcher Zimmerman (1990) decided to take a different approach to shedding light on the relationship between perceived control and behaviour. Instead of concentrating on the downward spiral of learned helplessness, Zimmerman focuses on investigating the upward spiral of learned hopefulness. Hence, while learned helplessness looks at the experience of lack of control Zimmerman (1990) developed a theory of learned hopefulness, which focuses on the experience of an event that leads to successful control. According to this theory, as a result of a positive experience, individuals make causal attributions for the event, which in turn shape their expectations for future events. The expectation that events are controllable consequently generates learned hopefulness characteristics such as increased psychological empowerment, proactive behaviour and reduced alienation. These characteristics clearly oppose learned helplessness symptoms such as withdrawal, alienation and depression (Zimmerman, 1990).

Thus, the theory suggests that experiences that enable individuals to go through a process of learning and employing skills also enable them to develop a sense of control, such as in the experience of voluntary citizen participation. This process, in turn, ultimately leads to psychological empowerment and can help buffer problems in life. Additionally, in Zimmerman's theory of learned hopefulness perceived control is multidimensional and encompasses self-efficacy, motivation to control and locus of control. The function of all three domains is defined as psychological empowerment. Thus, while learned hopefulness is understood as the process whereby skills are learned and employed psychological empowerment represents the product of learned hopefulness. Indeed, the results of Zimmerman's study (1990) testing this theory provided support for the associated statistical model and Zimmerman found a direct effect of voluntary participation on psychological empowerment in the community as well as in the student sample. The notion that an experience of effective participation facilitates motivational power and can induce a more optimistic outlook is also put forward by other researchers (see Kaplan, 1990; Lee, 1994).

However, it is now known that hopelessness and helplessness regarding global problems increases with age among young people. It is assumed that this is explained by the fact that adolescents are more capable of realising the full extent and complexity of the problem than children are (Ojala, 2012b; Eckersley, 1999; Hicks, 1996). The reason why hope seems especially promising in this context is that, unlike most other positive emotions, hope emerges in rather dark and difficult situations. People who are expecting the worst yet long for something better experience hope (Lazarus, 1994). According to positive emotions researcher Fredrickson (2013), "hope creates the urge to draw on one's own capabilities and inventiveness to turn things around. The durable resources it builds include optimism and resilience to adversity" (p. 4).

Research literature suggests that there may be a distinction between optimism and hope. While the optimistic person trusts that things will work out *somehow* the hopeful person believes in her or his own ability to create a favourable future (Alarcon, Bowling, and Kahzon, 2013). Nevertheless, historically, hope has also experienced some criticism as it was supposed to constitute a manifestation of naiveté, maladjustment, and psychopathology (see Peterson, 2000).

Nowadays, however, this perspective has changed, as a great variety of research findings present hope in a different way. Alarcon *et al.* (2013), for instance, conducted a meta-analysis of optimism and hope and found hope to be positively associated with happiness and negatively associated with stress and depression. In another meta-anaylsis, Yarcheski and Mahon (2014) identified predictors of hope and their associated effect sizes. It was shown that five predictors of hope had large mean effect sizes, namely positive affect, life satisfaction, optimism, self-esteem, and social support. Depression had a medium effect size and negative affect, stress, academic achievement and violence had small effect sizes. A further trivial effect size was ascribed to gender.

Findings from health psychology further showed that people with high levels of hope are more capable at absorbing health information as well as implementing it (Snyder, Rand, and Sigmon, 2002). Moreover, people with high hope can deal with problems more constructively (Drach-Zahavy & Somech, 2002), take action and find ways to better achieve their aims than people with low levels of hope (Snyder, 2000).

Strauss, Niven, McClelland and Cheung (2014) investigated the role of hope in different organisational settings and found that hope played a particular role in supporting employees to continuously adapt to change. Moreover, in a study by Rego, Sousa, Marques and Cunha (2012) hope and self-efficacy were found to predict the creativity of retail employees and in a longitudinal study over two years hope also predicted students' academic achievement (Marques, Pais-Ribeiro, and Lopez, 2011).

Summarised, in current research, hope presents itself as a resource whose development should be promoted and the emotional nature of hope is highlighted as a provider of motivation and energy to act even in times of uncertainty (Courville & Piper, 2004; McGeer, 2004). However, it is important to be aware that it remains unclear yet whether all sources of hope have a positive impact on engagement, as hope could be equally based on denial (e.g. see McGeer, 2004; Snyder *et al.*, 2002).

Against the backdrop of these research findings, it becomes increasingly valuable to specifically understand the role of hope in the context of coping with environmental threats. Unfortunately, this subject exhibits only a comparably scarce body of research thus far.

There is some research on adults' coping strategies in relation to environmental threats as exemplified in Homburg, Stolberg and Wagner's studies (2007). Homburg *et al.* measured coping using eight subscales which are based on Lazarus' (1994) coping approach and can be differentiated in problem-focused/action-centered versus deproblematisation-focused coping[6]. In their three validation studies they found that the problem-focused and action-centered scales as Problem Solving, Expression of Emotions and Self-Protection were positively correlated with proenvironmental behaviour. The other coping scales showed, as expected, no or negative correlations with proenvironmental behaviour with the surprising exception of the Wishful Thinking scale. Wishful Thinking was defined by the authors (2007) as "cognitive coping covering alternative solutions, based on hope and anticipation of a positive outcome" (p.757) and was found to be positively correlated with proenvironmental behaviour in study three. However, in this study, hope was not specifically integrated as a variable within the context of coping with environmental threats.

Fortunately there are now some recent studies by researcher Maria Ojala, which focus exactly on this subject (Ojala, 2008; Ojala, 2012a; Ojala, 2012b; Ojala, 2013). In an early study Ojala (2008) found an interaction effect between worry and hope in a sample of young adults (n = 422). It was shown that individuals who revealed a low degree of worry about environmental problems and a high degree of hope appeared to be reluctant to behave proenvironmentally, possibly indicating denial of the problem. In turn, for those individuals who showed a high degree of worry and high levels of hope, hope was positively related to behaviour.

In another study with teenagers and adults, Ojala (2012a) specifically explored whether hope influences proenvironmental behaviour when controlling for associated well-known predictors and when integrating hope based on denial. The quantitative hope measure that was used to assess this included a "hope based on denial" item and items representing "constructive hope".

The aspects of "constructive hope" were identified in a previous study (Ojala, 2007) in which Ojala qualitatively assessed underlying sources of hope that were, due to her selective actively-engaged sample, likely to be positively related to proenvironmental behaviour. The three main themes representing "constructive hope" were positive reappraisal such as putting things into a historical perspective, trust in sources outside oneself such as environmental organisations and trust in one's own ability to influence environmental problems in a positive direction.

Thus, the measure of hope concerning climate change (Ojala, 2012a) included all of the above-mentioned sources of hope. The results of this study revealed that, indeed, when controlling for well-known explanatory factors such as values, gender, social influence and knowledge, hope based on denial was negatively related to behaviour whereas constructive hope had a unique influence on proenvironmental behaviour. Based on these results Ojala (2012a) concluded that a focus on values in environmental education cannot replace a focus on hope.

Taking up on Folkman's (2008) suggestion Ojala (2012a) understands hope as a facilitator of problem-focused coping concerning climate change by providing the space to look for solutions and to gather the needed strength in order to face the problem.

---

6 Six of their eight subscales fitted this two-dimensional metastructure with Problem Solving, Expression of Emotion and Self-Protection representing the problem-focused coping and Denial of Guilt, Relativization and Pleasure representing deproblematization-focused coping. For a more detailed description of the subscales see chapter 4.3.5.1.

In an additional study Ojala (2012b) concentrated on identifying the different coping strategies concerning climate change in children and adolescents. The identified coping strategies were problem-focused coping such as thinking about the problem and searching for information and emotion-focused coping such as distancing from and de-emphasising the problem as well as seeking social support by talking to others about it. The third strategy was meaning-focused coping which incorporated positive reappraisal of the situation, existential hope, that is acknowledging the problem but focusing on positive aspects, and trust in sources outside of oneself such as other actively-engaged people, politicians and scientists. The results showed that, in all age groups, hope primarily originated from meaning-focused coping strategies such as positive reappraisal and trust. Moreover, in a further study (Ojala, 2013) it was shown that problem-focused and meaning-focused coping were positively correlated with felt environmental efficacy and environmental behaviour even when controlling for well-known predictors as values and gender. De-emphasising the threat, however, was negatively associated with the same measures. Unsurprisingly, the more adolescents used problem-focused coping, the more likely they experienced negative affect in everyday life, assumedly because of a higher degree of worry about climate change. Meaning-focused coping on the other hand was positively associated with well-being and optimism. According to Ojala (2012a) these results support previous findings about stress at a micro level which showed that meaning-focused coping strategies differ from denial as they represent a constructive way of coping when facing a stressor that cannot be immediately removed or solved (e.g. see Folkman, 2008).

Thus, positive reappraisal as part of meaning-focused coping, that is perceiving the threat yet being able to change perspective and activate positive emotions, can support facing the complex and worrying situation of climate change (Ojala, 2012a). Similarly, trust in other actors as another aspect of meaning-focused coping, constitutes an important form of coping, as the environmental situation obviously cannot be solved by one person alone. Moreover, the above presented results revealed that hope based on the trust that non-professionals together can make a difference is positively associated with proenvironmental behaviour. This demonstrates that this source of hope seems to motivate rather than lead to a diffusion of responsibility. Consequently, Ojala (2012a) stresses the significance of integrating the collective dimension of hope in the context of climate change in the future and to acknowledge that collective rather than only individual action can equally facilitate hope.

2.1.3 The human disposition to imitate
Humans carry a natural disposition to imitate, which brings about double-edged consequences when it comes to the matter of sustainability.

On the one hand, imitation can keep us trapped in ecologically harmful behaviour patterns as they are exhibited by a majority of people around us. On the other hand, fortunately, our disposition to imitate also means that we can start to change behaviour by imitating alternatives presented to us (Harré, 2011).

Behavioural imitation often arises unconsciously and automatically and essentially applies to everything that a person can observe in others such as motor movements and behaviour (Chartrand & Lakin, 2013). As experts in the field, Chartrand and Lakin (2013) explain, "humans alter their behaviour to blend into social environments" (p.

288), a phenomenon called "the chameleon effect". This was demonstrated in an experiment (Chartrand & Bargh, 1999) in which participants were either presented with a face-touching or foot-shaking confederate who was supposedly co-working with them on a fake task. Importantly, participants and confederates did not know each other and confederates did not display particularly welcoming behaviour. Regardless, the results showed that participants exhibited more face-touching when they were working with a confederate who touched their face than with one who shook their foot. Moreover, participants could not remember what kind of behaviour the confederates displayed and thus which behaviour they copied, which underlines the unconscious nature of the participants' action.

Such imitation behaviour has been researched regarding a large range of motor movements such as yawning (Helt, Eigsti, Snyder, & Fein, 2010), food consumption (Herrmann, Rossberg, Huber, Landwehr, & Henkel, 2011), pen playing (Stel *et al.*, 2010), cospeech gestures (Goldin-Meadow & Alibali, 2013) and health-related behaviours (Webb, Eves, & Smith, 2011)[7]. However, imitation does not only occur in the form of motor movements. For instance, people also imitate facial expressions (Dimberg, Thunberg, & Elmehed, 2000) and emotional reactions of interaction partners (Hawk, Fischer, & Van Kleef, 2011). Especially the imitation of emotional reactions often starts at an exceptionally early age as Meltzoff and Moore (1983) demonstrated in their study with 40 newborn babies in a Seattle hospital. In front of the babies, an adult model switched between intervals of repeatedly opening his mouth for four minutes and poking out his tongue for four minutes. An independent rater who could not see the model rated 26 of the 40 babies to perform more mouth opening when the model did so and also more tongue poking when this was actually produced by the model. The study illustrates just how deeply rooted imitation is in human nature.

However, in order to fully understand the scope of this disposition it is important to introduce the so-called mirror neurons (Harré, 2011).

Mirror neurons reinforce the notion of a strong relationship between perception and action as proposed in psychological models of imitation (Iacoboni, 2009). They represent cells, which respond equally to merely watching a goal-directed activity and to actually executing the activity (Byrne, 2005). Thus, actions of someone else are mirrored in the brain of the observer in the same way as though the observer was doing the action her or himself.

This phenomenon has been initially observed in monkeys. In one experiment Fogassi, Ferrari, Gesierich, Rozzi, Chersi and Rizzolatti (2005) trained a monkey to pick up food and eat it and to pick it up and place it in a container. As soon as the behaviours were learnt the researchers measured the neuronal activity in the parietal lobe while the monkey performed the tasks. As the next step, they then trained the monkey to observe a person either picking up food and eating it or putting the food into the container whilst measuring the monkey's brain activity in the same region. Fogassi *et al.* found that the neuronal activity for the observed actions matched the pattern that was recorded when the monkey performed the actions itself, both for picking up the food and eating it as well as for picking up the food and placing it in the container.

---

7   For reviews focusing on behavioural immitation see Chartrand and van Baaren (2009) or van Baaren, Janssen, Chartrand and Dijksterhuis (2009).

Harré (2011) draws three implications from this study. Firstly, the results imply that our brain automatically mirrors part of the experience of the observed person. Secondly, imitation may be so tempting because seeing an action at least partly activates the same part of the brain which also mirrors the motor action itself and thereby puts it in a state of alert (Harré, 2011). The third implication from Fogassi *et al.*'s study (2005) is that the actions "picking up food and eating it" and "picking up food and placing it in a container" excited two widely different sets of mirror neurons. Thus, the determining factor for the particular set of neurons to be activated was the end-goal of the observed action. Even when the experimenters placed the container into the monkey's mouth to make the two actions as similar as possible the resulting set of activated mirror neurons only overlapped 25 per cent with "placing the food in the mouth and eating it". In line with this research, Iacoboni (2009) suggests that actually two thirds of the activated set of mirror neurons respond to the goal instead of the mere motor action.

There are now some fMRI studies, which suggest that humans, too, have a mirror neuron system that seems to work similarly to that of monkeys (see Rizzolatti & Sinigaglia, 2010) and the importance of the formerly described goal orientation in the context of human imitation behaviour has been subject to a great deal of research. A famous example is a study conducted by Bandura, Ross and Ross (1961). In their study, preschool children observed an adult acting either aggressively or non-aggressively towards a toy called the "Bobo" doll. Then, the children were left alone in a room with the doll and other toys. Unsurprisingly, children who had watched the aggressive model before displayed much more aggression towards the doll than those ones who had not. Intriguingly, the children in the "aggression" condition not only demonstrated aggressive actions as formerly witnessed but they also engaged in non-imitative, non-demonstrated variations of the acts of aggression they previously observed. This indicates that the children most likely responded to the perceived goal of the model instead of merely imitating the motor actions of it. In a similar but modified study Bandura (1965) also showed that it is not only the goal of an action that draws attention but also the resulting consequences the model has to face. Children, for instance, displayed less similar behaviour toward the model when they witnessed that the model got punished following his actions.

What this shows is that ecologically responsible behaviour poses a difficult challenge if we are constantly surrounded by people modelling ecologically harmful behaviour.

Furthermore, against this backdrop, it appears useful to illuminate why we, as humans, imitate and whom we are prone to imitate.

Research shows that imitation behaviour does not only come easy to us but it also plays an important role in our social interactions. Imitation has been called the "social glue" that builds affiliation and empathy between interacting people (Lakin & Chartrand, 2003) and it is closely related to and moderated by our connectedness to others (van Baaren, Janssen, Chartrand, & Dijksterhuis, 2009). In fact, little imitation in a human interaction even has been found to increase cortisol levels in the participants' bodies indicating stress as a result of the implication of rejection (Kouzakova, van Baaren, & van Knippenberg, 2010). Imitation automatically appears to a greater extent when participants in the interaction aim to create rapport or when it already pre-exists, when they feel they resemble each other, when they have a high prosocial orientation or are in a positive mood (Chartrand & Lakin, 2013). People that express agreement with their interaction partners on various viewpoints are more often imitated that those who disagree (Drury & Van Swol, 2006). Moreover, interactants imitate friends more than strangers and likable strangers more than unlikable ones (McIntosh, 2006).

In this light, it is not surprising that also in the realm of social and environmental engagement the social influence from family and peers has been found to be particularly important (e.g. Bögeholz, 1999; Chawla, 1999; Grønhøj & Thøgersen, 2009; Grønhøj & Thøgersen, 2012).

2.1.4 The influence of social norms

As outlined in the previous section people unconsciously utilise imitation to get others to like them but it is also an effective strategy that can result in prosociality, empathy, smoother interactions, in helping behaviour between interaction partners as well as in changes in consumer behaviour and product preferences (Chartrand & Lakin, 2013). Thus, imitation appears to be an important social tool that people regularly apply in their everyday lives and which affects behaviour. Yet, imitation refers solely to the tendency of people to directly copy each other.

However, there is an additional powerful influence at play, namely social norms, which evoke the tendency to copy what we perceive as normal in any given situation (Harré, 2011). From an evolutionary perspective, social norms help us by serving as low-cost short cuts to identify the most adaptive behaviour in any given situation (Boyd & Richerson, 2009).

In the context of conservation behaviour, the effect of social norms has been studied widely. Nolan, Schultz, Cialdini, Goldstein and Grieskevicus (2008), for instance, found that a message providing information on the energy consumption of the average homeowner led to a greater reduction of energy use than a message emphasising environmental protection, self-interest and social responsibility. Intriguingly, the respondents rated social norms as least influential in their conservation decision and environmental protection and social responsibility as the most important explanations for their conservation behaviour. This shows clearly that we are unaware of the influence of social norms on our behaviour and that thinking of ourselves as ethical does not necessarily translate into behaviour.

In another experiment Cialdini, Reno and Kallgren (1990) put a handbill on windscreens of cars. Some of these cars were parked in highly-littered environments and others in a clean environment. When the car owners returned to their car they witnessed a confederate either dropping litter on the ground or merely passing through. Cialdini *et al.* (1990) then recorded whether the car owners dropped their handbills on the ground or not. Overall, more people littered in the highly-littered environment than in the clean one. People littered most when they previously watched the confederate littering into the littered environment. However, the least littering occurred when the car owners watched someone drop litter into a clean environment, most likely because this highlighted a violation of the prevailing social norm in that environment, that is, societal objections to littering. In a review on environmental modelling Schultz, Tabanico and Rendón (2008) found this to be a common phenomenon.

Presenting environmentally friendly behaviour as normal has been consistently proven to be more effective than appeals to protect the environment when aiming to encourage proenvionmental behaviour. In a study Goldstein, Cialdini and Grieskevicus (2008) varied bathroom messages which were meant to encourage the guests of a hotel to re-use their towels. One card in the bathroom invited the guests to "help save the environment" and the other version invited to "join the fellow guests in helping to save the environment". Goldstein *et al.* (2008) found significantly more towel re-use when it was presented as the normal behaviour than when it was merely described as an act to help save the planet.

In this context, it is important to highlight, though, that norms can also backfire as Schultz, Nolan, Cialdini, Goldstein and Grieskevicus (2007) showed in their study including 290 households in a Californian community. The households were divided into two energy consumption groups: lower and higher than average. Both groups were then informed how much energy they consumed and how they performed compared to the average. This minor intervention led to a six percent energy reduction in the higher-than-average group but to a nine percent increase in consumption in the initially lower-than-average group. Thus, the overall consumption of both groups combined increased. However, as soon as the experimenters valued the lower-than-average group by placing a smiley face on their information sheet the increase of energy usage was reduced to two percent from their baseline rates.

To conclude, norms pull people both above and below average toward the average. This means people who already act proenvironmentally have to be reinforced and valued in order to prevent the decline in engagement observed by Schultz *et al.* (2007) (Harré, 2011).

2.1.5 Environmental identity and the social environment

As the power of attraction of social norms and imitation already illustrated, the need to belong and feel accepted is inherent in human nature. This is similarly reflected in the importance of identities that we hold as part of ourselves.

Identities serve as a frame for systematising information about an individual using personal attributes, social roles and relationships or social categories (Clayton & Myers, 2011). A person experiences identities both as a sense of self and as defined by others. Therefore, the living environment is crucial for the development of identities, as it determines the way we are perceived and the way we perceive ourselves. Ultimately, identities are beliefs that we collect about ourselves which are in constant development as they are outcomes of the experiences we have. They become noticeable through the way we respond emotionally and cognitively to the outer world, for instance as focusing mechanisms or motivational forces (Clayton & Myers, 2011).

An environmental identity develops through a variety of means. As people often experience nature in their role as a member of a social group or community, one of these means is the social environment. Simply put, someone who acts to conserve the environment suggests a different social identity from someone who does not, and is therefore also perceived differently by others. As Sadalla and Krull (1995) found out, this is a culture sensitive matter, too. In their study, they asked college students to imagine the probable personality of someone who acts to conserve environmental resources, and found that the described person was uniformly associated with lower status. The authors concluded that in most cultures consumption indicates higher status. Therefore, in order to illuminate why some people do not engage in proenvironmental behaviour it is important to understand what kind of social identity may be attributed to conservation behaviour by the social reference group as well as what kind of image the individual wishes to convey within her or his social environment (Clayton & Myers, 2011).

The important role of the social environment is also revealed in a study by Zavestoski (2003). Zavestoski interviewed highly nature-dedicated workshop participants to find out how they were able to uphold their environmental identities in a rather unsupportive society. Many of the workshop participants nominated two social environments as beneficial for their dedication, namely a career that is compatible with their identity and supportive social networks. However, many felt that their nature connectedness was not appreciated or respected by the majority of people in their everyday lives.

In the quest for promoting proenvironmental behaviour a great focus has been placed on attitudes. One of the theories which gained most support in explaining the relationship between behaviour and attitudes is the Theory of Planned Behaviour (TPB; Ajzen, 1991). According to the TPB, proenvironmental behaviour is likely to arise when people hold a positive attitude towards conservation behaviour, when they hold descriptive or perceived injunctive social norms, namely when they think that significant others already engage in such behaviour or when they think significant others believe it should be performed, and when there is perceived behaviour control. Notably, the theory aims to illuminate planned behaviour and may not account for habitual behaviour (Steg & Vlek, 2009). Unfortunately, even though attitudes turn out to be good predictors of environmental behaviour they tend to explain only specific behaviours. That is, a positive attitude toward recycling most likely leads to recycling behaviour but does not necessarily imply using public transport instead of the car. It is in this light that more stable factors as values and identity seem promising in affecting a greater range of behaviours as a person perceiving her or himself as an environmentally friendly person might also engage in a wider range of proenvirornmental behaviours. Indeed, Gatersleben, Murtagh and Abrahamse (2012) found in their studies that values and identities were good predictors of proenvirornmental behaviour and identities explained behaviour over and above attitudes. As identities mediated the association between values and behaviour, the authors concluded that identities may represent broader concepts, which include values. This is in line with other studies on the relationship of environmental identity and behaviour (e.g. Clayton, 2003; Whitmarsh & O'Neill, 2010; Sparks & Shepherd, 1992).

In two experiments Fritsche and Hafner (2012) tested how people's motivation to protect nature changes in the face of existential threat. They found out that the participants' motivation to protect nature for its own sake was reduced when death awareness was induced. Intriguingly, this decrease was eliminated if protecting nature was presented as beneficial for humans or if participants scored moderately high on environmental identity. Thus, distancing from nature under death awareness is neutralised if nature is relevant to the human race or to the self.

Correspondingly, Clayton and Myers (2011) argue that adopting an environmental identity may generally foster a sense of self as a member of a collective in the way that it embodies the experience of being part of something larger than oneself. In the context of environmental threats, Clayton and Myers (2011) see great value in adopting such a collective identity, as individuals will have to take responsibility for group-level outcomes and collective identity is known to facilitate group-oriented behaviour (see *e.g.* DeCremer & Van Vugt, 1999).

2.2 The relational and experiential dimension of human care for nature

2.2.1 Environmental identity and the experience of nature

Over time, different terms emerged to label an "environmental identity" (Weigert, 1997; Clayton & Opotow, 2003) such as "ecological identity" (Thomashow, 1995) or "environmental self" (Cantrill, 1998). The common ground of all of these diverse terms is the notion that people's relationship to nature can be a relevant part of their self-concept and that nature experiences may influence the way people define themselves to themselves and to others (Clayton & Myers, 2011).

As we know, identities generally develop through the experiences we make. In the last section we have focused on the development of identities in social environments. However, especially in the context of the development of an environmental identity, it is only logical to assume that experiences of the natural environment are of importance, too. The question arises as to how the experience of nature may impact our sense of self and what actually constitutes the experience of an environmental identity or ecological self.

According to Bragg (1996), the experience of an ecological self entails the recognition of analogies and one's own relatedness to other natural elements. As a consequence, Bragg pursues, people may not differentiate anymore between threats to nature and threats to themselves. This viewpoint resembles Borden's (1985) reflections on the environmental crisis. Borden suggests that the environmental crisis also reflects a crisis within the self, as materialism and competition unfavourably impact nature but also many people's sense of self and of the world. Borden (1985) sees nature experiences as potential pathways to spark ecological insight and regain understanding about the deeply interconnected nature of oneself with the world. This in turn, Borden (1985) speculates, may trigger a reassessment of responsibility and action in people.

Clayton and Myers (2011) extract four rationales for ways in which nature may affect the sense of self. Firstly, the authors argue, the natural environment supplies the optimal level of sensory stimulation, which means that it is neither overwhelming nor boring. This is especially beneficial for the development of children as vividly outlined by Chawla (2007). However, importantly, nature thereby provides optimal space for self-reflection (Herzog, Black, Fountaine, & Knotts, 1997) promoting inner peace and self-discovery especially when in solitude (Long, Seburn, Averill, & More, 2003; Korpela, 1989; Korpela, 1992; Korpela, Hartig, Kaiser, & Fuhrer, 2001).

The second rationale is the satisfaction of the human desire for autonomy. As social regulations and consequences are rare in nature, nature can enhance the individual's sense of autonomy. Simultaneously, people bear the desire for connection or belongingness, the third rationale, which seems to be answered in so-called transcendent experiences (see chapter 2.2.4). These kind of experiences include feeling part of something greater or taking part in a deeper meaning and appear to be facilitated by nature (Williams & Harvey, 2001). Transcendent experiences, the associated basic kinship, belongingness and a profound sense of connection to nature were found in many studies on nature experiences (e.g. Williams & Harvey, 2001; Chawla, 1986; Korpela, 1989; Korpela, 1992). The last rationale that Clayton and Myers (2011) invoke is that nature calls the individual to take responsibility for her or his personal needs. Nature not only provides the space for self-sufficiency but exposure to the elements also requires an increase of proactivity in the sense that a person has to continuously handle unpredictable and constantly changing circumstances just like hot sun calls for finding a shady spot and rain for a dry shelter (see Scherl, 1989; Fredrickson & Anderson, 1999).

Thus, it is proposed that experiences in nature bear the potential to alter one's self-concept or identity and, as shown in the previous section, a strong environmental identity affects behaviour. Moreover, Bragg (1996) assumes that a strong environmental identity also affects sensitivity for environmental information, nature connectedness and attraction to activities facilitating nature connectedness.

2.2.2 Nature connectedness

As the importance of nature to human identity gained increasing acknowledgement, more and more ways to assess this human-nature connection arose (Clayton & Myers, 2011). For instance, Kals, Schumacher, and Montada (1999) developed a measure which conceptualised "emotional affinity toward nature" representing the emotional bonds and cognitive interest in nature. Clayton (2003), on the other hand, uses the term "environmental identity" which describes a sense of connection to the natural world and inherits the belief that nature is significant to humans and a significant part of them. Mayer and Frantz (2004) delineate connectedness to nature as the "individual's experiential sense of oneness with the natural world" (p. 504). Altogether, there are at least nine measures of nature connectedness which Tam (2013) excellently summarises in his review and which all appear to assess connectedness to nature effectively.

Ultimately, connectedness to nature is an affective construct, which varies in its expression across individuals and is based on experience (Mayer & Frantz, 2004). That is, people who feel strongly connected to nature seek more contact with nature and people who are in contact with nature to a greater extent feel more connected to it (e.g. Hinds & Sparks, 2008). In accordance, a study on affinity toward nature showed that affinity was most significantly predicted by the amount of time in nature and the amount of time in nature during childhood (Kals, Schumacher, & Montada, 1999). Additionally, it seems as though change requires long-term or repeated experiences in nature (Schultz & Tabanico, 2007) which is in accordance with meta-analyses on environmental education programmes which revealed that extended programmes are more likely to result in change than shorter ones (Rickinson, 2001; Zelezny, 1999).

A widely known theory that provides an important background for a large proportion of research on nature connectedness is the biophilia hypothesis proposed by Wilson (1984). Wilson (1984) described biophilia as "the connections that human beings subconsciously seek with the rest of life" (p. 350). According to this theory, based on human evolution in the natural world over millions of years, humans have developed and inherited a need for, and connection to, other living things.

The notion of connectedness to nature has also a long history in ecopsychology and ecology. The ecologist Leopold (1966) believed that if humans were to perceive natural land as part of the same community of life they would start to treat it with respect and love. As a consequence, according to Leopold, proenvironmental behaviour would arise naturally.

The increase of protective behaviour as a result of a sense of community has been, indeed, supported by social psychologists researching interpersonal relationships. Scientists found that among humans empathy and willingness to help increases with relationship closeness namely attachment (Cialdini, Brown, Lewis, Luce, & Neuberg, 1997). Researchers such as Mayer and Frantz (2004) or Schultz (2002) adopted this social-psychological concept of interpersonal closeness and transferred it to their approach to the human-nature relationship.

Veritably, connectedness with nature has been shown to be not only linked with environmental concerns (e.g. Brügger, Kaiser, & Roczen, 2011) but also with self-reported proenvironmental behaviour across measurements (Frantz & Mayer, 2014). For instance, the shorter revised version of the Connectedness to Nature scale (CNS-R) predicts proenvironmental behaviour across college students, children and a general adult population with correlations ranging from .35 to .58 (Frantz, Mayer, Gordon, & Handley, 2010; Frantz, Mayer, & Sallee, 2013; Gordon, Frantz, & Mayer, 2012). Whilst most of these results rely on self-reports, Frantz and Mayer (2014) were recently able to additionally demonstrate an association between connectedness to nature and actual conservation behaviour namely individuals' electricity use.

Ultimately, it seems as though people who feel connected to nature also feel the urge to protect it. For this reason many researchers now request that connectedness to nature should be promoted as an integral part of environmental education (Frantz & Mayer, 2014). However, in order to be promoted connectedness to nature needs to be understood more deeply.

Tam, Lee and Chao (2013), for instance, addressed the common assumption underlying many environmental campaigns that anthropomorphism[8] of nature highlights the similarity between nature and humans and therefore leads people to show more concern toward nature. This is already hinted at in past research findings which revealed that the more people think a nonhuman entity, such as a robot, to be able to feel the more hesitant they are to harm it (Gray, Gray, & Wegner, 2007). Moreover, the more people ascribe mental abilities to animals the more they empathise with them (Hills, 1995) and the more they advocate their rights (Plous, 1993). However, in their experiments Tam *et al.* (2013) not only focused on the anthropomorphism-behaviour association but also on its potential underlying psychological mechanism.

Literature generally suggests that anthropomorphism is motivated by our human innate need for social connection as a way to support survival and mental health (Baumeister & Leary, 1995). It is hypothesised that when a non-human agent is anthropomorphised, it becomes a source of social connection (Epley, Waytz, & Cacioppo, 2007). Indeed, there are studies supporting this hypothesis, for instance, by indicating that lonely people find non-human entities such as dogs or God to be more like humans than those who feel less lonely (Epley, Akalis, Waytz, & Cacioppo, 2008).

Against this background Tam *et al.* (2013) examined how anthropomorphism affects people's connectedness to and behaviour toward nature in three different experiments. Indeed, their experiments revealed that participants who assigned human qualities to nature to a greater extent also reported a stronger connectedness with na-

---

8   Anthropomorphism of nature refers to the assignment of human qualities to nature.

ture, which in turn led to conservation behaviour. Thus, connectedness mediated the link between anthropomorphism and proenvironmental behaviour.

However, there are more benefits of a strong connectedness to nature. There is now good evidence that connectedness to nature robustly correlates with indicators of well-being, for instance, people who report feeling connected to nature also report more happiness even after controlling for other subjective connections, they also report greater contentment with life and greater positive affect than their counterparts (Mayer & Frantz, 2004; Tam, 2013; Zelenski & Nisbet, 2014).

Also nature connectedness appears to be associated with psychological resilience as Ingulli and Lindbloom (2013) found. Based on qualitative studies revealing a positive association between connectedness to nature and one's ability to cope during difficult times (e.g. Glassman, 1995) Ingulli and Lindbloom (2013) conducted a survey study on psychological resilience and connectedness to nature. They found moderate positive correlations between self-reported psychological resilience and connectedness to nature for the entire sample. However, this result seemed to be related to the socioeconomic status associated with the data collection site in the sense that study participants from schools associated with higher socioeconomic status revealed a stronger relationship between connectedness and resilience than those with a lower socioeconomic status. The authors suggest that this finding might support other research results indicating that environmental awareness is related to socioeconomic factors (Ingulli & Lindbloom, 2013).

A further construct which seems to be particularly associated with connectedness to nature and well-being is meaning in life (Cervinka, Roderer, & Hefler, 2012). As Cervinka *et al.* elaborate:

> *Meaningfulness, in contrast to depression, is understood as a developmental motive, referring to a human's need of being in the world and experiencing a sense of purpose in life. People scoring high on meaningfulness conceive their lives as fulfilling and relatively free from feelings of powerlessness, helplessness, fear and depression. They feel accepted by others and experience social connectedness and high satisfaction in their lives.* (p. 384)

Howell, Passmore and Buro (2013) asked 311 undergraduates to complete several measures of connectedness to nature, meaning in life and well-being and found in their mediational analysis that meaning in life fully mediated the link between connectedness and well-being. Furthermore, in a second study, Howell at al. (2013) were able to demonstrate the same type of mediation via meaning in life for the link between well-being and religiousness. Altogether, their results support previous findings on the significance of meaning of life for well-being, and, moreover, give rise to the association between meaning in life and nature connectedness. Based on their second study Howell *et al.* (2013) further suggest that experiences, which involve transcendence beyond the self such as nature or religious experiences, influence and enhance well-being as a consequence of their association with enhanced meaning in life.

Similarly, Kamitsis and Francis (2013) found an analogous mediation between connectedness to nature and well-being, only this time via spirituality, a related construct of meaning of life. In their study spirituality was assessed via the Mysticism Scale (MS) (Hood, 1975), a measure free of religious interpretation, which reflects a sense of experience or unity with the outside world. As such, this measure rather assesses the "meaning-making" implied by a spiritual orientation than a potential religious component (Kamitsis & Francis, 2013). They found that spirituality significantly mediated the association between nature exposure and psychological well-being as well as between connectedness to nature and psychological well-being. The authors conclude that spirituality and its innate "meaning-making" might function as a source, which facilitates the benefits of nature experiences (Kamitsis & Francis, 2013).

In a further set of studies Howell, Dopko, Passmore and Buro (2013) focused on mindfulness, nature connectedness and various indices of well-being. Their studies revealed that "feeling good" indices of well-being were less reliably associated with connectedness to nature than "functioning well" indices representing psychological and social well-being. Moreover, it was rather the awareness scales of the mindfulness measures, thus awareness of experiences in nature, which correlated with nature connectedness than the acceptance scores that is the non-judgemental acceptance of the nature experiences.

Summarised, there seems to be a recurring stable association between nature connectedness and well-being. However, based on a content analysis of the Connectedness to Nature Scale (CNS) items by Perrin and Benassi (2009) Zhang, Howell and Iyer (2014) question whether it is actually the emotional connection, which is assessed via nature connectedness or rather people's cognitive belief about their connection to nature. In order to ensure tapping the emotional connection to nature they decided to include the Engagement with Natural Beauty scale (Diessner, Solom, Frost, Parsons, & Davidson, 2008) in their investigation of the relationship between nature connectedness and well-being, a scale which reflects emotional and physiological arousal in response to the perception of beauty in the natural world. Indeed, Zhang *et al.* (2014) found that the relationship between connectedness and well-being was moderated by the tendency to engage with natural beauty. The authors conclude that people who are more emotionally attuned to nature's beauty also gain most positive effects from being connected to nature.

Even though self-reported connectedness to nature seems to entail a great variety of benefits for humans and more of its facets are continuously revealed there are still grey areas as Vining, Merrick and Price (2008) intriguingly pointed out. Vining *et al.* (2008) conducted three studies sending out open-ended questionnaires asking randomly selected participants to report on their connection to nature as well as on their definition of natural and unnatural environments. The majority, that is 76.9 percent of the participants, considered themselves as part of nature. Yet, contradictorily, when asked to define nature participants generally excluded humans from the natural world and rather described preserved land unaltered by human beings. Indeed, some participants elaborated that they feel separate from nature even though they see themselves as a part of it and explained this discrepancy with a lack of contact and a lack of everyday closeness. The authors take up on the participants' explanations and see the present contradiction as a consequence of an increasing lack of contact with nature and a simultaneously increasing omnipresent contact with built environments. They furthermore suggest that it is worthwhile to consider that the human-nature relationship might not be strictly dichotomous in the sense that humans either feel part of nature or separate from it but that both perceptions can co-exist at the same time (Vining, Merrick, & Price, 2008).

Up to date, research into connectedness to nature gains increasing attention in the scientific field mostly focusing on its benefits for humans and proenvironmental behaviour. However, the studies of Vining at al. (2008) highlight that the human-nature relationship is immensely complex and possibly difficult to assess via the present categorisations and measurements in use. Given that nature connectedness does play the promising role that is suggested in the literature more insight needs to be gained into the processes and factors promoting such a connection. For this purpose it is worthwhile turning to qualitative research and particularly the research field of Significant Life Experiences (SLE) as a source of environmental commitment (Ernst & Theimer, 2011).

2.2.3 Formative experiences in the course of life

The course of individual lives is not always continuous, as Bandura noted (1982), but often shaped by chance encounters and events which can have lasting effects, change people's interests and can lead people into new trajectories of life. In line with this observation, Tanner (1980) discovered that biographies and autobiographies of environmental activists often started off with childhood memories of their nature experiences. This led him to open a new research field, that is, the study of Significant Life Experiences (SLE) as a source of commitment to environmental protection. He began to interview leaders of conservation groups asking them for memories of formative experiences, which ultimately led them to their work and passion. He found that these leaders mostly mentioned time spent in natural places, often in childhood, followed by influential teachers and parents, books and the loss of a natural area (Tanner, 1980).

This kicked off a growing body of research on people's reasons for commitment to working to protect the environment or educate others about it. Intriguingly, all of these studies report similar results in places all across the world such as Australia, Canada, Greece, Hong Kong, Slovenia, South Africa, Sri Lanka, Uganda, UK, Norway and the U.S. (e.g. Chawla, 1998; Bögeholz, 1999; Palmer *et al.*, 1998; Sward, 1999). Most frequently, the interviewees credited their commitment to environmental conservation or environmental education to special childhood places and people. Half to over 80 percent of the interviewed environmental educators and activists named childhood experiences of nature as a significant influence and equally often or second important family members and other role models who showed them the value of the natural world through their own appreciative attention to it. This was followed by membership in environmental or outdoor organisations, education and witnessing the destruction of a valued place.

Similarly, Chawla (1999) was interested in life experiences of Norwegian and North American environmental activists and educators, which formed their intention to act. Chawla, furthermore, specifically asked them about the period of life associated with these significant experiences. With the collected data Chawla (1999) was then able to construct a life path of predominant sources of commitment at different ages. Chawla's results revealed that the time of childhood is mostly associated with time spent in natural places, which was when a first bond with the natural world was formed and with family members who modelled an appreciation for nature. From junior high throughout university years education becomes important, and, unsurprisingly, with the beginning of university continuing into adulthood, friends turn into crucial role models and sources of encouragement. Throughout life, organisations such as girl scouts or environmental organisations can be important as they often bring about the possibility to spend time outdoors but also to get active together with others and thereby to acquire learning strategies and skills in groups. In adulthood, it is additionally the influence of job experiences and concern for the future of children that becomes apparent.

However, the thus far presented research on SLE is descriptive mostly referring to environmental activists and educators. This way, no comparison is possible with people who vary in their level of engagement, which is an important prerequisite in order to understand the dynamics of the environmental movement (Chawla, 2001).

Fortunately, there are now a number of comparative studies, which strengthen the descriptive research. For instance, a large survey study, including randomly selected American adults, showed that activities in natural places during childhood predicted proenvironmental attitudes and behaviour such as recycling and "green" voting (Wells & Lekies, 2006). Interestingly, exploring nature with others was not a significant predictor in this study. However, this does not contradict former findings, as research revealed that it is not the mere presence of others that is important but what these others do (Chawla, 2007).

Similarly, in a German survey sample (Kals *et al.*, 1999) interest in, and affinity for, nature as well as indignation at its inadequate protection was significantly associated to firstly, time spent in nature, including time spent during childhood, and secondly, to the meaningful presence of family members and teachers. Affinity, interest and indignation moreover predicted the willingness to conserve nature. Thus, while nature experiences had only a marginal direct effect on behaviour they did predict emotional affinity toward nature, which in turn predicted behaviour.

In a further study, 1243 surveys of 10 to 18 year-old Germans were collected. The sample included environmentally engaged students as well as non-active ones. The study revealed that the best predictors for the intention to protect nature were nature experiences, ecologically responsible behaviour of the parents and the behaviour of peers (Bögeholz, 1999).

Summarised, research on ecologically responsible behaviour shows that there is no single all-potent experience but several experiences together that seem to generate engaged citizens (Chawla, 1998). In addition, no direction of influence can be established, yet, and there are some aspects to consider when interpreting these results. For instance, some children may carry a special affinity for nature, hence seek and experience it more, and thereby elicit similar behaviour in adults and teachers. Also, children and adults have interactive relationships, thus caretakers could similarly decide to keep their children from free play in nature (Chawla, 2007). Further, people who are not committed to the environment could have had a similar amount of nature experiences as those who are committed but could have felt alienated in nature. Reversely, urban conservationists might have had little of the typical formative experiences but are nonetheless committed to proenvironmental causes (Chawla, 1998).

These considerations seem to be partly reflected in Myers' study (1997). Myers (1997) interviewed two groups of undergraduates who either majored in environmental studies or in other areas. Both groups rated their environmental concern as moderate to very strong and no difference was found with regard to incidences of positive natural place experiences in childhood, to positive feelings in nature, or to negative reactions to the destruction of a familiar natural habitat. However, Myers

(1997) detected a few more positive wilderness experiences, more family role models and more spontaneous accounts of positive childhood experiences of nature in the interviews with the environmental majors. But, intriguingly, the primary difference he found was that the environmental majors were more likely to express meaningful identification with a natural area. This, in fact, resembles research results of Brixler and Morris' (1997) study where the indicative group difference was not nature experiences as such but those ones, which socialised recreation seekers compared to non-seekers into interpreting nature in a positive or meaningful way. Myers (1997) concludes from his results that experiences such as positive nature experiences in childhood, positive feelings in nature, or negative reactions to the destruction of a familiar natural area fail to predict commitment to an environmental career. The crux, Myers (1997) argues, is to shift the focus of SLE research from solely knowing people's experience to understanding how individuals construct their significance. The self-reported cluster of reasons for the respondents' environmental engagement mirror how individuals make choices in their lives and most importantly, how they make sense of their lives. Thus, the essential question to be answered in SLE research is "how individuals (and groups) construct 'significance' both 'in' (during) and 'out' (after) of 'the' experience" (Payne, 1999, p.370).

According to Chawla (1998), another aspect missing in SLE research thus far is the investigation of the "internal environment" of individuals such as their needs, emotions, abilities and interests, which may be essential in the process of attributing significance to external events. While most SLE research focuses on the external environment of natural places or social mediators, the way the individual receptively responds to them, thus the exchange between an external and internal environment, remains the "silent side" of these experiences. "In all", Payne (1999) warns, "the inner/outer nature dualism is to be avoided" (p. 377).

2.2.4 Transcendence and the human experience of nature

While the former chapter highlighted, inter alia, the importance of experiences in nature this chapter focuses on the phenomenology of nature experiences, particularly significant nature experiences, and concomitant phenomena.

Obviously, qualitative dimensions of individuals' experiences in nature have been more challenging to assess empirically (Mayer & Frantz, 2004). Considering that engagement with nature is a subjective, lived experience, it is qualitative methods which are called for when researching the depths of human encounters with nature (Hinds & Sparks, 2011). As each human experience is an interplay of setting, individual identities and situational influences, each individual uniquely creates meaning, often by creating a story of their experience within the limits of what can be perceived, a notion called situated freedom (Patterson, Williams, Watson & Roggenbuck, 1998). This is reflected in a study with canoeists (Patterson, Williams, Watson, & Roggenbuck, 1998). Patterson *et al.* found that participants defined challenge as part of their canoeing experience very differently. For some challenge was positive, for others negative or ambivalent, for some it was the defining characteristic of their experience, others saw it simply as making a good story. Moreover, meaning seemed to change over time, which highlights the emergent nature of experiences, the influence of the environment on-site and situational circumstances (Patterson *et al.*, 1998).

Even though experiences in the natural world are highly individual, nature offers some fundamental features, which seem to create an especially beneficial environment for humans. Roggenbuck and Driver (2000) identified some of those as congruent with Kaplan's (1995) four critical components of restorative environments: being away, fascination, extent and compatibility. According to Roggenbuck and Driver (2000), wilderness most of the time means "being away" from everyday distractions, it harbours innumerable entities and processes that catch attention and elicit fascination, it is by definition vast and for a lot of people nature is highly compatible as exemplified in many activities in nature that directly respond to deeply rooted, over centuries inherited human endeavours such as hunting, collecting food, hiking, caring for pets, bird watching and tracking. Thus, nature seems to provide best prerequisites for people's restoration.

But as research shows, people report many more psychological rewards from their nature experiences than mere restoration, such as personal growth, creativity and inspiration (McDonald, Wearing, & Ponting, 2009), wonder and pleasure (Hinds & Sparks, 2011) or feelings of happiness and inner calm of being close to nature (Eigner, 2001). In accordance, self-reports of connectedness to nature encompassed a variety of descriptions such as calmness, wholeness, wonder and peacefulness but also joy and awe (Hegarty, 2010).

Hinds (2011) suggested that wonderment with nature facilitates an uncomplicated state of mind similar to mindfulness and that a diary-based account of engaging with nature can lead to mindful awareness, an "awareness that arises through intentionally attending in an open, accepting, and discerning way to whatever is arising in the present moment" (Shapiro, 2009, p. 556). As outlined in chapter 2.2.2, mindfulness indeed has been shown to enhance the experience of nature and nature connectedness (A. J. Howell, Dopko, Passmore, & Buro, 2011). Richardson (2013) examined the process of keeping a diary throughout repetitive nature exposure. He found that initially the writer rather observed nature with the desire to understand it but then, once the level of connectedness increased over time, the writings mirrored personal fulfilment in nature in the form of an emotional connection to the natural environment, satisfaction through immersion in nature, recognising nature's beauty and viewing nature as a fundamental life source which nourishes body, mind and soul. Mindful awareness became more and more evident in the entries once the connection to nature was built. The author concluded that a diary-based account of systematic engagement with the local environment can indeed establish a pathway to mindfulness.

Furthermore, some people consciously engage in activities such as walking, gardening and meditating in nature specifically for self-healing purposes (e.g. see Hegarty, 2010), which Snell and Simmonds (2012) see as evidence for the capacity of natural environments to evoke spiritual experiences. Although several studies emphasise the importance of the spiritual dimension of nature experiences (e.g. Fredrickson & Anderson, 1999; Williams & Harvey, 2001), the empirical exploration of the character of significant experiences that contribute to the spiritual value of nature is still scarce (Terhaar, 2009). This is surprising, especially in the light of the increasing popularity of the concept of connectedness to nature which some researchers see as an essentially spiritual phenomenon (e.g. Dutcher, Finley, Luloff & Johnson, 2007).

Snell and Simmonds (2012) interviewed twenty voluntary Australian participants on their spiritual experiences in nature. They found that, as part of their experience, participants noticed a switch in their state of mind from analysing and thinking to a rather meditative and reflective state. In this state, participants described, their personal issues resolved which led to profound changes in their beliefs, identity and emotions (Snell & Simmonds, 2012). According to Snell and Simmonds (2012) this process resembles the process outlined in the Attention Restoration Theory by Kaplan and Kaplan (1989).

Kaplan and Kaplan (1989) propose that attention restoration takes place in four stages: clearing the head, restoration of attention, confrontation with cognitive leftovers from previous days and, lastly, reflection of life, aims and opportunities. It is in this final stage where participants often report spiritual experiences as awe, wonder, connectedness, and unity and several researchers believe that this is where spiritual experiences in nature occur (e.g. Williams & Harvey, 2001).

Spiritual experiences in nature are often associated with the dissolution of the boundaries between the natural world and humans, almost like an out-of-body connection, and with the alteration of the sense of time and space (Fredrickson & Anderson, 1999). Importantly, self-reports revealed that it was, indeed, the natural environment, which allowed for the profound experiences to take place. Reported essential wilderness aspects were vastness, inherent physical challenges and long time spans of solitude (Roggenbuck & Driver, 2000) but also the absence of distractions, pressure and concerns of the human world (McDonald *et al.*, 2009). Studies have shown that profound experiences in nature are often coupled with a sense of oneness, unity, wholeness, and/or connectedness (Talbot & Kaplan, 1986) and a strong sense of meaning and purpose as a consequence of experiencing oneself in the setting of a vast natural environment. For participants, on the one hand, this setting emphasised the great value of life and, on the other hand, participants realised this way the transience of their personal issues (see Kaplan & Talbot, 1983; Fredrickson & Anderson, 1999).

The latter aspect even has been researched in experimental tests. Mayer, Frantz, Bruehlman-Senecal and Dolliver (2009) conducted studies to investigate whether exposure to nature actually facilitated individuals' ability to reflect on a life problem. In a series of studies, participants either took a 15-minute walk in an urban or natural environment or they watched a 15-minute video of a natural or urban environment. In all studies, nature enhanced the participants' ability to reflect on a life problem. The effect was more dramatic for the natural than for the virtual natural environment. Notably, this was partly mediated by enhanced nature connectedness but not at all mediated by increases in attentional capacity. Thus, it is not merely enhanced attentional resources that enable personal reflection but at least partly a sense of connection that arises from the experience in nature. Furthermore, the comparison between settings clearly points towards the significant influence that actually being in nature, rather than being exposed to an urban or even virtual natural environment, has on complex socioemotional processes such as dealing with a life problem (Mayer, Frantz, Bruehlman-Senecal, & Dolliver, 2009).

Hedlund-de Witt (2013) investigated phenomenological descriptions of her study participants' nature experiences. As a result, three interrelated clusters of themes emerged persistently – namely presence, interconnectedness and self-expansion. During their nature experience, participants started to tune in with their senses making them feel more present in their bodies and to the current moment, which also invoked in them the sense of truly participating in the world. Another common theme was interconnectedness, which has been found in other studies, too (e.g. Kaplan & Talbot, 1983; Fredrickson & Anderson, 1999; Williams & Harvey, 2001), and which encompassed the realisation of being tied in with the natural world, a sense of belonging as well as feeling one with something greater. Participants reported that this sense of interconnectedness made them realise that their actions have consequences, which appeared to lead to greater environmental awareness and behaviour by making them feel more responsible. The third theme cluster was self-reflection and self-expansion. Participants described experiencing themselves differently, for instance, as feeling more real, stronger or more like themselves. Some reported suddenly gaining access to parts of themselves that usually drown in everyday life such as a sense of inner peace, empowerment or meaning. This sense of self-reflection or self-expansion, in turn, seemed to highlight for participants their abilities and "better sides" and made them feel more inspired and empowered.

All in all, the majority of participants stated that such experiences had a crucial impact on their lives, influencing their world views, their environmental responsibility and in some cases even career choices (Hedlund-de Witt, 2013).

This is in accordance with the outcomes of a ten-year long research programme which has shown that such profound wilderness experiences can evoke broad psychological changes altering participants' perspectives on the world, nature and life but also personal priorities and engagement (Kaplan & Talbot, 1983; Talbot & Kaplan, 1986). As Hedlund-de Witt (2013) aptly summarised, "it appears that precisely when experiences in nature are particularly profound and meaningful to participants, a spiritual dimension is encountered, and the experience's potential to provide a sense of environmental responsibility is enhanced" (p.24).

However, notably, it seems as though it is not only human care for nature, which is altered but also the way humans relate to each other. Studies by Weinstein, Przybylski and Ryan (2009) showed that participants who were asked to actively immerse themselves in nature by paying attention to the various details in nature reported greater willingness to establish lasting relationships than less immersed individuals. More precisely, participants who were exposed to natural environments and who indicated immersion also communicated increased intrinsic and decreased extrinsic aspirations[9]. However, for those individuals who were exposed to non-natural environments immersion did not predict intrinsic aspirations but an increase of extrinsic ones. Importantly, this was the case even though Weinstein *et al.*'s studies proved these effects for nature on immersion merely in a laboratory setting by simply exposing the study participants to slides and plants. The authors conclude, "that nature [...] brings individuals closer to others, whereas human-made environments orient goals toward more selfish or self-interested ends" (p. 1327). This is in line with the studies of Zhang, Piff, Iyer, Koleva and Keltner (2014), which demonstrated the prosocial benefits of beautiful na-

---

9   As Weinstein *et al.* (2009) elaborated "intrinsic aspirations concern the pursuit of goals that in themselves satisfy basic psychological needs [...]. Extrinsic aspirations focus on externally valued goods that are not inherently rewarding but are sought to derive positive regard or rewards from others [...]" (p.1316).

ture. In four studies they showed that participants who perceived natural beauty more readily also reported higher prosocial tendencies (e.g. empathy). Further, participants who were exposed to more beautiful images of natural environments were also more trusting and generous and exposure to more beautiful plants in the lab increased the participants helping behaviour (Zhang *et al.*, 2014).

At any rate, these results indicate that nature inherently bears the potential to not only evoke transcendent or personally profound experiences that are beneficial for personal growth but also to transcend self-interest and to positively contribute to the quality of human interpersonal relationships.

3

The human-nature relationship through the lens of an expanded worldview

As already hinted at in the previous sections, whether experiences influence our lives depends on the meaning we ascribe to them. This, in turn, seems to shape our future experiences and perception (Myers, 1997) and is to a large extent influenced by the prevailing worldview (Chawla, 1999). Therefore, depending on how we choose to frame or understand the human-nature relationship, different implications for our perception, experience and behaviour arise. As Schultz (2002) aptly elaborates:

> *To what extent are humans part of nature? The answer to this question ripples through any ethic. If humans are part of nature, if they are connected symbiotically with nature, then perhaps they have a responsibility to protect nature. In contrast, if humans are not part of nature, then they do not have a moral responsibility.* (p. 64-65)

Schultz (2002) thereby gets right to the heart of the impact of such meaning-making. Simultaneously, this raises doubts as to whether the worldview, thus understanding of the human-nature relationship, nowadays actually serves the human and planetary well-being. But above all, considerations like this spark the question of how an expanded worldview might contribute to the human-nature relationship and how this might change our perception and behaviour.

However, in order to think outside the box of the prevailing worldview we need to become aware of it. Therefore, analysing scholarly insight into the human-nature relationship and the way this relationship has been conceptualised and researched over time seems indispensable in order to understand its extensive influence and the potential benefits of expanding our worldview (see also Russell *et al.*, 2013).

3.1 A brief history of the human-nature relationship

As cultural scientist and philosopher Alexandra Gusetti (2014) unravels in her book *Headfirst into Nature*, in the cultural history of nature humans embarked on a strange journey that led to the invention of a nature concept that excludes us. This leads to the valid question: What are we if not nature[10] (Gusetti, 2014)?

Most likely in the Palaeolithic Age humans rather experienced themselves as an integral part of the great variety of natural entities. This is suggested by cave paintings from that time, which mostly depict animals but only rarely humans, indicating identification with the wider natural world, in particular the animal kingdom. This self-perception changed with the agricultural use of land (in Europe approximately 7000 B.C.), which led humans to experience their creative influence and power as seemingly sophisticated creators.

However, there was a narrow pre-Socratic period when philosophers tried to explain the primal root of existence with nature itself. For instance Thales (625-546 B.C.) proposed water as the basic substance of life. This short moment in the cultural history of nature passed with Plato and Aristotle, who made a clear cut between nature and the hierarchical more sophisticated intellectual world. Furthermore, in Plato's myth of the creation of the world there is the all-embracing supremacy of God who is presented as the only architect and superior creator similar to Aristotle who presented God as pure perfection, which attracts the imperfect. Attacking Plato's idea of the supremacy of "the God who creates all" Giordano Bruno (1548-1600) argued that, consequently, everything which God had created must be equally divine, too. Bruno even went as far as to put human consciousness on the same level with nature and its creative character.

Meanwhile Vesalius (1514-1564) published his first anatomy book, which broke the medieval taboo in research and gave way to a new kind of science that aspired to understand nature by directly researching it. However, the extra-worldly God proposed by Aristotle as the primary initiator still prevailed.

Unanswered, in this context, remained the question of how to explain the inner drive and impulses in nature, which was why magic as a potential supplement to the scientific world became more the focus of scientific interest. Paracelsus, for instance, saw nature itself as a female magician and teacher and developed a vision of a new medicine that only accepted nature as a teacher. Paracelsus furthermore believed that humans bear just the same self-healing powers as nature. The attempt to integrate natural-magical thinking in the scientific discourse was characteristic for the 15th and 16th century but it quickly faded away.

With Descartes (1596-1650) came the crucial switch in thinking. Descartes regarded humans as sophisticated scientists who have the ability to analyse the mystical logic of nature. Also, according to Descartes, nature was available to humans as a mere research object free of perception. Following up on this notion, Newton (1642-1726) understood the world as steered by God who created simple and logical laws that rule the cosmos. For Newton, nature was God's work and his vocation was to recognise the laws working within. He established complex mathematics, which suddenly made the world describable through a scientific mathematical scheme. What was formerly within the scope of theologians was now left to experts highly capable of abstraction.

---

10   The following section will be based on the historical summary provided in Gusetti's book.

The image that arose during that time is one of intellectual scientists who "peer down at nature, observe the cosmos and draw conclusions" (Gusetti, 2014, p. 75).

This development troubled Kant (1724-1804) greatly. He pondered how to integrate liveliness and diversity in this worldview, as both could not be derived from natural laws. Nature and humans were facing each other, alien to each other yet akin.

This circumstance occupied many poets' minds during Romanticism and they saw art and poetry as a way to communicate with and understand nature. Nevertheless, they too remained separate from nature as they positioned themselves superior through their self-ascribed ability to understand and interpret nature. This way, Gusetti (2014) elaborates, nature was still not regarded "as a partner [...] but as an inferior lover" (p. 89).

The natural sciences meanwhile continued to experience a boom, as scientific experiments seemed to suggest that nature could indeed be broken down and analysed in isolated pieces. This assumption, however, was threatened around the end of the 19th and the beginning of the 20th century with the emergence of more and more scientific inconsistencies, which in turn encouraged the efforts of unconventional thinkers. For instance, Hans Driesch (1867-1941) showed in his famous experiment with sea urchins that another independent larva could develop from the original mutilated larva which proved the fascinating ability of organisms to reproduce and self-organise. With this Driesch furthermore demonstrated the presence of the whole in its parts as a fundamental specific feature of organic life. This was supported by Goldstein's findings on brain-lesioned soldiers from the First World War. Goldstein observed that the healthy areas of the brain started to take over the tasks of the injured ones, a finding which the human-machine-metaphor could no longer account for. Developments in physics paralleled those in biology that called into question a simple mechanistic view of the world. With the discovery of the quanta, at the end of the 19th century, it became evident that nature could not be understood as a random accumulation of atoms and that not everything could be explained mathematically. Specifically, quantum physics revealed that a quantum object could not be understood via the isolated states of its particles but that the whole must be accepted as the fundamental condition. Thus far, humans had been used to view the world as consisting of countless single objects that one can draw conclusions from. However, in the light of the world that quantum physics revealed, the only statements admissible seemed to be the ones about relational structures. Even though quantum physics is, thus far, only applicable to the very micro-level of our physical world, its existence does raise the question of how the "quantum reality" may relate to our "experienced reality" or, at the very least, what kind of implications this entails for our current scientific paradigm (for further elaborations on this topic see Walach & Stillfried, 2011).

After all, it remains an astonishing fact, as Gusetti (2014) aptly points out, that the concept of life is still not mentioned, not even in physical-philosophical holistic models. Gusetti argues that if there is space, time and matter and everything can be derived from it then life is an immanent phenomenon of the cosmos and should be addressed. However, apart from Schrödinger (1887-1961), this topic was not brought up in the physical context and the physical inorganic research areas were maintained separate from the organic and real world.

With the post-war economic upswing, consumption in the Western world increased massively, so that in the 1970s, the first extensive environmental problems became obvious. During that time eco-feminism arose and feminists started to question the dualism of science, rationality and masculinity versus nature and femininity. Feminist researchers saw danger in the masculine-rational separation from nature, which was why the feminist movement intentionally emphasised being part of nature. Today, it is widely recognised in gender studies that the development of Western thinking about nature is inseparable from the notion of human mastery over objectified nature and violence against women.

The increasing presence of environmental problems also entailed the reappearance of old philosophical questions and natural philosophers started to switch perspectives from "humans within surrounding environments" to "humans as only one living being amongst many".

However, this view opposes the religion-based supremacy that humans ascribe to themselves as well as the prevailing separation between rational human self-awareness and the surrounding, purely material nature as part of our contemporary worldview (Gusetti, 2014). Gusetti (2014) concludes that throughout the cultural history of nature humans have always reserved for themselves supreme competences as the observer, researcher and interpreter of nature. By drawing on the historical and long-established argument of possessing consciousness, a soul or rationality humans have persistently made sure not to become fully a part of nature.

3.2 Expanding the contemporary worldview

3.2.1 A critical examination of the contemporary worldview

It seems as though nature in our contemporary worldview is still regarded as separate from us, objective and analysable. There is now vast scientific knowledge about human as well as non-human nature. However, as Gusetti (2014) points out, within the realm of classical science it is still not orthodox to connect this knowledge with our own inner knowledge and experience of being a part of nature ourselves. Trusting our own intuition in this way is often dismissed as esoteric or naive (Gusetti, 2014). In Gusetti's (2014) opinion, physicality and sensuality as our human innate nature became alien to us as soon as we handed over the expertise to designated external scientific experts. In that sense, today science not only produces knowledge but also limits this individual knowledge, which derives from deeply experiential subjectivity. As biologist and philosopher Andreas Weber (2013) aptly elaborates the paradoxical aspect of this circumstance:

> *A worldview that can explain the world only in the 'third person', as if everything is finally a non-living thing, denies the existence of the very actors who set forth this view. It is a worldview that deliberately ignores the fact that we are subjective, feeling humans – members of an animal species whose living metabolisms are in constant material exchange with the world.* (p. 11)

Thus, humans have to overcome a considerable obstacle, as "the subjective experience of nature is, of course, the antithesis of the objective stance that science has come to insist on as an accurate way to understand existence" (Fish, 2005, p.104). Due to the scientific obligation to be unemotional and precise we are bound to the Cartesian view of nature as separate and inanimate. Nevertheless, ironically, it is also revolutionary scientific discoveries that can cause us to rethink our approach to nature and potentially cause changes in perception. This was demonstrated in the rise of quantum mechanics, which revealed nature's building blocks as highly interconnected and very much alive (Rader, 2009). However, as Gusetti (2014) argues, if intellectual understanding is not followed by a profound personal process and experiences these insights most likely remain superficial and disembodied (Gusetti, 2014). Yet, unfortunately, significant life events and exceptional experiences have been systematically excluded from conventional research in conjunction with the appreciation and acknowledgement for such experiences. Fatally, this robs us from different kinds of knowledge and keeps conventional research narrow (Braud & Anderson, 1998). As Braud and Anderson (1998) point out this not only causes frustration for researchers but also for the research consumers.

This circumstance actually refers back to the persistent research gap, as highlighted in the previous section, namely the lack of explanation for the phenomenon of life itself (Gusetti, 2014). As Weber (2007) criticises, this is the case even in biology where definitions of life remain distant from the experiences that we continuously make in our lives. However, according to Weber (2007), it is fundamental for biological sense-making to include the reality of subjective experience. Therefore, demanding a relational way of thinking, Weber (2007) calls for the integration of third-person science with a first-person science that embraces bodily experiences, feelings and sensations. Weber (2007) welcomes the constant paradoxes, which arise naturally when both are combined as, in Weber's view, life is all about moment-to-moment resolution and expression of complexity and contradictions.

In his book *Everything Feels* Weber (2007) further expounds how contemporary scientific discoveries, in fact, start to reveal subjectivity as a fundamental principle in nature. Weber (2007) clearly describes that with increasing ability to examine micro-levels of life, evidence for life's complexity and intelligence accumulates. According to Weber (2007), an organism appears as a unit, which is bound together via its feelings, namely feelings that inform the organism what does it good and what harms it. Furthermore, this "new biology", as Weber (2007) calls it, demonstrates that feeling as a phenomenon can explain consciousness as well as all life processes. As a consequence, Weber (2013) suggests complementing the enlightenment position with "enlivenment", that is with "the 'empirical subjectivity' of living beings, and with the 'poetic objectivity' of meaningful experiences" (p.11).

Weber (2013) sees the contemporary lack of attention ascribed to actual, lived and felt human existence in science, society and politics as one of the fundamental barriers to realising sustainability. The notion of dissolving relationships into entities or dead objects creates a metaphysic of death, which explains, as Weber argues (2013), why so many people nowadays feel depressed. Weber eloquently further infers that a relationship which is thought to be dead will be treated as such, which reflects the way humanity currently treats the earth. Weber (2013) therefore puts forth "a new cultural orientation towards the open-ended, embodied, meaning-generating, paradoxical and inclusive processes of life" (p.12).

The importance of integrating open-endedness in our worldview is in line with Gusetti's (2014) argument. She regrets that in classical-mechanistic science as well as in the history of holistic thinking the tendency to produce closed systems still prevails. In her opinion, this endeavour is bound to fail, as it is an empirical reality that a coherent whole is merely the exception and all components of the system along with all their associations can never be discovered entirely. Consequently, she proposes, as the only reliable truth, that nature is constituted of multidimensional connectivity and entanglement, which ultimately demands the recognition of the premise of unknowingness, thus, the recognition of nature as an inclusive, infinite and open system. Following up on this view, Weber (2013) further emphasises the utmost importance for humans to experience this connectivity, as it is what essentially makes us feel alive. He concludes as follows:

> *The freedom that the Enlightenment has sought to advance is the individual's personal autonomy to be one's own master. The freedom that the Enlivement seeks to advance is our freedom as individuals and groups to be «alive-in-connectedness» – the freedom that comes only through aligning individual needs and interests with those of the larger community. Only this integrated freedom can provide the power to reconcile humanity with the natural world.* (p.12)

The position of enlivement seems to at least partly touch on the notion of "reenchantment" (Griffin, 1988). Establishing a personal relationship with the living earth as an expansion of the prevailing scientific paradigm is put forth by various writers from diverse fields (Abram, 1997). This kind of personal relationship is called by many a "reenchanted" relationship with the natural world and gives rise to a way of knowing which includes sensory engagement, dimensions of wonder and joy as well as an expanded sense of identity (Barlett, 2008). More specifically, Barlett (2008) describes this as "the process by which nonrational, experiential, deeply meaningful relations with nature are reconstructed as a legitimate part of our contemporary worldview" (p.1080).

3.2.2 A brief introduction to deep ecology

In line with the above illustrated notions, working towards expanding our contemporary worldview, is the environmental philosophy "deep ecology" as founded by Arne Naess (1973). Deep ecology developed as an antidote to the more anthropocentrically driven form of environmentalism, which reinforces nature conservation for the purpose of protecting humanity (Merkl, 1995). Naess (1973) used the word "deep" to distance this philosophy from such "shallow" ecology, which, in his view, only deals with the symptoms of a much deeper ecological crisis.

According to Naess, the position that deep ecology adopts is not an intellectual construction but corresponds to deeply grown convictions that are rooted in the holistic understanding of nature, which developed throughout the course of human history (Diehm, 2006).

Naess also strongly insisted on the need to separate natural ethics and spiritual worldviews (Diehm, 2006). He believed that no aspect of nature, including humanity, can be superior to another, a principle which he called "biospheric egalitarianism" (Naess, 1973). Furthermore, according to Naess, each part of nature bears an intrinsic value, independent of its usefulness for human purposes (Naess, 1989). This notion, however, is not necessarily reflected in the Western worldview. As values deeply penetrate our thinking and actions, deep ecology demands deep questioning of the prevailing worldview and the associated meaning of truth (Devall & Sessions, 1985). Thus, it can be a long and painful process until an individual is actually able to experience and re-establish "a felt sense of identity that extends deep into the non-human world" (Rader, 2009, p. 18).

An expansive or transpersonal sense of self is one of the central elements in deep ecology and is referred to as the "ecological self" (Bragg, 1996). Naess (1988) simply defined an individual's ecological self as "that with which he identifies" (p. 22). Identification, in turn, is explained by Naess (1985) as "a spontaneous, non-rational process through which the interest or interests of another being are reacted to as our own interest or interests" (p. 261). Bragg (1996) researched the deep ecology literature and summarised these reactions as emotions, behaviours, perceptions and transcendent experiences.

Firstly, an experience of the ecological self can encompass emotional resonance with another non-human being similar to compassion or empathy. The second and more perceptual aspect of identification is the experience or recognition of similarity in another being. The third aspect of experiences of ecological self falls within the scope of spiritual experiences and describes a more cosmic connection and identification with all there is, which Fox (1990) referred to as ontologically-based identification. Fox (1990) further added a cosmologically-based identification, which represents a sense of connectedness with the rest of the natural world and roots in the realisation that all living beings are part of the same reality.

Finally, the fourth aspect of experiences of ecological self that Bragg (1996) extracts from the literature is that of spontaneous ecological behaviour. As a result of expanding the sense of self to all life forms humans naturally take care of the planet, obviating any need for environmental ethics. Deep ecologists believe that widening circles of identification also leads to extending the boundaries of our self-interest. This also implicates that the sense of self is regarded as flexible. As James Hillman (1995) eloquently elaborated in his essay *A Psyche the Size of the Earth*:

> *Since the cut between self and natural world is arbitrary, we can make it at the skin or we can take it out as far as you like–to the deep oceans and distant stars. But the cut is far less important than the recognition of uncertainty about making the cut at all.* (p. xix)

In the literature deep ecologists propose a wide range of methods for amplifying the ecological self (Bragg, 1996). For instance, Fox (1990) suggests spiritually based practices such as Zen Buddhist practices whereas Devall (1988) advises wilderness experiences and rituals as a way to familiarise with one's local region along with environmental activism and a simple life-style.

However, it is especially nature experiences and immersion that are repeatedly promoted as a way to assist the process of self-realisation, of developing a sense of biospheric equality, ecological self (Holloway, 1991) as well as of developing the desire to serve others and the planet (Roszak, 1992).

An example for such a practice, the Solo in nature, will be described in more depth in the following section.

3.3 An ancient practice revisited – Solos in nature

3.3.1 Introduction

The solo journey has a long pan-cultural tradition amongst others advocated by Christ, Kant, Confucius, Emerson, Thoreau and Muir, and it can take on many shapes such as walking, hiking, biking, or paddling in solitude (Smith, 2005).

For instance, solo walking is a famous Aborigines practice called "walkabout", which traditionally serves as a rite of passage. The walkabout can last months and the walked paths bear spiritual but also pragmatic significance as they also reveal sources of water (Smith, 2005). Even though the walkabout involves solo walking, while the Native American "vision quest" involves a static Solo waiting at a sacred place, both have in common that they reflect the hero's journey as outlined by Joseph Campbell (2008).

Studying myths from around the world Campbell (2008) recognised that heroic journeys usually follow a certain pattern: it starts with the hero leaving everyday life to search for a personal vision and gather special knowledge. This typically leads to a confrontation with personal fears and challenges, which need to be fought and overcome. The journey from the known to the unknown changes the hero forever and he returns to his community with new knowledge and gifts (Campbell, 2008). As a metaphor for personal growth and self-discovery Solos in nature are often understood as a hero's journey (Smith, 2005).

As Joan Halifax wrote, "Nature's wilderness is the locus for the elicitation of the individual's inner wilderness, the great plain of the spirit" (Galland, 1980, p. 115). Therefore, nature can give rise to a process of self-discovery, which is accompanied by switching from a focus on the outside to a focus on the inside (Smith, 2005). In particular, solitude in conjunction with the absence of everyday distractions provides optimal space for personal reflection. Such introspection, in turn, facilitates insight into self and, as part of a Solo in wild nature, brings about an awareness for one's potential and capabilities, as participants have to face their fears and take responsibility for their own well-being (Smith, 2005). Even though Solos can involve a great deal of contemplation of personal relationships it is knowledge about self that can be directly extracted from it (Smith, 2005).

However, Solos can also lead to unique experiences of the connections with the natural world. As ecopsychologists believe, this might be essential for psychological, social and cultural health (Roszak, 1979). No matter how narrow or extensive the timeframe the Solo provides an opportunity to experience such effects (Smith, 2005) which includes the experience of psychological interconnectedness with the non-human world. As Romanyshyn (2007) put it:

> *The ecological reality is this – we are completely dependent for our survival on the rest of nature. Physically, we cannot exist as encapsulated beings. We would argue that this is the case psychologically too – our psyche is sustained by its connection to the 'soul of the world'.* (p.17)

This psychological dependency is also elaborated by Weber (2013). Throughout human history we have continuously extracted mental concepts and inspiration from the natural world. This, in turn, has enabled humans to experience the symbolic and experiential side of being. For humans to be mirrored by non-human nature is necessary and irreplaceable as Weber (2013) explains:

> We need the experience of engaging with a «living inside» that stands in front of us, displaying itself as a fragile, mortal body. We need other organisms because they are in a very real sense what we ourselves are (biologically and psychically), but they give us access to those hidden parts of ourselves that we cannot see – precisely we cannot observe ourselves while observing. There is always a blind spot central to the establishment of our own identity. Seen from this point of view, other beings are the blind spot of our self-understanding. (p.34)

In Weber's (2013) opinion, the process of "becoming fully human by relating to the non-human" is of utmost importance for as long as we carry an inner uncertainty about self we won't be able to embrace "the other" and this inability to relate ultimately opposes the preservation of life.

As such, this process is also a crucial element that the Solo experience offers to the soloist.

3.3.2 The structure of the Solo as a rite of passage

As already stated, Solo times in nature can take many forms. However, in the following section I will describe the Solo time in the format of a rite of passage, as this resembles mostly the structure and overall intention of the 24-hour Solo programmes under investigation in the present work. The description is based on Bodkin and Sartor's (2005) outline of the rites of passage vision quest, which usually includes more extended Solo periods of three to four days.

A Solo facilitated to serve as a rite of passage can help people to specify life transitions and bring about the opportunity for psychological healing when initiated with intention, clarity and heart. Traditionally, a rite of passage was undertaken to confirm the movement from one life stage to the next by rising to a challenge of body, mind, soul and spirit. This can include transitions from childhood to adult life as well as transitions of adult life (Bodkin & Sartor, 2005).

Nowadays, in Western culture, these rites of passage have largely disappeared. However, people still feel the urge to mark transitions in life in meaningful ways. This especially affects adolescents wanting to move on to adulthood. Examples of widely acknowledged modern rites of passage from adolescence to adulthood are getting a driver's licence or graduation but often youth also start to create their own informal, non-intentional and peer-sanctioned rites of passage that are rather risky and destructive, such as binge drinking or being initiated into a gang. The crux with the latter kind of rites is that they lack fundamental elements of a genuine initiatory passage, namely appropriate challenges, elders as guides and witnesses and a celebration of the gained new status by the wider community (Bodkin & Sartor, 2005).

Foster and Little (1996) transferred Arnold Van Genepp's (1960) model of traditional rites of passage to the modern form of a vision quest as a rite of passage. According to this model, the three stages that a participant undergoes are severance, threshold and incorporation.

Severance represents the first phase when a person starts to leave behind modern everyday life. As part of a programme this includes the process of firstly, committing to the programme, traveling into wilderness, setting up a base camp and then leaving base camp to enter the Solo time. The threshold stage defines the space between the old self and the new self where the participant spends a designated time alone in the wild.

According to Bodkin and Sartor (2005), any initiatory rite requires a certain degree of risk as this gives the participant the opportunity to explore her or his boundaries, which enables self-discovery. The main challenges that a modern vision quest inherits are solitude, fasting and the exposure to the elements during the Solo time by merely taking a sleeping bag and a tarp as protection.

With the end of the Solo time and coming back to base camp starts the phase of incorporation, which is marked by the return to the wider community where the participant brings "the wisdom and inner truth of the experience back into the world" (Bodkin & Sartor, 2005, p. 34).

Each of the three stages described above include several elements that are covered as part of the programme. Part of the severance stage is the preparation for the Solo, which includes talks and exchanges in the group about safety issues, physical challenges, aspects of the flora and fauna in the area and procedures in cases of emergencies. However, a considerable part of the preparation is also dedicated to potential psychological challenges, personal fears and the clarification of the personal intention for undertaking a Solo time. The more aware the soloists are of the feelings that can arise as part of the Solo experience and of their personal intention the more they can learn from them (Knapp, 2005). Usually, these aspects are addressed using the council format of listening and talking from the heart in the group (see chapter 4.3.3.1). Participants are further sensitised to perceive all elements of nature as teachers. As Bodkin and Sartor (2005) elaborate:

> *Rather than relating to the earth intellectually, as an it, we suggest that people relate to everything they encounter as a thou. This brings the natural world to life and more fully opens the realm of intuition. A participant might have the experience of being perceived and known by wilderness itself. This point of view can be experienced directly by speaking and listening to the earth, and does not require belief.* (p. 38)

After the preparation phase follows the Solo as the transition time. This is the time when participants are on their own and what happens during this time is highly individual. Some participants describe having talked to elements and animals, some experienced boredom, hunger and loneliness, others experienced deep love and joy, relationships are evaluated, some cry a lot or have significant dreams or animal encounters (Bodkin & Sartor, 2005).

The incorporation phase includes the return to the group and everyday world and the processing of the experiences. Usually, participants are welcomed with a generous meal to break the fast. After a period of rest the group gathers in circle to start sharing their experiences one-by-one. Here, the programme guides take on the role of elders as they listen to the stories and mirror back elements of significance and meaning of the soloists' stories. As Knapp (2005) elaborates:

The role of facilitators can be described as helping others with meaning-making. Briefing and debriefing, when done well, increase the value of the experience to the learner. The more skills and information a facilitator has about the goals of the solo, site location, and the person taking it, the better that leader will be able to guide the learner in making sense of the experience and in achieving deeper understandings. The key goal for the vision seeker is to know how to apply what is learned in the future. (p. 21)

A further council then concentrates on the return back home which for most people poses a challenge, as in contemporary western culture there is mostly no special welcome as would be expected in traditional cultures. The invitation and purpose of the Solo time, however is to return to everyday life and share the gathered gifts with one's people. Some people find it difficult to return because they mourn the uplifting and profound experience of their Solo time and the feelings of safety experienced in group councils. Another difficulty can be to return very enthusiastic but soon relapse into old habits. Therefore, the phase of incorporation always includes a period of time in which participants share their concerns regarding going home, explore sources of support and share commitments they want "to make to embody the gifts of their Solo" (Bodkin & Sartor, 2005, p. 41).

3.3.3 Research findings

Throughout history and across cultures quietness and solitude have been appreciated as a way to facilitate personal growth, insight and creative thinking (e.g. see Fredrickson & Anderson, 1999; Knapp & Smith, 2005). For this reason, time in solitude has emerged as a significant part of contemporary outdoor and adventure programming and has gained as such increasing empirical credibility. The Solo, as a structured experience of solitude in nature, can appear as a core component of a programme or as one of several components. Commonly, in these programmes, Solos take place in a designated safe location and can last between 24 hours and several days (Nicholls, 2009).

Even though research interest in these experiences has increased, a lot about the soloist's experience, thus the internal component, remains unknown (Maxted, 2005). In the following I will give an overview of associated research findings and practitioners' expertise.

3.3.3.1 Framework of the Solo

As Smith (2005) aptly pointed out, the way in which facilitators frame a Solo experience is of great importance for the participants' experience. Experiences can vary a great deal depending on whether the Solo was initially framed as a vision quest, walkabout, survival task, way of connecting with nature, time for reflection and relaxation, or as part of a monastic tradition. These frameworks create the mindset, which make the time in solitude more meaningful for participants and prepare them for the experience. This view is in line with Maxted (2005) who emphasised the significance of Solo preparation in order to help participants to truly engage with their surroundings. As excellent examples Maxted (2005) describes "mini-solos" which take place prior to the "real" Solo and include observational and reflective tasks in nature. Preparation, Maxted (2005) believes, can determine whether the experience turns out to be negative or a growth opportunity for the soloist, which especially applies to adolescents, as they rather "need to be jolted out of potential solo boredom in order to connect with nature" (p. 135).

This is in line with the outcomes of Kalisch, Bobilya and Daniel's (2011) study, which compared solists' experiences of different ages. They found that younger participants struggled with boredom more than older ones. Maxted (2005) argues that the Solo bears the potential to lead to deep thinking if there is appropriate reflective skill-building as a preparation for the Solo and draws on reports which indicate that adolescents compared to pre-adolescents may receive better gains from the Solo due to better reasoning skills which allow for deeper self-examination (Larson, 1997).

Bobilya, McAvoy and Kalish (2005) researched 126 college students who participated in Solos between 24 to 60 hours as part of an 18-day wilderness programme. Participants repeatedly indicated the importance of their own expectations for the experience. In all programmes the instructor turned out to greatly influence the participants' Solo experience through the preparation for, facilitation during and discussion after the Solo and sometimes this influence was directly connected to the participants' personal expectations for the Solo. Another key factor that Bobilya *et al.* (2005) found in their study was the environment in which the wilderness programmes took place. Ninety-six percent of the participants indicated that the environment influenced their perception of the Solo experience.

3.3.3.2 The experience of solitude

As Nicholls (2009) pointed out, the notion that solitude, as part of a Solo, is generally a positive experience leaves aside the fact that people can have a lot of different emotional reactions to being alone. Most likely preparation for a Solo is especially crucial in the Western world as people in our culture only rarely experience solitude. Even more so, being alone may be negatively associated with unnecessary risk-taking or antisocial traits (Buchholz, 1997), as well as with forms of punishment or bullying during childhood (Maxted, 2005). Studying 48-hour Solo experiences of adolescents over four years Maxted (2005) found a number of fears arising in participants. Maxted (2005) categorised them into fears regarding nature aspects and unexpected encounters with other people as well as fears of being alone and of the unknown within. The author warns about the danger of romanticising longer Solos as spiritual growth opportunities while for some adolescents a Solo may be perceived and experienced negatively.

However, Kalisch, Bobilya and Daniel's (2011) study showed that those Solo characteristics which participants found most difficult were simultaneously the most enjoyable ones. In their study the greatest number of participants firstly perceived the Solo as a beneficial experience, secondly was primarily excited to enter the Solo, and thirdly reported feeling peaceful during the Solo time. The rate of those participants who reported feeling anxious dropped from 22 percent entering the Solo to merely six percent during the Solo. Concurrently, the number of respondents who reported feeling peaceful more than doubled from 28 percent entering the Solo to 58 percent during the Solo time, which suggests an increase of the familiarity with the situation. Moreover, the qualitative data showed that the decrease of anxiety was also due to the calming effect of nature. Despite a culture of fast-paced lifestyles, participants appreciated the opportunity for rest and reflection on self, relationships, life issues and the future.

However, the most frequently stated enjoyable characteristic was solitude, indicating the participants' receptivity to the experience (Kalisch *et al.*, 2011). This was followed by reports of lack of activity and journaling as the most enjoyable characteristics of the Solo. Solitude was simultaneously the most enjoyable and the second most difficult aspect of the Solo followed by boredom and preceded by fasting. Even though fasting was the most frequently mentioned challenging aspect of the Solo, many participants also reported valuing the fasting experience. It was evident that fasting contributed to an increase of focus, a new gratefulness, empathy for others, and an increased awareness of their dependency. The authors concluded that challenges also contain an enjoyable quality, which can serve as a programme enhancement. Furthermore, this points towards the positive role of optimal stress in wilderness programmes which according to Hendee and Brown (1988) facilitates personal growth. Notably, the above-presented findings of Kalisch *et al.* (2011) represent a summary of congruent results for two different samples and programmes. While one sample included younger participants between 13 and 18 the other included mainly 18-year-olds. Furthermore, in the latter sample the Solo was more spiritually-focused whereas the Solo in the other sample was implemented with the purpose of giving the participants a true wilderness experience and an opportunity for reflection, self-reliance, resourcefulness, and confidence building (Kalisch *et al.*, 2011). Therefore, the authors conclude that the experience of a Solo in nature does seem to have common components regardless of age, programme details and location.

3.3.3.3 Life significance of a Solo experience

Daniel (2005), on the other hand, was interested in the life significance of a spiritually oriented wilderness Solo experience. His sample included 227 participants who went on the programme between 1976 and 2000. Findings of this 25-year retrospective study indicate that indeed the Solo is retrospectively viewed as a significant life event. The Solo experience seems to incorporate important characteristics of significant life events as it was described as a novel, unique and extraordinary experience, it took place in an inspirational environment, it posed mental, physical, emotional and spiritual challenges and offered time and space for reflection in solitude and silence. Participants reported to have extracted life lessons and that it provided a reference point and perspective in their lives. Additionally, the Solo enhanced the exploration of self in relationship to nature, others and God (Daniel, 2005).

4

Mixed methods enquiry of immersive experiences in wild nature

4.1 Overarching aims and objectives

As elaborated in the previous chapters, in the face of global change sustainability matters become increasingly apparent. A substantial issue, in this context, is the role of human behaviour in particular the issue of the way humans act on the natural environment. This automatically draws the attention towards the contemporary view on the human-nature relationship which seems to lack thorough research attention (see Schultz, 2002). Particularly with regard to the decrease of nature in our everyday lives it appears crucial to start investigating how we as humans are interconnected with it on the various levels of our being which evidently exceed the purely physical one as outlined in the literature section.

Undeniably, there is a fair amount of research on the relationship between ecological and social behaviour and values, attitudes and social norms. However, in respect to ecological behaviour the influence of concepts such as nature connectedness or the ecological self, which take nature into consideration as part of human identity have only begun to emerge in mainstream research.

Therefore, the present research focuses on practices, which facilitate a more personal and intimate encounter with the natural world. In these practices the purely knowledge-based approach to nature is extended to a deeply experiential exploration of nature and self. This, in turn, allows for the investigation of the phenomenology of immersive experiences in wild nature as a first step to better understand the event itself and the human-nature relationship that reveals itself in it. Further, I aim to track the influence of these kind of experiences on the individual's personal development and possibly behaviour.

I realised the empirical investigation of this topic through a long-term evaluation of a 14-day outdoor programme for young adults, which aims at facilitating such experiences in particular through a 24-hour Solo spent in nature[11].

Furthermore, I assessed an additional group of participants, which took part in a one-week programme exclusively focusing on the Solo time in nature. Thereby, the

---

11 Additional aspects and the flow of the programme will be described at a later stage in chapter 4.3.3.1.

Solo-only sample serves as a reference sample to identify the particular features and effects of the Solo time in nature. Overall, both programmes constitute the foundation for this explorative applied research approach.

While the explorative, basic research dimension aims to create a more thorough understanding of immersive experiences in wild nature, the applied research dimension serves the purpose of responding to a very practical problem, which represents a popular point of criticism in sustainability research and related fields of research such as environmental psychology and other areas focusing on the science of human behaviour. However important it is to scientifically identify predictors of behaviour, the current and pressing question as to how this knowledge may be put into practice is often bypassed. Therefore, by evaluating concrete potentially useful practices for facilitating change in attitude, awareness and level of activism, the present research aims to create knowledge, which is valuable to both the practitioner and researcher alike and thereby intends to bridge the gap between science and practice.

A further objective of this research is to extend research methodology by probing new ways of investigating complex topics of enquiry such as personally meaningful experiences in nature. Thus, I intended to go beyond either/or approaches, to endorse various ways of knowing and to thereby strive for an approximation of seemingly antagonistic forces in research as reflected in the divide between the subjective and objective, the qualitative and quantitative. This endeavour is reflected in the inclusion of dreams as a potential source of knowledge[12] and in the inclusion of the researcher's self-reflexivity and intuitive ways of knowing (see chapter 4.3.7) as an integral part of the research process.

Moreover, I applied fairly new research methods, instruments and approaches such as the intersubjective-heuristic enquiry, applied thematic analysis, questionnaires like the Phenomenology of Consciousness Inventory (PCI) (Pekala, 1991) and the overarching mixed methods approach. By virtue of explicating the rationale for exploring new scientific territory these implementations will occasionally entail a contextualisation within the history and philosophy of science, as will be evident in the following chapters.

Summarised, the overarching aims and objectives of the present research project are:

a. to explore the phenomenology of immersive experiences in wild nature,
b. to evaluate these experiences as a potential facilitator for personal development and behaviour change by means of longitudinal data,
c. to bridge the gap between science and practice by researching concrete practices which are feasible and applicable,
d. and to tackle and extend the limitations of common research methodology by probing new methods, approaches and instruments.

---

12 Notably, even though the dream study, along with the associated literature, methods, results and discussion, will be presented in an additional chapter (see chapter 5) it is nevertheless explicitly regarded as part of the mixed methods enquiry.

4.2 Extracted hypotheses and research questions

4.2.1 Quantitative research questions and hypotheses
In the following section, the hypothesis for the analysis of the quantitative data will be presented next to the explored areas of change, which I assessed via standardised questionnaires as part of the longitudinal evaluation of the Butterfly Effect programme[13].

The general purpose of the quantitative research was to longitudinally evaluate the effects of the Butterfly Programme by depicting trends in the group, which exceed the limited number of the interview sample. Furthermore, I aimed to test the applicability of various standardised psychological instruments to the context of evaluating experiential outdoor programmes such as the Butterfly Programme. This additionally applies to the Solo time in nature as I probed to quantify this experience and explore a potential pattern of consciousness in Solo time participants. I realised this by utilising a standardised questionnaire (PCI), which is usually utilised in order to assess content of consciousness in meditation or hypnosis sessions (Pekala, 1991).

Summarised the quantitative research strand aims to answer the following research questions:
1. Is there a common pattern for content of consciousness during the Solo time?
   a. Is the PCI applicable to the context of the Solo time in nature?
2. What are the immediate and/or long-term effects of the Butterfly Programme in the following areas:
   - relationship with nature
   - personal value system
   - attitude towards others and life
   - empowerment
   - actual environmental behaviour and community engagement?

4.2.1.1 Relationship with nature
Based on the intimate character and focus of the encounter with nature through the 24-hour Solo but also due to outdoor living throughout the Butterfly Programme and other nature-based exercises I assume that participants will report changes in this area as assessed via the Inclusion of Nature in Self, Coping with Environmental Problems, Affinity towards Nature and Connectedness to Nature Scale.

4.2.1.2 Personal value system
Based on the emphasis on nature, personal and group processes as well as on the ongoing invitation to reflect on the input and experiences provided through the Butterfly Programme I assume that participants will report changes in their personal value system. These potential changes will be explored by utilising a standardised questionnaire the Life Values Inventory.

---

13 In the present work the Butterfly Effect programme may be occasionally abbreviated as Butterfly or BE programme.

4.2.1.3 Attitudes towards others and life
Based on various implemented practices such as council and the overall approach of the programme to combine the confrontation with global, community and personal challenges with joy and a positive attitude towards life I assume that participants will report changes in this area, namely in constructs such as hope via the Miller Hope Scale, Gratitude, Capacity for Love and Trust scale.

4.2.1.4 Empowerment
As the various programme components focused on personal empowerment I assume that participants report changes assessed via constructs such as the Civic Attitudes and Skills Questionnaire and Individual Community-Related Empowerment.

4.2.1.5 Environmental behaviour and community engagement
Based on the literature and theoretical models which point towards the influence of values, experiences, awareness and attitudes on actual behaviour I assume that Butterfly participants will report changes in Proenvironmental Behaviour as well as in the Participation Scale of the Individual Community-Related Empowerment construct.

4.2.2 Qualitative research questions
The purpose of the qualitative research strand is to explore the participants' experiences of the Butterfly Programme with particular focus on the phenomenology of immersive experiences in wild nature and associated processes.

Furthermore, I aspire to explore the Butterfly participants' perceived changes in their lives and in themselves after the programme.

The emergent research questions can be summarised as follows:
1. What constitutes an immersive experience in wild nature?
2. Which process or features facilitate these experiences?
3. What are the common or distinct features between the Butterfly participants' immersive experience in wild nature and those that experienced solely a Solo time in wild nature?
4. What are the effects of such immersive experiences in wild nature and of the overall Butterfly programme on the participants' lives and how do participants explain these?

4.2.3 Mixed methods research question
I addressed the research questions using the mixed methods approach. Consequently, I assessed different types of data in order to gather complementing information:

Qualitative Data: assessed via retrospective semi-structured interviews, which allow participants to consciously reflect on both presented and self-chosen topics.

Quantitative Data: via standardised questionnaires to assess specific and potentially relevant psychological constructs.

"Intuitive" Data: extracted via self-reported dreams of the participants and researcher, which occurred during programme time. I used these to assess the unreflected, subconscious processing of their experience which, due to the particularity of the topic, I will present in a separate chapter 5.

All in all, I aspire to explore in which way the different types of data work together and create a comprehensive map of the topic of enquiry. Consequently, the mixed methods research question is:

How are the different types of data interconnected and what can be learnt from integrating them?

4.3 Method

4.3.1 Introduction to the mixed methods approach

Up until today it is not a widely adopted practice to mix methods, namely qualitative and quantitative approaches to research. The degree of separation between the two approaches varies from discipline to discipline (Creswell & Plano Clark, 2007) and springs from a long nurtured divide between the two major prevailing orientations towards scientific understanding.

In the development of a science of human behaviour, two major social science models dominated. One model, known as the positivist/empiricist approach, emulated the natural science emphasising the researcher's distance in the process of observation and analysis. Typically, this model utilises quantitative methods to retrieve knowledge. The other model, on the other hand, is characterised by the constructivist/phenomenological orientation and is associated with qualitative methods. Here, the emphasises lies on understanding the subjective world through immersing in an engaged process of interpretation as it is believed that human action is influenced by individual thought, experience and intention (Gergen, 2013). However, because of the major break-throughs that the natural sciences accomplished philosophers became increasingly interested in pinpointing the rational foundation of such science in order to make it transferable to all of academia. This led to the "mainstream science" as we know it today, called empiricism. Within this framework the goal is to generate universal objective knowledge and thus a systematic account of the world through experiments and processes of predicting and controlling. Notably, in these processes, political and ideological values are seen as a potential bias and remain disregarded.

Clearly, this approach contrasts with the interpretative character of qualitative enquiry and against this background qualitative research does not meet the proposed criteria for "good research" (Gergen, 2013). However, even though quantitative methods contribute to the justification of scientific ideas the question of the foundational logic of the idea itself remains. Indeed, as Popper (1959) proposed there is no such thing as a foundational logic for an initial idea. Rather, ideas and propositions arise from a context of discovery. This in turn appears to be inherent in qualitative approaches to research. It is in this capacity that qualitative research is accepted from the empiricist perspective. However, there are far more merits of the qualitative approach and it is now even increasingly applied within the context of justification such as in evaluation research (Gergen, 2013).

Nevertheless, traditional dualism arranged for the two approaches to maintain a competitive relationship (Howe, 1988) rather than a synergistic one, not the least because of their opposing worldviews. Paradigm purists have argued for the incompatibility thesis, which represents the belief that paradigms could and should not be mixed

(Tashakkori & Teddlie, 1998), an issue which is still debated today (Creswell & Plano Clark, 2007). The opposing camp on the other hand argues that social phenomena are complex and multiple realities do exist, which questions the reasonability of assigning superiority to only one philosophical paradigm and the capability of capturing such complexity by means of only one method (De Lisle, 2011). Conceptions like this led to the evolution of mixed methods research succeeding solely quantitative and qualitative approaches and by many researchers pronounced as the "third methodological movement" (Tashakkori & Teddlie, 2003). Creswell and Plano (2007) define mixed methods research as follows:

> *Mixed methods research is a research design with philosophical assumptions as well as methods of inquiry. As a methodology, it involves philosophical assumptions that guide the direction of the collection and analysis of the data and the mixture of qualitative and quantitative approaches in many phases in the research process. As a method, it focuses on collecting, analysing, and mixing both quantitative and qualitative data in a single study or series of studies. Its central premise is that the use of quantitative and qualitative approaches in combination provides a better understanding of research problems than either approach alone* (p.5).

The development of mixed methods research is fairly young and still ongoing. Therefore, up until today there are still areas which demand further work and discussion such as issues concerning mixed methods designs, worldviews and associated implications (Creswell & Plano Clark, 2007).

However, many researchers already recognise the value of this approach. Followers argue that based on the complexity of emergent research problems either/or approaches of the past are no longer suitable and need to make room for more multifaceted and socially relevant considerations (Rorty, 1999). The flexibility that derives from combining inductive and deductive processes within a broader research cycle allows for new questions to arise and for new ways to pursue them (Teddlie & Tashakkori, 2009).

4.3.2 The applied mixed methods approach

4.3.2.1 Defining the research process and design

The present multiyear research project incorporates a combination of basic research with classical evaluation research. On the one hand the research interest focuses on the evaluation of the outcomes and impact of the Butterfly Effect programme and on the other hand on the basic exploration of the phenomenology of immersive experiences in wild nature. In effect, both purposes were simultaneously immanent in the same studies as illustrated in Figure 2.

The applied mixed methods research design is the convergent parallel design. The convergent parallel design in this research project implies the concurrent collection of quantitative and qualitative data within one study as apparent when reviewing Figure 2 with each of the dashed boxes encompassing one study. Altogether, I carried out three studies with the third one being a follow-up study of the first one.

Figure 2 illustrates the research process in relation to the type of data, which I collected in each study and concurrently highlights the priority of the two strands

Figure 2. Overall research process and design. Lower- and uppercase letters reveal which research strand, qualitative (qual) or quantitative (quan), was emphasised in each study. Identical spelling (e.g. Quan + Qual) signifies equal emphasis.

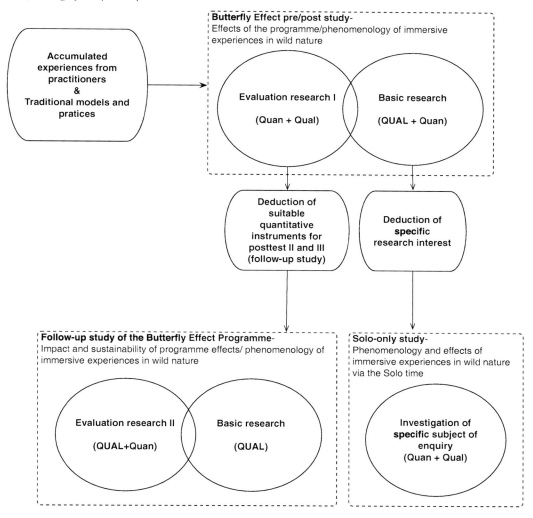

within each study as indicated by either capital or lower case letters. As apparent when studying the figure, in basic research, as a result of its strongly explorative nature, I put more emphasis on the qualitative strand (QUAL + Quan). During the Butterfly Effect pre/post study survey and interview data played an equally important role regarding the evaluation of the programme as I addressed the same content areas using both methods (Qual + Quan). This was also true for the Solo-only study as I assessed the Solo experience via the Phenomenology of Consciousness Inventory (PCI) as well as via interviews. However, during the follow-up study of the initial Butterfly Effect programme evaluation (pre/post study) I shifted the emphasis from equal importance towards prioritising the qualitative strand. The reason for this shift emerged from the experiences gathered during the Butterfly Effect pre/post study. The qualitative data from the pre/post study simply proved to be more informative than the quantitative data and simultaneously revealed that the level of exploration that was needed could not be sufficiently met by standardised questionnaires. Furthermore, the shift was supported by the broader and more explorative research focus of the follow-up study on the changes in and the programme's impact on participants' lives after a longer period of time.

Another considerable aspect of the research process is the starting point for the investigation of the topic of enquiry. Intervention research often implies a theory → adaptation research process, which was not the case in this particular research process. For the present research project the starting point of the research process was neither an existing theory nor established scientific knowledge but rather built on the knowledge and reports reflecting the practice of professionals who utilise Solo times in nature and on long-established pristine knowledge and practices. Thus, the rational for researching the Butterfly programme and the Solo time in particular, is the observed successfulness of these practices in the field and the aspiration to explore the emerging phenomena (see Figure 3).

The phenomenon studied in this work is an immersive experience in wild nature and constitutes the focus of the basic research strand. As this represents a phenomenon that has not been extensively researched thus far, I reviewed and explored the experience with regard to specific intrinsic features or dimensions. In order to realise this I analysed qualitative data from all three studies (pre/post study, follow-up study and Solo-only study). Furthermore, and as a result of the numerous preeminent reports on the Solo time during the first phase of data collection, I deducted a more specified research interest, namely the role and sole effects of the Solo time in nature (see Figure 3). In order to assess this, I collected data from a small reference sample consisting of participants of a Solo-only programme.

This exemplifies well that even though the mixed methods design was fixed at the start of the research process, the research design and interest was partly emergent, too. Apart from the phenomenology of immersive experiences in wild nature, an additional aspect of the basic research in this project can be found in the testing of the utility and transferability of a standardised questionnaire, the PCI, initially designed to assess content of consciousness to the context of a Solo time in nature.

The evaluation effort, on the other hand, I realised by means of a panel study, a type of longitudinal design, which indicates data collection from the same participants at different points in time. The applied evaluation model and process is illustrated in Figure 3.

As the baseline measurement (pretest), two weeks prior to the start of the programme, I handed out an extensive survey to the Butterfly programme participants. The same assessment of survey data took place during the last two days of the programme along with the qualitative data collection such as interviews on the observed effects and the experience of the programme (posttest I). Furthermore, eight weeks after the programme I contacted the participants again and asked them to fill out a substantially reduced online-version of the survey (posttest II). In order to assess the sustainability of the effects as detected in the pretest/posttest comparison, the follow-up study took place one and a half years after the Butterfly programme (posttest III). Here, participants went through the same limited online-survey as implemented at posttest II and I interviewed the previous interviewees again regarding their personal estimations of the impact of the programme on their lives.

Figure 3. Applied evaluation model and design.

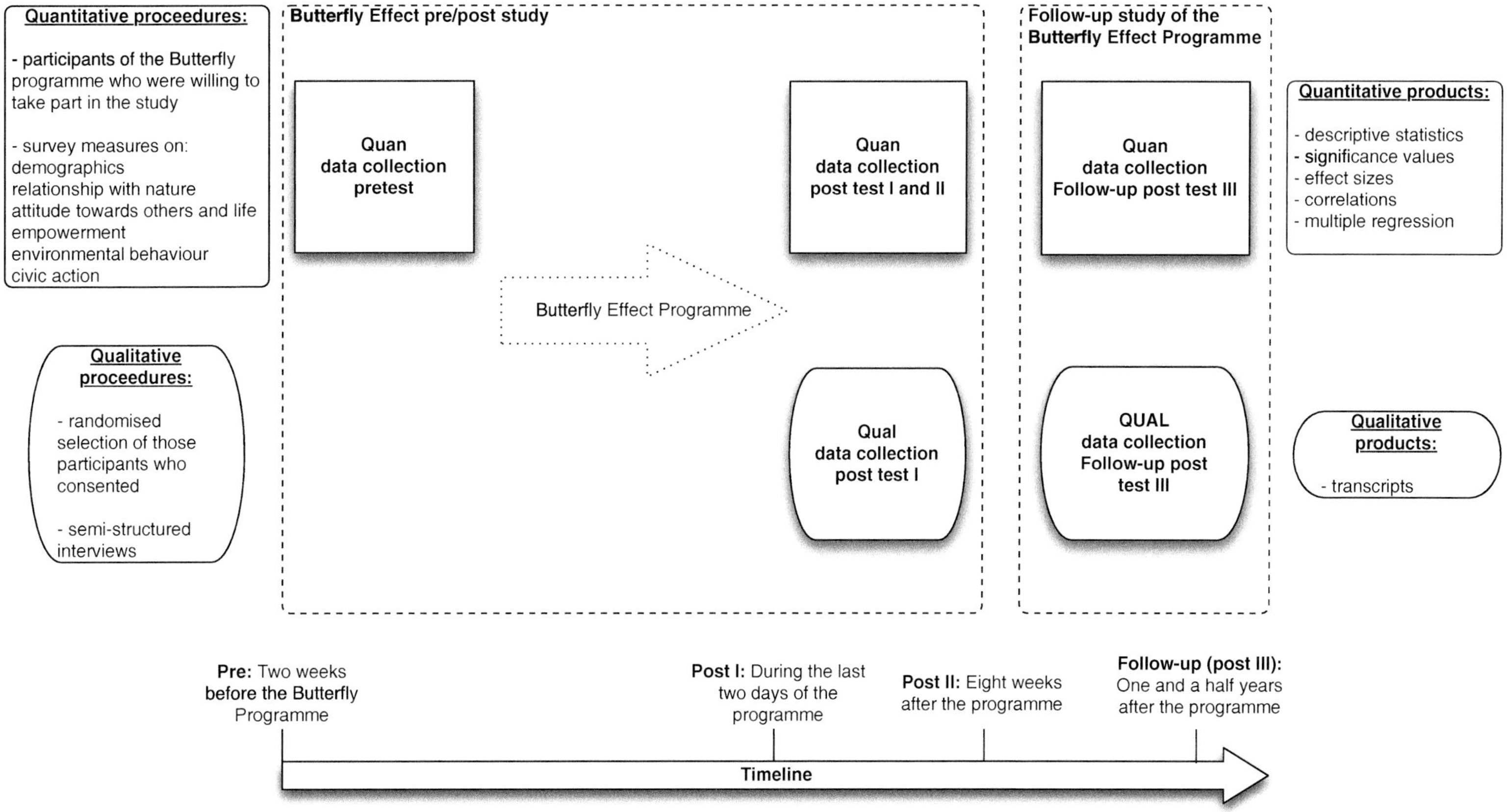

Quantitative procedures:
- participants of the Butterfly programme who were willing to take part in the study
- survey measures on:
  demographics
  relationship with nature
  attitude towards others and life
  empowerment
  environmental behaviour
  civic action

Qualitative procedures:
- randomised selection of those participants who consented
- semi-structured interviews

Butterfly Effect pre/post study

Quan data collection pretest

Butterfly Effect Programme

Quan data collection post test I and II

Qual data collection post test I

Follow-up study of the Butterfly Effect Programme

Quan data collection Follow-up post test III

QUAL data collection Follow-up post test III

Quantitative products:
- descriptive statistics
- significance values
- effect sizes
- correlations
- multiple regression

Qualitative products:
- transcripts

Timeline

Pre: Two weeks before the Butterfly Programme

Post I: During the last two days of the programme

Post II: Eight weeks after the programme

Follow-up (post III): One and a half years after the programme

4.3.2.2 Defining the worldview and philosophical assumptions

As the previous sections have repeatedly shown, the epistemology and general philosophical orientation to research have a considerable, far-reaching and often overlooked effect on various aspects of research such as research design, the role of the researcher, outcomes and outcome interpretation. Therefore, one of the benefits that comes with applying mixed methods is the researcher's opportunity to become aware of the philosophical foundations and assumptions underlying her or his scientific enquiry. Simultaneously, it becomes a methodological requirement to explicate these assumptions in mixed methods research projects and reports (Creswell & Plano Clark, 2007).

In order to realise this endeavour I used the classification of worldviews and associated implications for practice, as illustrated by Creswell (2007, p. 24), as a guideline.

In terms of the ontology, the project incorporated a pragmatist stance taking single and multiple realities into account via applying multiple methods of data collection to inform the research problem. The pragmatist view also applied to the axiology, as I included biased and unbiased perspectives depending on the method in use. This is also true for the methodology and rhetoric for I collected and mixed both qualitative and quantitative data as well as put formal and informal writing styles into practice.

However, when it came to the epistemology I applied a constructivist approach, as I aimed for closeness to the experience and accompanied participants at their site.

4.3.2.3 Rationale for the applied mixed methods approach and additional applications

The previous sections have already indicated by degree the rationale for applying mixed methods in this research project.

Evidently, different methods were needed in order to address the different research questions. On the one hand, in order to detect general trends and changes in the group, I applied the commonly known pre/post outcome evaluation model by means of quantitative measures. However, on the other hand, I also aspired to identify context components and processes that facilitated the outcomes, which are highly relevant to ensure the programme outcomes and the effectiveness of an intervention. Additionally, due to the explorative character of this research and in order to achieve completeness, I aimed to provide space for those aspects to emerge that I did not directly address via questionnaires. As it was a major research concern to explore the phenomenology of immersive experiences in wild nature, evidently additional in-depth accounts of participants were required by means of qualitative methods such as interviews.

Thus, on balance, one data source alone was insufficient to address the research questions. Moreover, mixing methods allowed for further examination of the quantitative exploratory results in view of the qualitative outcomes and vice versa and thereby contributed to the credibility of the results. This is closely related to the most commonly used argument for mixing methods, which is that of greater validity via triangulation of the findings. By virtue of mixing methods the reliability of counts can be integrated with the validity of experience and perception (Wheeldon & Ahlberg, 2011). Indeed, research can be scientifically significant without providing practical significance. As qualitative research is sensitive to context and often transmits a broader view of an experience it contributes greatly to the utility of findings for practitioners (Creswell & Plano Clark, 2007).

In summary, in this study I chose the mixed methods approach by virtue of enhancing validity, utility, credibility, completeness and in order to do justice to the different research questions (see Creswell, 2007).

4.3.2.4 Expansion of the applied mixed methods approach

To complete the depiction of the pursued approach I added one further complementary aspect to the mixed methods approach in the present research project. As already touched on in previous sections, it is the aspect of the researcher's self-reflexivity which will be explicitly woven into the several stages of this academic work. By making relevant aspects of my experiences as a researcher transparent I aspired to add to the validity and credibility of this work and to extend research methodology towards a more inclusive account of meaningful variables of the research process, such as self-reflexivity and different means of knowing (see chapter 4.3.7). Therefore, instead of keeping self-reflexivity and other means of knowing as an intention and practice that takes place "behind the scenes", I probed ways of in-text implementation. In this way I permitted these aspects to appear on equal footing just like any other commonly reported part of the research process.

Hopefully, this element of the work may be seen as a further development and inspiration as well as a basis for dialogue and discussion for fellow researchers.

4.3.3 Evaluated programmes

4.3.3.1 The Butterfly Effect Programme

Roots of the programme and the team

The Butterfly Effect Programme 2011 was a follow-up programme of the "*Butterfly Effect – Creative Sustainability Youth Exchange*", which ran in 2009 in Findhorn, Scotland and was supported by Youth in Action funding[14]. The Butterfly Effect 2011 was also Youth in Action-funded and organised by the Learning Partnership for Creative Sustainability (LPCS).

The members of the LPCS come from various European countries and are professional and voluntary youth workers and trainers with previous experience of Youth in Action projects as organisers and /or participants. Many of them have taken part in international training programmes and seminars focused on youth work, nature-based methods, non-formal learning and outdoor education and are active in local environmental and cultural initiatives. The team of the Butterfly Programme 2011 consisted of eight facilitators who came from the UK, Austria, Switzerland, Germany, Italy and the Czech Republic.

Time and place

The Butterfly Effect was a twelve-day programme, which ran from 13th to 26th of August 2011. The programme took place in a camp setting near to Findhorn eco-village in the North East of Scotland, which is known as a model eco-village in the field of development for sustainability.

---

14 European programme, which financially supports the implementation of projects for young people in the areas of formal and non-formal education.

Throughout the programme the example of the Findhorn eco-village and community was frequently revisited for learning and reflection about the many levels and elements of sustainability.

Camp structure and setting

The practical learning aspect of the Butterfly Programme consisted of sessions exploring the different levels of sustainable living and was framed by camp management and daily so-called 'service and care' periods. As the campsite was only partly set up there was still a lot to be done when participants arrived. Completing the camp structure, for instance, building the outdoor toilets but also collecting firewood for daily use was part of the "service and care" slots. Furthermore, the daily meals were prepared in the camp kitchen with a designated team of participants supporting the cook from the Findhorn community. Moreover, participants lived in tents throughout the entire programme and programme activities happened mostly outside or in the wooden structures and marquees on the campsite. In this way participants experienced their interrelations with nature on a very practical level as well as living in a community in a camp with light-weight and low-impact lifestyles.

Overall focus

The overall focus of the programme was sustainability and self-development with the aim to inspire a sense of interconnectedness with the wider community of life, promoting responsible citizenship and active participation in the transition towards a culture of sustainability.

During the project, nature-based methods and outdoor education were essential. Most of the techniques used were methods based on deep ecology or adapted practises of traditional cultures, such as the 24-hour Solo time in nature and the practice of council.

Deep ecology work offers practices and exercises that allow connecting emotionally to the extent of the destruction and suffering that is taking place in the world towards both human and non-human communities. The implemented chosen group exercises were directly inspired by The Work That Reconnects, developed by environmental activist and sustainability educator Joanna Macy (Macy & Brown, 1998). The exercises included, for instance, activities such as blind-folded walks through nature to establish trust among the group and activate the senses.

The implemented council sharings were inspired by the Way of Council, originated by the Ojai Foundation in California. Council is a practice that facilitates the space for authentic encounter by creating a setting to listen to what is alive for the different persons in the group. Typically, people sitting in council with each other follow four intentions: speaking from the heart, listening from the heart, being concise and allowing spontaneity (Zimmerman & Coyle, 1996). During the Butterfly Exchange this method was used almost daily in different contexts for sharing experiences of exercises, learning and reflections. On a broader level this method was implemented to learn from each other, tap into the wisdom of the group and thereby creating a sense of connection amongst participants.

In addition, the programme included typical non-formal learning methods such as open-space technology, workshops, simulations, brainstorming, daily group reflections and excursions.

Flow of the programme

The flow of the programme may be separated into three phases, which will be drafted in the following. A detailed description of the daily activities of the programme are presented in a table in Appendix C.

The first four days at Findhorn were oriented towards experiencing new tools and sharing new ideas and techniques. The focus during this time period was to get to know the camp routine and to create a healthy group dynamic.

The second phase of the programme took place at the Culbin Estate, a large woodland in the highlands. Team and participants hiked there and together set up a provisional camp site for the core of those four days on-site was the 24-hour Solo experience in nature. In this way the lifestyle was further simplified as a way to ease participants' into their Solo time in nature.

In order to identify their intention to spend 24 hours alone in nature, the day before the Solo participants "crossed a threshold", an exercise used a number of times during the programme. The term "crossing the threshold" stems from the idea to find a visible or imaginary threshold in nature, for instance a piece of wood, and by stepping over it facilitating and marking the entrance into a different space where all mental elaborations can be dropped and the whole person orients towards observation and perception of inner and outer events. This space is visited for a brief period of time and the visitor usually crosses the threshold with a particular intention or question. By observing what is seen, heard or felt, often through concrete encounters with the natural world, the person may extract insights or deepen her or his understanding of the question they came with. This understanding is then retrieved back into everyday life by crossing the threshold again.

The Solo in this programme lasted from sunrise until the next sunrise, thus participants were invited to spend 24 hours including the night alone in nature. Typically for a Solo time, participants neither bring a tent nor food, limiting their belongings to water, a sleeping mat and bag, warm clothes, a first aid kit and a tarp. This is supposed to narrow down possible distractions and facilitate openness to and awareness for the surroundings and for what is alive for the person in the present moment.

The aim of the 24-hour Solo as part of the programme was to offer participants an opportunity to discover the richness of nature and question their own role within it but also to provide participants with a space to confront their fears. Summarised, being left to oneself and exposed to nature is meant to offer participants a container for self-reflection, insight, inspiration and connection with oneself and nature.

When participants returned, the provisional campsite was dismantled and the group returned to their campsite in Findhorn. This marked the beginning of the third and final phase of the programme.

Participants firstly shared their experiences within circles of smaller groups. One-by-one participants gave an account of what they experienced or understood during their Solo time and their stories were then "mirrored" by the trained facilitators. In this context "mirroring" means that the facilitators offered a personal summary of the participant's stories by echoing back features that stood out to them. This practice means to support the incorporation of the participants' experiences during their Solo time and led to the final programme point.

The very last days of the programme served as a space for sharing practical information on how to become more empowered in everyday life as well as for sharing inspirational ongoing programmes, initiatives and projects all over the world. Also, all participants who shared the same country of origin were encouraged to sit together and think about how to follow-up on and possibly implement the gained skills, competences and knowledge within their own lives and communities for instance by creating own projects in their local communities.

4.3.3.2 The Solo-only programme

The team
The team of the Solo-only programme consisted of one female and one male facilitator who were both trained in nature-based work, particularly in Solo time facilitation. Both facilitators are, furthermore, members of the LPCS and were involved in the previous Butterfly Programmes.

Time and place
The general framework of the Solo-only programme was set up on the farmyard of a community project in Bavaria, Germany and lasted for five days in May 2012. Apart from their Solo time in nature, participants lived in a house on the farmyard during the preparation and incorporation phase of the Solo-only programme.

Overall focus
Clearly, the overall focus of the Solo-only programme was different to that of the Butterfly Programme as it centred only on the Solo time in nature. Furthermore, as members of the participant group already knew each other beforehand, no emphasis was put on group building exercises. However, the way stories and experiences were shared during this programme was via councils as described in the previous section.

The Solo-only programme was offered to the participants during the final phase of a one-year peace programme that they took part in. Thus, the Solo was facilitated with the intention to provide participants with an opportunity to deal with that specific up-coming change in their lives.

Flow of the programme
The Solo-only programme consisted of three major phases, which are typical for Solo rituals in nature: the preparation of the Solo time, the actual Solo time and the incorporation of the Solo time.

The first phase of preparation in the case of this particular programme included an additional one-day taster experience a week prior to the actual five-day Solo programme. This day served the purpose of giving the group an idea of the specific approach to nature, which is immanent in the Solo time ritual. This taster experience included going out into nature individually with a "threshold exercise" (see description of Flow of the programme in chapter 4.3.3.1). In this way it was intended to give group members the opportunity to experience nature from the angle of this particular tradition and to support the person in their decision of whether or not to participate in the full Solo programme.

The actual first three days of preparation during programme time consisted of smaller "threshold exercises" which in the beginning involved the participants' reflection on their lives. Then, the exercises slowly led participants into a process of pinpointing what is currently alive for them in their lives. As touched on in chapter 3.3.2. Solo rituals often serve the purpose of closing what has been, celebrating what is, or simply marking a transition in life. In that sense, through the exercises participants were supported in finding an intention for their Solo time and additionally became acquainted with the teachings of an ancient nature-based psychological map, the Four Shields of human nature (see Foster & Little, 1999), which serves the purpose of helping the individual to locate her or his current position in life.

After the first three days the group transitioned to a forest nearby where facilitators built a provisional base camp, whilst participants were sent out to find their spot for the overnight Solo.

Participants then communicated their rough location in the area to the facilitators and the group gathered around the threshold circle to symbolically step into their Solo time (see description of the Solo time in the Butterfly programme in chapter 4.3.3.1).

Once the participants returned at sunrise the camp was packed and the group returned to the community farmyard. This was followed by the final phase of the programme, the phase of incorporation, where stories were shared with the whole group and mirrored by the facilitators (see description of the mirroring process in chapter 4.3.3.1).

4.3.4 Sample description and data collection

4.3.4.1 The Butterfly sample

Sample selection and data collection procedure
Generally, the Butterfly participants were selected by the national partner organisations of each country, which participated in the Youth in Action programme. The partner countries were the United Kingdom, Belgium, Germany, Austria, Italy and the Czech Republic. The national organisations who agreed to be part of the Butterfly Effect Programme all work with young people on different themes, most of them primarily focusing on the environment, sustainability and empowerment. The young people who participated in the programme were either already associated with the organisations or were friends with previous participants of the Butterfly Programme 2009. Thus, participation was voluntary.

The initial recruitment of the survey sample for this research project, however, was realised through the programme facilitators, as most of the participating countries were also represented in the international team of facilitators. In each participating country a pre-meeting was organised by one of the facilitators as an information and orientation meeting for the enrolled Butterfly participants. If a facilitator was unable to attend I asked another representative from the sending organisation to take her or his place. During the pre-meetings, which took place roughly two weeks before the start of the programme, the present research endeavour was briefly introduced and participants were handed out an information sheet and consent form and asked to fill out the first set of questionnaires as the baseline measurement. Out of the 36 participants of the Butterfly Effect Programme 2011 26 took part in the pretest measurement. The completed questionnaires were collected by the facilitators or representatives and then handed over to me at the start of the programme on-site in Findhorn, Scotland.

In order to assess content of consciousness during the Solo time in nature I implemented the PCI after the participants' Solo experience, precisely right after the sharing and mirroring in the group. Here, not only those participants who took part in the baseline condition reported back but also some of those who decided not to take part in the initial survey measurement. Therefore, the sample size for the PCI data (N= 31) from the Butterfly group is slightly larger than the size of the survey sample.

On the last day of the Butterfly programme I asked the Butterfly participants to again fill out the same questionnaires as at the pretest measurement. I collected the completed questionnaires directly on-site.

Furthermore, during the last two days of the programme I conducted the qualitative interviews. I selected the interview sample (N= 9) randomly from all of those programme participants who agreed in the consent form to take part in an interview at the end of the programme (for further description see section 4.3.6).

For posttest II, eight weeks after the programme, I contacted participants via email. A limited version of the questionnaire which I handed out at pretest and posttest I was attached as a Word document, which I asked participants to fill out and send back to me via email.

For the follow-up study, posttest III, one and a half years after the programme, I contacted participants again via email. I sent out the same limited version of the initial questionnaire in the form of an online survey with the slight variation of including a couple of extra items. Moreover, as part of the follow-up study, I contacted the same interview partners as for posttest I for a second interview. Out of nine interviewees at posttest I eight interviewees took part in an interview again (for further description see section 4.3.6).

Participation in any part of the research phases was voluntary and without any payment.

Interview sample characteristics

At posttest I the average age of the nine interviewees was 24 years with a gender distribution of six males and three females. After one and a half years the average (m= 24.13) was only slightly higher as the oldest participant dropped out. The interviewees came from Austria, Italy, Belgium and the UK at both points of time.

Table 2

Distribution of age and gender in the Butterfly interview sample

	Total N	Age		Gender	
		M (SD)	Min- Max	N male	N female
Posttest I	9	24 (3.87)	18- 31	6	3
Follow-up	8	24.13 (3.04)	19- 29	5	3

Notes. N = number of participants; M (SD) = mean (standard deviation); Min = minimum; Max = maximum.

Survey sample characteristics

In order to realise a measurement of change within the group of Butterfly participants I collected the data at four measurement points, as illustrated in the sample selection. Due to dropouts the sample size slightly varied for the different measurement points.

Two months later, at posttest II, and one and a half years later, at posttest III, 19 participants reported back.

The distribution of age and gender according to the measurement points is presented in Table 3.

Furthermore, the distribution of nationalities at the different measurement points as well as the distribution of the residential areas of participants in their home countries is presented in the following Table 4. At each measurement point over 60 per cent of the sample was at home in urban areas.

Additionally, I asked participants to rate their past contact with nature during their childhood years from age seven to twelve. The rating scale ranged from one to four with one indicating a lot of contact with nature and four very little. The mean and standard deviation for the samples according to the measurement points is illustrated in Table 5.

Table 3

Distribution of age and gender in the Butterfly survey sample

	Total N	Age		Gender	
		M (SD)	Min- Max	N (%) male	N (%) female
Prestest/ Posttest I	26	23.15 (3.37)	18- 31	8 (30.8)	18 (69.2)
Posttest II	19	22.68 (2.83)	18- 28	3 (15.8)	16 (84.2)
Posttest III	19	23.17 (3.35)	18- 29	4 (21.1)	15 (78.9)

Notes. N (%) = number of participants (percentage of participants); M (SD) = mean (standard deviation); Min = minimum; Max = maximum.

Table 4

Distribution of nationalities and residential areas in the survey sample

		Pre/Posttest I	Posttest II	Posttest III
		N (%)	N (%)	N (%)
Country of origin				
	Germany	4 (15.4)	4 (21.1)	2 (11.1)
	Austria	5 (19.2)	4 (21.1)	5 (27.8)
	Italy	5 (19.2)	4 (21.1)	4 (22.2)
	Belgium	6 (23.1)	3 (15.8)	4 (22.2)
	Czech Republic	1 (3.8)	1 (5.3)	1 (5.6)
	UK	5 (19.2)	3 (15.8)	2 (11.1)
	Total	26 (100)	19 (100)	18 (100)
Residential area				
	Urban	17 (65.4)	12 (63.2)	12 (66.7)
	Rural	9 (34.6)	7 (36.8)	6 (33.3)

Note. N (%) = number of participants (percentage of participants).

Table 5

Past contact with nature during childhood in the Butterfly survey sample

	Total N	"During my childhood (age 7-12) I spend a lot of time in nature." Range 1 ("a lot") to 4 ("very little").
		M (SD)
Prestest/ Posttest I	26	2.35 (.89)
Posttest II	19	2.11 (.81)
Posttest III	19	2.17 (.92)

Notes. N = number of participants; M (SD) = mean (standard deviation).

4.3.4.2 The Solo-only sample

Sample selection and data collection procedure

The participants of the Solo-only programme were simultaneously participants of "project peace", a voluntary peace year for young adults between 18 and 25 years. The Solo-only programme was part of a variety of activities and events that were offered to the "project peace" participants throughout their yearlong volunteer time. The Solo was proposed to the volunteers during the final two months of their volunteer time as a way to reflect on their year and current lives. Before the Solo-only programme started the volunteers already completed half a year of volunteering abroad and an extensive time living and working together on the farmyard in Bavaria, focusing on topics like peace, sustainability and community.

The Solo-only programme was introduced by the two facilitators prior to the actual start of the programme and the volunteers subsequently freely decided whether to take part or not. At the preceding "taster day" (see section 4.3.3.2) the "project peace" programme manager also briefly introduced the present research endeavour to the participants and handed out an information sheet and consent form. In the latter participants were additionally asked whether they would be willing to participate in an interview at the end of the programme.

After participants returned from their Solo time and their stories were shared in the group and mirrored by the facilitators participants completed the PCI. On the last day of the programme I handed out an additional open-ended storytelling question, which was completed by nine of the participants.

Furthermore, during the last day of the programme I conducted the qualitative interviews. I selected the interview sample (N= 4) randomly from all of those programme participants who consented to take part in an interview at the end of the programme.

Participation was voluntary and without any payment.

Interview sample characteristics

The interview sample consisted of one male and three females with a mean age of 20. All of the participants were German (Table 6).

PCI sample characteristics

As the research focus in the Solo-only programme was the phenomenology of the Solo time in nature there was only one point of measurement by means of the PCI directly after the storytelling and mirroring. All project peace volunteers who decided to take

Table 6

Distribution of age and gender in the Solo-only interview sample

Total N	Age		Gender	
	Mean	Min- Max	N male	N female
4	20	19- 21	1	3

Notes. N = number of participants; Min = minimum; Max = maximum.

Table 7

Distribution of age, gender and original residential area in the Solo-only PCI sample

	Total N	Age		Gender		Residential area[a]	
		M (SD)	Min- Max	N (%) male	N (%) female	N (%) urban	N (%) rural
Solo-only programme	11	20.64 (2.11)	18 – 26	2 (18.2)	9 (81.8)	4 (36.4)	6 (54.5)

Notes. N (%) = number of participants (percentage of participants); M (SD) = mean (standard deviation); Min = minimum; Max = maximum; [a] one missing value.

part in the Solo-only programme also took part in the study. The sample size for the PCI assessment comes to eleven subjects.

The distribution of age and gender as well as of the original residential area of the participants is presented in Table 7.

Additionally, I asked participants to rate their past contact with nature during their childhood years from age seven to twelve. The rating scale ranged from one to four with one indicating a lot of contact with nature and four very little. The mean for this item was 1.64 with a standard deviation of .67.

4.3.5 Quantitative research strand

4.3.5.1 Quantitative outcome measures

Inclusion of nature in self (INS)

The Inclusion of Nature in Self (INS) is a single-item measure of the perceived relationship between nature and self created by Schultz (2001). As Schultz (2002) states "the psychological analysis of inclusion focuses on the understanding that an individual has on her place in nature, the value that s/he places on nature and his or her actions that impact the natural environment (p.67)."

The measure represents a modification of Aron, Aron and Smollan's (1992) Inclusion of Other in Self (IOS) scale which assess closeness in interpersonal relationships. The scale roots in research revealing that in close relationships each person incorporates aspects of the other as part of her or his concept of self (Aron & Fraley, 1999). Thus, the INS is a graphical measure, which was developed to assess the extent to which an individual includes nature within her or his cognitive representation of self (see Figure 4).

Figure 4. The Inclusion of Nature in Self (INS) scale by Schultz (2001).

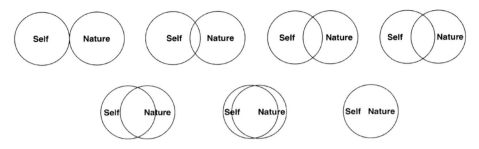

The person is asked to choose from seven overlapping circles labelled "self" and "nature" which circle best describes the person's relationship with the natural environment. The corresponding question is: how interconnected are you with nature? Scores range from 1 (*upper left circle*) to seven (*lower right circle*). The circle with the least overlap represents a person who perceives her or himself as separate from nature and the completely overlapping circle a person who perceives her or himself as the same as nature.

The measure has been shown to be reliable across time in test-retest and it correlates positively with biospheric environmental concerns (r= .31), the Perspective Taking (PT) subscale of the Interpersonal Reactivity Index (IRI) (r= .3), self-reported environmental behaviour (r= .41) as well as the New Environmental Paradigm (NEP) Scale (r= .2) which measures the degree to which a person perceives humans as an integral part of the natural environment, rather that separate (Schultz, 2002).

An advantage and distinctive feature of this instrument is that it is a graphical single-item measure and therefore economical to use. However, this also prevents an estimation of the accuracy of the measurement.

Coping with Global Environmental Problems (GEP)

The Coping with Global Environmental Problems (GEP) Scale was developed by Homburg *et al.* (2007) and measures how people respond to and cope with environmental stressors such as pollution impact, accidents and disasters and global environmental problems.

Coping is measured using eight subscales which are based on Lazarus' (1994) coping approach and can be differentiated in problem-focused versus deproblematisation-focused coping. Six of the eight subscales fit this two-dimensional metastructure with Problem Solving, Expression of Emotion and Self-Protection representing the problem-focused coping and Denial of Guilt, Relativization and Pleasure representing deproblematisation-focused coping. Wishful Thinking and Resignation, however, represent the non-integrated scales and may be subject of further research. Each subscale is illustrated with a sample item in Table 8.

All-together forty-one items make up the scale and respondents are asked to "Please read each statement carefully and decide whether each statement does apply or does not apply to your own reaction."

The subscales use a 6-point Likert scale, ranging from 1 (*not at all true*) to 6 (*exactly true*) and the mean score is recorded for each subscale. A high score indicates that an individual fits that subscale category exactly. Only the subscale scores are used and no total score is created for this scale.

Table 8

Subscales of the Coping with Global Environmental Problems (GEP) Scale by Homburg et al. (2007)

Subscale	Sample item
Problem Solving	It is important for me to talk to others about such global environmental changes and to look for solutions in everyday life.
Expression of Emotion	I become angry, when I talk about these environmental problems.
Self-Protection	Due to the air pollution, I tend to avoid roads with heavy traffic for longer.
Denial of Guilt	I do not feel responsible for this situation.
Relativization	I think there will be a way out.
Pleasure	If possible, I feel comfortable despite the environmental changes.
Wishful Thinking	I wish there would be a sudden change and everything would get readjusted.
Resignation	The problems of global environmental changes cannot be solved.

The subscale Problem Solving involves cognitions and actions centering on the current problem to be solved such as starting to accumulate knowledge on the topic. This scale excludes mechanisms such as avoiding the problem. A high score on this subscale indicates that a person is likely to use this approach when coping with environmental problems.

The subscale Expression of Emotion measures the degree to which a person copes by showing emotional reactions to environmental issues such as anger or sadness. A high score on this subscale indicates that a person is likely to use this approach when coping with environmental problems.

The subscale Denial of Guilt measures the degree to which people fail to assume responsibility for environmental problems. A high score on this subscale indicates that a person is likely to use this approach when coping with environmental problems.

The subscale Relativization measures the degree to which a person believes that despite the discrepancy between the actual and the target state a solution will somehow manifest. A high score on this subscale indicates that a person is likely to use this approach when coping with environmental problems.

The subscale Wishful Thinking measures the emphasis a person puts on wishing for a sudden change and disappearance of all problems. A high score on this subscale indicates that a person is likely to use this approach when coping with environmental problems.

The subscale Self-Protection measures a behavioural coping style that focuses on personal health. It represents the degree to which a person exhibits healthy behaviour as a way of coping with environmental problems for instance via avoiding polluted areas. A high score on this subscale indicates that a person is likely to use this approach when coping with environmental problems.

The subscale Pleasure measures the individual's focus on her or his own well-being despite the environmental problems. A high score on this subscale indicates that a person is likely to use this approach when coping with environmental problems.

Finally, the subscale Resignation measures the degree to which a person accepts the problem to be and believes that the problem is unchangeable. A high score on this subscale indicates that a person is likely to use this approach when coping with environmental problems.

The authors (Homburg *et al.*, 2007) promote researching coping as "coping processes play a decisive role as mediators or moderators between environmental impacts, appraisal of these impacts, and physical and psychological consequences (p.755)" and are widely discussed as a decisive predictor of proenvironmental behaviour. Indeed, as expected, the problem-focused and action-centered scales Problem Solving, Expression of Emotions and Self-Protection were positively correlated with proenvironmental behaviour. All coping styles correlated positively with psychological stress apart from Denial of Guilt and Relativization, which correlated negatively with stress. In all of their three studies (N = 265; 275; 225) the authors were able to replicate the scales and the scale structure (Cronbach's α= .63 to .90) (Homburg *et al.*, 2007). Homburg *et al.* (2007) recommend the scales for the evaluation of programmes that aim to reduce environmental stress and facilitate proenvironmental behaviour.

Emotional Affinity toward Nature (EAN)

Emotional Affinity toward Nature (EAN) is a construct developed by Kals, Schumacher, and Montada (1999) as a counterpart to the cognitive concept of interest in nature. Their conceptualisation of emotional affinity is composed of four aspects and therefore four subscales were developed: Love of Nature, Feelings of Freedom in Nature, Feelings of Security in Nature, and Feelings of Oneness with Nature (see Table 9).

Each subscale is rated on a 6-point Likert scale, ranging from 1 (*complete disagreement*) to 6 (*complete agreement*) and the mean score is recorded for each subscale. Higher scores on the subscales indicate that the associated aspect of emotional affinity toward nature is more highly pronounced.

The measure was presented to 281 adults in Germany and factor analyses confirmed that all items of the four subscales loaded on the same factor, with Cronbach's alpha between .80 and .92 for all subscales. Furthermore, the authors showed that emotional affinity is more closely related to environmentally relevant commitment and behaviour than mere cognitive interest in nature. Multiple regression analyses revealed that 39% of emotional affinity toward nature traces back to present and past experiences in natural environments (Kals *et al.*, 1999).

Connectedness to Nature Scale (CNS)

The Connectedness to Nature Scale (CNS) (Mayer & Frantz, 2004) provides a measure of an individual's trait level of feeling emotionally connected to the natural world. It was designed to assess the extent to which a person generally feels as part of the natural world and emotionally connected to it. This measure consists of 14 items rated on a 5-point Likert scale, with a rating ranging from 1 (*strongly disagree*) to 5 (*strongly agree*). Respondents are asked to "Please answer each of these questions in terms of the way you generally feel. There are no right or wrong answers. Using the following scale, in the space provided next to each question simply state as honestly and candidly as you can what you are presently experiencing." Scores are summed and the total scale score ranges from 14 to 70. Higher scores reflect a higher degree of affective connectedness to nature. Sample items are depicted in Table 10.

Table 9

Subscales of the Emotional Affinity toward Nature (EAN) measure by Kals et al. (1999)

Subscale	Sample item
Love of Nature	Spending time in nature today, I feel a deep feeling of love towards nature.
Feeling of Freedom in Nature	When I spend time in nature today I feel free and easy.
Feelings of Security in Nature	When I spend time in nature today a feeling like security arises.
Feelings of Oneness with Nature	By getting in touch with nature today I get the feeling of having the same origin.

Table 10

Sample items of the Connectedness to Nature Scale (CNS) by Mayer and Frantz (2004)

Sample Items of the Connectedness to Nature Scale
I often feel a kinship with animals and plants.
I feel as though I belong to the earth as equally as it belongs to me.
I often feel that all inhabitants of Earth, human and nonhuman, share a common "life-force".
Like a tree can be part of a forest, I feel embedded within the broader natural world.

The psychometric properties of the scale were tested in five studies, which confirmed the single-factor structure and high internal consistency. The authors highlight the scale's economical use and reliability (Cronbach's alpha= .79 to .84) as the CNS is a multi-item instrument as opposed to the INS. Furthermore, the CNS relates to other related constructs such as the NEP (New Environmental Paradigm) scale, identity as an environmentalist, perspective taking for nature and the INS and also reveals positive correlations with subjective well-being, ecological behaviour and anitconsumerism (Mayer & Frantz, 2004).

Life Values Inventory (LVI)

The Life Values Inventory (LVI) was developed by Brown and Crace (1996) to provide a brief and economical assessment of intrapersonal values that guide behaviour and is intended for the high school and adult population. The LVI contains 42 items that measure 14 values assessed via three items each. Instead of letting the respondents rate the items in terms of importance as commonly known in values instruments the respondents are invited to think about values that guide their behaviour. Thereby, the authors aim to address positive response bias that might otherwise occur as individuals have the tendency to assign more importance to positive values (Brown & Crace, 1996). Thus, respondents rate each item in a Likert format, which reflects how much each item guides the respondent's behaviour (1 = almost never guides my behaviour; 3 = sometimes guides my behaviour; 5 = almost always guides my behaviour). The values measured by the LVI are Achievement, Belonging, Concern for the Environment, Concern for Others, Creativity, Financial Prosperity, Health and Activity, Humility, Independence, Interdependence, Objective Analysis, Privacy, Responsibility, and Spirituality. For each value scale the ratings of the three items are summed up. The subscales with their associated value profile are depicted in Table 11.

Table 11

Subscales of the Life Values Inventory (LVI) by Brown and Crace (1996)

Value subscale	Value profile
Achievement	It is important to challenge yourself and work hard to improve.
Belonging	It is important to be accepted by others and to feel included.
Concern for the Environment	It is important to protect and preserve the environment.
Concern for others	The well-being of others is important.
Creativity	It is important to have new ideas or to create new things.
Financial Prosperity	It is important to be successful at making money or buying property.
Health and Activity	It is important to be healthy and physically active.
Humility	It is important to be humble and modest about your accomplishments
Independence	It is important to make your own decisions and do things your way.
Loyalty to Family or Group	It is important to follow the traditions and expectations of your family or group.
Privacy	It is important to have alone time.
Responsibility	It is important to be dependable and trustworthy.
Scientific Understanding	It is important to use scientific principles to understand and solve problems.
Spirituality	It is important to have spiritual beliefs and to believe that you are part of something greater than yourself.

The LVI has a high sensitivity to cultural values, a stable factor structure and its scales maintain internal consistency (Cronbach's alpha between .55 and .88 for the adult population). The convergent validity was assessed by correlating LVI scale scores with items from the Rokeach Values Survey (RVS). 27 of the 30 predicted correlations with the RVS were significant for adults in the expected direction (Brown & Crace, 1996). Temporal stability of LVI scales was examined with test-retest reliability coefficients. The retest coefficients on all scales were significant over an interval of about 18 days. Retest coefficients for adults ranged from .57 on the Concern for Others scale to .90 on the Spirituality scale. Criterion validity was examined by sending a Behavioural Rating Scale (BRS), which was designed to assess behaviours associated with the values on the LVI to a person who knows the respondent well. Eight of the correlations between the BRS and analogous LVI scales were statistically significant with an additional one approaching significance (Brown & Crace, 1996).

Miller's Hope Scale (MHS)

The Miller's Hope Scale (MHS) (Miller & Powers, 1988) measures hope in adults and stems from the field of nursing research. It consists of 39 items that are rated using a 6-point Likert format from 1 (*very strongly disagree*) to 6 (*very strongly agree*). The scale consists of three subscales: (1) Satisfaction with Self, Others and Life, (2) Avoidance of Hope Threats and (3) Anticipation of a Future. Sample items are presented in Table 12.

For all three scales individual scores can be generated with higher scores indicating higher hopefulness. As the last item[15] of the Anticipation of a Future scale references hopefulness in the context of health or illness I decided to exclude it from the survey

---

15   Item 40: I can find reasons to stay positive about my health.

Table 12

Subscale sample items of Miller's Hope Scale (MHS)

Subscale	Sample item
Satisfaction with self, others and life	My life has meaning.
Avoidance of hope threats	I am so overwhelmed, nothing I do will help.
Anticipation of a future	I look forward to an enjoyable future.

due to the lack of relevance for my research sample. Therefore the possible overall score ranged from 39 to 234 in the present study.

Experts on content and measurement reviewed the instrument, which ensured content validity. Psychometric properties of the instrument were tested in 522 healthy adults. Cronbach's alpha was .93 with an overall test-retest reliability of .82. Criterion-related construct validity was established by correlating the MHS with psychological well-being (r= .71) and purpose and meaning in life (r= .82). Miller viewed hope in the development of this instrument as a multidimensional construct that exceeds goal attainment and represents a state of well-being (Miller & Powers, 1988).

International Personality Item Pool (IPIP) Scales

Three scales were obtained from the International Personality Item Pool (IPIP) (Goldberg, 1999): Trust, Gratitude (GRA) and Capacity for Love (CAP).

The IPIP is an international scientific collaboratory for the development and cultivation of personality inventories, which are accessible through public domains and which scales can be applied in scientific and commercial contexts.

The IPIP Trust scale belongs to a group of IPIP scales, which were developed to measure constructs similar to those in the 30 NEO PI-R facet scales developed by Costa and McCrae (1992). The IPIP Trust scale therefore depicts the NEO PI-R trust facet of the factor "agreeableness".

The IPIP Trust scale was constructed by a procedure that applies to most IPIP scales which is to identify those IPIP items, which as a scale correlate highly with an existing measure, in this case the corresponding NEO facet. The correlation of the IPIP trust scale with the NEO facet "trust" is r= .79 and the alpha coefficient of the IPIP 10-item trust scale is .82. Respondents rate the items on a 5-point Likert scale ranging from 1 (strongly disagree) to 5 (strongly agree) with a high overall score indicating higher trust.

Gratitude (GRA) and Capacity for Love (CAP) are two of 24 IPIP Values in Action (VIA) scales which are revised versions of the VIA scales developed by Peterson and Seligman (2004). The VIA is a self-report assessment to measure 24 character strengths which correlate substantially with self-nominations of strengths. The test in general shows good reliability on measures of internal consistency and test-retest correlations (> .70). In three large sample studies, the scales correlated modestly with rewarding aspects of work, love, and play and for most scales including Capacity for Love and Gratitude robust correlations with life satisfaction were found.

CAP belongs to a class of strengths called "humanity" (Peterson & Seligman, 2004) which represents strengths that emphasise the human strength of tending and befriending others. CAP in that matter represents generally valuing relationships especially those, which include reciprocally sharing and caring for each other. The revision

Table 13

Sample items for Trust, Gratitude (GRA) and Capacity for Love (CAP) from the International Personality Item Pool (IPIP)

Scale	Sample item
Trust	I believe that others have good intentions.
Capacity for love	I am willing to take risks to establish a relationship.
Gratitude	I feel a profound sense of appreciation every day.

of the original scale was accomplished by omitting one item from the scale and thereby improving the internal consistency to alpha= .70.

Gratitude belongs to a class of strengths called "transcendence" which represent strengths that establish connections to the larger universe and meaning in life. GRA in this context represents an individual's awareness of the positive things in life and the individual's ability to expressively acknowledge this. The 8-item GRA scale was refined by omitting two items from the original scale, which led to an alpha coefficient of .79.

Higher numbers on both scales reflect more of the strength.

A sample item for each scale is depicted in Table 13.

Civic Attitudes and Skills Questionnaire (CASQ)

The Civic Attitudes and Skills Questionnaire (CASQ) (Moely, Mercer, Ilustre, Miron, & McFarland, 2002) is a questionnaire that was originally designed to evaluate service-learning outcomes.

Service-learning is an pedagogical approach that is implemented in educational curricula and which connects cognitive learning with the promotion of academic and civic engagement and actual assumption of responsibility. It is assumed that service-learning produces changes in six major areas (Stukas, Clary, & Snyder, 1999), out of which two have been focused on for the purpose of the present research. This was realised by implementing three of the associated scales of the CASQ. One of the targeted major areas of change is self-enhancement indicated through self-esteem, personal efficacy and confidence. The associated CASQ scales that were applied in this research are "Interpersonal and Problem-Solving Skills" and "Leadership Skills".

"Interpersonal and Problem-Solving Skills" in the context of the CASQ scans an individual's ability to listen, work cooperatively, take over perspectives, communicate, think logically and solve problems. Regarding "Leadership Skills" respondents are asked to rate their leadership ability and effectiveness in that role.

The second area monitored in the present evaluation study is value-expression, which Moely (2002) summarises as the "expression of humanitarian and prosocial values through action and plans for future involvement in community service (p.1)." The monitoring of this particular area was realised by implementing the associated CASQ scale "Civic Action" which asks respondents to evaluate their intention to show community engagement in the future. Items of all subscales are rated on a five-point Likert scale ranging from 1 (strongly disagree) to 5 (strongly agree) with higher scores indicating better skills or more action.

Sample items for each of the applied subscales are shown in Table 14.

Table 14

Sample items for each of the applied subscales of the Civic Attitudes and Skills Questionnaire (CASQ)

Subscale	Item
Civic Action	I plan to do some volunteer work.
Interpersonal and Problem-Solving Skills	When trying to understand the position of others I try to place myself in their position.
Leadership Skills	I feel that I can make a difference in the world.

The internal consistency of the CASQ was tested in two undergraduate student samples (N's= 762, 725), which revealed alphas of α = .79 and α = .80 for "Interpersonal and Problem-Solving Skills", α = .79 and α = .79 for "Leadership Skills" and α = .86 and α = .88 for "Civic Action". Test-retest reliability was assessed while keeping constant social desirability with resulting coefficients of r_{tt} = .56 and r_{tt} = .62 for "Interpersonal and Problem-Solving Skills", r_{tt} = .81 and r_{tt} = .72 for "Leadership Skills" and r_{tt} = .74 and r_{tt} = .71 for "Civic Action" (Moely et al., 2002).

Individual Community-Related Empowerment (ICRE)

The Individual Community-Related Empowerment (ICRE) scale (Kasmel & Tanggaard, 2011) is an adaption of the Individual Mobilisation Survey (Jakes & Shannon, 2002).

Individual Empowerment (IE) reflects a person's belief that what one is trying to accomplish is actually realisable and is viewed as an efficient strategy in empowering young people (Reininger et al., 2003). The concept of ICRE, however, is understood as an active type of community orientation and involves the individual's desire to create her or his own role and context as well as feeling able to do so (Zimmerman, 2000). Against this background the ICRE scale served as an appropriate instrument to assess changes regarding perceived empowerment in the Butterfly participants' lives.

The ICRE scale embraces five subscales that emerged from the factor analysis: Self-Efficacy (seven items) in combination with self-confidence, Participation (three items) reflecting the level of engagement in collective action, Motivation (three items) to be involved in one's community, Intention (four items) to become involved and Critical Awareness (one item) of the seriousness of the issues present in one's own community. For the purpose of the present study only Self-Efficacy, Participation, Motivation and Critical Awareness were assessed as the intention to become involved was already assessed as part of the CASQ subscale Civic Action. All items are rated on a five-point Likert scale ranging from 1 (strongly agree) to 5 (strongly disagree) with lower scores indicating higher ICRE.

Sample items for each subscale are depicted in Table 15.

The subscales were implemented before and after the programme apart from Participation. The Participation subscale was implemented three times throughout the project (pretest, posttest II and follow-up) in order to depict the participants' actual behaviour change that is actual lasting community engagement.

Content validity of the ICRE scale was accomplished by an expert panel of six which is reflected in the resulting high ratio (0.98) that was calculated using Lawshe's formula

Table 15

Sample items for the applied subscales of the Individual Community-Related Empowerment (ICRE) scale

Subscale	Item
Self-efficacy	I have the knowledge and skills to influence the community.
Intention	I want to get involved in my community.
Participation	I volunteer for community projects.
Motivation	I am motivated to get involved in my community.
Critical Awareness	I think that the problems in my community are serious.

(Lawshe, 1975). The internal consistency, Cronbach's alpha, of the total empowerment scale was $α = 0.86$ and for the subscales Self-Efficacy $α = 0.88$, Intention $α = 0.83$, Participation $α = 0.81$ and Motivation $α = 0.69$. As Critical Awareness comprised only one item the matter of internal consistency was not relevant for this subscale.

Proenvironmental Behaviour Scale (PEB)

The Proenvironmental Behaviour (PEB) Scale used in this work is a shortened version of the PEB Scale as utilised by Schultz, Gouveia, Cameron, Tankha, Schmuck and Franek (2005). The scale was implemented by virtue of evaluating changes in the Butterfly participants' actual behaviour as was the case with the Participation subscale of the ICRE questionnaire. For this purpose the scale was applied at three points in time: pretest, posttest II and follow-up.

The PEB Scale assesses proenvironmental behaviours asking how often respondents engaged in behaviours such as recycling behaviours, conservation behaviours, consumer behaviours and transportation behaviours in the past month. Respondents rate the frequency of the listed behaviours on a four-point scale, ranging from 4 (*daily*), 3 (*weekly*), 2 (*monthly*), to 1 (*never*). If there was no opportunity for a certain behaviour in the past month respondents have the option to circle NA (*not applicable*) which is treated as a missing (Schultz *et al.*, 2005). The total score is created by calculating the mean of the ratings. Scores therefore range from one to four with higher scores indicating a higher level of proenvironmental behaviour. Sample items are shown in Table 16.

Social Desirability Scale-17 (SDS-17)

The Social Desirability Scale-17 (SDS-17) is modeled after the Marlowe-Crowne Scale (Crowne & Marlowe, 1960) and was constructed with the intent to modernise the content of the latter. The SDS-17 assesses an individual's tendency to describe her or himself with socially desirable attributes. This is realised by presenting the respondent with statements regarding their behaviour. These behaviours are either socially desirable but commonly infrequent or socially undesirable but commonly frequent.

Sample items are depicted in the following Table 17.

Respondents of the SDS-17 rate 16 statements in a forced-choice answer format (*true* or *false*) indicating, according to the respondent, whether the statement describes them or not. Each answer that is given in the socially desirable pattern as described above is awarded one point. These points are added across items and on a scale between

Table 16

Sample items of the Proenvironmental Behaviour (PEB) Scale

Proenvironmental Behaviour Scale sample items
I looked for ways to reuse things.
I conserved gasoline by walking or bicycling.
I purchased products in reusable or recyclable containers.

Table 17

Sample items of the Social Desirability Scale-17 (SDS-17)

Social Desirability Scale-17 sample items
I sometimes litter.
I always admit my mistakes openly and face the potential negative consequences.
I never hesitate to help someone in case of emergency.

0 and 16 the result depicts the individual's tendency to answer socially desirable with higher scores indicating a greater social-desirability response bias.

Overall, the psychometric studies investigating this scale (Stöber, 2001) revealed high internal consistency of the SDS-17 (Cronbach's alpha= .80). Furthermore, this coefficient did not differ greatly between age groups.

The SDS-17 scores proved to be sensitive to social-desirability provoking instructions and further results demonstrated appropriate convergent validity with other lie or social desirability scales.

This questionnaire was implemented in order to capture the respondents' general tendency to respond in a socially desirable appropriate way, as the target behaviours in this study, community engagement and proenvironmental behaviour, are most likely sensitive to this issue. In the present evaluation study the SDS-17 score is used to statistically control for the social desirability bias when evaluating other self-report measurement outcomes.

Sense of Community Index II (SCI-2)

The Sense of Community Index II (SCI-2) (Chavis, Lee, & Acosta, 2008) is a revised version of the Sense of Community Index (SCI) developed by Chavis, Hogge, McMillan and Wandersman (1986). The SCI-2 is based on McMillan and Chavis (1986) theory of sense of community. Contrary to the SCI the SCI-2 covers all of the elements of sense of community as described in the theory, which includes four elements: membership, influence, meeting needs, and shared emotional connection. Therefore the SCI-2 contains 24 items that can be divided into four subscales with six items each that reflect one of the four elements. The first subscale deals with the Reinforcement of Needs, the second one with Community Membership, the third one with the perceived individual Influence within the community and the fourth one with the Shared Emotional Connections within the community. Respondents rate how well each statement reflects their feelings about their community using a four-point Likert scale ranging from 0 (*not at all*) to 3 (*completely*). Scores can be generated for the individual subscales ranging between 0 and 18

Table 18

Subscales and sample items of the Sense of Community Index II (SCI-2)

Subscale	Item
Reinforcement of Needs	I get important needs of mine met because I am part of this community.
Membership	Being a member of this community is part of my identity.
Influence	This community can influence other communities.
Shared Emotional Connection	Members of this community care about each other.

as well as for the whole survey ranging between 0 and 72 with higher scores indicating a stronger sense of community. Sample items for each subscale are depicted in Table 18.

The SCI-2 is a very reliable instrument with Cronbach's alpha of $\alpha = .94$ and alpha scores of .79 to .86 for the four subscales.

The SCI has been utilised in a variety of different fields and cultural contexts and proved to be correlated with perceived environmental performance demands and interpersonal support and networks (Pretty, 1990). For the purpose of this study the SCI-2 was used as a control variable and implemented by virtue of investigating the impact of the felt sense of community in the Butterfly group on other possible changes in constructs and self-reported behaviour.

Phenomenology of Consciousness Inventory (PCI)

The Phenomenology of Consciousness Inventory (PCI) (Pekala, 1991) is a self-report inventory that is used to quantify states of consciousness that are linked with a specific experience or stimulus condition. The respondent is requested to recall her or his experience and retrospectively answer 53 items that relate to this experience. Thereby, a quantitative profile of the individual's quality of consciousness at that time is generated along 26 dimensions that are grouped into 12 major dimensions (Positive Affect, Negative Affect, Altered Experience, Imagery, Attention, Self-Awareness, Altered State of Awareness, Internal Dialogue, Rationality, Volitional Control, Memory, and Arousal). Five dimensions of those are averages of subdimensions while the other 21 are independent. The 26 dimensions with their meaning, rating and grouping are shown in Table 19. Each item is rated on a continuum ranging from 0 to 6 on a 7-point Likert scale. This way the respondent determines the position of the experienced quality of consciousness dimension on a continuum between two poles or expressions of a particular quality of consciousness (see Table 19).

Furthermore, the PCI includes five Reliability Item Pairs (RIP) that are implemented in order to assess the consistency of a respondent's answers. The RIP are spread across the questionnaire and each pair consists of two questions that are similar but are presented with reverse polarity. The suggested guideline is that if the average RIP score exceeds 2.0 the respondent may be unreliable in her or his answers.

Pekala provided detailed information and data on the validity and reliability of the instrument (Pekala, 1991, chap. 5-7). In order to validate the PCI Pekala and colleagues created a baseline state of consciousness of sitting quietly with open eyes for four minutes (N= 112) and another baseline condition of sitting quietly with eyes closed (N= 217). The internal consistency of the PCI is excellent with alpha coefficients between .70 and .90 (Pekala, Steinberg, & Kumar, 1986). The German version

Table 19

The 26 Dimensions of the Phenomenology of Consciousness Inventory (PCI), Clustered into 12 Major Dimensions

PCI Dimensions	Dimensions on Left (0) … Right (6) Poles of Scale
Altered Experience	*Average of:*
Body image	Bodily feelings: within skin … expand into world
Meaning	Insight, awe, reverence: none … strong
Perception	World's appearance: no difference … strong difference
Time sense	Flow of time: no change … strong change
Altered awareness	*State of awareness: normal … strikingly different*
Physical arousal	*Muscular tightness, tension: low … high*
Attention	*Average of:*
Inward direction	Attention: directed to external world … to internal world
Absorption	Attention: distracted, low concentration … completely absorbed
Imagery	*Average of:*
Amount	Amount of visual imagery: low … high
Vividness	Imagery: vague, dim, diffuse, normal … vivid like real-world objects
Internal dialogue	*Silent talking, internal dialogue: none … strong*
Memory	*Memory: blurred, hazy, vacant … sharp, distinct, complete*
Negative affect	*Average of:*
Anger	Anger, rage, upset: none … strong
Fear	Fear, terror: none … strong
Sadness	Sadness, unhappiness, dejection: none … strong
Positive affect	*Average of:*
Joy	Ecstasy, extreme happiness, joy: none … strong
Sexual excitement	Sexual feelings: none … strong
Love	Feelings of love, living-kindness: none … strong
Rationality	*Thinking: unclear, obscure, irrational … clear, distinct, rational*
Self-awareness	*Self-awareness, self-consciousness: low … high*
Volitional control	*Control over thoughts, attention: none … high*

of the PCI was developed by Ott (Rux, 2002) and demonstrated lower internal consistency with an alpha coefficient of .69. The authors ascribe this circumstance to the questionable motivation of their sample subjects.

However, the PCI has been successfully applied in its original domain of hypnotic susceptibility and up until today its domain of validity has extended to the study of a great variety of subjects such as meditation, out-of-body experiences, stress management techniques, drumming, firewalking and trance dancing to name a few (see MacDonald, Friedman, & Kuentzel, 1999).

For the purpose of this study I further widened the domain of application to the experience of immersive experiences in wild nature, thus, right after the telling and mirroring of their stories, I asked Butterfly participants as well as participants of the Solo-only programme to rate their 24-hour Solo experience in the woods based on how they felt at the time of their experience.

This endeavour breaks new territory as the 24-hour time span is indeed exceeding the conventional use of the PCI. The time span of an experience, which Pekala sees as assessable via the PCI, encompasses a maximal duration of 20 minutes. Furthermore, its conventional use requests very recent recalls shortly after the original experience. However, in the context of the present research project I assessed the Solo experience deliberately not until after the mirroring process, which took place up to a day later. The reason for choosing this procedure was that the storytelling and mirroring is understood to be an essential and inseparable part of the Solo experience as a whole (see chapter 3.3). Pekala (1991) emphasises that both cases, assessing experiences of longer durations as well as allowing for longer time intervals between the experience and the PCI assessment, may entail the risk of relying on inference rather than on memory, which may distort the assessment of the phenomenological features of the original experience. Pekala (1991) further warns that experiences of longer durations than 20 minutes may lead to a recall bias of rather referring to the first several minutes or last several minutes of the experience. However, in the case of this study Solo participants intensively re-enacted their 24 hours through the storytelling in the group and went into further elaboration of aspects of their stories through the mirroring process right before completing the PCI. This makes common recall effects such as the primacy effect unlikely. Nevertheless, with a time span of 24 hours it seems reasonable to assume that Solo participants average or infer their subjective experience of this time span. While this may be a distortion when aiming to assess a comprehensive map of all the phenomenological features of the original experience as objectively as possible, averaging or inferring a subjective account of the Solo experience exactly meets the intention of the current study. The purpose of the application of the PCI in the context of the Solo experience is to assess the major qualities of consciousness during the Solo time as participants retrospectively and subjectively recall them. The Solo time is a ritual that intentionally invites participants to tap into a space of myth and into their personal stories and relationship with the wider world and thereby calls for personal meaning-making and purposely emphasises subjectivity. The purpose of applying the PCI in the present research project is to gain descriptives of what participants subjectively extract from this experience and to investigate potentially common ground.

Another essential part of the commonly applied PCI procedure is the baseline condition as a way to contrast the stimulus condition. Even though Pekala (1991) provides conversion tables for raw PCI scores as a way to categorise the obtained PCI data, comparison is only possible with data from the stimulus condition "eyes closed sitting quietly" and "eyes open sitting quietly". Evidently, these conditions do not resemble the Solo experience and therefore cannot act as a suitable baseline condition for the Solo time. However, in the context of the data collection for the present research project, thus during the programmes themselves, it was not possible to implement further extensive measurements for the baseline condition. Thus, in order to be able to still facilitate interpretability of the data, I endeavoured to find the best possible fit in terms of already conducted PCI data that bear the potential of serving as a useful touchstone for evaluating the Solo time PCI data.

The PCI study that could best support this endeavour was the study on religious and spiritual experiences from Wildman and McNamara (2010) who modified the typical PCI procedure and utilised ordinary and happy experiences as a baseline condition for religious experiences. As both joyful and transcendent or spiritual qualities are frequently reported to be part of immersive experiences in wild nature (see chapter 3.3), drawing upon religious and happy experiences as a reference point for understanding and categorising the PCI Solo time data appear useful. The ordinary experience on the other hand as assessed in Wildman and McNamara's study may serve as a useful representation of what is experienced during an ordinary everyday life event and therefore additionally may help to highlight distinctive features of the Solo time. Thus, all three conditions will serve as reference points for further reflection on the Solo time data in the results section.

Wildman and McNamara's (2010) sample consists of 39 voluntary participants with a mean of age of 34. All participants were asked to recall three separate experiences from within the last year: an ordinary experience, which was neither specifically religious nor specifically intense, a religious experience and a happy experience. The recall prompt was "I want you to tell me about a personal experience from within the last year that you remember as being X[16]. Now I want you to take a moment to think about this X event. You may even close your eyes and think about all of the X events you have experienced. Then think about one X event, conjure it up, relive it, and then tell me about it [...] (p.232)." After narrating their experiences participants dated it, answered questions about it, renarrated it and then filled out the PCI on the basis of how they felt during the experience X.

Although this process differs from the recall procedure of the Solo experience there are important congruencies such as firstly going through a process of reviving the experience through storytelling and then processing the experience by means of answering questions about it as in Wildman and McNamara's study and in the case of the Solo ritual by means of mirroring the participants' stories. Furthermore, in both scenarios participants completed the PCI retrospectively directly after narrating and processing their experience.

Demographic information and control items

In addition to the above listed questionnaires I assessed selected demographic information and single questions.

Demographic information included age, gender, nationality and the residential area (rural or urban).

The single questions served the purpose of additionally controlling for potential confounding variables that were either already known from the literature or anticipated.

At pretest, I asked respondents to indicate the frequency of contact with nature during their childhood (age 7 to 12 years) and also currently, as well as whether they plan to spend more time in nature in the future, on a five-point Likert scale ranging from 1 (absolutely true) to 5 (not true at all) with lower ratings indicating highly frequent contact with nature or the plan to spent more time in nature in the future.

At posttest I, respondents rated the degree to which they felt the evaluation was disturbing their personal process during programme time as well as the degree to which they felt language difficulties disabled them from properly answering the questionnaires on a four-point Likert scale ranging from 1 (not at all disturbing) to 4 (disturbed a great deal).

---

16 X acts as a place holder for either religious, happy or ordinary.

Figure 5. Overview of the assessed constructs at the various points of measurement.

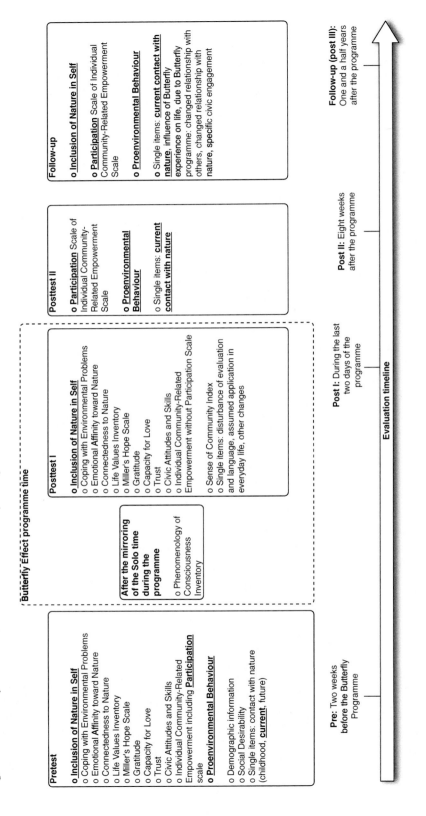

At posttest I, one further item assessed the degree to which participants felt they can apply what they learned during the programme in their everyday lives on a four-point Likert scale ranging from 1 (not at all applicable) to 4 (a great deal applicable).

Additionally, an open-ended question provided space to write down other important changes participants noticed in themselves that had not been addressed in the questionnaires.

An overview of the assessed constructs at the points of measurement is illustrated in Figure 5. I assessed all items and constructs, which are underlined in Figure 5 longitudinally.

4.3.5.2 Quantitative data analysis

I submitted the hypotheses presented in chapter 4.2.1 to robust exploratory statistical tests assuming convention 5% levels for controlling errors.

In principle, I adopted the following statistical strategy:

Firstly, I analysed the data visually by means of histograms in order to determine whether the data were normally distributed. The vast majority of variables did not prove to be normally distributed, which is why I chose to apply non-parametric procedures.

As the data were skewed I employed robust statistics, the Wilcoxon matched-pair signed-rank test, for testing pre-post-differences. I then calculated approximate effect sizes for the differences using Rosenthal's (1991) equation (see box below) to convert z-scores into the effect size estimate r.

$$r = Z/\sqrt{N}$$

As in exploratory research there is always the danger of committing type II errors and overlooking effects, I refrained from adjustments for multiple testing and instead documented effect sizes and interpreted also the consistency of changes and patterns.

Furthermore, I employed non-parametric correlations in order to investigate the patterns of change. Here, I focused on analysing the relationship between already assessed relevant changes in test scores across time reflected in effect sizes. In other words, to find out to what extent a change in one construct was related to a change in another I calculated differential values[17], which I then used to determine correlations. Due to the small sample size of the pre- and posttest comparison I chose to rely on Kendall's tau (τ) (see Howell, 1997) and on the significance level .05.

Additionally, I correlated the control variables, namely residential area, contact with nature during the childhood, gender, age and social desirability, with the calculated differential values of the above described relevantly changed test scores.

I carried out the statistical analysis using SPSS 21.0.

Furthermore, I replaced the missing values for all of those scales that demanded the calculation of total scores. The procedure for the replacement was to firstly identify the with the missing value associated subscale and then to replace it with the calculated mean of the individual's existing values of this subscale. Otherwise, if the scale did not include subscales, the missing value was replaced with the intraindividual mean of the entire scale.

However, I did not replace missing values whenever the scoring procedure for scales and subscales merely required the calculation of means. In this case, I simply calculated the mean score by using the remaining intraindividual values of the associated scale.

---

17 Differential values depict the difference between pre- and post test scores.

4.3.6 Qualitative research strand

4.3.6.1 Open-ended storytelling question

In order to assess a greater variety of meaningful experiences exceeding the interview sample of the Solo-only sample, I implemented an open-ended storytelling question at the end of the Solo-only programme. Here, I asked all of the programme participants to "write down their story of a moment or situation during the programme when something personally meaningful has been learnt or understood." I administered this question in order to gain more insight on the nature and areas of personal change that are triggered in programmes that facilitate immersive experiences in wild nature. I added all transcripts of the answers to the qualitative data pool.

4.3.6.2 Qualitative interview approach and procedure

As repeatedly touched on in the previous chapters I intended to thoroughly document the research process and include my own experiences throughout the research process as part of the qualitative data. To achieve this objective I kept a research diary from the start of the research project. The research diary comprises research-related thoughts, experiences and dreams throughout the entire research process as well as field notes that I took during the Butterfly Programme. Especially as a preparation for the latter I engaged in an exercise of focused self-reflexivity in order to become aware of my own expectations regarding the research outcomes. In qualitative research this method is called bracketing and is thought to lessen the potentially distorting effects of the researcher's preconceptions on the research process by bringing them into awareness.

To realise this I went into nature and, after taking a moment of quiet, started to note down in an associative manner personal fears, wishes and expectations regarding the data collection process and the research outcomes. I kept the results in my research journal, which I revisited before the start of the interviews at the end of the programmes. The captured specific wishes, expectations, fears and potential projections amounted to five personal guidelines for the process of data collection which served me as a reminder and supported me to maintain an open mind and to the greatest extent possible unbiased perception. The guidelines are illustrated in Table 20.

Furthermore, in advance to the programmes, I took time to clarify and set my intentions for the research project. This endeavour is in line with Braud and Anderson's (1998) case for the importance of creating a supporting atmosphere of a research project by bringing personal intentions into awareness and explicating them. My intentions were largely mirrored in the suggestions by Braud and Anderson (1998, p. 63).

Table 20

Personal guidelines for the process of data collection

Guidelines
Do not hear only what you know from your own experience.
Do not read your own experience into what is said.
Let go and be perceptive for whatever may unfold.
Do not anticipate what is going to happen.
Stay authentic.

In order to be able to revisit the intentions throughout the entire research process I recorded them in writing in my journal. The associated excerpt of the research journal is depicted in the following.

> *May there appear the "right" persons in the sample, may they be able to know and express the most useful material relevant to the topic. May I be able to receive, understand and express new learnings in the most useful way; ways that are useful to me, to the participants, to the future reader of this work, to the research field, and to society as a whole.*
>
> *May I hear all the voices.*

The excerpt also reflects my overall understanding of research as a vehicle for possible transformation for everyone involved.

In the mixed-methods chapter I already explained the general purpose of the qualitative research strand. However, the purpose of exploring a so-far little known phenomenon, in this case of immersive experiences in wild nature, entails also practical implications for conducting the interviews such as not yet knowing the most appropriate interview questions and equally important how to ask them in the most comprehensible way. Thus, in the present work the refinement of interview questions and the extraction of knowledge represent a simultaneous process and reflect the fluid and dynamic approach taken in the qualitative strand of this research project.

The conducted interviews were all semi-structured and I made adjustments to the interviews in real time when necessary. A good example for an adjustment was the interview guideline question "Do you feel your experience of nature during the Butterfly programme changed your sense of self in some way?" I initially used the expression "sense of self" in order to avoid the implicit assumption of duality when talking about self and nature. However, it quickly became evident that this way it was not clear to interviewees what the question aimed at or referred to so that I returned to the question of "potential changes in the individual's relationship with nature".

The dynamic approach is further reflected in the use of structure and the simultaneous preservation of the inductive nature of qualitative enquiry. Accordingly, I ensured that all relevant subject areas of the semi-structured interviews were covered yet the order of topics, the flow of the interview and excursions to novel relevant topics were initiated and co-created by the interviewees. For instance, if a question was naturally answered as part or the result of the participant's response to another topic I refrained from repeating the question at a later stage in the interview. This resulted in a more natural style as I was able to follow the rhythm and flow of the participant's thoughts and arising topics without imposing an artificial framework. This, alongside the familiarity between the interviewees and myself due to my presence throughout both, the Solo-only and the Butterfly programme, contributed to building rapport. Against the backdrop of aiming to conduct illuminative qualitative data this constitutes an important foundation for exploring and sharing personally meaningful experiences in an interview. Indicators for a good rapport between myself, the interviewer, and the interviewee were reflected in several interviews where interviewees directly expressed gratitude and appreciation for having been interviewed.

Table 21

Main areas of focus according to the interview samples

Area of focus	Butterfly post I	Butterfly follow-up	Solo-only
Overall personal rating	Of programme and Solo	Retrospectively of programme as a life event	Of Solo
Nature (-related changes)			In-depth account of the content of the Solo experience
	Effects of Solo (ritual) and outdoor setting of the programme regarding one's experience of nature		Effects of Solo (ritual) regarding one's experience of nature
	Perceived resulting changes in the relationship with nature	Perceived manifested changes in the relationship with nature	Perceived resulting changes in the relationship with nature
Triggers and types of inner re-orientation or change	Moment of shift, insight or revelation		Moment of shift, insight or revelation
Other areas of growth/ changes	Regarding relationship with oneself	(Most significant) actual changes in life due to Butterfly	Regarding self
	Regarding relationship with others		
	Regarding relationship with world		Regarding relationship with world
	Regarding focus in life		Regarding focus in life
(Anticipated) changes in pro-active behaviour	Lifestyle	Actual lifestyle changes	
	Engagement	Actual engagement	

Another aspect of the interview approach was inductive probing, which I applied by virtue of clarifying participants' expressions and associated meanings. Notably, due to the internationality of the Butterfly sample, mostly neither me nor the interviewees spoke their mother tongue during the interview. Therefore I used inductive probing not only to support participants in deepening their story and explicating their experiences but also to minimise possible misunderstandings due to language difficulties. In order to be able to estimate the validity of the interview data in regard to this potential distortion I implemented a survey item at posttest I which assessed whether participants felt that language issues impaired their ability to properly answer the questions. Participants rated this question on a score ranging from 1 (not at all) to 4 (a great deal). The statistical analysis revealed a mean of 1.8, which means that the average answer to this question was positioned in between "not at all" and "not very much". For the Solo-only sample this issue did not arise at all as interviewer and interviewees spoke in their mother tongue German.

Due to the different nature of the Solo-only and the Butterfly programme the interview guidelines for both samples differed to some extent. Key areas, however, remained similar or the same. The different and converging main areas of focus are illustrated in Table 21. The empty spaces in the table indicate areas, which I did not explicitly include in the interview guideline. For instance community building was an integral part of the Butterfly programme but not of the Solo-only programme as participants of the latter already lived in community together before the programme started. Therefore, I did not focus on community as a potential area of change during

Table 22

Sample size, interview length and interview setting categorised by interview sample

	Sample size	Interview duration (in minutes)	Interview setting
Butterfly sample posttest I	9	15 (min) to 58 (max), 30 (mean)	Face-to-face, outdoors, Scotland
Butterfly sample follow-up	8	21 (min) to 60 (max), 36 (mean)	Via Skype™, virtual
Solo-only sample	4	19 (min) to 39 (max), 28 (mean)	Face-to-face, outdoors, Germany

the interviews with the Solo-only sample. It is important to note that the table merely reflects the conversational areas as planned in the different interview guidelines and not the themes as they emerged.

As already mentioned in the sample descriptions, I selected the interview samples randomly from all of those programme participants who agreed in the consent form to take part in an interview at the end of the programme. Thereby I aimed to allow for a variety of voices and viewpoints to surface and to avoid an unintended selection bias. All of the interviews were conducted by myself. The sample size, interview length and interview setting categorised by the interview sample is depicted in Table 22. I recorded all face-to-face interviews on a voice recorder and later on transformed them into Waveform audio format (WAVE). The follow-up interviews took place via Skype™. I recorded them in real time using the open source programme Audacity® and subsequently transformed them into WAVE.

4.3.6.3 Qualitative data transcription

Part of the interviews from the Butterfly sample was transcribed by a bachelor student whose thesis was affiliated with the present research project. The remaining interviews were transcribed by myself. Furthermore, I performed several revisions of all of the transcripts and when necessary I consulted an English native speaker.

The method of transcription, which I applied, followed the overarching aim of achieving best possible readability and comprehensibility while ensuring the maintenance of the statement and meaning of the original sentence. For this purpose I did not transcribe feedback words and sounds within a sentence unless necessary for meaning-making. I transcribed paralinguistic actions and events, incomprehensible text segments, accentuations and other transformations according to an adapted version of Legewie and Petzold-Teske's (1996) rules of transcriptions (see Appendix A).

4.3.6.4 Qualitative data analysis

I performed the data analysis using an online qualitative and mixed methods research tool called Dedoose.

The theoretical underpinning and guideline for the data analysis was a process introduced by Guest, MacQueen and Namey (2012) called Applied Thematic Analysis (ATA). Guest *et al.* (2012) emphasise that ATA is not a new approach to data analysis. According to the authors researchers have been applying similar types of analysis techniques for a long time with the only difference being an absence of a methodological framework for the application process.

The primary concern of ATA is to depict peoples' stories and experiences in the most understandable and accurate way. ATA therein orients towards serving the needs of applied research endeavours and allows for the combination of multiple qualitative analysis techniques. In practice, this may encompass elements of grounded theory such as identifying and comparing common themes in order to detect a potentially underlying theoretical model. Simultaneously, however, applied research is often not primarily concerned with generating theory but with understanding feeling, behaviour and thinking of people in a specific context as is characteristic for phenomenology. Both approaches offer valuable contributions to understanding and the distinctive feature of ATA lies in the combination of these approaches with additional other analytic means to make a case as for instance via quantification. Thus, when using ATA the research question is addressed through a synthesis of various interpretive and quantitative techniques.

The practical purpose of the analysis of the present research data was to evaluate the effects of the Butterfly Programme and the phenomenology of immersive experiences in wild nature, to complement the quantitative data and to look for clues that may build an explanatory theory.

Thus, the analytic purpose was to identify common themes in the interview data in relation to predefined areas of interest and to explore emergent themes and codes and their interrelations. Furthermore, for a more targeted analysis and in order to add comparative context to the data I addressed differences and similarities between extracted themes in the Butterfly data and the Solo-only data through a cross-site analysis.

Even though I maintained awareness for different types of in-text clues, I placed the initial focus of attention in the theme and code extraction process on repetitions across transcripts. The underlying assumption of this theme-recognition technique is that re-occurring themes or codes are likely to reflect an important inherent theme in the data. A critical number of repetitions is commonly not fixed and relies on the theme's relevance to the research objectives and the researcher's judgement (Guest *et al.*, 2012).

Nevertheless, I repeatedly indicate code counts throughout the results section of the present work. Notably, code counts potentially include code applications from all three studies and represent the number of interview excerpts. This means that the code count does not reflect the number of interviews that contained a specific code but the code's general intensity of occurrence within one interview and/or across interviewees.

The data proved to be sufficiently rich and nuanced to allow for a detailed analysis or more figuratively spoken for the construction of a comprehensive map from "street view to global" (Guest *et al.*, 2012). The nuanced analysis initially generated an extensive number of codes, which exceeded the sensible scope of data display. Thus, in an iterative process of coding I reduced the number of codes substantially. I realised this by means of thematically categorising and merging codes and by subsequently linking them to the matching overarching theme. In that sense, themes usually describe what a unit of codes is about and codes, which are directly linked to the raw interview data segments, represent the more nuanced aspects of the associated theme. I collected all themes and associated codes in a codebook, which contained the working titles of the extracted themes and codes as well as their preliminary definition. Clearly, I continuously modified the codebook throughout the several stages of analysis. Serving as a guideline for assigning codes to interview segments the codebook allowed for a more rigorous interpretation of the data and helped to reduce ambiguity in the coding process.

Moreover, part of the coding process was also the application of so-called marker codes, which served the purpose of indicating all of those interview segments that were, for instance, specifically linked to the Solo time. Hereby, I was able to analyse later on which themes or codes emerged especially frequently in certain contexts.

After the coding process I explored the codes for intercorrelations by virtue of searching for triggers and processes that may account for common experiences. I was able to realise this particularly via the online analysis tool Dedoose, which offers a variety of data visualisations including correlation tables of the applied codes across data sets. Dedoose provides a visual overview of the pattern in the data through coloured tables indicating the frequencies of certain code co-occurrences. This function facilitated the localisation of potentially meaningful relationships between codes and their associated text segments. By reviewing the excerpts, which simultaneously included the two codes under investigation, I was then able to determine the nature of their relationship.

As will be evident in the results section, the extracted themes partly freely emerged and are partly identical with the predefined areas of focus from the qualitative interview guideline. As regularly addressed in the interviews, the predefined topics naturally also occurred as themes in the data. However, the constitution of these themes, for instance the exact nature of "changes in the relationship with the world", is explained through the associated emergent codes.

Furthermore, in some cases of particular areas of interest, instead of concentrating on commonalities across individuals the goal of the analysis was to provide an exhaustive picture of the data and thus all the differing emergent aspects of a phenomenon regardless of their quantitative weight. This was the case for instance when asking the participants about their experience of the effects of the ritual surrounding their Solo time. In the case of ritual effects I chose this different approach because firstly this topic could be easily broken down into definable aspects and was manageable in its range of responses and secondly because this topic appears particularly relevant for practitioners and in-field implementation.

Such deviations exemplify well the fundamental purpose and flexibility of ATA. Therein, the level of detail, the type of analysis and the chosen format of depicting the results all vary, always orienting towards the best fit for the research questions, the research purpose and audience without ignoring the need of a rigorous set of procedures that allows for a transparent and credible way of analysing the data (Guest *et al.*, 2012).

4.3.6.5 Reliability and validity of the qualitative research strand

The previous section gave an overview of the applied procedures in the process of analysing the qualitative data of the present research. Especially from a quantitative viewpoint, naturally questions about the validity and reliability of the findings arise. As it is the concept of mixed methods research to combine qualitative and quantitative approaches it appears worthwhile to stay present to both perspectives on indicators for valuable research. In quantitative research indicators of the latter are psychometric criteria namely reliability and validity. In qualitative research, however, the overall goal is not to replicate findings, thereby achieving maximum reliability, but more focus is directed towards validity (Guest *et al.*, 2012).

Significantly, qualitative and quantitative approaches seem to be reflected in the origins of the word validity already. Validity and value both root in the Latin word valere, which translates as having worth and importance or being strong. But the same word, value, also indicates a specific numeric quantity. This reveals two ways of looking at validity. The latter is well known as it represents the common scientific approach to validity. However, simultaneously, validity captures a qualitative perspective which reflects a subjective impression of importance (Braud & Anderson, 1998) and will be revisited in more depth in the following section on extended views of validity.

However, in the context of mainstream qualitative enquiry validity may as well be expressed by the terms of credibility and accuracy of the research procedures and outcomes. This points towards the important role of the face validity of a qualitative study, as it is ultimately left to the individual's judgement, based on the available descriptions of the research procedures and outcomes, whether or not the presented outcomes can be considered as valid (Guest et al., 2012).

These reflections provide a broad overview of reliability and validity in qualitative research. Beyond this, however, are concrete efforts that can be undertaken to enhance the validity and reliability in qualitative research or in other words the trustworthiness of the findings.

On the research design level of the present research, I enhanced validity by using multiple methods, which allowed for the triangulation of the findings. Thereby, intrinsic biases immanent in single-methods and single-theory studies can be reduced and the weaknesses of the applied methods can compensate each other.

At a data collection stage, I furthermore endeavoured to avoid common biases that can decrease the validity of a qualitative study. For instance, I held the effect of the interviewer constant across time and samples as I alone conducted the interviews. This ensured that the data collector always knew the purpose behind the questions and could explicate them consistently when necessary.

At a data analysis stage, I enhanced the validity by employing a rigorous transcription protocol when transforming the recorded data into written text. Furthermore, the construction of a codebook helped to reduce ambiguity in the process of interpreting the interview data.

In terms of face validity I frequently underpinned the extracted codes and themes presented in the results section by direct quotes. This discloses my interpretations as the direct connections to the actual statements become visible and thereby ensures transparency.

4.3.7 Expanding the view of validity

The previous section briefly introduced conventional ways of enhancing validity. In contrast, this chapter is concerned with an expanded view of validity as proposed by Braud and Anderson (1998)[18] by means of introducing rather unconventional indicators of validity respectively different ways of knowing.

---

18 As Transpersonal Research Methods for the Social Sciences (Braud & Anderson, 1998) is one of the very few books dealing with expanded views of validity the present chapter primarily follows and relies on this reference.

The requirement that needs to be met in order for this chapter to serve its purpose of addressing validity is the willingness of the reader to accept that the purely intellectual approach has its limits and that science is an on-going process, which can always only depict part of reality.

Indeed, looking back on the gain of knowledge throughout history we come to understand that "the counterintuitive glimmerings of yesterday become the accepted actualities of today (Braud & Anderson, 1998, p.215)." We also see that even research that is conducted in accordance with the contemporary scientific worldview, such as physics or mathematics, reveal intriguing evidence for the incompleteness that comes along with the application of only one system or worldview, repeatedly inviting scientists to think outside of the box. This is for instance shown in Gödel's incompleteness theorems where it becomes a fact "that no formal system that is sufficiently complex to be interesting can be finitely describable, consistent, or complete within itself (Braud & Anderson, 1998, p.215)."

Clearly, when turning towards different kinds of knowledge such as intuitive knowledge, we enter into a realm that cannot be tapped through conventional instruments of measurement and that lacks a fixed procedure or protocol that needs to be followed. Nevertheless, big thinkers and scientists describe intuition as an integral pathway leading them to their cutting-edge scientific discoveries. A famous example is Einstein who explained about his own research process that "there is no logical path to these laws [universal elementary laws]; only intuition, resting on sympathetic understanding of experience, can reach them (as cited in Braud & Anderson, 1998, p.221)."

This may cause feelings of discomfort and may even appear as the counterpart of validity. However, Braud and Anderson (1998) make an intriguing point when they present empirical research findings that challenge the assumptions underlying conventional validity and thereby shed new light on the essential question of what is real.

A representative example for such a study is one conducted in 1952 by Ayrapetyants and colleagues (cited in Razran, 1961, pp.91-92). The research team introduced air or solutions into patients' bladder fistulas, which naturally increased the pressure in their bladders. Respiration, electrodermal activity, intrabladder pressure and the subjective report on the patients' urgency to urinate were assessed. In the beginning all indicators reflected the physically induced pressure appropriately. Naturally, when no physical pressure was induced but the pressure meter falsely indicated high pressure the physiological and psychological indicators did not respond. Then, the researchers exercised classical Pavlovian conditioning by inducing a number of times high physical pressure into the bladder while presenting the patients simultaneously with high pressure meter reading. After that patients displayed almost on all objective and subjective indicators responses to high physical pressure in the bladder even though no pressure was induced and they were merely presented with a faked high pressure meter reading. Intriguingly, this was also true the other way around. Patients showed no objective and subjective response to actually induced high physical pressure when the pressure meter falsely suggested that no pressure was applied. Thus, the patient's subjective and, noteworthy, objective responses solely relied on the revealings of the pressure meter regardless of the physical reality of actually induced pressure. This example demonstrates the influence learnings from the past can have on the perception of reality in the present and addresses the question tackled at the beginning, namely What is real?

What are we to draw upon as a basis for decision-making when determining reality or truth? Is it the physicality of the actually induced pressure or the physiological and psychological criteria (Braud & Anderson, 1998)? Or both?

The previously presented study is one of many examples that reveal such ambiguities and present us with the possibility of multiple realities. Indeed, inner events we experience as human beings are not visible physically, yet they are *there*. Moreover, they can appear even more real to the individual than the physical reality and can have a substantial impact on one's personal life (Braud & Anderson, 1998). Once accepting the possibility of multiple realities, addressing these realities through pluralistic means of knowing suddenly does not seem that dubious anymore.

In Braud and Anderson`s (1998) understanding "validity has to do with whether one's findings or conclusions are faithful or true to what one is studying (p.213)". Against this backdrop they suggest including various means of knowing as indicators of validity such as bodily wisdom, emotions and feelings, aesthetic contributions, intuition, coherence of aspects and sympathetic resonance, all of which can occur at various points throughout the research process.

Bodily wisdom addresses events that occur in relation to the research, such as feeling something "in the pit of the stomach", feelings of chills or tensions. Sometimes a physical reaction in the researcher, participants or readers may indicate that something is true or very wrong. Most people have experienced such bodily wisdom in various situations in their everyday lives already.

Similarly, *emotions and feelings* can inform about the validity of the research and research findings. Braud and Anderson (1998) state that "when feelings of excitement, surprise, and delight are supplemented by feelings of awe and gratitude, researchers can be assured that they are being true to the experiences that are being explored and that their approach and findings are valid (p.219)."

The *aesthetic contribution* as an indicator yields towards the validity of conclusions, methods and conceptual models or theories. A rather extreme but clear example is the physicist Paul Dirac who claimed that in his equations it was the presence of beauty which assured him that he was on the road to success (Braud & Anderson, 1998). A further aesthetic feature may also be seen in the experiential adequacy experienced in the elements of research, namely whether something rings true because it is in line with the experience of the persons confronted with the research.

Probably the most frequently and naturally used indicator of validity in everyday life is *intuition*. Comparable to a state of feeling, intuition may be described as a state of knowledge (Braud & Anderson, 1998). Reflected in an inner confidence and the perpetual feeling that one's research findings are true, intuition can indeed serve as guide to validity in the research process, just as Einstein's experience emphasises in the section above.

Especially throughout the research process of the present work another indicator of validity was found in nocturnal dreams. In the context of the already presented indicators, dreams can include intuitions and constitute largely uncensored reflections of feelings and emotions that partly may not even have risen to awareness yet (see chapter 5).

All of these indicators of validity can occur simultaneously and can represent different layers of one experience. Braud and Anderson (1998) suggest that *coherence* amongst the partakers of the research, but possibly even more essentially the coherence of these different layers, may be what we as researchers are "seeking in our quest for validity (p.223)."

Furthermore, all of the so-far mentioned indicators of validity are immanent in *sympathetic resonance* as a barometer for fidelity and fullness of the research. This refers to reader resonance as well as co-researcher resonance and relates to a phenomenon known from physics. Physical experiments revealed that, given that the structure and operating rules are similar, one system will respond to the call of another, with the complexity of the response always reflecting the complexity of the call. Thus, if for instance experiential descriptions in the research are presented authentically and sufficiently richly, they will evoke resonance in a reader familiar to those experiences (Braud & Anderson, 1998).

Clearly, the challenge of the presented means of knowing is that they always bear the possibility to be misinterpreted and to occasionally even "lie" (Braud & Anderson, 1998) for instance when coming from places of wishful thinking or fear. Furthermore, although these different ways of knowing partly represent deeply rooted human instincts, we need to be aware that they also oppose the contemporary concept of knowledge, worldview and scientific process of insight. As a result, intuition and the like take on the role of a taboo at least within the field of research, which can lead to personal insecurities when it comes to trusting in and making use of different ways of knowing as part of scientific enquiry. Clearly, such insecurities complicate the matter as they hold the potential of distorting the contributions that different means of knowing may bear for validity.

For this reason, pledging for uncontrolled and blind use of emotions, intuitions, dreams and bodily sensations would be disproportionate within the research context. However, the unfamiliarity and insecurities can also be seen as an invitation to start sharpening these means of knowing again by paying them more careful attention and, as realised in the present research, by making use of intersubjective validation processes through co-researchers (see chapter 5.3.1).

Evidently, as outlined before, many of the most successful researchers throughout history have made use of these other means of knowing and experienced not only highly beneficial effects but also experienced them as an inseparable part of scientific discovery. Thus, in the present work the described additional means of knowing are seen as a rewarding way to broaden and compliment the range of indicators of validity in research and beyond this as an overarching guideline for the research process.

4.3.8 Self-reflection on different ways of knowing in the research process

Intuitive ways of knowing as a way to validate my research more or less stole their way into my thesis. Sometimes it literally felt as though I was sticking my hands into a black box and started to feel my way through the darkness. And translating a felt sense into words seemed impossible at times. I did not plan for any of this to actually show up within the framework of my thesis but at some point it felt inevitable to provide a rightful and equitable place that would not belittle or betray what I could gather from these other places. With places I refer to the different ways of knowing as outlined in the previous section, the black box of sensing, feeling and knowing intuitively. And as touched on before, what is experienced there can be as real or more real than the physical reality. This is depicted emphatically in an interview excerpt presented in Braud and Anderson's (1998) book on research methods. Here, Marie-Louise Franz (1989) described part of an interview that she conducted with C.G. Jung:

> He talked about a crazy girl and said, "She was on the moon," and talked about it as if it had been very real. Being rational, I was indignant and said, "She hasn't been on the moon." Jung said, "Yes, she has." I thought, "That cannot be" I said, "That satellite of the earth there-which is unhabited-she hasn't been there." He just looked at me and said, "She has been on the moon." (filmed interview)

This excerpt sparked in me a vivid dream I had, which, in fact, captures my personal research process in respect to the theme of this chapter. I dreamt this dream at a time when I was much concerned with methodologies and formal frames, strongly searching for a way to integrate different ways of knowing into a standard format of a dissertation. So in terms of travelling to the moon I was especially concerned with the question whether the moon could be connected to the earth and if so, how. Along with this quest I also carried some self-doubt, asking myself whether this venturesome undertaking could be legitimate at all and whether I could trust my black box of knowing enough to report it to some degree.

In response to this particular process it was the following dream, which seemed to validate my search for integration and helped me to proceed into the unknown:

> A teacher gives a task to his class of students. They are standing on a meadow and in the background in the sky hangs an enormous planet like the moon or the sun. Only the planet looks quite extraordinary as it is strewn with huge sunflowers. The students' task is to jump as high as possible and at their peak of jumping to wish wholeheartedly to be able to pick a sunflower. The teacher explains that at this peak of wish intensity and high jumping a force will suck the student up to the planet so that she or he can quickly pick a sunflower before falling down again.
>
> The students do as they are asked and one after the other accomplish the combination of high jumping and wish intensity so that they can bring back a flower. However, one student stays behind undecided. This student doubts to be able to jump that far and pick the sunflower quickly enough and also feels resistant to try it in front of all the eager other students. Everyone is done with the task but the teacher gave a couple of days to accomplish it so that this student has time to start practicing alone. Secretly, the teacher is watching. He knows that this student was always a bit peculiar.

Then, the student actually somehow reaches the planet. But instead of quickly picking the flower and falling back to earth the student lands on the planet. It is clear that the student does not want to pick the sunflower forcefully and follows quite a different method of obtaining the flower. He or she picks up a part of a flower and converts it into some kind of a clapping instrument. Generating a baseline rhythm with this new instrument the student starts to sing a song to the sunflowers while wandering through the sunflower fields. By singing to them, this is clear in the dream, the student wants to sweet-talk the sunflowers into giving themselves to the student voluntarily.

Meanwhile on earth the teacher watches the scenery. He already started to grade the task, which was also handed in in written form by the other students. Eventually, the teacher arrives at the report card of the remaining single student and a close-up of the report card shows that the teacher already wrote down the top mark on the report card. In brackets, however, he noted that this grade will only come into effect once the student actually returned to earth. The teacher silently calculates the time that is left for the student to return. He is relieved that he granted more time for this task so that this student had the space to try out this new method. Simultaneously, he simply knows that the student will return in time and bring back many sunflowers.

The next day I had a Skype scheduled with my co-researcher and supervisor of the dissertation. Again, I experienced the value of consulting with a co-researcher and of sympathetic resonance as an indicator of validity. It was through a poem, which resonated in my co-researcher while listening to my dream that I understood the full circle of the process that needed to take place. The poem my dream reminded her of is one by Samuel Taylor Coleridge (1817, as cited in Radin, 1997).

> *What if you slept,*
> *and what if in your sleep you dreamed,*
> *and what if in your dreams you went to heaven*
> *and there you plucked a beautiful flower,*
> *and what if when you awoke*
> *you had the flower in your hand?*
> *Ah, what then?*

Listing to my silent and wistful answers that arose in response to the poem I heard:

…Then, I would know that I have actually been there and that the dream was as real as waking up.

… Then, there would be a pathway between both worlds.

… Then, I would know for sure that multiple realities do exist.

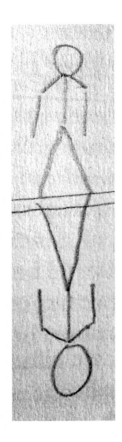

Figure 6. Scribble while daydreaming about, "What is real?"

It seemed to me as though the story of my dream dealt with a crossing-over within my own dream world, from the sunflower planet to earth. The crux was to bring my gathered treasures back. The poem of Coleridge, however, raises this crossing-over onto another plane by pointing directly towards the line between the waking and the dream reality and then letting this line beautifully fade away. Thereby, he revealed to me the realms of possibility that lie therein, encouraging me to overcome my insecurities and to hold on to the treasure of my dream world. This is clearly the art and the venture that lies within the integration of different ways of knowing, thus, colliding worldviews or multiple realities.

Indeed, it is a wondrous experience to persistently cross over this fine line, at times seemingly wearing it off more and more and occasionally even standing directly on it, mirrored in both worlds at the same time.

After all, my dream did leave me with a very real flower. As a result I picked up on my initial attempts and started to create spaces within this dissertation where first-person events, the research process and different ways of knowing could manifest.

4.4 Results

After an initial separate analysis of the qualitative and quantitative data set, I firstly integrate the qualitative and quantitative data in the quantitative results section. As the quantitative data set is based on a small sample and a non-experimental design this procedure helps substantiate the statistical outcomes via qualitative contextualisation at an early stage. However, the results section is followed by an additional, more interpretive and literature based, integration in the discussion.

4.4.1 Phenomenology and underlying processes of immersive experiences in wild nature

The underlying data for this chapter consist of the qualitative longitudinal Butterfly data and Solo-only interview data. Obviously, the Solo-only interviewees only referred to their Solo time in nature and their preparation and incorporation phase (see the description of the Solo-only programme in chapter 4.3.3.2). However, it is important to note that Butterfly participants immersed in nature through a variety of different means in addition to the Solo time such as through full-time outdoor living, deep ecology exercises and threshold walks (see chapter 4.3.3.1), which will be immanent in the accounts of their nature experience. Therefore, when necessary, I will explicate the experiential contexts of certain themes or codes.

Generally, all the themes and codes that I present in this section are inherent in both samples, Butterfly and Solo-only, with only one exception, which I will identify as such in the associated section.

4.4.1.1 Experiencing interconnectedness with nature

The emergent high-level theme in the interviewees' descriptions of their encounter with nature was the *experience of interconnectedness with nature*.

Further analysis revealed the presence of multiple layers of experiential interconnectedness, which I will further elucidate in the following as the *practical, physical, emotional, transpersonal* and *psychological dimension* of experiencing interconnectedness with nature.

The practical dimension

The practical dimension of the participants' experience of interconnectedness with nature was exclusively reflected in the Butterfly participants' experiences. This dimension describes the participants' experience of a reciprocal and practical dependency between humans and nature. Participants experienced the relationship between their everyday needs and the associated natural resources and thereby realised the practical dimension of their interconnectedness with nature. Logically, in the interviews, this dimension primarily appeared in the context of living outdoors and running an outdoor camp, which likely explains why this theme did not occur in the Solo-only sample.

A statement of one of the Butterfly interviewees exemplifies this descriptively. Here, the interviewee explains that she feels part of nature but at the same time at nature's mercy. She then continues to elaborate that she feels treating nature carelessly will eventually backfire.

When I enquired where this awareness came from the interviewee stated:

> *Being that exposed, being outdoors and because we slept in a tent for such a long time and did everything ourselves. Having heated the water ourselves, having set the fire ourselves so that we can keep warm, having cooked ourselves, transported the firewood and that way you somehow clearly see the interrelations* (BF4[19]).

The physical dimension

As part of the physical dimension of experiencing interconnectedness with nature participants gave descriptions of experiencing and recognising that human life is embedded within a wider physical system and that within this system all living organisms follow the same principles of life.

Describing her Solo experience an interviewee stated:

> *And I became aware of this cycle. […] And that was somehow like a clock! We actually live according to the sun. And that everything moves in circles, spinning and moving on and on. That's what I have come to understand the most* (B4).

---

19 The identifier depicts the sample membership. B= Butterfly interviews posttest I, BF= Butterfly follow-up interviews, S= Solo-only interviews.

The emotional dimension

Generally, at heart, the emotional dimension of the participants' experience of interconnectedness with nature reflects their experience of an inner readiness to respond to nature on a fundamental emotional level: merely by being in nature an instant emotional connection and reaction arises. This was particularly reported as part of the participants' experiences during their Solo time (see chapter 4.4.1.2, Figure 1).

Even though in the data the emotional dimension of interconnectedness encompasses a variety of emotional states, there are some evoked emotional states that were reported remarkably frequently. This includes narratives of calming down, having the feeling of "returning to something pure" and feeling confident that "everything is right the way it is". However, most commonly participants reported feeling "safe" and "home" when out in nature.

In one case I enquired more deeply and asked the Butterfly interviewee who was a stranger to the Scottish landscape what exactly he meant by "home". He replied, "Familiar to that land. Not just protected. Very familiar (B2)."

The analysis revealed no remarkable differences between the prevalence of this code in interviews with participants from the UK and for instance in interviews with participants from Germany, Belgium or Austria. This illustrates that the presence of an emotional connection with nature in the sample is not dependent on actual familiarity with the land or the place of birth but rather that it depicts a connection with the natural world that is intrinsic and universal in nature.

"Safe" on the other hand was explained as feeling completely accepted and held by nature regardless of all the personal emotional issues and flaws there may be.

On the broadest level, the emotional dimension of experiencing interconnectedness was mirrored in frequently used expressions such as "feeling connected with nature" or "feeling part of nature". In some cases, this experience was even taken a step further and specifically linked with the reciprocal aspect of interconnectedness as is reflected in realisations such as "If I accept nature then nature will accept me (BF6)."

The transpersonal dimension

The transpersonal dimension embraces a variety of nature experiences that transcend the other dimensions. The common ground for this dimension consists in reports of immersive experiences in nature that dissolve or extend the participants' boundaries of their sense of self. This experience was often coupled with strong emotions such as deep feelings of awe, sadness and/or connection as well as with moments of personal insight.

Some interviewees for instance reported experiences such as taking over nature's perspective. As part of her Solo experience one of the interviewees shared:

> *I have experienced pain about wars or ecocide before. But this was without any felt distance and went under my skin at a different level. Somehow more personal. I talked to nature the whole time. AND I started to mix everything. I could not separate anymore: ecocide is sad for me because it is bad for the world and I feel sad now because my childhood was bad. Everything was completely mixed-up* (S3).

In some cases these experiences included events that exceeded the rationally explicable, as apparent in an account of an interviewee describing a moment of personal break-through during his Solo time:

> *While meditating [...] I started to hear music coming from the forest. Which is ridiculous somehow. [...] It was like classical music coming from the trees from the other part of the valley. And somehow that music helped me to go inside. And what I saw there – I remember I had this kind of vision [...]* (BF2).

The interviewee continues to describe how this vision made him see and understand an essential and difficult part of himself, which ultimately resulted in making peace with it.

Other reports revealed states of bliss and oneness that were accompanied by a sense of awe and wonder as exemplified in an experience that another interviewee had during her Solo time:

> *I sat in the bushes and I realised "everything is connected" at another level. I saw all the animals, the plants, experienced everything that was taking place as a wonderful composition; everything was linked and happened exactly when it was supposed to happen. Everything is wonder* (S3_A).

The psychological dimension

This dimension includes the participants' experience of their psychological interconnectedness with nature. Here, participants recognise their personal stories, intentions, issues, or thoughts as real-life metaphors in natural landscapes or objects. In the reports, these reflections often have an impact on the participants' initial experience of the subject and stimulate an inner psychological process.

> *When I entered my Solo with the intention "I let go and trust" I encountered this trust in all the plants, animals, rocks, clouds... Just being themselves. For me it is so encouraging and healing to experience the way the beech tree is being a beech tree. Clear and genuine, self-sufficient in its being and trusting in being just fine the way it is. To be enough and accepted and taken care of as oneself* (S10_A).

As evident in the previous and following example, participants describe experiences where a certain quality of nature activates that very quality in themselves.

> *For me it is so important to have the openness in the landscape. Yes. In the landscape and in nature. Because it helps a lot, it helps me a lot, to have a wide view myself* (B3).

While being out in nature participants started to perceive their inner landscape in the outer landscape quite literally. Participants reported that as a consequence well-known personal states or situations were perceived more clearly:

> [...] *And then it started to rain heavily so I had to sit down under a tree. And I glimpsed out underneath the tree, which protected me from the rain, it was a fir tree with branches that hung very low to the ground. In front of it I saw many broken branches. Chaos. And in between there were little, beautiful flowers here and there. And yes, that somehow did remind me very clearly of what I bore inside myself at the moment* (S3).

Participants seem to experience nature as a mirror through an on-going dynamic interplay between their own psyche and the natural world. Reports revealed that being confronted with unexpected situations or events in nature also brought about the potential of acquiring additional self-knowledge.

> *I had this experience with the deer* [...], *a mother deer and a little fawn. And when they saw me the mother ran away and left the child behind. That shocked me, I was really frightened and did not know what to do.*

> *It reminded me, or made it clear to me, why I have not really arrived here* [in her home country] *yet. I have felt the same way when I left Nepal leaving all the children from the orphanage behind.*

> *And because of that* [situation] *I realised that I have to let it go and also why it is so difficult for me. Because obviously my own impression is that I let them down* [the children from the orphanage]. *And I think that was the most important thing.*

> [...] *I do think it* [the realisation] *happened because of nature. Because I have not thought of it before, I was thinking about totally different stuff and then it suddenly hit me. I suddenly stood right IN FRONT of the fawn because I did not realise that it did not run away. And then I noticed how it lay there so small and helpless. I do think I came to understand that because of nature* (S2).

4.4.1.2 Contextualising the experience of interconnectedness with nature

As indicated in the introductory section the interview data encompass the Butterfly sample and the Solo-only sample. The fact that the Butterfly participants were in touch with nature through a variety of means, as well as the emphasis in this research on Solo times as a space for immersive experiences in nature to emerge, gives rise to specifying the contexts in which the different dimensions of interconnectedness with nature were experienced.

This was achieved by quantifying the qualitative results.

In the following Figure 7 the dimensions are depicted according to their frequency of occurrence in descending order. It can be seen that the most frequently reported dimension of interconnectedness with nature was the emotional one followed by the psychological, practical, physical and transpersonal.

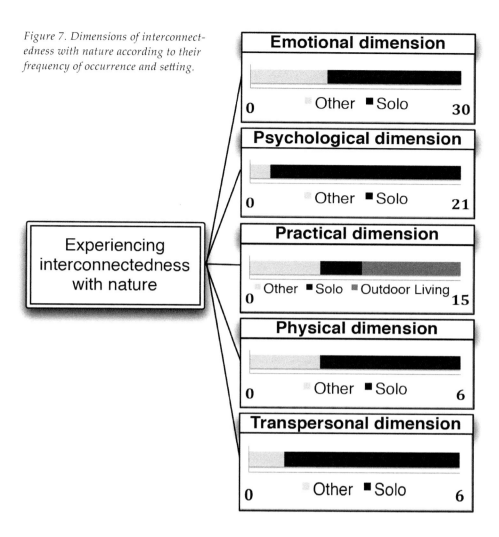

Figure 7. Dimensions of interconnectedness with nature according to their frequency of occurrence and setting.

Each dimension is presented along with a corresponding bar, which reflects a continuum of the code count ranging from zero to the total number of code occurrence. Further, the bar is divided in segments, which are differently shaded from light grey to black. The different segments indicate the type of context in which participants experienced the particular dimension of interconnectedness and thereby inform about the context's potential relevance as a trigger for such an experience.

The figure reveals that, apart from the practical dimension, all the other dimensions were mainly experienced during the participants' Solo time. Primarily the psychological, emotional and transpersonal dimensions were referred to as part of the interviewees' Solo experience. The practical dimension was predominantly experienced in the context of outdoor living during the Butterfly programme. The category "other" includes all those reports that were not linked with a specific nature context. Thus, this category may include nature experiences that took place during the Solo time but were not explicitly stated as such.

4.4.1.3 Perceptual state and attitude when in nature

A theme that kept arising across interview partners was the participants' description of the particularity of their perceptual state and attitude when out in nature. According to the interviewees, this state and attitude had a substantial impact on their experience in and at times of nature and was also influenced by elements of the ritual surrounding the Solo time.

Participants most frequently reported that being in nature, primarily during their Solo time, caused them to *switch from being in the head to arriving in the present moment*. A major contributing factor for this switch was the experience, often described as novel, of not feeling distracted by anything.

> *I am not distracted by people or busy surroundings or "things to do" at home. Instead you can just be. And watch. Watching trees or how the grass is waving in the wind. For me, this leads me more easily to this inner space* (B4).

Furthermore, interviewees reported that being in nature triggered and enlivened the use of all their *senses*.

Elaborating why she felt more connected with nature during her Solo time an interviewee stated:

> *Because I was not distracted, because I had the time to observe my surroundings with a loving eye. Especially the flies, all the insects and all the- well, I was able to make use of all my senses in order to allow nature to permeate through me* (B8).

Unsurprisingly, the code "use of the senses" co-occurred in the interview data with "switching from being in the head to arriving in the present moment". Accordingly, when interviewees described that they immersed themselves in nature by means of enlivening their senses they also frequently reported that they were able to free themselves from mental and everyday distractions, thus arrived in the present moment.

4.4.1.4 Psychological effects of the Solo time ritual

In addition to the above-mentioned aspects there are specific elements of the Solo ritual which contributed to the particularity of experiencing and perceiving during the 24 hours of being alone in nature.

Interviewees informed about the impact of entering nature with an intention, the impact of fasting for 24 hours as well as the impact of the ritual as a general overarching frame for their experience.

In line with the configuration of the Solo ritual every participant set a personal, individual *intention* before going out (see programme description in chapter 4.3.3.1). However, it turned out there also appeared to be a shared implicit intention, which commonly occurred in the interviewees' accounts. This implicit intention, which seemed to have naturally arisen when participants entered the 24-hour Solo time, was to experience nature as a mirror. This indicates the presence of a strong preliminary openness in the interviewees to enter into a more personal relationship with nature and is often subject of the preparation phase of the Solo time.

Furthermore, reports revealed that going out with an individual intention impacted the way participants experienced nature. The following table accumulates the most

Table 23

Roles and effects of the Solo intention on the participants' Solo time

Roles and effects of the intention
Intention as a personal indicator of completion
"I went into the Solo to ask for more clarity and more energy. And I found it (B3)."
Intention as a reference point throughout the Solo time
"It was an important ingredient. [...] I did try to connect with my intention repeatedly throughout my Solo time (S3)."
Intention as a facilitator for a different nature perception
"I did meet nature more consciously. I had many moments in which I found myself somewhere suddenly perceiving something I have never seen before (S3)."
Intention as a facilitator for clarity of mind
"You have a different way of approaching things, you are really focused and not so concerned about what is going to happen (B3)."

commonly reported ways, in which going out with an intention influenced the participants' Solo time along with brief illustrative excerpts from the interview data.

The effects of *fasting* on the perceptual state and attitude when being in nature were generally described as bodily changes, such as becoming weaker and slower. However, there were also accounts pointing out that not eating resulted in extra energy, which would be otherwise used for digestion.

Participants agreed that fasting affected the way they perceived during the Solo time. The distinct perception was described as switching from a thinking mode to a mode of experiencing, as well as generally perceiving from a state of calm. Further reports revealed that fasting supported the time in nature by distributing more meaning to the Solo time and by eliminating eating as a potential distraction.

The reported effect of the *overall Solo time ritual* on the participants' nature experience encompassed the enhancement of their experience of nature as well as the enhancement of their awareness during that time. Interviewees elaborated that the ritual served the purpose of creating a meaningful, valuable and protected space for their experiences to unfold by clearly marking a beginning and an end. Participants further reported that this personal space appeared unique and separate from their everyday life and thereby freed them to do and approach things differently than they normally would. One interviewee, for instance, shared that she uncharacteristically allowed herself to rely on her gut feeling and completely focused on what she actually needed in the present moment throughout her entire Solo time.

4.4.1.5 The underlying process in nature experiences – from attaining self-access to gaining insight

One of the most frequently reported benefits participants experienced in nature was facilitated self-access[20]. The descriptions in the interviews suggest that self-access is part

---

20 The term "self-access" is used as a synonym for the German word "Selbstzugang". It describes the ability to be aware of self-relevant information such as personal needs, desires, previous experiences, thoughts and emotions (Quirin & Kuhl, 2015).

Figure 8. The participants' process in nature leading to self-access and insights based on within-code relationships. Bracketed numbers = total code count across samples; one-directional arrows = accounts of causal relationships; bidirectional arrows = accounts of a reciprocal enhancing effect between codes; pie chart pieces = content of insights.

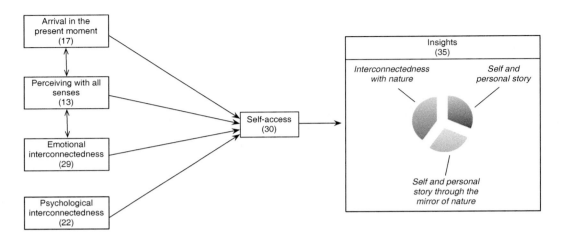

of a personal process participants experienced in nature, which inevitably led to the gain of personal insights.

The pattern emerging from within-code relationships revealed important elements that helped to establish self-access as well as the different areas of content of the resulting personal insights. The emergent pattern is shown in Figure 8 with the bracketed numbers reflecting the total code count across samples. Further, the arrows illustrate the nature of the code co-occurrence with the bidirectional arrows representing frequent accounts of a reciprocal enhancing effect between codes and the one-directional arrow reflecting accounts of rather causal relationships.

Accordingly, nature invited participants to enliven their senses and to become present to the moment, one mutually influencing the other. In nature, there are only little distractions as known from everyday life and by experiencing the richness of each moment participants came to access what is lying within themselves. This way it appears as though getting to the bottom of what is going on in nature entailed the interviewees' penetration to the bottom of what was going on within their inner worlds.

> *I am not distracted by irrelevant things there. Whether I can access Facebook or not is not relevant for my life but nevertheless it seems important to me in my everyday life. And when I am in nature and this is NOT accessible then I look at my toes and fingers and at the trees and I touch them and feel so much more authentic and more pure. So much more immersed in what is really going on. And I think that it is in this state that I can access much more easily the essence of the question or my personal need that I went out with. (BF8)*

The perceptually receptive state when being in nature also enhanced the participants' experience of feeling emotionally interconnected with nature and vice versa.

As evident in the following quote, participants recognised the Solo time as especially supportive of experiencing this interaction:

> *Every single part of nature suddenly becomes really special. Yes, if you include all the different senses, not only seeing but also feeling and smelling then you feel more easily that you are one part of a whole* (B4).

The experience of emotional interconnectedness with nature was often essential for participants in order to be able to open up. Various times participants explained their gaining self-access with the emotional state that nature evoked in them. Interviewees described a calming and harmonising effect of nature as well as feeling home and protected. This, in turn, provided them with confidence and a safe space to penetrate deeper into their own inner worlds.

When I asked an interviewee why he held the belief that the Solo time was a crucial prerequisite for uncovering a personal issue, he stated:

> *Because […] you can find out these kind of things only when you are in complete harmony with yourself. And I find myself in harmony with myself only when I am in nature. Or play music. Or stay connected with nature* (B2).

Another gateway for participants to access their inner workings was the experience of psychological interconnectedness with nature. As already elaborated in the associated code description above, nature seems to serve as a mediator through which participants can access their personal stories and perceive themselves in a unique way.

An interviewee described the way perceiving nature as a mirror has affected her:

> *Ultimately, it helped me to look at myself better. Because when I usually look at myself it often happens with my head. And when I go into nature and imagine that nature mirrors myself I see only what is me because otherwise I would not see it. […] Now* [during the Solo-only programme] *it became entirely clear to me that I can TRULY see what occupies my mind. […] And this is how I came to realise that it is easier when I look at myself in nature than when I look at myself through ME* (S1).

Throughout the programmes participants gained various types of insight which are depicted in the pie chart in Figure 8. Notably, 30 of the 35 insight-associated interview excerpts were part of the participants' Solo description, thereby indicating the particularly beneficial space and experience that the Solo ritual seems to offer for participants.

Participants gained insights regarding three broader content areas: insights regarding their personal interconnectedness with nature, insights regarding their personal processes and stories and a mixed category. In the latter category, participants reported insights that regarded their personal lives and processes, which also at the same time included an elaboration of how this was mirrored to them by nature. Thereby, the category simultaneously encompasses the participants' realisation of their interconnectedness with the natural world.

Table 24

Means (standard deviations) of the PCI dimensions for the Solo, religious, happy and ordinary experience

	Solo	Religious	Happy	Ordinary
Altered experience	3.57 (0.80)	2.61 (1.50)	1.76 (1.26)	1.20 (1.01)
Body image	3.84 (1.04)	2.24 (1.89)	2.08 (1.73)	1,36 (1.45)
Unusual meanings	4.19 (1.07)	3.54 (1.68)	1.96 (1.36)	1.17 (1.39)
Perception	2.58 (1.3)	1.82 (1.66)	1.14 (1.32)	0.74 (0.99)
Time sense	3.67 (0.99)	2.54 (2.0)	1.89 (1.75)	1.56 (1.71)
Attention	3.42 (0.74)	3.89 (1.16)	3.11 (1.04)	3.26 (1.19)
Absorbtion	3.75 (1.03)	4.60 (1.03)	4.03 (1.41)	4.37 (1.42)
Direction of attention	3.08 (0.96)	3.49 (1.44)	2.42 (1.53)	2.51 (1.58)
Imagery	3.45 (1.08)	1.36 (0.97)	2.46 (1.33)	2.23 (1.26)
Imagery amount	2.98 (1.46)	5.62 (3.26)	1.74 (1.49)	1.51 (1.64)
Imagery vividness	3.87 (0.99)	2. 41 (1.88)	3.17 (1.58)	2.91 (1.45)
Negative affect	1.42 (1.12)	1.71 (1.38)	0.46 (0.7)	0.945 (1.22)
Anger	1.62 (1.64)	1.53 (1.70)	0.28 (0.61)	1.31 (1.71)
Fear	1.08 (1.39)	1.53 (1.91)	0.49 (0.89)	0.49 (0.97)
Sadness	1.6 (1.7)	2.04 (1.88)	0.51 (0.95)	1.03 (1.41)
Positive affect	3.63 (1.12)	2.24 (1.32)	3.49 (1.03)	1.61 (1.18)
Joy	3.66 (1.41)	2.72 (2.13)	4.81 (1.03)	2.24 (1.61)
Love	4.43 (1.2)	3.51 (1.90)	4.38 (1.52)	2.06 (1.77)
Sexual excitement	2.79 (1.94)	0.47 (1.20)	1.29 (1.76)	0.53 (1.01)
Altered state of awareness	3.61 (1.03)	2.97 (1.96)	1.72 (1.59)	0.99 (1.46)
Self-awareness	4.2 (1.08)	4.45 (1.29)	4.63 (0.9)	4.71 (1.21)
Arousal	1.82 (1.1)	2.18 (1.60)	1.51 (1.43)	1.67 (1.52)
Internal dialogue	3.14 (1.81)	3.21 (1.64)	2.00 (2.06)	2.36 (1.90)
Memory	4.41 (0.95)	4.75 (1.08)	4.87 (1.12)	4.85 (1.01)
Rationality	3.5 (1.31)	4.46 (1.39)	5.06 (1.05)	4.88 (1.41)
Volitional control	2.72 (0.96)	3.32 (1.38)	4.41 (1.06)	4.96 (1.22)

When asked about a moment of personal insight a Solo-only participant reported:

> *I followed my gut feeling and ended up by a lake. I let nature tell me that it is time for me to let go of my fear of not being pretty enough or of not being able to satisfy pretences. Many little signs told me this. In the end, this was confirmed by the sound of chimes in the distance. Simply incredible (S8)!*

4.4.1.6 The Solo time through the lens of the Phenomenology of Consciousness Inventory (PCI)

The overall PCI sample (N= 42) consists of the two subsamples of 11 Solo-only participants and 31 Butterfly participants. Only one case had to be excluded from the sample

Table 25

Effect sizes (Cohen's d) for the differences of mean between the Solo experience versus the religious, happy and ordinary experience

	Religious	Happy	Ordinary
Altered experience	.80	1.72	2.6
Attention	.49	.34	.15
Imagery	2.04	.82	1.04
Negative affect	.23	.70	.41
Positive affect	1.14	.13	1.76
Altered state of awareness	.41	1.41	2.07
Self-awareness	.21	.43	.45
Arousal	.26	.24	.11
Internal dialogue	.04	.59	.42
Memory	.33	.44	.45
Rationality	.71	1.31	1.01
Volitional control	.51	1.67	2.04

as its RIP score exceeded 2.0 (see description of the Phenomenology of Consciousness Inventory in chapter 4.3.5.1).

Visual analysis by means of histograms revealed that some of the PCI (sub-) dimensions were not normally distributed. Therefore, as a way to determine whether both samples could be merged into one, I analysed the differences of means between both groups using the non-parametric Mann-Whitney test. The statistical analysis revealed no significant differences of means between groups regarding the individual PCI dimensions (see Appendix B). As a consequence, I decided to merge the Solo-only PCI data with the Butterfly PCI data.

For the purpose of a more detailed analysis of the phenomenology of the Solo time, I examined not only the major dimensions but also the subdimensions of the PCI and compared them with characteristics of religious, happy and ordinary experiences as assessed by Wildman and McNamara (2010, see description of the Phenomenology of Consciousness Inventory in chapter 4.3.5.1). Table 24 illustrates the means and standard deviations for the PCI dimensions regarding the Solo, religious, happy and ordinary experience.

In order to be able to estimate the differences of means between the conditions Solo, religious, happy and ordinary experience I calculated effect sizes using Cohen's d based on pooled standard deviations. Table 25 depicts the effect sizes (Cohen's d)[21] for the differences of mean between the Solo experience versus the religious, happy and ordinary experience.

Altered experience

Altered Experience is one of the major PCI dimensions, which is represented by four subdimensions. When comparing the associated means of the Solo experience with those of the religious, happy and ordinary experience it became evident that Solo

---

21 Cohen (1988) provides the following estimates for d: 0 to .1: no effect; .2 to .4: small effect; .5 to .7: medium effect; .8 to ≥ 1.0 large effect.

Figure 9. Intergroup comparison of means for the subdimensions of Altered Experience.

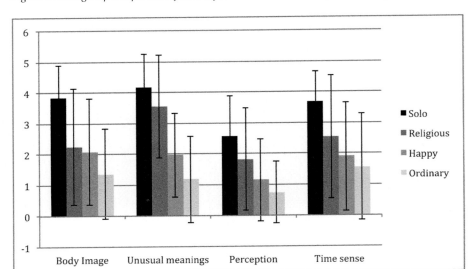

participants retrospectively assigned this major dimension a relatively strong presence during their Solo experience (see Figure 9).

The mean scores for the associated four subdimensions reflect the participants' experiences of their Body Image, Unusual Meanings, Perception and Time Sense during their Solo time. As visible in Figure 9 participants seem to have experienced their bodies differently than usual during their Solo time. The higher the mean for the subdimension Body Image the more participants indicated in the questionnaire that their bodies extended beyond the boundaries of their skin and that they experienced unity with the world/environment. Compared to religious, happy and ordinary experiences this appears to have been particularly pronounced during the Solo experience. Remarkably high was also the degree to which participants reported awe and wonder toward the world as well as the degree to which they experienced profound insights of certain ideas and issues during their Solo time as represented by Unusual Meanings. Furthermore, a comparably high mean on the Perception subdimension reflects the participants' reports of perceiving the objects in the world around them differently. Solo participants also reported a change in their perception of the Flow of Time, which seems to have been more strongly pronounced during the Solo time than in other extraordinary experiences such as in a religious or happy experiences.

Summarised, regarding the PCI major dimension Altered Experience, the statistical analysis revealed large effect sizes for the differences in means of the Solo experience versus the religious ($d= .8$), happy ($d= 1.72$) and ordinary ($d= 2.6$) experience.

Attention

The major PCI dimension Attention is represented by the two subdimensions Absorption and Direction of Attention. Low means for Absorption indicate a state of

Figure 10. Intergroup comparison of means for the subdimensions of Attention.

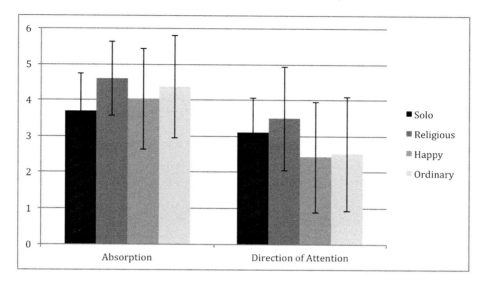

low concentration and distraction during the experience under investigation whereas high means represent a state of being completely absorbed in the experience. The visual analysis of Figure 10 revealed a lower degree of Absorption during the Solo time than during the religious experience. However, this difference decreases compared to the happy and ordinary experience.

The dimension Direction of Attention illustrates whether the attention during the experience was rather directed to the external world as indicated by a low mean or rather directed to the internal world as indicated by a high mean. For the Solo time compared to an ordinary or happy experience the direction of attention appears to have been slightly more directed to the internal world resembling the trend of the religious experience.

However, both subdimensions Attention and Absorbtion do not seem to reflect strikingly distinct features of the Solo time. In line, effect sizes regarding the major dimension Attention were only small for religious ($d= .49$) and happy ($d= .34$) experiences and no effect was detected when the Solo time was compared with the ordinary experience ($d= .15$).

Imagery

The Imagery dimension consists of two subdimensions Imagery Amount and Imagery Vividness.

Low means for the amount of visual imagery perceived during the experience indicate a small amount of imagery and vice versa. Vividness expresses whether the perceived imagery was rather diffuse as reflected in low means or rather vivid like real-world objects as represented by high means. As reflected in Figure 11 the imagery amount during the Solo time seems to have been greater than in ordinary or happy experiences but lower than in religious experiences.

In Wildman and McNamara's sample the imagery perceived during a religious experience appears to have been slightly more diffuse than during a happy or ordinary

Figure 11. Intergroup comparison of means for the subdimensions of Imagery.

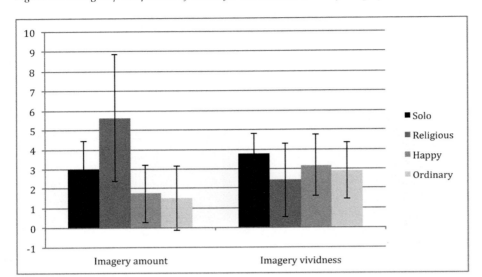

experience. However, the reported imagery during the Solo time seems to be more vivid than for the other three conditions.

This is furthermore reflected when comparing the means of the overarching major dimension Imagery. Compared to the mean of the Solo time large effect sizes were detected for religious (d= 2.04), happy (d= .82) and ordinary (d= 1.04) experiences indicating that this dimension of consciousness appears to be markedly pronounced during the Solo time.

Negative affect

The negative affect dimension is composed of the subdimensions Anger, Fear and Sadness. As evident in Figure 12 all three subdimensions seemed to be generally low for all of the assessed experiences.

Naturally, the means of all three subdimensions of Negative Affect are the lowest in the happy experience, followed by the ordinary experience. The religious and Solo experience, on the other hand, tend to incorporate comparably more negative affect. The mean of the major dimension Negative Affect was slightly higher for the religious experience than for the Solo experience as is reflected in a small effect size of d= .23. However, the mean for the Solo experience was higher than for the happy experience as indicated by a medium effect size of d= .70 as well as for the ordinary experience (d= .41).

Positive affect

The positive affect dimension encompasses the subdimensions Love, Sexual Excitement and Joy. All three subdimensions were more strongly present in the Solo experience than in the ordinary and religious experience (see Figure 13).

Moreover, the presence of feelings of love during the Solo time matches the degree as reported by people that were asked to remember a personal happy experience.

Figure 12. Intergroup comparison of means for the subdimensions of Negative Affect.

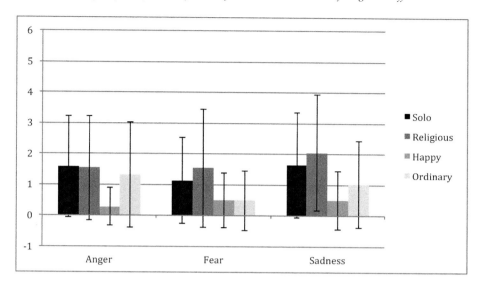

Figure 13. Intergroup comparison of means for the subdimensions of Positive Affect.

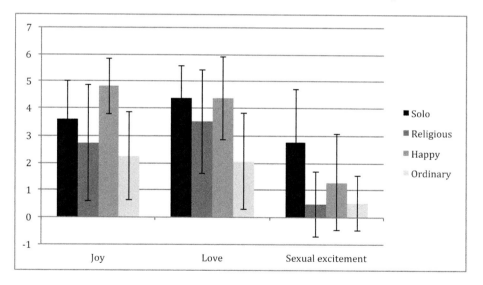

Further, sexual feelings seem to have played a comparably greater role during the Solo time than during either one of the other types of experiences.

Concurrently, the mean of the associated major dimension Positive Affect was higher for the Solo experience than for the religious and ordinary experience as underlined by large effect sizes for both the religious (d= 1.41) and ordinary (d=1.76) experience. Notably, no effect (d= .13) was found for the difference between the Solo and the happy experience indicating how strong the presence of positive affect was during the Solo time.

The remaining seven major dimensions

The higher the mean of the major dimension Altered State of Awareness the more unusual participants perceived their state of awareness during the experience under investigation. Compared to the ordinary experience (d= 2.07) as well as to the other two extraordinary experiences as the religious (d= .41) and happy one (d= 1.41) participants of the Solo time reported to have experienced a strongly altered state of awareness which is reflected in small to large effect sizes (see Figure 14).

Figure 14. Intergroup comparison of means for the dimensions Altered State of Awareness, Self-Awareness, Arousal and Internal Dialogue.

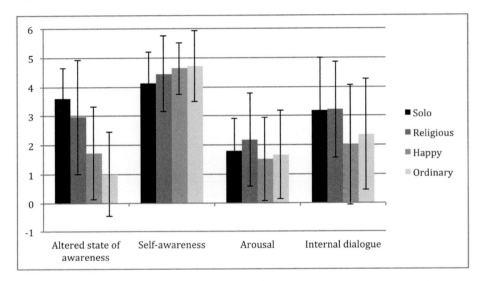

Figure 15. Intergroup comparison of means for the dimensions Memory, Rationality and Volitional Control.

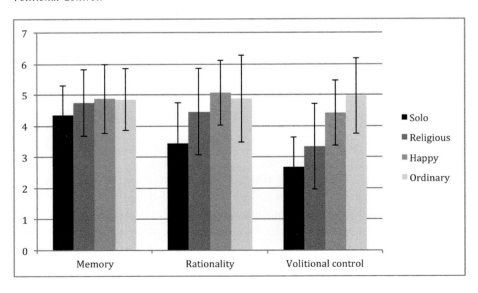

Self-awareness on the other hand seemed to have been commonly high during the Solo time with a commonly rather low muscular tension (see Figure 14). The major dimension Internal Dialogue was similarly present during the Solo time as in the religious experience (d= .04). However, compared to the ordinary (d= .42) and happy (d= .59) experience this dimension was more strongly pronounced in the Solo experience indicating a greater amount of silent talking during the Solo time (see Figure 14).

Further, participants were well able to remember what they experienced with only small effect sizes for the differences of means when comparing the Solo time with the religious, happy and ordinary experience (see Figure 15).

Interestingly, participants reported remarkably less rational thinking during the Solo time and less volitional control over their thoughts (see Figure 15). This was further reflected in medium to large effect sizes for the differences of means when comparing the Solo with the other types of experiences regarding both major dimensions, rationality and volitional control.

The relationship between the major dimensions of the PCI

Based on the analysis of the significant (p< 0.01) two-sided non-parametric Spearman correlations I was able to extract a pattern of relationships between the major dimensions of the PCI. For economical reasons and in order to avoid capitalisation of chance I regarded only the major dimensions and only those correlations that met the significance level of p< 0.01.

The correlations are presented in Table 26.

Table 26

Two-sided non-parametric Spearman correlations between the major dimensions of the PCI

	Altered experience	Positive affect	Negative affect	Imagery	Self-awareness	Altered state of awareness	Arousal	Rationality	Volitional control	Internal dialogue
Altered experience	1	.47**	-.2	.44**	.27	.43**	-.12	.17	-.26	.27
Positive affect	.47**	1	-.16	.21	.08	.26	.02	.15	.05	-.21
Negative affect	-.2	-.16	1	-.06	-.31*	-.24	.51**	-.46**	.34*	.16
Imagery	.44**	.05	-.06	1	-.07	.06	-.18	.00	-.14	.46**
Self-awareness	.27	.14	-.31*	-.07	1	-.04	.02	.41**	.37*	-.32*
Altered state of awareness	.43**	.20	-.24	.06	-.04	1	-.12	.39*	-.26	.31*
Arousal	-.12	.02	.51**	-.18	-.02	-.12	1	-.14	.12	-.06
Rationality	.17	.15	-.46**	.00	.41**	.39*	-.14	1	.19	.01
Volitional control	-.26*	.05	.34*	-.14	.37*	-.26	.28	.12	1	-.37*
Internal dialogue	.27	-.21	.16	.46**	-.32*	.31*	-.1	.06	-.37*	1

Notes. * p < .05; ** p < .01.

Evidently, the reported Altered Experience during the Solo time was positively correlated with Positive Affect, a more strongly pronounced Imagery dimension as well as with a perceived Altered State of Awareness. Further, there was a positive association between Internal Dialogue and Imagery, indicating that during the Solo time increased internal dialogue was associated with more intense imagery. Apart from Internal Dialogue notably all of these dimensions were most strongly present during the Solo experience compared to all reference samples thus religious, happy and ordinary experiences.

Higher reported Arousal, thus muscular tightness and tension, was associated with more Negative Affect, representing anger, fear and sadness, during the participants' Solo experience. Further, negative affect was also negatively correlated with Rationality. This suggests that the stronger participants felt that negative affect was part of their Solo time the more they tended to experience less rationality, namely less ability to think clearly and distinctly. Rationality was further positively linked with higher Self-Awareness during the Solo time. However, even though self-awareness and rationality were associated the means for both of these dimensions were comparably low in this sample.

Summary

The Butterfly and Solo-only sample did not differ significantly in their means of the assessed dimensions of consciousness. Thus, aspects of the Solo experience appear to be shared among the Solo-only participants and the Butterfly participants regardless of differences between both groups such as differences in location and context.

Furthermore, against the background of the reference conditions religious, happy and ordinary as assessed by Wildman and McNamara (2010) specific features of the Solo time were distinguishable.

In addition, participants appeared to perceive their state of awareness as well as their experience during the Solo time as altered. Their altered experience was reflected in the participants' indications of their bodies extending the boundaries of their skin, experiences of unity with and awe and wonder towards the world as well as in the gain of profound insights regarding ideas or issues. During the Solo time participants seemed to perceive the surrounding objects and the flow of time differently than usual and they also indicated perceiving pronounced imagery.

The Solo, furthermore, seemed to be marked by strong feelings of love, joy and also by sexual feelings. Sexual feelings, however, did not stand out due to a particularly high mean for the associated subdimension but merely because this dimension was even less frequently reported during the happy, religious and ordinary experience.

Significant positive correlations revealed a strong association between the participants' altered experience and their positive affect, imagery and their altered state of awareness during the Solo time.

There was no remarkably strong presence of negative affect during the Solo time. However, negative affect was indicated to a greater extent than assessed in the ordinary experience. Correlations revealed that negative affect during the Solo time positively correlated with arousal and negatively correlated with rational thinking.

It appears that there was a greater amount of silent talking during the Solo time than in the referenced ordinary experience. Furthermore, more silent talking during the Solo experience was associated with more intense imagery.

Solo participants indicated comparably less volitional control over their thoughts and less rational thinking during their Solo time. Less rational thinking, in turn, was associated with more negative affect and lower self-awareness. Nevertheless, based on the means for negative affect and self-awareness both dimensions did not seem to have been unusually strongly present during the Solo time.

4.4.2 Further emergent contributing features and processes of the Butterfly Effect programme

In order to be able to understand the long-term impact of the Butterfly programme on the participants' lives as depicted in the next chapter it is important to draw a complete picture of what Butterfly participants perceived as fundamental and inseparable aspects of the Butterfly Effect programme exceeding their nature experiences. These further contributing aspects of the programme emerged as additional themes in the interview data and are summarised under the high-level theme *community experience*. I briefly introduce the subthemes in the following.

4.4.2.1 Common ground

Repeatedly, Butterfly participants regarded the perceived common ground in the Butterfly group as exceptional. Participants ascribed this to the fact that everyone in the group faced the same challenges and shared transformative experiences. The common ground was perceived as extraordinary as it was established despite the great number of nationalities and people who were initially foreign to each other. Moreover, interviewees cherished that values and attitudes seemed to be mutually shared in the group.

> *Maybe it is because I thought that whoever is here has to have a bit of madness that makes him a friend. You know, I do not know him or her but I am sure that we have something to share because we are both here. So the question is: why should I come here, live in the open air, in tents with the rain, cold and compost toilets and so on. And I think that if someone is doing this that he surely has something to talk about, share. And this gave me the chance to go and talk. It was helpful* (B2).

Participants' accounts revealed that the common ground was not only the result of shared values and shared experiences but also of a group process where participants started to mutually reinforced each other to progressively open up emotionally.

4.4.2.2 Role models for the practicability of change

Participants frequently highlighted the power of role models they encountered throughout the Butterfly programme. For the interviewees these role models acted as real-life evidence for the practicability of change.

Particularly, role models were recognised in other participants, the Butterfly team and in Findhorn as a model for ecological community living on a larger scale.

Interviewees described to have benefitted from witnessing the transformation that the other participants underwent during the programme. Observing how the other participants opened up, interacted and worked with each other as well as witnessing the ideas and visions in others served as an important role model for themselves.

> *It was the people that were there and the visions that they had. And those were ideas that were greater than the ones that I allowed myself to have and which I might not have perceived as important at that time. But through the experience I realised, Wow, this can be done and I can connect like this and this way it is possible to, in turn, do something for other people! And it felt so meaningful. Yes, there is something that is good and that I want to do and I felt a lot of energy then (BF8).*

Through the team of facilitators, interviewees reported to have learned that a career can actually follow the heart. By observing how the team worked voluntarily merely because they believed in the effect of their work, lived their values and facilitated transformative experiences for others, interviewees felt inspired and encouraged to activate their own abilities, to work for change and to believe in its practicability.

> *You know, meeting the LPCS team, extraordinary people living their values. Doing it not for money or big companies. […] I'm sure they also have fears but they are doing it. And I would say, okay, if they can do it, if they are investing time and money and energy for changing young people like this I can do it on my way also (BF7).*

Findhorn as a community and ecovillage on the other hand worked as a role model for change on a larger scale and revealed to participants that change is happening in different places in the world.

> *To be in Findhorn [is] to see that change will happen, that they are making a change here and that there are other parts in the world where they are doing a change, too (B6).*

4.4.2.3 Feasibility of community

A further subtheme of the overall Butterfly community experience was the participants' realisation that people are actually able to live in community harmoniously.

> *Something I really learned in Findhorn with the Butterfly is that it [community] is actually REALLY working. It is SO powerful. Before I was like, it is a nice concept. I was really WILLING to believe that this is working but I have never experienced it. So […] I could not teach it, I could not really use it and I do not think it is usable or understandable unless you have really experienced it. Here, I really experienced it. Here we all agree that it is really like, Phew (B7)!*

Following their outdoor camp experience interviewees further recognised that building a community is not only generally possible but also feasible even under quite simple living conditions where not all of the standard needs and comforts might be met.

4.4.2.4 Interconnectedness with others

Notably, as emergent in the participants' nature experience (see chapter 4.4.1.1) Butterfly interviewees also described experiences of interconnectedness with others as part of the overall Butterfly experience. As part of the participants' community experience the theme of interconnectedness with others inherited three dimensions of interconnectedness: the emotional, practical and psychological, which I will introduce in the following.

The *practical dimension* of interconnectedness with others describes an experience and emerged understanding of the reciprocal benefits of working together. Most commonly this was experienced during the "Service and Care" slots as part of the camp management during the Butterfly programme (see chapter 4.3.3.1). One interviewee explained her belief that one can make a difference with her "Service and Care" experience:

> *Because you realise [...] if everyone just covered a small part* [of the work] *then in the end you did it anyways. It does not matter whether you have to help build something or whether you have to clean something as part of "Service and Care". If everybody contributed just a little bit then it is clean in the end. And it is done* (B4)!

The *emotional dimension* of the participants' experience of interconnectedness with others was by far the most frequently emergent one. It embraces experiences of feeling part of a whole, exchanging emotional support as well as feeling deeply connected with others and was often linked with a heightened awareness for the fact that people, indeed, bear the ability to positively influence each other.

> *And when you receive like that you just want to give back ten times more and continue to build on each other. Because you see also the others evolving. And you see what you have said- the impact that it can have on the other person is like, Wow, that is so cool* (B7)!

As part of the described emotional exchange within the group interviewees recurrently reported personally defining moments, which appeared to be concentrated on the experience of compassion. These accounts included both, reports of personally felt compassion and observing true compassion in others.

An interviewee described such a moment as part of the storytelling in the group after his Solo experience:

> *A special moment was hearing everybody's stories and me telling mine. C* [team member] *was crying. I was telling him quite personal things. You know, to see that emotion from someone that does not really know me, a man especially, that was quite a special moment. [...] But it* [the crying] *was not out of sadness, it was out of support. It was not out of sympathy, he really FELT it from his HEART and I think that is the one thing* (B9).

The *psychological dimension* encompasses the interviewees' reports of recognising themselves in others and other people's stories. This is expressed in the participants' realisation that seemingly personal life issues are shared among humans.

Listening to the story of another participant an interviewee experienced a moment of personal insight:

> [I realised] *that other people can have similar relationships like me and for me it is beautiful that I am not an isolated case. Or maybe it is an isolated case but not TOTALLY isolated for it is recurring. And that it feels nice to share this* (B8).

As part of this dimension participants recurrently came to realise that the relationship they have with others simultaneously mirrors the relationship they have with themselves.

> *Because when I am looking at the negative side* [of people] *and I am judging people I am usually doing that because I am doing that to myself. And I am not being as happy with myself. So I am looking out to other people and I have learned to look at the good in people and see the good in people and to look at their qualities because when I look at their qualities and I look at the good in them I can see that in myself* (B5).

4.4.2.5 Attaining self-access through others and associated supportive aspects of the Solo ritual

Through the experiences with others interviewees frequently reported experiencing facilitated self-access. Further elaboration of the relationship between aspects of these experiences by means of analysing code co-occurrences revealed an associated process and specific context.

The crucial starting point for this process seems to lie in their experience of personally sharing in the group. This was frequently highlighted by descriptions of the power immanent in listening to other people's stories as well as in sharing one's own story with the others. Notably, this was mostly reported in connection with a specific format of sharing, namely through Council (see chapter 4.3.3.1). This format was implemented as part of the Solo ritual by means of sharing each others' Solo experiences as well as practiced at various additional points of time throughout the programme.

The context in which the power of story sharing was mentioned in the interviews is illustrated by the pie chart in Figure 16. Evidently, story sharing was most frequently mentioned with regard to the Solo time followed by sharing in a regular Council and finally followed by a small category reflecting those accounts that did not allow for specification of the context of sharing.

It is in these contexts that interviewees experienced the story sharing as a facilitator for the experience of emotional and psychological interconnectedness with others (see flow chart Figure 16). The amount of co-occurrence between the codes is reflected in the numbers attached to the dotted arrows.

Mediated through their experience of interconnectedness with others interviewees described having been able to gain access to personal aspects of themselves. In order to reflect this mediation the code relationship between story sharing and self-access is

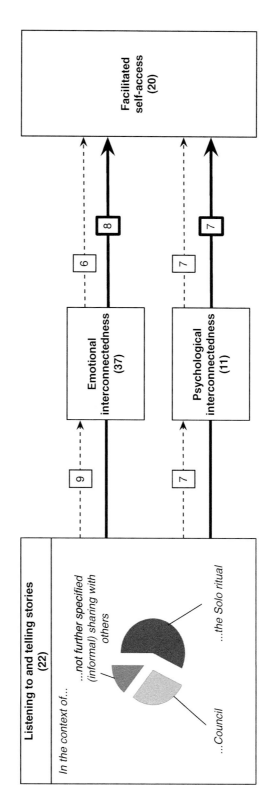

Figure 16. The initiated process and context of sharing stories according to code co-occurrence and code frequency. Numbers in brackets = overall code frequency; Numbers attached to the dotted arrows = Amount of co-occurrence between codes; Numbers attached to bold arrow = Number of excerpts that included all three codes at once.

presented in two steps via the dotted arrows as well as through an unbroken bolder arrow which represents the number of excerpts that specifically included all three codes at once. As depicted in Figure 16, the experience of access to the self through the experience of psychological interconnectedness with others has been solely reported as part of the story sharing whereas self-access through the emotional dimension of interconnectedness was not necessarily directly linked with listening to and telling stories as evident in the following interview excerpt.

> *I have the feeling that we* [the group] *are more open, that we can deal with our emotions more easily or that we can show them now or that we do not shy away from them anymore. Or maybe in this context it is me who is more open now because I realised that others are able to open up, witnessing that and realising that it feels good when I do, too* (B8).

Put in a nutshell, by listening to and sharing stories with each other participants reported the experience of feeling part of a larger whole, exchanging emotional support and/or experiencing connection and compassion which mirrors the experience of emotional interconnectedness with others. Moreover, by sharing their stories participants were able to recognise their own story and own workings in the other person's and herein experienced the psychological dimension of interconnectedness. These experiences further served as facilitators for self-access which is reflected in the participants' accounts of being able to more easily accept their own fears and vulnerabilities, to better understand themselves, to embody their experiences, to open up emotionally and to gather new perspectives on themselves.

> *Definitely you recognise yourself in most of the stories you hear. And you feel a lot of gratitude* […] *like when you say "Thank you for sharing this" it is a real Thank you. You really feel blessed to be there and to hear all this stuff and to be able to receive so much* […]. *That definitely builds a deep sense of connection. It really ROOTS. Your story is not just something from the brain but it really gets rooted in yourself and you really embody all those stories and this thinking you had. All these experiences become embodied through Council, I feel* (B7).

The same themes and patterns were found in the Solo-only sample indicating that the Solo experience also inherits a community dimension alongside the focus on the nature experience.

The bar diagrams in Figure 17 illustrate which themes of the Butterfly community experience were shared with the Solo-only reference sample[22].

Evidently, the only congruent themes are the psychological and emotional dimension of interconnectedness with others as well as the attainment of self-access through others. Further data analysis revealed, indeed, that self-access in the Solo-only sample was especially gained through the psychological but also through the emotional dimension of interconnectedness as part of the storytelling after the Solo time, as exemplified in the account of a Solo-only interviewee describing why the storytelling helped her.

---

22 Notably, the Solo reference sample encompasses four in-depth interviews and is thus considerably smaller than the Butterfly samples. Therefore, the diagrams and code counts cannot be compared in terms of their relational significance but merely indicate congruent themes across samples.

Figure 17. Comparison of code occurrences in the area of "community experience" across samples.

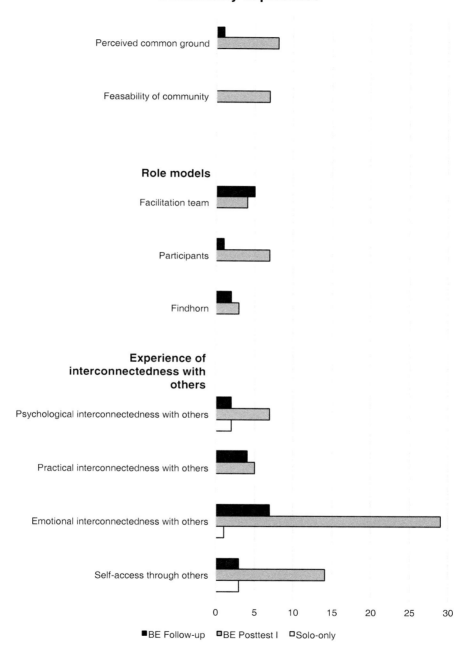

> *I think just by seeing that I am not alone with these new experiences and insecurities. Also before we went out regarding fears- that everyone went through almost the same process. Well, everyone had different issues but it was the trappings. And that made it easier for me to accept and embrace my fears for example* (S2).

Another social aspect of the Solo ritual, which affected the processing of the gathered experiences, was the mirroring of the Solo stories through the guides (see chapter 4.3.3.1).

Clearly, participants not only gained new perspectives on themselves and their stories through the storytelling but also due to the mirroring afterwards. Most interviewees described either gathering different perspectives on their story or being able to understand it better as a consequence. Participants furthermore described that they felt their stories were appreciated and/or they could themselves appreciate their stories more through being mirrored by the guides. Some interviewees further reported that the mirroring confirmed for them that their experiences were "real".

> *Especially due to the mirroring and by listening to the others' stories by means of Council I came to realise how much symbolism there was in my Solo experience and the parallels that I find and that it, indeed, WAS something huge. Namely a great diversity of symbols that I can connect with my life* (B8).

4.4.3 Qualitative evaluation of the long-term effects of the Butterfly Effect programme

Naturally, the results presented in this section rely on the qualitative follow-up data, which I collected from the same interview sample one and a half years after the programme ended.

However, most of the themes that emerged one and a half years later had already emerged in the interviews at post test I and numerous themes simultaneously occurred in the four interviews with the Solo-only interviewees.

Thus, the applied analysis procedure which underlies this follow-up section followed the principle of firstly detecting all the emergent dominant themes in the follow-up interviews and then, if applicable, underpinning them with related excerpts from the other interview samples. The rationale for applying this procedure was to accumulate a greater quantity of narratives so that I could better understand and depict the true nature and different nuances of each code.

All changes described in this chapter are changes that Butterfly interviewees specifically ascribed to the perceived impact of the Butterfly programme on their personal lives.

4.4.3.1 Nature-related changes

Realisation of one's own adaptability

When I asked the interviewees one and a half years later how their relationship with nature has changed, one theme that repeatedly emerged was the interviewees' realisation of their own adaptability to a simpler life-style. Due to living so closely with nature during camp time and also due to facing the challenge of being alone in nature without distractions, a shelter or food during the Solo time Butterfly participants reported having reflected on and having learned how adaptable they actually are as well as having gained new perspectives on their assumed needs.

> [I learned] *that we do not need as many things as we think we need. You remember that, the Solo. 30 hours without eating, without a phone, without reading, writing and talking to anyone! Do we really need to eat meat everyday? Do we need to have a shower everyday? Do we need to do most of the things we think we need? These are the things I think I learned there. And it became physical. I think better with my body since that experience* (BF2).

Power of attraction to nature

Frequently, participants reported to generally feel more attracted to nature as well as to actually seek more time in nature.

This is exemplified in the following statement of an interviewee elaborating the changes in her life back home.

> *I noticed that there is this deep wish inside of me to be outdoors and to sleep outside that keeps coming back. Somehow to be more in touch again. And that I am looking for that in the city and it is because of that that I have small plants or flowers in my room. BECAUSE I can see them this way and because they are there this way and when they are not there I miss something* (BF8).

The way of relating to nature

The most complex and frequently appointed nature-related change in the participants' lives was the way in which they described to relate to nature one and a half years later. The way of relating to nature serves as an umbrella for five subthemes that highlight its specific aspects.

In order to describe the way in which their relationship with nature has changed Butterfly interviewees often drew upon aspects of their *previous relationship with nature*.

In this context participants reported that they used to visit nature for rather practical, recreational or distractive purposes, as some stated, without appreciation for the surroundings. Other interviewees reported having perceived nature as rather frightening.

Moreover, interviewees gave descriptions of having perceived humans and nature as separate, nature as inanimate or even non-existent.

> *I really didn't grow up with a connection to nature. My parents didn't bring me to the forest, you know. It was more that I was going to the tennis club or was doing theatre […]. So I didn't have this nature education. I was like, there are humans and then there is nature* (BF6).

One and a half years later participants still reported to *perceive nature more with their senses* as a result of their Butterfly experience.

As an interviewee described the perceived change:

> *Now it* [the relationship] *has completely changed. When I say completely I mean right from the start. Do you remember what we did with A* [team member], *experiencing nature with the different senses? So touching things, smelling things, you name it. Nature is not just a great beautiful picture to look at and sometimes people walk through it. It is also something highly new. Always highly new* (BF2).

Further, interviewees noticed a change in their *awareness and perception of nature* such as paying more attention to nature, perceiving it more consciously, seeing more nuances and aspects of it and noticing a change in their attitude towards nature.

> *Before the Butterfly* […] *I used to go for example with my parents every Sunday* […] *to have great walks in nature. And every time I think back to it I think, What a waste! I did not have any perception. I did not have a clue of what I was doing! And if I could do it again now I would probably do it differently, yeah* (BF2).

Personification of nature

An interesting aspect that stuck out during the analysis of the interview data was the interviewees' frequent use of expressions that turned nature into an active dialogue partner as though referring to a conversation with a friend. This was reflected in recurring expressions like "the forest/the river/nature told me" which were mostly used in the context of depictions of insights they gained about themselves. These expressions were found in interviews with the Solo-only interviewees as well as with the Butterfly interviewees one and a half years after the programme.

Moreover, interviewees independently started to utilise the process of making friends with other people as a metaphor to explain how their relationship with nature has changed due to their nature experiences during the programmes.

> *Yes, it changed. We are a little more friends I would say* […]. *We have a bit more confidence in each other maybe* […]. *We broke the ice a bit. I already broke the ice with nature a bit before* [the Butterfly] *but this* [the Butterfly experience] *was really strong. And nowadays it* [nature] *feels like a friend to me.* […] *I try to be aware of it. It is not easy to remember every day that you have a good friend. But, yes, when you need it you know it is there* (BF3).

As evident in the element of mutually gained confidence in the latter quote the newly built relationship seems to be based on reciprocity and equality as is further illustrated in the following interview excerpt.

> *Nature rather became a counterpart, I think. It was more of a relationship that developed between me and nature. But at eye level* (S3).

As mentioned before, this phenomenon also manifested in accounts of the Solo-only interviewees right after the Solo programme possibly pointing towards the Solo time as a potential trigger for such a switch in relationship.

As part of the description of how she perceived nature differently during the 24-hour Solo in the woods a Solo-only interviewee stated:

> *Maybe* [I perceived it] *more as a human being or something like that? So not anymore like it* [nature] *is somehow surrounding us but this is someone I can really talk to. In this way. Maybe it changed in that direction* (S2).

When I interrogated why she thought this emerged during her Solo time the interviewee explained:

> *Simply because I just REALLY had time. And I had peace and quiet and I did not need to do anything, which was nature-unrelated. Yes. I think that was the main thing* (S2).

A very similar depiction was given by a Butterfly interviewee only this time reflecting on the change in relationship one and a half years after the Butterfly experience.

> *The way I am with nature now, when I have the pleasure to be with nature again, is deeper than before. Because back then* [during the Butterfly] *it was two full weeks full of that* [nature]*, you know. It is like* [the difference between] *seeing someone for one day or seeing someone for two weeks. When you have a relationship with someone for two weeks it is stronger. You see this person for two weeks every day and afterwards you know he will be your friend forever. You have shared something. When it is just one day you know that the person you have met was nice. You had one day and you were speaking all the time and it was so amazing* […]. *But it is one day. And it is harder then to keep in touch. Often it eventually starts to become a souvenir and you remember this amazing person that you have met for one day. But two weeks is SO strong and that you cannot forget and you have to revisit this person again* (BF6).

Summarised, it appears as though participants created a sort of relationship resembling human friendships. Herein, especially in comparison to their previous relationship with nature as described earlier, interviewees seem to have undergone a process of personifying nature. On the extreme ends this process encompassed a transformation of perception, which ranged from perceiving nature as a mere surrounding or thing to perceiving nature as an intimate friend.

Approximately 61 per cent of the excerpts referring to this shift are simultaneously accounts of the interviewees' Solo time.

Emotional interconnectedness with nature

In contrast to the previously described emotional dimension of the experience of interconnectedness with nature (see chapter 4.4.1.1) this theme embodies reports of the already established emotional bond with nature as an outcome of the programme. In this way, follow-up accounts of emotional interconnectedness with nature can be understood as sustained outcomes of the participants' experience of interconnectedness with nature.

Elaborating why her emotional bond with nature is stronger nowadays a Butterfly interviewee reflected on her Butterfly experience and Solo time:

> *In a way you can say I was connected with nature before because nature helped me when I had a low-energy level or something like that. Or when I felt anger […] I could just look at a tree and forget about it. […] But there was still a distance. […] It was more superficial but not: I KNOW that we are connected and I KNOW that nature is really important and that we need it. So maybe it used to be more mental and with the Butterfly […] it was more a question of FEELING. Before it was more, Nature is important so I have to take care of that! But then, I never spent 24 hours just in nature. […] So just THAT, to be really WITH nature for TWO days. To wake up and have my feet in the grass, to hear nature when I wake up and sleeping in nature with no protection around me. That is something you feel more deeply because you feel safer then. [Before] I was not totally connected to every part* [of nature]. *I think it* [the Solo experience] *goes deeper because you feel nature with all the five senses. You learn how to really FEEL this nature and how to really totally live with nature. And that was something new* (BF6).

Accounts of emotional interconnectedness as a programme outcome include a variety of expressions such as "feeling nature more deeply", reports of a sense of connection, a persistent sense of home, feeling an emotional bond, feeling part of nature, as well as reports of experiencing emotional reactions to nature such as feeling responsible for and protective of it.

Fourty-four percent of the excerpts reflecting on this change were part of the interviewees' accounts of their Solo time. Furthermore, the analysis of code patterns revealed that emotional interconnectedness repeatedly co-occurred with reports of an altered awareness and perception of nature as well as with indicators of having entered into a "human friendship" with nature via personification as described previously.

4.4.3.2 Changes related to others

Awareness for the importance of others
Another part of the assessed areas of change was whether interviewees perceived changes in their relationship with others due to the Butterfly programme.

In this context participants reported a heightened awareness for their interconnectedness with others and for the importance of community and other people in their lives.

The heightened awareness is illustrated in the following statement of a Butterfly interviewee describing what he has learned from the Butterfly.

> *I show myself at my best when I am in a supportive environment while I sometimes I do not show my best in an unsupportive environment. So yes, my perception of community and of myself changed because I am more conscious about the fact that I need a cooperative and supportive community* (BF3).

Attitude towards others

As a result of the Butterfly interviewees reported changes in their attitude towards other people. Accounts included trusting other people more, carrying a more positive attitude towards and feelings of gratitude for others as well as being more open.

As a Butterfly participant stated one and a half years later: "I am able to just go to people and speak to people a lot more (BF1)."

Notably, participants that were interviewed right after the Butterfly programme already perceived this change in themselves as evident in accounts like "I believe in people a lot more (B9)." or "I learned to listen to my heart, follow my heart and to look at the good in other people (B5)."

Interaction with others

As a further change in their lives interviewees reported an altered interaction with others. This encompasses an increased willingness to collaborate and share with other people as well as to interact with other people in more considerate ways.

Moreover, participants reported having learned to listen to other people. This was often perceived as one of the key learnings participants took back home and was repeatedly attributed by them to their Council experiences during the Butterfly.

> *As far as I am concerned I can say: the one thing was to listen to others and to myself. That was the thing that changed the most. I could not immediately get what exactly had changed. I knew something had changed but what exactly? I mean, it was nothing practical you could see with your eyes. But the most important thing* [that had changed] *was my* […] *ability to listen to others and to myself. Since we did a lot of Council activity,* [during the Butterfly] *it was mostly about speaking with your heart or listening with your heart* (BF2).

In this context interviewees also often disclosed to have integrated Council in their everyday lives, formally or informally.

> *Now, often when we have a problem or discussion in the team* [at work] *I propose to use the Council way. So that is a concrete action that we use often and even in discussions with my boyfriend I propose to him this kind of way of speaking if we have an argument* (BF6).

Urge to pass something on to others

As a result of the Butterfly experience interviewees described to bear an inner wish to pass their experiences on and share what they experienced or learned with other people. In the interviews participants reported to realise this either by intentionally embodying certain values and approaches to life or by directly talking to other people and by explicitly working on facilitating similar experiences for other people.

This is exemplified in the following quote of an interviewee describing this shift in herself since the Butterfly programme.

> *I tell other people* [about the Butterfly experience] *and enjoy it.* [...] *I do not tell everybody. Only when I feel that it is well treated. So I do not necessarily tell people who might perceive it as crazy or "hippie" or who might not like it or simply think: "That is ridiculous!" But when I know there is this seed somewhere then I do tell with GREAT pleasure and I share fully. And I try to motivate others as well. Something that I before felt was "Well, whatever!" But now it is a personal need of mine that others are able to experience it as well. And that is something I did not care about before* (BF8).

4.4.3.3 Changes related to self

Ability to influence

In the follow-up interviews participants revealed to have realised their own strength and ability to make a difference. Participants reported to have recognised that small groups and even individuals can influence situations and other people greatly, which often entailed growing faith in the power of a simple small act.

> *Most of the people have the impression that they are nothing and that they have no impact and they feel so small. And with this kind of experience* [the Butterfly] *you understand that you're not small at all and that everyone counts and has an impact* (BF6).

Self-confidence

Participants frequently reported a gain of self-confidence, which they linked directly to the Butterfly experience. Mostly, interviewees used expressions as self-confidence and faith or belief in oneself. However, occasionally participants would describe this shift by reporting to have lost fear. In this context interviewees related the gain of self-confidence repeatedly with having faced and managed the challenges of the Solo time.

Specifically, 35 per cent of the time this inner change was brought up as part of the interviewees' accounts of their Solo time.

In the context of having just shared his Solo experience with me a Butterfly interviewee concluded:

> *That is what nature can do! From an anger-life made of stress* [...] *to something made of peace, of faith. FAITH. IN. ME. Which I did not have. That is something that switched. And that changed me* (BF2).

Trust in own intuition

Interviewees indicated to have gained trust in their own intuition due to the Butterfly experience, which was mostly described in the context of their Solo experience (57 per cent of this code's occurrence).

Interviewees expressed the gain of trust in their intuition in various ways such as switching off the head and following their gut feeling or heart as well as listening to and following their inner voice.

When I asked a Butterfly participant what she was able to take back home from the Butterfly programme she responded:

> *Staying connected, listening to myself* […] *to what my body is saying, to what my intuition is saying and not just being on two wheels and keeping on going forward* (BF7).

Authenticity

According to the interviewees a further outcome of the Butterfly was an increase of personal authenticity. Participants described having learned to be more authentic due to the Butterfly experience. They described having freed themselves from what other people think and from the pressure they sense in society to be someone else. Interviewees not only reported to be now able to accept their own weaknesses and to cope with them better, but also to simultaneously meet their inner strength with more awareness and appreciation, as evident in the following excerpt:

> *I think I have accepted that I have limits and that I am not good at everything. And that I TELL people* [now]. *Not just keeping that to myself helps other relationships with people a lot. For collaboration… when you accept yourself fully with your bad and good sides. And before I just tried to be good at everything and be the best at everything. And now I just accept that I am perfect when I am NOT good at everything.* […] *So yeah. That is the gift I received* (BF6).

Forty-five percent of the reports of this inner change were mentioned in the context of the interviewees' accounts of their Solo time.

Self-awareness

A theme that repeatedly emerged in the interview data was heightened self-awareness. This manifested in interviewees' reports of greater understanding, clarity or awareness of their inner workings and was most commonly described in the context of revelations that arose while experiencing aspects of the programme. Markedly, 61 per cent of the reports of this inner change were mentioned in the context of the interviewees' accounts of their Solo time.

An example of such statements is exemplified in the brief following excerpt.

> *And I have learned from all this stuff and it has been good, you know, to be aware of myself and I learn from my own feelings* (B5).

4.4.3.4 World and life-related changes

Sense of connection with the world and life

Butterfly participants explained to feel more connected with the world and to their lives and described this as an inner change they experienced during the Butterfly programme. Interviewees reported having experienced that they are part of a larger whole, an insight, which stayed with the interviewees until today. Some depicted this experience as a process from initially feeling rather alone in the world to realising through the Butterfly that they are in fact never alone. Moreover, participants revealed to have also gained a sense of place and belonging on earth as evident in the following excerpt.

> *Those experiences of being a lot in the nature, in very free contact with nature helped me to realise that I am part of a great body. And most of the time we live in great cities, which help us to forget that. Now, I am just MORE aware of who I am here on earth and what the earth is* (BF2).

Approach to life

The reported change of the interviewees' approach to life encompasses a variety of aspects, such as engaging with life or work more passionately, having readjusted life objectives, being able to perceive more depth, purpose or quality in life, having incorporated a more caring, trusting, open-minded, mindful and appreciative attitude towards their lives, as well as a broader awareness for world affairs.

The following excerpt gives an example for such a change.

> *I know it is something stupid and obvious to say but we always think that money is the goal to reach in our life. No! That is not real. We have something else. We have the special feeling of feeling part of something, which is truly better. And yes, that changed. The life objective, the point of life has probably changed for everyone* (BF2).

Urge to contribute to the world

One and a half years later, interviewees reported that the Butterfly programme had evoked in them the urge to contribute something to the world. This frequently co-occurred with the interviewees' urge to pass something on to others, which was often stated in reference to their nature experience. However, while the latter is located on a micro-level in the sense of wanting to specifically contribute to other people's range of experience the urge to contribute to the world is addressing the macro-level in the participants' lives. This was reflected in their arising wish to be generally useful and serve a purpose in the world. Interviewees repeatedly described that they were able to gain a clearer vision of the type of contribution they wanted to offer to the world. Concretely, participants described that the Butterfly experience activated in them the need to realign their career-related paths with their gained sense of self and the world. Thereby this particular change speaks to the central question and personal investigation of one's purpose in the world.

Unsurprisingly, the urge to contribute to the world co-occurred with a reported increase in authenticity as evident in the following report.

> *Through the Butterfly I realised that I want to live my life, and I mean all my life, and to be the director of my life and to live my values. And not just having the Butterfly Effect in the summer and then being disconnected the rest of the year just doing normal stuff. So I started to think, Ok, now I have to apply what I have seen, I have to apply what I really- where I really feel good. The aim in life is to feel good at any moment and to go into that direction. This is a lot connected to the fact that I want to live my emotions. I want to live my values* (BF7).

4.4.3.5 Activism and motivators for behaviour change

Thus far, the analysis and related results focused on the phenomenology of immersive experiences in wild nature, its underlying process, additional contributing features and processes of the Butterfly programme as a vehicle for such experiences and the associated perceived changes of interviewees in terms of their relationship with nature, self, others and the world one and a half years later.

However, the question remains whether the Butterfly experience led to activism or actual behaviour change. This question takes up the initial problem statement, which is concerned with the psychological root of environmental problems and with the question of what is needed to cross the Rubicon from knowledge to action.

Proenvironmental behaviour

Apart from one case all Butterfly interviewees reported to have adopted additional proenvironmental behaviours. However, some interviewees revealed that they had adopted additional changes right after the Butterfly programme, which they could not sustain indicating that interviewees might had to find a balance between a personally realisable and their desired state as exemplified in the following excerpt.

> *I became a vegetarian for a period. […] It lasted for nine months and then I was a pescetarian for a while. But now I am back to normal again (LAUGHTER). So yeah. Just a few things like that* (BF5).

The same interviewee continued to describe the changes that persisted:

> *When I am hill walking up a mountain I might just pick up some litter and I am just more caring to animals, you know, take my mother's dog out […]* (BF5).

The reported stable behaviour changes ranged from consuming less, recycling, picking up litter to switching modes of transport for example exchanging the car for a bike. As already evident in the last excerpt, another perceived change in behaviour was to be more caring towards animals and plants, which caused some participants to literally start bringing living plants into their apartments as a result of the Butterfly programme.

Practical engagement

Continuous personal engagement as a result of the Butterfly programme was reported back by all but one interviewee.

Practical engagement that interviewees felt was triggered by their Butterfly experience encompassed implemented career changes, such as fully pursuing a career path in line with personal values and visions, as well as initiating own Youth in Action programmes, attending trainings and programmes which broadened their own skills, or voluntarily supporting new projects dealing with global social change. Notably, a lot of these actions were often connected with nature awareness work or sustainability matters.

> *Now, I am attending a training to become an outdoor trainer. This is an important ingredient, which also resulted from the Butterfly. Because there I got to know people who were concerned with this topic and who partly also teach this training. […] So for me quite a network developed from this […] and now I do this outdoor training. […] Before I was aware that nature is somehow important to me but I did not realise that working with groups in nature is so great. That it can actually create an impact. It was just not relevant, it was not strongly present in my surroundings* [before] (BF8).

Perceived triggers of implemented action

Naturally, in the context of reported behaviour change it is essential to understand what triggered participants to undergo such change. Figure 18 illustrates the perceived triggers of the implemented actions from the participants' retrospective point of view and will be further elaborated in the following.

Retrospectively, participants mostly ascribed the changes in proenvironmental behaviour to their former experiences of emotional and practical interconnectedness with nature, and the resulting persisting feeling and knowledge of this interconnectedness.

In the following a Butterfly interviewee describes the root of her behaviour change.

> *Now I just feel more aware of my responsibility, or yes, more aware. Not just more responsibility but a greater awareness for my responsibility. […] Because I did this Solo in nature and because that* [Solo] *spot sheltered me during that time and I was allowed to stay there and also I took everything that belonged to me back with me, so I did not leave anything behind which nature could not digest. Because of that it felt like, Yes, now, this is my "counter-responsibility" for having been allowed to stay there* [Solo spot] (BF8).

The motivators mentioned for practical engagement, such as organising and running projects and programmes or realigning career paths, differed compared to those for environmental behaviour.

What appeared to have greatly impacted the interviewee's willingness to engage on the community level was their encounter with role models embodied through the facilitation team of the Butterfly programme, other participants or the Findhorn community (see chapter 4.4.2.2).

An illustrative example is the following statement of a Butterfly interviewee describing why the Butterfly programme helped him to take action back home.

Figure 18. Butterfly participants' perceived triggers of the implemented actions.

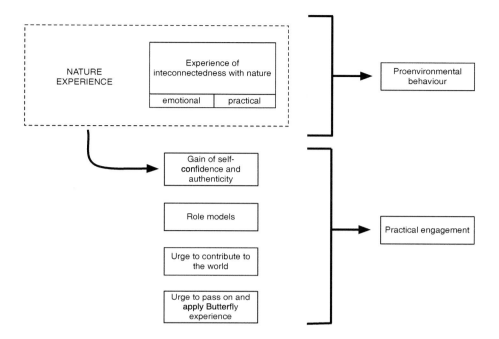

> *Just by looking at Findhorn and at the village and also the people that were there. That some of them did really extraordinary things gives you a lot of energy and the feeling that [...] I can do whatever I want. Findhorn village was something really nice for me but* [it is] *also something, which is quite hard to realise. So I thought if someone was able to create Findhorn I can do what I want in X* [home country] (BF3).

Furthermore, interviewees described the root of their motivation as an inner urge to pass on and apply what they experienced during the Butterfly programme as well as in their urge to contribute something meaningful to the world, as evident in the following excerpt.

> *Since the Butterfly I took part in maaany different [...] activities in my everyday life. [...] Environmental activities, voluntary activities and with my association we applied for own "Youth-in-Action" programmes. And that is it, you know. Being part of SOMETHING or working for SOMETHING, for SOMEONE, for the community helped me realise that it is not useful to stay in my room and [...] play computer games* (BF2).

As mentioned before, motivators for environmental behaviour and practical engagement differ but nonetheless it is difficult to draw a line between the two as they merely address different types of engagement. Environmental behaviour takes place on a rather individual "daily routine" level whereas the reported practical engagement entails creating something with and for others. The entanglement of the two becomes evident in an additional motivator for community engagement, which was the interviewees' perceived gain of self-confidence as a result of the Butterfly programme. Interestingly, in the interviews participants repeatedly attributed this gain to their nature experiences such as having managed to live fully outdoors and having accomplished and experienced the 24-hour Solo in the woods.

This way the data appear to reveal a twofold connection between the participants' nature experience and their practical engagement one and a half years later. On the one hand, their nature experience seems to be reflected in the content of the programmes and initiatives that they came to realise later on and on the other hand, as a more direct outcome, participants reported to have gained self-confidence through their nature experiences. In turn, according to the interviewees, it was largely their gain of self-confidence, which enabled them to personally engage on a community level after the Butterfly programme.

An illustration of this link can be found in the following response of an interviewee to my question whether he would actually ascribe his reported engagement to the Butterfly experience.

> *(LAUGHTER) This is a good question! I don't know. [...] Maybe. Because during my day outside* [the Solo] *I felt that if anything would go wrong I would handle it. So that really gives me the self-confidence to do something which sometimes may frustrate you a lot. [...] Coming back with this self-confidence gave me the energy to work also when you feel that you are trying to do something very hard. I do not know how to explain this. The self-confidence to be at the end really happy with who you are gives you the energy to* [do] *work which may not always turns out as you hope* (BF3).

4.4.3.6 Comparison of code occurrences across samples

As touched on earlier, the previously presented results in this section rely on the follow-up data, which was collected one and a half years after the programme ended.

However, as most of the themes that emerged one and a half years later already emerged at post test I, and numerous themes simultaneously occurred in the four interviews with the Solo-only interviewees, code occurrence by sample is depicted in the bar diagrams in Figure 19.

In this way the code occurrence can be viewed separately for each sample and congruent effects of the sole Solo experience and the sustainability of the effects from post test I to the follow-up become evident at a glance.

Clearly, the changes that Solo-only and post test I Butterfly interviewees reported are immediately perceived changes right after the Butterfly respectively Solo-only experience and do not depict long-term effects.

Evidently, the Solo-only participants consistently anticipated most nature-related changes as well as changes in their relationship with themselves. However, one self-related change, which was repeatedly emphasised by Butterfly participants, was absent in the Solo-only sample, namely the realisation of their own ability to influence or make a difference in the world. Unsurprisingly, changes in the relationship with others also constituted a missing aspect in the reports of the Solo-only sample. Obviously, this does not mean that these elements were generally not present in the Solo-only participants.

Figure 19. Comparison of code occurrences in the areas of assessed changes across samples.

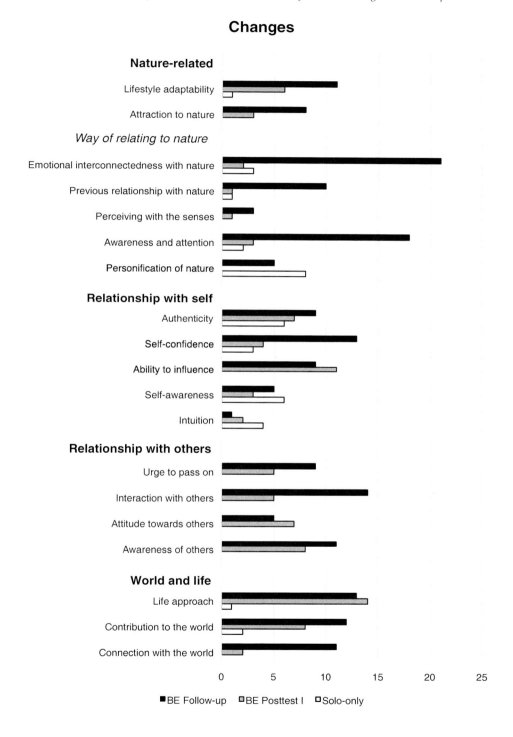

However, it does indicate that the interactional level of the Solo-only programme mainly focused on the relationship with oneself and nature, as opposed to equally providing a learning environment to deeply explore group dynamics and interrelations with others that expand the social aspects of the Solo ritual (see chapter 4.4.2.5).

Notably, the encounter with other participants, the facilitation team and Findhorn as role models as well as the growing urge to pass their experiences on to other people were essential triggers for taking action as described by the Butterfly participants.

This circumstance possibly makes a case for the importance of integrating interconnectedness in its fullness when aiming to facilitate activism. That is, to follow the immanent logic of the interconnectedness of all of life by acknowledging that the sense of interconnectedness between humans and nature and the sense of interconnectedness among humans are mutually reinforcing and, indeed, inseparable. Potentially, both interconnections need to be equally consolidated in order to feel involved and empowered enough to truly engage with the world and take action.

4.4.4 Quantitative immediate effects

4.4.4.1 Relationship with nature and coping with environmental problems

Due to the intimate character and focus on the encounter with nature throughout the 24-hour Solo but also due to outdoor living throughout the Butterfly Programme and other nature-based exercises, I assessed the participants' relationship with nature also via standardised scales.

Specifically, I asked participants to rate their overall emotional connectedness to nature, assessed via the Connectedness to Nature Scale (CNS) and Inclusion of Nature in Self (INS) as well as specific aspects of their Emotional Affinity towards Nature (EAN) in order to specify the particular areas of change in the participants' relationship with nature. Furthermore, I monitored the participants' way of Coping with Global Environmental Problems (GEP) before and after the Butterfly programme to see how their nature experiences might have affected psychological coping (for a summary of statistical parameters for each scale see Table 27).

According to the Wilcoxon signed-rank test result there was a significant increase from pretest (Mdn = 53.5) to posttest I (Mdn = 58) in the participants' reported connectedness to nature, $z = 3.391$, $p < .05$, and the increase was medium-sized ($r = .48$).

Regarding the emotional affinity towards nature, there was no significant difference from pretest (Mdn = 5.25) to posttest I (Mdn = 5.5) in the participants' level of love of nature, $z = .949$, $p > .05$, $r = .14$ as well as no significant difference from pretest (Mdn = 4.75) to posttest I (Mdn = 5.38) in the participants' level of feelings of security in nature, $z = 1.878$, $p > .05$, $r = .27$.

However, there was a significant increase from pretest (Mdn = 4.75) to posttest I (Mdn= 5.31) in the participants' level of feelings of freedom in nature, $z = 2.234$, $p < .05$, $r = .32$, as well as a significant increase from pretest (Mdn = 4.88) to posttest (Mdn = 5.25) in the participants' feelings of oneness with nature, $z = 2.161$, $p < .05$, $r = .31$.

Of the eight subscales of the Coping with Global Environmental Problems (GEP) Scale two subscales changed significantly. Statistical parameters for all eight subscales are presented in Table 27.

There was a significant increase from pretest (Mdn = 4.2) to posttest I (Mdn = 4.4) in the participants' usage of the coping style Problem Solving, $z = 1.961$, $p < .05$, $r = .27$. Furthermore, there was also a significant increase from pretest (Mdn = 3.1) to posttest I (Mdn = 3.5) in the participants' adaptation of the coping style Relativization, $z = 2.268$, $p < .05$, $r = .31$.

Figure 20 shows boxplots of pre- and posttest scores for each subscale. The visual analysis revealed that the coping styles Resignation (RES), Denial of Guilt (DEN) and Self-Protection (SPR) were, from the start, only relatively weakly incorporated by the Butterfly participants. Pleasure (PLE), Problem Solving (PS) and Wishful Thinking (WT) on the other hand appeared to be the strategies, which participants generally adopted to a greater extent.

Notably, Pleasure and Wishful Thinking are coping styles that rather emphasise the individual's ability to still enjoy things in life and to strongly wish for a turn for the better in the face of global environmental problems (see chapter 4.3.5.1) whereas Problem Solving represents a rather pragmatic approach of looking for solutions and acquiring knowledge.

Interestingly, effect sizes suggest that the greatest increase took place on the subscales Problem Solving as well as Relativization, which reflects the individual's belief that things will work out.

Summarised this reveals that participants, despite continuing to treasure the positive side of life and to wish for a better future, also started to believe that global environmental

Figure 20. Boxplots of pre- and posttest scores for the eight subscales of the Coping with Global Environmental Problems (GEP) Scale. RES = Resignation; DEN = Denial of Guilt; SPR = Self-Protection; REL = Relativization; EXEM = Expression of Emotion; PLE = Pleasure; PS = Problem Solving; WT = Wishful Thinking.

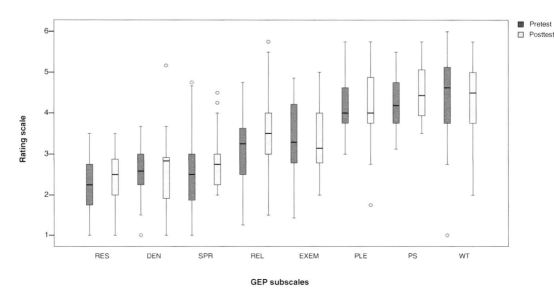

Table 27

Summary of statistical parameters for the implemented scales assessing the participants' relationship with nature

(Sub)scale	N	Median pre / post	p-value	z-value	Effect size r
Connectedness to Nature (CNS)	25	53.5 / 58	.001*	3.39	.48
Love of Nature (EAN)	24	5.25 / 5.5	.34	.95	.14
Feelings of Freedom in Nature (EAN)	24	4.75 / 5.13	.03*	2.23	.32
Feelings of Security in Nature (EAN)	24	4.75 / 5.38	.06	1.88	.27
Feelings of Oneness with Nature (EAN)	24	4.88 / 5.25	.03*	2.16	.31
Problem-Solving (GEP)	26	4.2 / 4.4	.05*	1.96	.27
Expression of Emotion (GEP)	26	3.4 / 3.2	.48	-.7	
Relativization (GEP)	26	3.1 / 3.5	.02*	2.3	.31
Wishful Thinking (GEP)	24	4.6 / 4.5	.69	-.4	
Self-Protection (GEP)	24	2.5 / 2.8	.1	1.64	.24
Pleasure (GEP)	24	4 / 4	.98	-.02	
Denial of Guilt (GEP)	25	2.6 / 2.8	.87	-.17	
Resignation (GEP)	24	2.4 / 2.5	.29	1.05	.15

Notes. N = sample size; * p < .05.

problems can be dealt with and focused even more on the coping style Problem Solving. Further, the authors of GEP (Homburg et al., 2007) found that Problem Solving is positively correlated with proenvironmental behaviour whereas Relativization together with Denial of Guilt are the only coping styles which are negatively correlated with stress.

4.4.4.2 Personal value system

I examined potential changes in the participants' value system via the Life Values Inventory (see chapter 4.3.5.1) covering 14 values altogether. It is important to note that I asked participants to indicate how strongly each value guided their behaviour in their lives before the programme and then during the programme time as assessed right after the programme at posttest I. Therefore, changes in this area do not depict lasting changes in the participants' value system but rather reveal which values guided their behaviour more or less strongly during the programme time compared to their everyday lives.

For each value sample size, median, p-value, z-value and effect size is depicted in Table 28 at the end of this section.

The Wilcoxon test showed that the Butterfly programme did not elicit a statistically significant change (p > .05) in the values Achievement[23] (z = .477), Scientific Understanding[24] (z = -.671), Belonging[25] (z = 1.197, r = .17), Creativity[26] (z = -1.299, r =

---

23 "It is important to challenge yourself and work hard to improve."
24 "It is important to use scientific principles to understand and solve problems."
25 "It is important to be accepted by others and to feel included."
26 "It is important to have new ideas or to create new things."

Figure 21. Effect size r for detected increases of value activation.

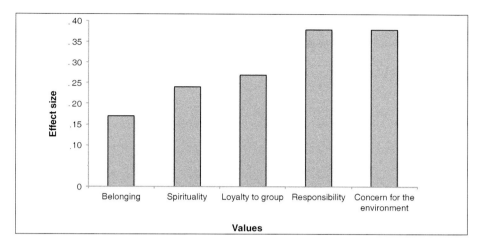

-.18), Loyalty to Family or Group[27] (z = 1.948, r = .27), Privacy[28] (z = -1.888, r = -.26), Spirituality[29] (z = 1.746, r = .24) as well as in the Concern for Others[30] (z = .911).

Notably, the median of the latter value Concern for Others was already considerably high at pretest (Mdn = 12.5) with the highest possible score being 15, which may be why it did not differ at posttest (Mdn = 12.5) and may indicate a ceiling effect.

As detected effect sizes do not always match up with the statistical significance they are presented separately in bar charts (see Figure 21 and Figure 22).

Statistically significant increases of behaviour-guiding value activation (p < .05) during the programme was measured in the values Concern for the Environment[31] (z = 2.746, r = .38) and Responsibility[32] (z = 2.715, r = .38). Effect sizes for all the increases in value activation, regardless of statistical significance, are depicted in Figure 21.

It can be seen that participants appear to have reported a small increase of the importance of belonging to a group, having spiritual beliefs and following the expectations of the group. Medium effect sizes were detected for the increase of the value Responsibility, representing an increased awareness for the importance of being dependable and trustworthy, as well as for the value Concern for the Environment, reflecting an increased awareness for the importance of protecting and preserving it.

Statistically significant decreases (p < .05) in value activation were detected in the values Humility[33] (z = -2.049, r = -.28), Health and Activity[34] (z = -2.298, r = -.32), Independence[35] (z = -3.034, r = -.42) and Financial Prosperity[36] (z = -3.782, r = -.53).

---

27 "It is important to follow the traditions and expectations of your family or group."
28 "It is important to have time alone."
29 "It is important to have spiritual beliefs and to believe that you are part of something greater than yourself."
30 "The well-being of others is important."
31 "It is important to protect and preserve the environment."
32 "It is important to be dependable and trustworthy."
33 "It is important to be humble and modest about your accomplishments."
34 "It is important to be healthy and physically active."
35 "It is important to make your own decisions and make things your way."
36 "It is important to be successful at making money or buying property."

Effect sizes for all decreases in value activation are shown in Figure 22.

Correspondingly, participants reported a small decrease of creativity, of the importance to spend time alone and of the importance of being modest about own accomplishments. Further, medium effect sizes were detected for the decrease of the importance of having to do things one's own way and for the importance of being healthy and physically active. For the latter 3-item scale, however, two and especially one of

Figure 22. Effect size r for detected decreases of value activation.

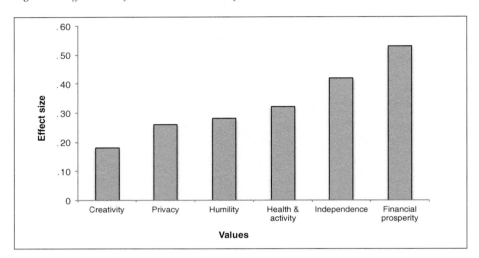

Table 28

Statistical parameters for each value

Subscale	N	Median Pre / post	P-value	Z-value	Effect size r
Achievement	26	11.5 / 12	.63	.48	
Belonging	26	10 / 11	.23	1.2	.17
Concern for the environment	26	13 / 13	.006*	2.8	.38
Concern for others	26	12.5 / 12.5	.36	.91	
Creativity	26	12 / 11.5	.19	-1.3	-.18
Financial prosperity	25	7 / 3	.000*	-3.78	-.53
Health and activity	26	10 / 9	.02*	-2.3	-.32
Humility	26	9 / 8	.04*	-2.05	-.28
Independence	26	12 / 11	.002*	-3.03	-.42
Loyalty to family or group	26	11 / 12	.05	1.95	.27
Privacy	26	12 / 11.5	.06	-1.9	-.26
Responsibility	26	12 / 13	.007*	2.7	.38
Scientific understanding	26	9 / 9	.5	-.67w	
Spirituality	26	12 / 13	.08	1.75	.24

Note. N = sample size.

the three associated items are rather athletically-oriented, targeting the importance of being good in a sport, which may be why the data mirrored a decrease of this value.

The largest effect size across all values was identified for the significant decrease of the value financial prosperity, representing how much participants felt their behaviour was guided by the importance of being successful at making money.

The following table summarises all relevant parameters for each value.

4.4.4.3 Attitudes towards others and life

In order to assess possible changes in the participants' attitudes towards others and life I implemented the Miller Hope Scale as well as a Gratitude, Capacity for Love and Trust scale (see chapter 4.3.5.1) and tested for pretest/posttest differences.

As evident in Figure 23, Butterfly participants reported a significantly higher level of hope at posttest I (Mdn = 196), thus right after the Butterfly programme, than at pretest (Mdn = 187), shortly before the start of the Butterfly programme, $z = 2.73$, $p < .05$, with a medium effect size $r = .38$.

Furthermore, participants indicated significantly higher scores on the subscale Satisfaction with Self, Others and Life (SSOL) after the programme (Mdn = 100) than before the Butterfly programme (Mdn = 92), $z = 2.088$, $p < .05$, $r = .29$, as visually depicted in Figure 24.

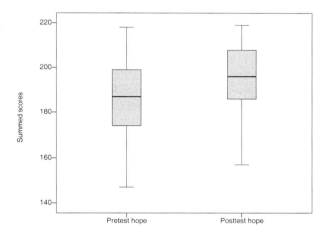

Figure 23. Boxplots of pre- and posttest scores for overall hope.

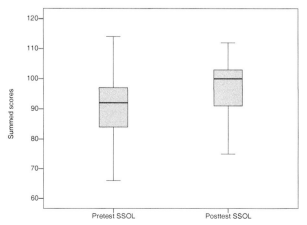

Figure 24. Boxplots of pre- and posttest scores for the subscale Satisfaction with Self, Others and Life (SSOL).

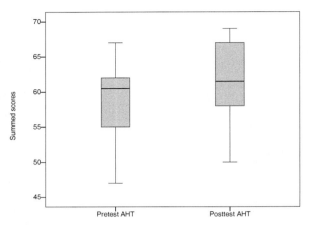

Figure 25. Boxplots of pre- and posttest scores for the subscale Avoidance of Hope Threats (AHT).

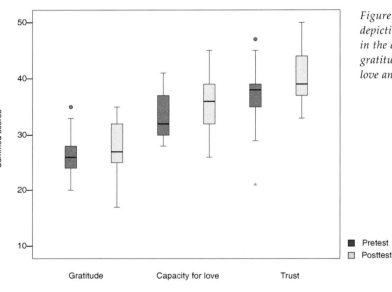

Figure 26. Boxplots depicting the changes in the distribution for gratitude, capacity for love and trust.

Table 29

Statistical parameters of the (sub-) scales assessing the participants' attitude towards others and life

Scales and Subscales		N[1]	P – value	Effect size r
MHS	Total	26	.006**	.38
	SSOL	26	.037*	.29
	AHT	26	.011*	.35
	APF	26	.097	.23
Gratitude		25	.018*	.33
Capacity for love		25	.002**	.44
Trust		26	.002**	.43

Notes. MHS = Miller's Hope Scale; SSOL = Satisfaction with Self, Others and Life; AHT = Avoidance of Hope Threats; APF = Anticipation of a Positive Future; N = sample size; * $p < .05$, ** $p < .001$. [1] The number of cases may differ for the tests as conventionally only paired scores are included in the calculations.

Consistently, participants reported lower levels of perceived hope threats[37] at posttest I (Mdn = 61.5) than at pretest (Mdn = 60.5), z = 2.532, p < .05, with a medium effect size r = .35 (see Figure 25).

However, there was no significant difference regarding the scores of the subscale Anticipation of a Future between pretest (Mdn = 35.5) and posttest I (Mdn = 37), z = 1.658, p > .05. Nevertheless, a small effect size (r = .23) was detected for the change between pre- and posttest scores.

Furthermore, the Wilcoxon signed-rank test result indicated a significant increase of the Butterfly participants' level of gratitude from pretest (Mdn = 26), before the Butterfly programme, to posttest I (Mdn = 27), z = 2.361, p < .05, and the increase was medium-sized (r = .33). This represents a significantly higher individual awareness of the positive things in life and the Butterfly participants' own ability to expressively acknowledge this.

Also there was a significant increase of the participants' capacity for love from pretest (Mdn = 32) to posttest I (Mdn = 36), z = 3.101, p < .01, r = .44, indicating that Butterfly participants generally valued relationships more especially those, which include reciprocally sharing and caring for each other.

A significant increase between pretest (Mdn = 38) and posttest I (Mdn = 39), z = 3.121, p < .01, was also found in the participants level of trust in others, r = .43.

P-values and effect sizes for each construct are summarised in Table 29.

Changes in the distribution for gratitude, capacity for love and trust are also visualized by means of boxplots in Figure 26[38].

4.4.4.4 Empowerment

I monitored the participants' empowerment via three scales of the Civic Attitudes and Skills Questionnaire (CASQ; Moely, 2002), namely Civic Action, Interpersonal and Problem-Solving Skills and Leadership Skills. In addition, I assessed four subscales of Individual Community-Related Empowerment (Kasmel & Tanggaard, 2011): Motivation, Critical Awareness, Self-Efficacy and Participation. As I utilised the latter subscale Participation in this study to assess actual long-term community engagement I will present results relating to this subscale in the next chapter 4.4.5.

Seeing that the data were skewed I employed the Wilcoxon signed-rank test. All relevant parameters of the test results for each subscale are presented in Table 30.

There was no significant change from pretest (Mdn = 6) to posttest I (Mdn = 6) in the participants' level of motivation to be involved in the local community, z = -.580, p > .05. However, as possible scores for this subscale range between 3 and 15[39] a median of 6 indicates that participants were already quite motivated at pretest. Furthermore, no significant change was detected from pretest (Mdn = 2) to posttest I (Mdn = 2) in the participants' level of critical awareness[40], z = -1.016, p > .05. Regardless of the statistical non-significance a small effect size (r = -.14) was found indicating a small increase in critical awareness for the problems in the individual's community. Like in

---

37 The ratings were coded so that higher scores on this subscale reflect a higher level of hope thus a lower level of perceived hope threats.
38 Note that all oft the three constructs include differing numbers of items which is why the summed scores cannot be compared with each other in this figure.
39 This subscale consists of three items with lower scores indicating higher motivation.
40 This subscale consists of a single item: „I think that the problems in my community are serious."

the case of the participants' motivation, it is important to note that the median critical awareness is considerably low at pretest, which indicates a high degree of critical awareness to start with and suggests that there might be a ceiling effect at stake.

Similarly, there was no significant change from pretest (Mdn = 4) to posttest I (Mdn = 4.3) in the participants' level of intention for civic action, $z = 1.737$, $p > .05$. However, there was a small increase in the level of intention ($r = .24$) as also revealed by the medians[41] at pretest and posttest I.

A further Wilcoxon signed-rank test indicated that the participants' perceived self-efficacy changed significantly from pretest (Mdn = 16.5) to posttest (Mdn = 16), $z = -2.036$, $p < .05$, $r = -.28$.

Table 30

Statistical parameters of the test results for each subscale of the Civic Attitudes and Skills Questionnaire (CASQ)

Subscale	N	Median pre / post	p-value	z-value	Effect size r
Self-Efficacy	26	16.5 / 16	.042*	-2.036	-.28
Motivation (to get involved)	26	6 / 6	.562	-.580	
Critical Awareness	26	2 / 2	.310	-1.016	-.14
(Intention for) Civic Action	26	4 / 4.3	.082	1.737	.24
Interpersonal and Problem-Solving Skills	26	3.0 / 4	.037*	2.080	.29
Leadership Skills	26	3.4 / 3.6	.002*	3.037	.42

Note. N = sample size; * p < .05.

Figure 27. Effect size r for changes on the empowerment subscales.

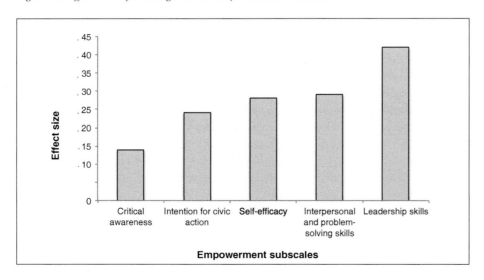

---

41 The score for the subscale Intention represents the mean of the individual's ratings which range between 1 and 5 with higher scores indicating greater intention.

Moreover, there was a significant increase from pretest (Mdn = 3) to posttest (Mdn = 4) in the levels of interpersonal problem-solving skills, z = 2.080, p < .05, r = .29. This change reflects an increase in the participants' ability to listen, work cooperatively, take over perspectives, communicate, think logically and solve problems.

Additionally, there was a significant increase from pretest (Mdn = 3.4) to posttest I (Mdn = 3.6) in the level of the participants' self-reported leadership skills, z = 3.037, p < .05, r = .42. This change indicates that participants perceived their leadership ability and effectiveness as greater than before the Butterfly programme.

Effect sizes for all presented changes are illustrated in Figure 27.

4.4.5 Quantitative long-term changes

4.4.5.1 Inclusion of Nature in Self (INS)

Butterfly participants reported a significantly higher level of interconnectedness with nature at posttest (Mdn = 6), thus right after the Butterfly programme, than at pretest (Mdn = 5), shortly before the start of the Butterfly programme, z = 3.67, p < .05, r = .51. The effect size[42] indicates a large increase in the participants' perceived interconnectedness with nature right after the programme.

Between posttest (Mdn = 6) and posttest III (Mdn = 5) no significant difference was found, z = -1.852, p > .05, r = -.3. Nevertheless, the associated effect size indicates a medium-sized decrease in the perceived level of interconnectedness with nature between the two measurement points. The boxplots in Figure 28 imply that the level of interconnectedness declined between posttest and posttest III.

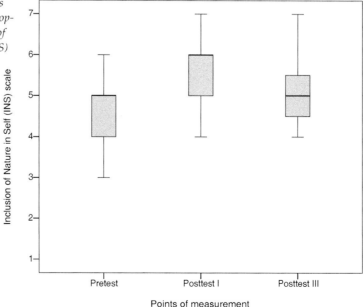

Figure 28. Boxplots depicting the development of Inclusion of Nature in Self (INS) across time.

---

42   Effect sizes r are interpreted according to Cohen (1988).

However, the level of interconnectedness one and a half years after the programme (Mdn = 5) still represents a change (r = .29) in the perceived level of interconnectedness compared to the initial level at pretest (Mdn = 5), suggesting that there was no decline back to the original level of interconnectedness, z = 1.81, p > .05, r = .29. All p-values, effect sizes and sample sizes are depicted in Table 31.

4.4.5.2 Proenvironmental Behaviour (PEB)

There was no significant difference in the participants' proenvironmental behaviour at pretest (Mdn = 3.6) and at posttest II (Mdn = 3.9), z = .959, p > .05, r = .16. However, the effect size indicates a small change between both measurement points, supported by the difference reflected in the medians, towards an increase of proenvironmental behaviour (see Figure 29).

Also proenvironmental behaviour did not significantly differ between posttest II (Mdn = 3.9) and posttest III (Mdn = 3.9), z = .828, p > .05, r = .15. Nevertheless, the effect size, again, indicates a small increase in proenvironmental behaviour. Similarly, proenvironmental behaviour did not significantly differ between pretest (Mdn = 3.6) and posttest III (Mdn = 3.9), z = .719, p > .05, r = .12.

This indicates that there may have been a small but non-significant change in the participants' proenvironmental behaviour as measured via the PEB. At first glance this seems to contradict the interviewees' reports, which revealed a general increase in proenvironmental behaviour. However, possibly the increase could not manifest in the quantitative data due to a ceiling effect. After all, in the international comparison in Schultz et al.'s study (2005) the highest PEB mean was found for the German university student sample with M = 3.29. It is also important to note that the data are based on an international sample, which means that composting and recycling, for instance, as assessed via the PEB might have been realisable only to a limited extent in some countries.

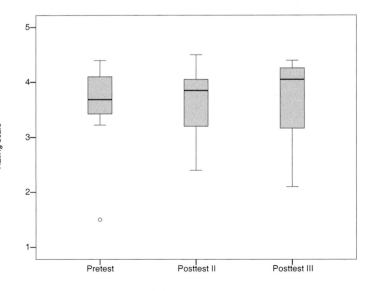

Figure 29. Boxplots depicting the development of proenvironmental behaviour (PEB scale) across time.

Furthermore, in the interviews Butterfly participants also reported an increase in their care for animals and plants as part of newly adopted proenvironmental behaviours. This exemplifies that the PEB naturally encompasses only a limited range of proenvironmental behaviours and therefore might not have addressed all of the relevant ones for the present sample. All p-values, effect sizes and sample sizes are depicted in Table 31.

4.4.5.3 Community participation

Butterfly participants reported a significantly higher level of participation[43] in their communities[44] two months after the Butterfly, at posttest II (Mdn = 5), than at pretest (Mdn = 6), z = -2.400, p< .05, and the increase was large (r = -.54). There was no significant difference in the level of community engagement between posttest II (Mdn = 5) and posttest III (Mdn = 6), z = .777 p >.05. However, a small effect size (r = .14) was detected which, together with the visual analysis of the boxplots (see Figure 30), suggests a small decline between posttest II and posttest III.

However, the level of the participants' community engagement one and a half years after the programme, at posttest III (Mdn = 6), was still significantly higher than at pretest (Mdn = 6), z = -2.116, p < .05. The effect size for the increase of engagement between the two measurement points is medium-sized (r = -.36). All p-values, effect sizes and sample sizes are depicted in Table 31.

The present pattern of participation therein suggests that the Butterfly programme caused an immediate and large increase in the participants' level of engagement, which then appears to have declined slightly one and a half years later. However, the decline does not reach back to the initial level of engagement but seems to balance out at a still significantly higher level of participation than before the programme.

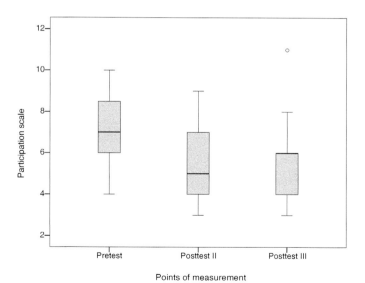

Figure 30. Boxplots depicting the development of community participation (ICRE scale) across time.

---

43 Community engagement is assessed via the Participation subscale of the Individual Community-Related Empowerment (ICRE) Scale
44 Higher levels of participation are reflected in lower scores on the scale.

4.4.5.4 Current contact with nature

There was no significant difference in the reported amount of current contact with nature between pretest (Mdn = 2) and posttest II (Mdn = 2), z = 0, p > .05. Equally, there was no significant difference in the amount of reported current contact with nature between posttest II (Mdn = 2) and posttest III (Mdn = 3), z = 0, p > .05 as well as between pretest and posttest III, z = .535, p > .05. All p-values, effect sizes and sample sizes are depicted in Table 31. Even though the results reflect no significant changes over time the median at pretest and posttest II indicates that participants declared the item "Lately, I have been spending a lot of time in nature" as "mostly true" (see Figure 31).

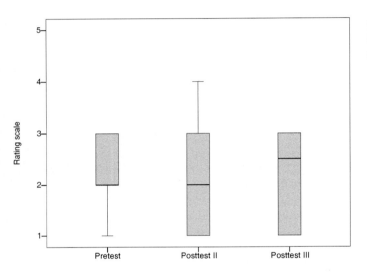

Figure 31. Boxplots depicting contact with nature across time.

Table 31

Overview of constructs, sample size, p-values and effect sizes

Construct	Measurement point comparison	N[a]	P – value	Effect size r
INS	Pre/ post I	19	.00	.51
	Post I/ post III	19	.064	-.30
	Pre/ post III	19	.07	.29
PEB	Pre/ post II	19	.337	.16
	Post II/ post III	16	.407	.15
	Pre/ post III	19	.472	.12
Participation (ICRE)	Pre/ post II	20	.016	.54
	Post II/ post III	15	.437	.14
	Pre/ post III	17	.034	-.36
Current nature contact	Pre/ post II	19	1.00	
	Post II/ post III	19	1.00	
	Pretest/ posttest III	19	.593	

Notes. N = sample size; INS = Inclusion of Nature in Self measure; PEB = Proenvironmental Behaviour Scale; ICRE = Individual Community-Related Empowerment Scale; [a] The number of cases may differ for the tests as conventionally only paired scores are included in the calculations.

This suggests that participants already spent a fair amount of time in nature before the Butterfly programme, which may explain why no significant change was detected over time. Nevertheless, the visual analysis shows that the distribution changed over time. That is, the variance seems to decrease. Thus, even though participants, on average, might not go out more often less participants report to go out very little.

This is an interesting result considering that spending time in nature is also highly dependent on weather, thus season. Notably, while pretest and posttest II measurements took place in summer and autumn posttest III was conducted in wintertime. In this context the fact that no significant decline in contact with nature was reported between summer and winter appears as a remarkable result itself. However, the lack of a control group allows for no further interpretation at this point.

4.4.5.5 Retrospective overall programme evaluation

One and a half years after the Butterfly programme I implemented three single items in the online survey in order to assess:
- how much the programme changed the participants' relationship with and perception of other people,
- how much the programme changed the participants' relationship with and perception of nature,
- and to which extent the programme influenced the participants' path of life.

The scale for all of the above items ranged from 1 (*not at all*) to 5 (*a great deal*). Table 32 shows that the overall trend of answers ranges between 4 and 5.

Figure 32 displays the associated boxplots conjointly visualising that Butterfly participants retrospectively, one and a half years later, categorised their experience of the Butterfly programme as highly influential regarding their relationship with nature, other people as well as their path of life. This result confirms the reports of the interviewees (N = 9), and suggests that the associated qualitative results also represent the trend in the larger Butterfly sample (N = 19) one and a half years after the programme ended.

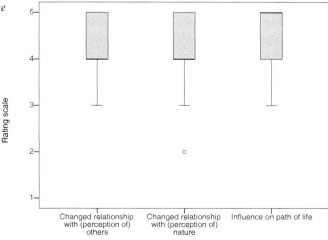

Figure 32. Boxplots for the rating of the overall programme evaluation items.

Table 32

Mean, standard deviation and median of overall programme evaluation items

Item	N	M (SD)	Mdn
Relationship with other people	19	4.32 (.67)	4
Relationship with nature	19	4.21 (.98)	4
Influence on path of life	19	4.37 (.83)	5

Notes. N = sample size; M (SD) = mean (standard deviation); Mdn = median.

4.4.6 Exploring quantitative patterns of change

Apart from a few designated exceptions[45] the reported patterns of change are based on multiple regression models and Kendall's tau (τ) correlations between the indicators of change, namely the differential values of the test scores[46]. Clearly, correlations with differential values only permit statements about the relationship between changes in variables and do not allow for statements about the direction of change. However, in the correlation analysis, I considered only the differential values of those of variables, which changed significantly over time or revealed a measurable effect size. Therefore, in these cases, I in fact knew the direction of change from the previous chapters where I presented medians, effects sizes and significance test results in detail. In this context, I will occasionally include the already captured direction of change in the reports of the correlations in order to bring together and thereby make sense of the thus far collected information.

As the long-term focus of this quantitative empirical work lay on changes in behaviour, namely proenvironmental behaviour and community engagement, the analysis of the correlations concentrated on this area.

The statistical exploration was specifically directed to significant associations between changes in the participants' relationship with nature and their proenvironmental behaviour and community engagement. However, emphasising the exploratory nature of this enquiry, I also considered meaningful emergent cross-links between variables just as potentially relevant relationships that I derived from the interview analysis.

4.4.6.1 Community engagement

Interestingly, the participants' change in community engagement[47] between pretest and posttest II (Δ Participation 1) was exclusively significantly related to the change in the participants' inclusion of nature in their sense of self between pretest and posttest (Δ INS), $\tau = -.42$, $p < .05$. The participants' change in community participation between pretest and posttest III (Δ Participation 2), on the other hand, was significantly related to how their connectedness to nature changed between pretest and posttest, $\tau = .41$, $p < .05$ (see Table 33).

---

45 Variables, which were only measured at one point in time are age, gender, residential area, time spent in nature during childhood, social desirability and sense of community. Furthermore, correlations and regression models that included proenvironmental behaviour are based on one-point measurement posttest values.
46 Differential values depict the difference between pre- and posttest scores and are symolised by the delta sign (Δ).
47 Community engagement is assessed via the Participation subscale of the Individual Community-Related Empowerment (ICRE) Scale.

Table 33

Significant correlations of community participation

	Δ Participation 1	Δ Participation 2
Δ Inclusion of Nature in Self (INS)	-.42* (.024)	
Δ Connectedness to Nature (CNS)		-.41* (.035)

Notes. Δ Inclusion of Nature in Self = differential value of INS (pretest/ posttest); Δ Connectedness to Nature = differential value of CNS (pretest/ posttest); Δ Participation 1 = differential value of Participation (pretest/ posttest II); Δ Participation 2 = differential value of Participation (pretest/ posttest III); * p < .05.

A potential contextualisation for this result can be derived from the qualitative results where interviewees revealed that their care for nature was often closely intertwined with the type of civic engagement they chose (e.g. outdoor education). Also it is important to note that connectedness to nature as measured by the CNS is related to the inclusion of nature in self as measured by the INS (Mayer & Frantz, 2004). This was found in previous studies and appears to be evident in this study, too. Despite the similarities of the two constructs previous research has also drawn attention to potential differences. The exact nature of these differences, however, is still subject to future research.

4.4.6.2 Proenvironmental behaviour

As proenvironmental behaviour (measured via the PEB Scale) appeared to be rather stable over time, thus the variance of this variable is small, I in this case refrained from analysing correlations between differential values but analysed associations between proenvironmental behaviour at posttest III and the values of the other constructs at posttest. The data revealed that the participants' proenvironmental behaviour one and a half years after the programme was significantly related to empowerment scales at posttest, namely the participants' intention for civic action, $\tau = .44$, $p < .05$, the participants interpersonal problem-solving skills, $\tau = .5$, $p < .01$ and the participants' leadership skills, $\tau = .46$, $p < .01$. Moreover, proenvironmental behaviour at posttest III was significantly related to how much participants incorporated the active problem-solving style (GEP scale) as a way to cope with environmental problems at posttest, $\tau = .35$, $p < .05$, to how much they engaged in their local communities two months after the programme, $\tau = -.39$, $p < .05$ and to the participants' inclusion of nature in their sense of self at posttest, $\tau = .47$, $p < .05$.

To examine the underlying patterns more closely I performed a hierarchical regression analysis. Two variables predicted the participants' proenvironmental behaviour one and a half years after the Butterfly programme significantly well. The predictors were Inclusion of Nature in Self and Leadership Skills at posttest.

In order to test whether the assumptions of a multiple regression were met, an analysis of standard residuals was carried out, which showed that the data contained no outliers (Std. Residual Min. = -2.22, Std. Residual Max. = 1.47). Tests to see if the data met the assumption of collinearity indicated that multicollinearity was not a concern (INS, Tolerance = .98, VIF = 1.02; Leadership Skills, Tolerance = .98, VIF = 1.02). Also the data met the assumption of independent errors (Durbin-Watson value = 2). The normal P-P

Table 34

Significant correlations with proenvironmental behaviour

	Civic action posttest	Interpersonal problem-solving skills posttest	Leadership skills posttest	Problem Solving (GEP) posttest	Partici-pation scale posttest II	INS posttest
PEB at posttest III	.44* (.011)	.46** (.003)	.46** (.009)	.35* (.041)	-.39* (.041)	.47* (.014)

Notes. PEB = Proenvironmental Behaviour scale; GEP = Coping with Global Environmental Problems measure; INS = Inclusion of Nature in Self scale; * p < .05, ** p < .01.

plot of standardised residuals, which showed points that were not completely on the line, but close, indicated that the data contained approximately normally distributed errors.

At step I Inclusion of Nature in Self contributed significantly to the regression model, $F (1, 17) = 6.04$, $p < .05$ and accounted for 26% of the variation in proenvironmental behaviour at posttest III. Introducing the variable Leadership Skills at posttest explained an additional 20% and this change in R^2 was significant, $F (2, 16) = 6.96$, $p < .01$. Together the two predictors explained 40% (adjusted R^2) of the variation in proenvironmental behaviour at posttest III (see Table 35).

The pattern that presents itself in the correlations indicates that engagement in one area is also associated with engagement in other areas. Moreover, proenvironmental behaviour or engagement one and a half years later was associated with the general readiness or intention right after the programme to socially engage in the future, as well as with a problem-focused and action-centered coping style regarding environmental problems. This supports previous research findings that found the Problem Solving subscale to be, indeed, associated with actual proenvironmental behaviour (Homburg *et al.*, 2007).

However, a further salient element of the correlations in this area is the interrelational aspect. This is reflected in the correlations of proenvironmental behaviour with improved interpersonal skills as well as with the participants' altered way of relating to nature after the programme, that is having integrated nature more deeply as part of their sense of self.

The latter relationship supports research findings (e.g. Kals, 1999), which indicate that the depth of our personal relationship with nature does, indeed, predict proenvironmental behaviour. This is also confirmed by the qualitative data where the participants' experience of their emotional interconnectedness with nature was named as a decisive trigger for changes in their proenvironmental behaviour after the programme.

The interpersonal element, on the other hand, possibly represents the social dimension of proenvironmental behaviour. In this context, it is particularly interesting that the associated variables are Leadership Skills and Interpersonal Problem-Solving Skills. Within the scope of the small sample size and its specificity this finding may be interpreted as a highlighted link between proenvironmental behaviour and the individual's ability to take the initiative and to act as a role model. Taking into account that green behaviour is not necessarily a mainstream practice it is easily conceivable that leadership skills or at least the associated self-ascribed competences as well as commu-

Table 35

Multiple regression model for the participants' proenvironmental behaviour one and a half years after the Butterfly programme

	B	SE B	β
Step I			
Constant	0.3	1.34	
Inclusion of Nature in Self (posttest I)	0.58	0.24	.51*
Step II			
Constant	-1.16	1.31	
Inclusion of Nature in Self (posttest I)	0.5	0.21	.44*
Leadership Skills (posttest I)	0.53	0.22	.46*

Notes. R^2 = .26 for step I, ΔR^2 = .20 for step II (p < .05); B = beta value; SE B = standard error of beta value; β = standardised β; * p < .05.

nication, cooperation and problem-solving skills are required in order to stick with this kind of behaviour in other social contexts (see also chapter 2.1.4).

After all, both elements, the nature-related and interpersonal, accounted for 40% (adjusted R^2) of the variation in the participants' proenvironmental behaviour one and a half years after their Butterfly experience.

Notably, the importance of both elements emerged already in the qualitative section, where triggers of action were reported to root in the participants' nature experiences but also in their experiences with others (see 4.4.3.5).

4.4.6.3 Activism, concern for the environment and nature connectedness

The participants' level of concern for the environment, which changed significantly over the course of the programme (see 4.4.4.2), did not significantly correlate with proenvironmental behaviour.

However, the change in the participants' level of concern for the environment was significantly related to the participants' change in their level of connectedness to nature, τ = .35, p < .05, to the change in their sense of responsibility, τ = .38, p < .05, and to the change in their sense of belonging to a group, τ = .34, p < .05.

Notably, this again seems to pick up on the twofold relationship that I touched on in the section regarding proenvironmental behaviour. While environmental concern is associated with the participants' sense of connectedness to nature it is also associated with their ascribed importance to belonging to the Butterfly group and with the increased importance of personal reliability, thus responsibility, as a behaviour guiding value.

This may be interpreted in a number of ways. Firstly, environmental concern is likely to have been part of the social norm in the Butterfly group, which is why it may correlate with the increased importance of belonging to and being a reliable part of the group.

Alternatively, however, the increased importance of belonging and responsibility may reflect a form of empowerment, in the sense that participants felt that they belonged to a group and perceived their own responsibility as a part of it, which in turn allowed them to give way to their environmental concern. The latter explanation refers

Table 36

Significant correlations for activism, concern for the environment and nature connectedness

	INS	Δ CNS	Δ Belonging	Δ Responsibility
Proenvironmental Behaviour (PEB) posttest III	.47**a (.014)			
Participation	-.42*b (.024)	-.41*c (.035)		
Δ Concern for the Environment		.35* (.024)	.34* (.031)	.38* (.016)

Notes. INS = Inclusion of Nature in Self; Δ CNS = differential value of Connectedness to Nature Scale (pretest/posttest); Δ Belonging = differential value of Belonging (pretest/ posttest); Δ Responsibility = differential value of Responsibility (pretest/ posttest); Δ Concern for the Environment = differential value of Concern for the Environment (pretest/ posttest); [a] correlation with INS at posttest; [b] correlation between Δ INS (pretest/ posttest) and Δ Participation (pretest/ posttest II); [c] correlations with Δ Participation (pretest/ posttest III); * p < .05.

to Lazarus' protection-motivation theory (Lazarus, 1966), which expects people who perceive high threats and low coping ability to turn to emotion-focused coping, such as normalising or denying the situation, whereas people who perceive high threats and high coping will utilise a problem-solving approach. Applied to this outcome, people who felt empowered by being part of a group could cope with higher concern for the environment and would not need to deny it.

Of course, an explanation for these correlations can as well lie in a combination of the previous two.

When investigating the relationship between environmental concern and action, the change in the participants' rational concern for the environment was neither significantly associated with reported proenvironmental behaviour nor with changes in community engagement. This is an interesting result, as it appears only natural to assume that social and proenvironmental engagement increases with the individual's increase of concern. However, variables that, indeed, were significantly related to both measures of engagement were the changes in the participants' emotional connectedness to nature and in the way they started to perceive nature more strongly as a part of their self. This may indicate that the emotional and cognitive proximity to nature in this sample has a different impact on the individual than the rational understanding that nature is in danger. That is, the emotional closeness to nature relates to actual behaviour whereas heightened concern for the environment does not.

4.4.6.4 Coping with environmental problems

Regarding changes in the way participants responded to and coped with global environmental problems two strategies increased the most, namely Relativization and Problem Solving (see chapter 4.4.4.1). For both coping styles, changes between pretest and posttest were significantly related to the participants' changes in various constructs representing nature connectedness (see Table 37).

However, over and above the correlations with nature connectedness, the GEP subscale Problem Solving was additionally significantly related to hope, gratitude and the participants' sense of responsibility as a behaviour guiding value between pretest and posttest (see Table 37).

Based on the high correlations I decided to run a hierarchical regression analysis with the variables Responsibility and Gratitude as predictors.

Table 37

Significant correlations with two styles of coping with environmental problems

	INS	CNS	Responsibility	Gratitude	Hope
Problem Solving	.33* (.037)	.34* (.022)	.5** (.001)	.39** (.009)	.37* (.01)
Relativization	.43* (.013)	.33* (.034)			

Notes. INS = Inclusion of Nature in Self scale; CNS = Connectedness to Nature Scale; * p < .05, ** p < .01.

Table 38

Multiple regression model for the coping style Problem Solving

	B	SE B	β
Step I			
Constant	0.01	0.12	
Responsibility	0.21	0.06	.60**
Step II			
Constant	-0.1	0.11	
Responsibility	0.17	0.06	.47**
Gratitude	0.08	0.03	.44*

Notes. R^2 = .36 for step I, ΔR^2 =.16 for step II (p < .01); B = beta value; SE B = standard error of beta value; β = standardised β; * p < .05; ** p < .01.

In order to test whether the assumptions of a multiple regression were met an analysis of standard residuals was carried out, which showed that the data contained no outliers (Std. Residual Min. = -1.77, Std. Residual Max. = 2.27). Tests to see if the data met the assumption of collinearity indicated that multicollinearity was not a concern (Responsibility, Tolerance = 1, VIF = 1; Gratitude, Tolerance = .9, VIF = 1.11). Also the data met the assumption of independent errors (Durbin-Watson value = 2.06). As the normal P-P plot of standardised residuals showed points that were close to the line the visual analysis indicated that the data contained approximately normally distributed errors.

The multiple regression revealed that at step I, the change in the participants' responsibility contributed significantly to the regression model, F (1, 23) = 12.83, p < .01 and accounted for 36% of the variation in the participants' change in Problem Solving. Introducing the participants' change in Gratitude as a further variable explained an additional 16% and this change in R^2 was significant, F (2, 22) = 12, p < .01. Together the two predictors explained 48% (adjusted R^2) of the variation in the participants' change in the coping style Problem Solving (see Table 38).

To summarise, the coping style Relativization represents the individual's belief that solutions will manifest despite discrepancies between the actual and target state and in the literature this style is found to be one of the few coping styles that correlates negatively with stress (Homburg *et al.*, 2007). As it turned out in this study, Relativization was associated with INS and the CNS. This may indicate that the increase of connectedness with nature is associated with the need to believe that "everything will work out fine" possibly as a kind of self-protective mechanism.

However, the increase of the deproblematisation-focused coping style Relativization was accompanied by an increase of the problem-focused and action-centered coping style Problem Solving which has been shown to correlate with proenvironmental behaviour in past research (Homburg *et al.*, 2007). Clearly, the simultaneous increase of both coping styles may seem conflicting at the first glance. However, as Relativization stands for the belief that "things will work out" it reduces stress and may allow for the preservation of a positive outlook towards the future, similar to hope. Nevertheless, the experienced change in Relativization was not related to the participants' change in their level of hope but hope was, indeed, associated with their changes in the utilisation of Problem Solving. Thus, while nature connection was associated with both Relativization and Problem Solving, the participants' change in hope was exclusively related to their change in Problem Solving.

The simultaneous increase of Relativization and Problem Solving over the course of the programme, as well as the association between hope and Problem Solving, may point towards the importance of maintaining a positive outlook on the future in the face of global environmental problems, as hinted at in the associated literature (see chapter 2.1.2).

Correspondingly, the regression model revealed that Problem Solving could be best explained by the participants' sense of responsibility but also by gratitude. Responsibility, as assessed in the present study, reflects the degree to which participants' felt that being reliable and trustworthy as well as meeting obligations guided their behaviour during the Butterfly. Furthermore, the Gratitude scale captured the participants' awareness of positive things in their lives and how well they were able to expressively acknowledge this. It can be seen that the participants' increase in their sense of responsibility and their increase in their gratitude in life throughout the Butterfly predicted their increase in the action-centered coping style Problem Solving. Notably, this again brings up the previously touched on positive outlook on life and its potential importance for action-centered coping strategies in the face of fear and uncertainty.

4.4.6.5 Values, beliefs and attitudes

Aiming to understand responsibility better I investigated associations with the change in the participants' sense of responsibility as a behaviour guiding value. The analysis revealed significant relations to indicators of nature connectedness, such as to the change in the participants' feelings of freedom in nature, $\tau = .34$, $p < .05$, in their feelings of oneness with nature, $\tau = .39$, $p < .05$, in the inclusion of nature in their sense of self, $\tau = .34$, $p < .05$, but also in their level of hope, $\tau = .36$, $p < .05$ (see Table 39).

Notably, the connection between responsibility and nature already emerged in the qualitative interview data as a trigger for activism. Here, interviewees indicated that their intimate experience and relationship with nature heightened their sense of responsibility and thereby brought about personal engagement as potentially reflected in the correlations between Problem Solving, nature connectedness, gratitude and responsibility and as evident in the following quote:

> *Now I just feel more aware of my responsibility, or yes, more aware. Not just more responsibility but a greater awareness for my responsibility. [...] Because I did this Solo in nature and because that* [Solo] *spot sheltered me during that time and I was allowed to stay there [...]. Because of that it felt like, Yes, now, this is my "counter-responsibility" for having been allowed to stay there* [Solo spot] (BF8).

Moreover, interviewees reported that their personal encounter with nature strengthened their self-confidence. In line with this, correlations with changes in the partici-

Table 39

Significant correlations with the participants' gain of responsibility

	Feelings of Freedom in Nature	Feelings of Oneness with Nature	Inclusion of Nature in Self	Hope
Responsibility	.34* (.039)	.39* (.015)	.34* (.046)	.36* (.015)

Note. * p < .05.

Table 40

Significant correlations with participants' increase of self-efficacy

	Feelings of oneness with nature	Hope
Self-efficacy	-.41** (.007)	-.34* (.018)

Notes. * p < .05, ** p < .01.

pants' self-efficacy[48] revealed a similar pattern. Hence, the change in the participants' self-efficacy was significantly related to the change in their feelings of oneness with nature, $\tau = .41$, $p < .01$, but also to the change in their level of hope, $\tau = -.34$, $p < .05$ (see Table 40). Notably, self-confidence, as a result of the participants' nature experience, also emerged as a facilitator for action in the interview data (see 4.3.5).

Evidently, the variable that constantly reappeared throughout the correlation analysis was hope. Hope particularly attracted attention, as it was often associated with variables that were identified as potentially relevant facilitators of engagement either via the qualitative or via the quantitative enquiry.

Firstly, as mentioned above, the participants' change in hope was significantly related to their change in self-efficacy, $\tau = -.34$, $p < .05$, as well as to their change in their sense of responsibility, $\tau = .36$, $p < .05$. Furthermore, the change in hope was significantly related to the change in the participants' application of problem solving, $\tau = .3$, $p < .05$, and to the change in their activation of self-protection[49] as a coping style with environmental problems, $\tau = .36$, $p < .05$. Notably, both coping styles are problem-focused and action-centered coping styles which are known to correlate with proenvironmental behaviour (Homburg et al., 2007) and which oppose strategies such as denial.

However, the participants' change in hope was also associated with changes in their feelings of oneness with nature, $\tau = .33$, (.031) $p < .05$, their capacity for love, $\tau = .45$, $p < .01$, their reported sense of community within the Butterfly group, $\tau = .41$, $p < .01$, and gratitude, $\tau = .37$, $p < .05$ (see Table 41).

While capacity for love[50] and sense of community seem to tap into the community experience of the participants, the feeling of oneness with nature clearly relates to the participants' nature experience as part of the programme. Gratitude for life on the other hand encompasses the participants' general attitude towards life. Notably, these

---

48 The ICRE Self-Efficacy scale simultaneously assesses self-confidence (see the description in chapter 4.3.5.1) and is reversely rated which accounts for the negative correlations.
49 The Self-Protection subscale represents the degree to which a person exhibits healthy behaviour as a way of coping with environmental problems for instance via avoiding polluted areas.
50 Capacity of Love represents valuing relationships, which include reciprocally sharing and caring for each other.

	Hope
Self-efficacy	-.34* (.018)
Responsibility	.36* (.015)
Problem solving	.3* (.010)
Self-protection	.36* (.017)
Feelings of oneness with nature	.33* (.031)
Capacity for love	.45** (.003)
Sense of community	.41** (.004)
Gratitude	.37* (.014)

Notes. * p < .05, ** p < .01.

Table 41
Significant correlations with the participants' increase of hope

variables[51] changed significantly over the course of the programme and were significantly related to the participants' change in their level of hope.

Indeed, though indirectly, hope appeared in the qualitative data where participants brought up role models and community living as experiences that enabled them to start to believe in the practicability of change in the world (see 4.4.2). Also the experience of deep relationships with humans and nature generated a substantial amount of emotions and, ultimately, of positivity in the participants as evident in the following quote:

> *Coming here has opened my mind, it has followed my heart and I have been SO happy at times and really quiet emotional and sad, you know. Yesterday I felt as if I had to keep stopping myself of crying and it was crying with [...] happiness, with love for my surroundings and my family. And [...] gratefulness for the opportunity to come here and to experience this LOVE that I felt in myself. And [...] this gives me so much hope for the future and I see my future very bright. And I'm looking forward to my future. And before, as I said, it was very DARK and NEGATIVE and did not have much hope* (B5).

The participants' increase of their overall level of hope throughout the programme may be explained by an argument Nicholsen (2002) made in her book *The Love of Nature and the End of the World: The Unspoken Dimension of Environmental Concern*. Here, she states that a "holding environment" is an important requirement for people to be ready to admit feelings. According to Nicholsen, this "holding environment" may be found in mentors, family or friends. In the context of the qualitative results it appears sensible to also consider adding nature to this list. After all, the qualitative outcomes revealed that the participants' experience of emotional interconnectedness with nature was essential for them in order to be able to open up. Various times participants explained their gain of self-access with the emotional state that nature evoked in them, namely feeling in harmony, calm, home and protected.

Possibly, it was the participants' nature and community experiences that provided a "holding environment" and prevented disempowerment despite the growing awareness for the generally difficult global situation as reflected in the simultaneous significant increase in the participants' environmental concern.

---

51 With the exception of sense of community, which was only rated once, at the end of the programme.

It is imaginable that participants instead drew hope from their experiences of being part of a strong and supportive group as well as from their sense of connection with the natural world, hence the association between hope and capacity for love, gratitude and feelings of oneness with nature. Furthermore, the hope springing from these empowering experiences may have supported participants in their ability to enter into a stronger engagement with the world, hence the association between hope and the participants' sense of responsibility, problem solving, self-protection and self-efficacy.

4.4.6.6 Sense of community

Because the Butterfly programme placed great emphasis on building a sense of community with nature but also with other people, I asked Butterfly participants to rate their perceived sense of community in the Butterfly group at the end of the Butterfly programme.

Looking at the relationship between the previously presented change variables and the participants' sense of community in the group seems important in order to identify those areas of change which are actually associated with this aspect of the programme.

The analysis of correlations revealed that the reported sense of community in the Butterfly group was significantly related to how much the participants' level of trust in others and life changed between pre- and posttest, $\tau = .34$, $p < .05$, as well as their level of hope, $\tau = .41$, $p < .01$, their level of gratitude for life, $\tau = .43$, $p < .01$, and their capacity for love regarding others, $\tau = .48$, $p < .01$. Furthermore, their sense of community was significantly related to the participants' gain of leadership skills between pretest and posttest, $\tau = .38$, $p < .05$.

However, the participants' sense of community in the Butterfly group was also significantly related to how much they changed in the degree of inclusion of nature in their sense of self between pretest and posttest, $\tau = .36$, $p < .05$.

While the associations with trust, gratitude, capacity for love, leadership skills and hope (see previous section) are rather self-explanatory, the correlation with INS seems to call for further consideration.

It is apparent that the sense of community in the Butterfly group was related to how interconnected participants felt with nature. Of course it is conceivable that this connection merely represents a simultaneous increase as a result of the simultaneous experience of both interconnectedness with others and with nature as part of the programme. Moreover, it is possible that the sense of community again represents an underlying social norm that promoted the interconnectedness with nature as part of the group identity (see 2.1.5).

However, the correlation may also indicate that the increasing feeling of interconnectedness with nature facilitated a sense of community in the group and vice versa,

Table 42

Significant correlations with the participants' sense of community

	Δ Trust	Δ Hope	Δ Gratitude	Δ Capacity for love	Δ Leadership skills	Δ INS
Sense of community	.34*	.41**	.43**	.48**	.38*	.36*

Notes. Δ = differential value (pretest/ posttest); INS = Inclusion of Nature in Self measure; * p < .05, ** p < .01.

reflecting the interconnectedness of all living systems as already touched on in chapter 4.4.3.5. Notably, parallels between the experience of interconnectedness with others and nature as well as between the associated psychological processes of attaining self access already became visible in the qualitative data. Opening up to one's own internal world and recognising oneself in the other or nature appeared as a common and similar process. Possibly, these experiences facilitated awareness for interconnectedness in general, which does not distinguish between nature and others but encompasses the whole of life and all living things.

Inevitably, the investigation of the relationship between interconnectedness with others and interconnectedness with nature constitutes a fascinating subject and calls for further research in the future.

4.4.7 The influence of the control variables

The control variable Residential Area correlated with none of the relevant differential values.

All significant correlations between the remaining control variables and the relevant differential values are presented in Table 43.

Evidently, the slight increase on the GEP subscale Resignation[52] was significantly related to how old participants were, $\tau = .33$, $p < .05$, and to how much time they had spent in nature during their childhood, $\tau = .37$, $p < .05$. This suggests that the increase of resignation in the face of environmental problems is associated with older participants and also with those who had spent less time in nature during their childhood.

Moreover, the increase on the Inclusion of Nature in Self (INS) measure between pre- and posttest (Δ INS) was significantly related to how old participants were, $\tau = -.33$, $p < .05$, indicating that younger participants were associated with greater change in this area. The increase on the Inclusion of Nature in Self (INS) Scale between pre- and posttest III (Δ INS 2), on the other hand, was negatively correlated with social desirability, $\tau = -.39$, $p < .05$, revealing that greater reported change between pretest and posttest III is associated with lower scores on the Social Desirability Scale (SDS). Accordingly, social desirability appears to not have threatened the validity of the results.

Furthermore, gender was significantly correlated with the increase of hope, $\tau = -.36$, $p < .05$, and gratitude, $\tau = -.36$, $p < .05$. As gender is coded with zero for male and one for female participants, the negative correlation indicates that males reported greater change in hope and gratitude between pretest and posttest.

Indeed, this is supported by the boxplots for hope at pre- and posttest split by gender (see Figure 33).

The visual analysis revealed that male participants started out at a considerably lower level of hope than female participants. However, the level of hope in female and male participants appears to assimilate at posttest I.

A similar situation can be observed when comparing gratitude at pre- and posttest split by gender (see Figure 34).

---

52   Resignation measures how strongly a person believes that environmental problems are unchangeable.

Table 43

Significant correlations between control variables and relevant differential values

	Sex	Age	Childhood time in nature	Social desirability
Δ Hope	-.36*			
Δ Gratitude	-.36*			
Δ Resignation		.33*	.37*	
Δ INS		-.33*		
Δ INS 2				-.39*

Notes. Δ = differential value (pretest/ posttest); INS = Inclusion of Nature in Self measure; Δ INS 2 = differential value of Inclusion of Nature in Self (pretest/ posttest III); * $p < .05$.

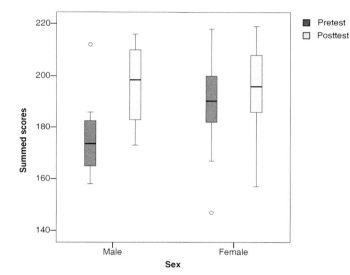

Figure 33. Boxplots for change of hope over time split by gender.

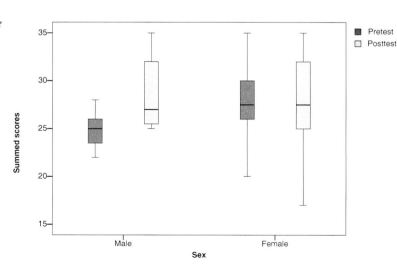

Figure 34. Boxplots for change of gratitude over time split by gender.

5

Intuitive dream enquiry

5.1 Introduction

As part of the evaluation of the Butterfly Programme I collected nocturnal dreams of the participants and myself during programme time. These dreams represent the foundation for the dream study, which I will present and examine in the following section. As dreams are a rather unconventional data source in evaluation research, I will briefly contextualise the approach within the philosophy of science followed by a short introduction to relevant dream research findings.

The prevailing conception of science and research is primarily dominated by empiricism. According to this positivist approach, knowledge is foremost based on sensory experiences and relies on observation and experiments as the method of choice. This appears useful in a large variety of scientific fields where the main objective is to discover general principles in outer relations, to predict and to control. As a consequence, however, domains of enquiry remain limited, just like the degree of depth to which certain aspects of human experience can be understood (Braud & Anderson, 1998).

The philosopher and mathematician Bertrand Russell illustrates this circumstance with a paradox. He points out that on one hand ordinary perception serves as the foundation for the constitution of physical theories but at the same time, and paradoxically, these generated physical theories do not seem to reflect everyday perception, which is full of interpretation and thus meaning (Russell, 2007).

Russell's work was greatly influenced by the philosopher and founder of American psychology William James, who put forth an epistemology, which he called radical empiricism. To James experiences were not mere derivatives of sensory data but a complex process full of meaning. James highlighted the circumstance that we experience the world as embedded and acting agents and therefore he considered experiences in all their variety of content as valid objects of study, not only including physical and mental phenomena but also the interconnections between them and their inner reflections (James, 1890). James was concerned about the general trend that leads away from concrete experience into abstract conceptual analysis for he felt that it is in concrete experience that deeper features of reality can be grasped (James, 1911).

The ecopsychologists Kerr and Key (2011) illustrate the limitations of the fields of study within the positivist paradigm by drawing upon Jahn and Dunne's model of mind-matter interactions (Jahn & Dunne, 2001).

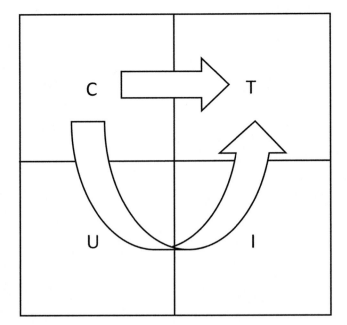

Figure 35. Kerr and Key's adaptation (2011) of Jahn and Dunne's (2001) model of mind-matter interactions. C = Conscious mind. U = Unconcious mind. I = Intangible events and processes of the physical world. T = Tangible events and processes of the physical world. Kerr & Key (2011) after Jahn & Dunne (2001).

As depicted in Figure 35 the positivist approach uses the conscious (C) mind to tackle tangible (T) events and processes of the physical world, which is represented by the two quadrants above the central x-axis. Hereby, everything which takes place in the unconscious (U) mind remains unacknowledged as well as intangible (I) events and processes of the physical world, as shown in the two quadrants below the central x-axis. Therefore, the area below the x-axis represents all the aspects of a psychological phenomenon, which remain disregarded and are somewhat difficult to assess limiting oneself to a positivist approach. Furthermore, the model implies that knowledge of a phenomenon acquired through the positivist approach might not be as complete as it seems, as the internal processes below the x-axis are entirely neglected yet part of the phenomenon as a whole. Indeed, as psychologist and philosopher Harald Walach (2014) laid out aptly, the positivist assumption that consciousness is only secondary to material processes has in fact by no means been proved.

When taking these considerations into account naturally methodological questions arise. Tapping the unconscious and intangible processes and then retrieving the gathered information back into the realm of the tangible physical world and conscious mind unquestionably poses a challenge for research and demands an innovative methodology (Kerr & Key, 2011).

This challenge is tackled in heuristic research where information originating from intuitions, dreams and imagery is deliberately included in the research process as valid data on a phenomenon. Thereby, it is aspired to perform this very movement as illustrated by the bent arrow in Figure 35.

However, before further elaborating the method, it seems valuable to gain a deeper understanding of dreams themselves. Therefore, research findings of relevant dream features and their application are briefly outlined in the following.

One of the most striking questions regarding dreams may be the question of their purpose. In dream research there is a fair amount of literature on the function of dreams yet, up until today, this mystery has not entirely been solved. There are, however, some aspects of dreaming which enjoy a good amount of scientific evidence.

It is assumed that dreams serve the activation and recombination of memories (Stickgold, Hobson, Fosse, & Fosse, 2001) as well as memory consolidation (Hobson, 1994). Moreover, outcomes of neuroimaging studies suggest that the brain is biased towards emotional processing during the REM (rapid eye movement) stage of sleeping, which is one of the well-known sleep stages correlated with dreaming (Stickgold *et al.*, 2001). The notion of emotional processing is also supported by studies on dreams. A study on dreams of traumatised children for instance showed that children with trauma experience more severe threats in dreams as opposed to non-traumatised or less traumatised children (Valli *et al.*, 2005).

This brings forth another feature of dreams, which is the selectiveness of the dream production mechanism. Over several years dream researchers Strauch and Meier (1996) collected a large body of dreams in their sleep laboratory and analysed over 500 REM dreams to learn about common features of dreaming regarding images, thoughts, and emotions.

In one study they examined 112 dreams in regard to references to the laboratory situation test persons were exposed to. They found that references were present in nearly every second dream. Not only did the dreams prefer laboratory stimuli from preceding days but they also showed the emotions that were triggered accordingly. When reviewing the temporal sources of dream elements, Strauch and Meier (1996) identified an intelligible dominance of day residues in the constitution of dreams, that is people, settings and objects from preceding days. It was shown that the occurrence of elements dating further back decreases in the dreams. Moreover, Strauch and Meier (1996) discovered in another experiment that personal matters of immediate concern were more easily induced into a dream than abstract attributes.

Another intriguing finding from their laboratory was extracted through the examination of dreams of children and youth. The data revealed that dreams reflect developmental stages, as the dream world transforms with the development of thinking and imagination. Strauch and Meier (1996) give the example of the development of self-image in children, which appears to be a prerequisite before a child can take an active role in its dream as well.

Evidently, dreams are not a mere product of chance but consist of the dreamer's subjective perspective on self and the world as well as of the dreamer's knowledge pool and preceding experiences.

But it is not only the experiences during wakefulness that influence the dream. Vice versa dreams also influence the mood of the individual after waking up (Schredl, 2000). Studies revealed that people tend to believe that dreams contain meaningful information and engage in motivated interpretation of their dreams which in turn impact their everyday lives (Morewedge & Norton, 2009).

Strauch and Meier (1996) emphasise in their summary the creative and surprising aspect of dreams as dreams combine waking experiences, memories and emotions, reorganise them and thereby recreate a novel internal reality and fresh experience for the dreamer. It is on this plane that they suggest that reviewing a dream's meaning might contribute to problem-solving and the understanding of waking experiences.

As a matter of fact, considerations like this are supported by anecdotes on the origination of several famous scientific discoveries (see Barrett, 2001). A well-known example is the discovery of the structure of benzene, the fundament of all aromatic substances by August Kekulé. Not only once did he gain insight on his subject of research through the content of his dreams. Kekulé himself described how he fell asleep at his desk one night and dreamt of the alchemistic symbol, the Ouroboros snake, a snake, which bites its own tail. This image brought about the long-desired solution for his research problem and led him to his vision of the structure of the benzene (Schultz, 1890).

Remarkably, it is only recently that these reports and associated implications attract interest to further investigate sleep and insight. Wagner, Gais, Haider, Verleger and Born (2004) set up an inventive experiment where subjects were asked to perform a cognitive task. In order to succeed test persons needed to learn stimulus-response sequences. They could either improve gradually by increasing response speed or abruptly by detecting a hidden rule underlying the sequences. The training of the task was then either followed by eight hours of nocturnal sleep, nocturnal wakefulness or daytime wakefulness. Wagner *et al.* found that more than twice as many test persons gained insight into the underlying rule after sleeping as after wakefulness and thus concluded that sleep inspires insight and facilitates the extraction of explicit knowledge by restructuring memory representations.

Even though the anecdotes of the above mentioned scientific insights mostly refer to the content of the scientist's dream, to date insight is primarily investigated in relation to the more general realm of sleeping.

Nevertheless, it appears to be particularly the aspect of dreaming that fascinates humans by their ability to offer insight through meaning-making. By reflecting dreams, aspects of being can be brought to consciousness that are otherwise difficult to tackle during wakefulness. This might be supported by the dream's characteristic to provide a setting free of challenges as social desirability, duties and self-censorship (Strauch & Meier, 1996).

For this reason dreams have also proved to be useful in therapeutic settings (e.g. Hill, Diemer, Hess, Hillyer, & Seeman, 1993). A famous pioneer in this field was the psychiatrist and founder of the analytic psychology C. G. Jung, who saw great therapeutic potential in dreams and ascribed to them a disclosing function and the ability to self-heal (Roesler, 2010). Up until today, by virtue of the dream's resourcefulness in the way it contextualises and reveals information on the emotional state of the dreamer psychotherapists found them beneficial in psychotherapy and in gaining self-knowledge (Hartmann, 1996).

This kind of utilisation seems to tap into an old cross-cultural heritage. Dreams have forever intrigued philosophers, physicians, writers and peoples around the world and veritably, the concept of gathering insight through dreams dates far back in history. In ancient cultures like Egypt, Greece, Mesopotamia and Rome dream interpretation was even considered a sophisticated art, which was applied when guidance for a particular problem was needed (Hughes, 2000).

5.2 Distilling the objective of the dream study

It is intriguing that the dreamer is the sole inventor of the dream yet the very inventor is unable to deliberately choose the dream's theme (Strauch & Meier, 1996). Seen from this perspective, dreams are indeed experiences that spring from the quadrants below the x-axis and emerge back into consciousness. This characteristic of dreams appears especially interesting when viewing dreams as a potential data source for research as it discloses information that is usually hard to access.

Nevertheless, it is important to note that although dreams are highly personal they also bear a collective dimension. People experience the world, they dream of their experiences in the world, and over and above everyone in the world dreams. As specified by Strauch and Meier (1996), "Dreams always have an individual touch as they reflect a dreamer's personality and life situation but dreams also bear a collective imprint because people are comparable in thinking, feeling, and behaviour and under certain conditions have similar experiences" (p.181).

Coming from a different field of study, the American mythologist Joseph Campbell followed a similar track. He studied myths and religion and particularly the human desire to create stories and images. In doing this, he discovered universal motifs and themes across time and cultures. In his corresponding book *The Hero with a Thousand Faces* (2008) he presents an intriguing analogy, where he calls myths depersonalised dreams and vice versa states that individual dreams are personalised myths. As Joseph Campbell further elaborates (2008):

> *Both myth and dream are symbolic in the same general way of the dynamics of the psyche. But in the dream the forms are quirked by the peculiar troubles of the dreamer, whereas in myth the problems and solutions are shown directly valid for all mankind*[53]. (p.14)

These considerations help to determine two main areas of interest that lead to the research question.

Looking at the matter of dreams from the perspective of experimental dream research the question of the collective imprint within the dream data arises.

On the other hand, through his analogy Campbell offers a different but equally interesting perspective, which sparks the question of how individual dreams may intersect with the wider world of myth, respectively the depersonalised dream and its phenomenology.

It is in this context that it appears worthwhile to explore the value of dreams when researching a particular human experience across individuals.

For this purpose the present study requires the incorporation of two levels. One level deals with the content of the dreams and the extractable supplemental knowledge on the investigated experience. The other level, however, is rather concerned with foundational methodological questions, for instance, whether dreams can serve as a source for meaningful data at all and which methods may be applied to best process and work with these kinds of data. Evidently, this undertaking calls for an explorative approach and therefore I propose no specific hypothesis. However, it appears viable to pose leading questions for the dream analysis and to define the overarching aims of the present study.

---

53   Copyright © Joseph Campbell Foundation (jcf.org) 2008. Used with permission.

The leading questions for the dream analysis are:
Q1: Are there shared themes across individuals underlying the dream data?
Q2: How does the shared experience of the programme unfold on a more subtle level and is there an immanent depersonalised dream?

The overarching aims of the present dream study are:
a. to explore dreams as a data source and the associated methodology,
b. and to complement the information as retrieved from the other data sources and thereby gaining deeper insight into the phenomenon as a whole.

5.3 Method

As a result of the proposed leading questions working with the dream data called for a twofold methodological approach.

In respect to the first question (Q1) I analysed dreams for shared themes using applied thematic analysis (APA) as a common practice in qualitative research.

However, it seemed indispensable to additionally pay respect to the fact that dreams undoubtedly represent a particular data type. As outlined before, dreams contextualise emotions, memories and experiences from wakefulness in a unique way and, unlike common interview data, reveal information in a more subtle often quite mystifying way. Their account does not necessarily follow a logical structure as known from a waking state of mind and images, symbols and surprising cross-references can appear. Furthermore, each dream report is the result of an effort to reconstruct a holistic experience, which is altered through language (Strauch & Meier, 1996). Thus, when intending to understand the shared experience through dreams in a more holistic way, it seemed sensible to implement a method that supports the dream's language by facilitating a dream-like state and thereby creating a space for the depersonalised dream to emerge. Unlike common theme extraction as practiced in the field of dream research this approach touches on subtler levels of the experience and possibly on the world of myth as a metaphorical map of human experience.

In an attempt to assess this and in order to relate to the second question (Q2) I applied the intersubjective-heuristic method as proposed by Kerr and Key (2011). As this is a novel method I will further elaborate the intersubjective-heuristic enquiry in the following chapter.

5.3.1 Outline of the intersubjective-heuristic method

As stated before, I realised part of the analysis by applying the intersubjective-heuristic method as proposed by Key and Kerr (2011). As their method is a modification of Clark Moustakas' (1990) heuristic method, I will briefly outline his approach in the following.

Heuristic enquiry aims to penetrate to the very core of an experience and to engage with the phenomenon as it is, instead of conceptualising it. This is mainly accomplished by means of rigorous self-enquiry on the part of the researcher. In order to gain a deeper understanding of the experience the researcher engages in an intensive process where she or he immerses with the chosen research question, which is familiar to the researcher and has left the researcher with the desire to fully understand the phenomenon. Thus, it can be argued that it is the question that adopts the researcher and not the other way around (Kenny, 2012).

In many ways heuristic research is contrary to the positivist approach as it requires the identification of the researcher with the topic of enquiry and deliberately involves intuition, self-dialogue, tacit knowledge and focusing. Focusing (Gendlin, 1978) is a technique which is used to access bodily-based knowing. As it constitutes an important part of the discovery process of heuristic research and was applied in this study it will be described in more detail at a later stage.

After the initial phases of engagement with the question and immersion with the subject of enquiry the researcher retreats into a period of "incubation" as a way to allow the material to process itself. All information, formal, informal or intuitive, is collected throughout the process of alternating engagement and reflection and is treated as potential data for the analysis. In order to create space for these data to emerge the researcher needs to initially allow for the relaxation into unknown space. This eventually leads to the next phase of illumination. Here, "aha" experiences take place, which is the point when all the different pieces of information come together anew. Finally, the phase of illumination is followed by the explication of meaning and by creatively synthesising the emerged understanding for instance through poetry and artistic expression (Braud & Anderson, 1998).

In order to introduce the intersubjective-heuristic method it is necessary to elucidate the underlying assumptions that come along with Kerr's and Key's backgrounds as ecopsychologists. In their work Kerr and Key (2011) recognised that experiences of psyche and nature become clearer if the skin-bound sense of self is extended to a wider interconnected self, also known as the "ecological self" (Naess, 2005). Clearly, the notion that the human psyche is interwoven with nature contrasts with positivist psychology, which understands the self as discrete and as a separated entity among others (Kerr & Key, 2011). In this regard, Key and Kerr (2011) propose a "new interconnected way of 'seeing'" (p. 53) in order to allow ecopsychological phenomena to become evident. This simultaneously supports and is supported by Capra's (1997) understanding of the ecological crisis as a crisis of perception for it reflects the consequence of the contemporary notion to view things as separated from each other.

Coming from the ecopsychology background, Key and Kerr (2011) identified four interconnected elements, which appear to be crucial when implementing the heuristic method in ecopsychology research. These modifications additionally take into account an intersubjective enquiry between researchers, ecological contextualisation, social activism and engagement with the unconscious.

Intersubjective enquiry between researchers refers to the circumstance that in heuristic research it is the individual researcher, who in the end makes meaning of the multifaceted data acquired. Key and Kerr (2011) see several benefits in turning the heuristic process into an intersubjective-heuristic process by engaging more than one researcher. Firstly, they see intersubjective enquiry as a way to support deeper relaxation into the process itself and specifically into the immanent encounter with the unknown. Furthermore, working with a co-researcher broadens the perspective on the phenomenon and thereby invites creativity and potentially useful creative tension between researchers.

As ecopsychology studies the relationship between human beings and the natural world, ecopsychology research evidently requires a contextualisation that not only includes the human but also encompasses the natural world. For this reason Key and

Kerr (2011) suggest the second modification of heuristic enquiry, which is the ecological contextualisation. They propose to enter into a dialog with the ecological context as a way to gain a deeper understanding of psychological phenomena and one's own research process. To accomplish this but also to test research theories Key and Kerr advocate continuous active engagement with the natural world throughout the entire research process.

Further, Key and Kerr (2011) elaborate that "ecopsychology has emerged to meet an urgent need for personal and social transformation in the face of ecological crisis, so ecopsychology research must lead to action" (p. 67). This contrasts with heuristic enquiry, which does not necessarily imply social action and as a consequence leads to Key's and Kerr's third modification: social activism. Key and Kerr (2011) emphasise the importance of setting the intention for positive social change as an integral part of their method. Stemming from their own experience Kerr and Key found that the transformation the researcher experiences throughout the intersubjective process can in turn empower the researcher's activism. By cultivating an attitude of being in service to each other and the earth, a sense of solidarity is created between researchers, which can also transfer to others. In this way a valuable frame is provided for the generated creative and intuitive insights to be utilised in the most vital way.

Finally, as the fourth modification, Key and Kerr (2011) make a case for the researcher's engagement with her or his unconscious. While dreams, intuitions and synchronicities can serve as valuable informants and give direction in heuristic enquiry Key and Kerr (2011) emphasise that this can also reflect areas of resistance and unconscious motifs of the researcher. According to Key and Kerr this should be acknowledged and brought to awareness in order to illuminate the complex process of research. Aside from the challenge that engaging with the unconscious in this way might imply, Key and Kerr suggest viewing this element also as an invitation to positively deepen the transformative power that heuristic research bears for the researcher's self-development.

5.3.2 Sample

I used a sample of nine dreamers who experienced the Butterfly programme including me, the researcher. I included only those nocturnal dreams that appeared throughout the programme. I assessed dreams of six of the dreamers as part of the interviews at posttest I. The number of dreamers is not equivalent to the interview sample size at posttest I, as three interviewees were not able to remember their nocturnal dreams or did not want to share them. Furthermore, I included two more dreams, which were shared with me by other participants of the programme. As two people shared two of their nocturnal dreams, eleven dreams were collected altogether (see Table 44). Three of the interviewees explicitly stated to have dreamt their dream during their Solo time.

In coherence with the collective dimension of dreaming as elaborated earlier my own dreams were included in the data set. I took part in the programme as an "embedded observer" closely following the programme, participants and staff. Furthermore, the process of the programme and the experience of the Solo was known to me from a participant's point of view, as I participated in the first Butterfly programme several years before.

Table 44

Composition of the dream sample

	Interview sample posttest I	Other participants (including researcher)	Total
Number of people	6	3	9
Number of dreams	7	4	11

5.3.3 Dream data

The majority of dreams were reported as part of the interviews from the Butterfly programme at posttest I. Therefore, interview equipment, duration and method of transcription corresponds to chapter 4.3.6.2.

I recorded the dreams that were separately reported by the other two participants in writing in my research journal. The same procedure applies to my own dreams.

5.3.4 Applied elements and stages of the intersubjective-heuristic method

5.3.4.1 The co-researcher

My co-researcher in this study supervised the various stages of research and, being a professional focusing practitioner, also led the focusing session.

The focusing session took place via Skype and was recorded online and later on transcribed.

5.3.4.2 Procedure of the focusing session

In order to prepare for the focusing session I read the dream material thoroughly several times. The focusing practitioner, in the case of this study, entered the session without prior knowledge of the dreams' content.

As the focuser enters the focusing session any mental elaborations on the dream material are deliberately dropped and the focuser arrives in a relaxed and altered state. Throughout the focusing session the focuser sits with closed eyes, verbally describing occurring contents of consciousness. This includes bodily sensations, imagery, thoughts and emotions. As Kerr (2008) aptly summarises the focuser's experience:

> *In focusing, one alternately dwells in the realms of experiencing and of symbolising – expanding one's awareness out from what is known about a phenomenon to what is not yet known. This takes time, and patient waiting, and the process of shifting between experiencing and symbolisation is iterative. With each shift, the focuser learns more. (p. 23-24)*

The focusing practitioner continuously paraphrases and minimally reflects back what has been said by the focuser. The session is finalised by the practitioner giving feedback on the essence she or he captured from the session.

Table 45
Stages of application of the intersubjective-heuristic enquiry

Stage	Purpose	Procedure
1	Data collection	Interviews of Butterfly participants, field notes and research diary
2	Immersion in data	1. Reading and re-reading transcripts of dreams 2. Reflection on researchers own experience of the dream data using focusing (Gendlin, 1978) along with feedback and reflection on focusing session from the co-researcher 3. Drawing, studying of field notes, taking notes on imagery that arose and discussions with co-researcher
4	Incubation	Setting aside data for two and a half weeks while spending time outdoors, practicing yoga, studying experimental dream research data and literature on the philosophy of science
5	Illumination	Experience of a moment of illumination or insight that brought about a shift in perception of the dream data
6	Immersion in data	1. Reviewing of dream data against the background of gathered insight 2. Reflecting with co-researcher on gathered insights
7	Incubation	Setting aside data for a month while working on literature review on dreams and thematic analysis of dream data, spending time outdoors and practicing of yoga
8	Explication	Examining what has arisen in the process and extracting meaning
9	Creative syntheses	Emerged understanding is brought together to a coherent expression

5.3.4.3 Stages of application

The stages of application of the intersubjective-heuristic enquiry are summarised in Table 45. The table represents the process as it took place in this study and adhere minor adjustments of Kerr's and Key's method.

5.4 Results

5.4.1 Results of the intersubjective-heuristic enquiry

5.4.1.1 Reflection on the process and emerged images
As intersubjective-heuristic enquiry constitutes a modified version of heuristic enquiry I will specifically point out novel elements in the following reflection on the process.

Furthermore, it appears vital for this chapter to allow for a conscious shift in narrative. As Kerr (2008) sensibly highlighted it is crucial to avoid the methodological pitfall of neither fully applying an objective approach nor fully allowing for subjectivity to unfold as required in heuristic research. On my side, as the researcher, this means to deliberately allow for my subjective experience to evolve and manifest as an equally valuable approach to scientific insight. Therefore, this section along with the section on the creative synthesis will closely illustrate my personal experiences, process and reflections on the emerged supplemental data and dream data.

The process of fully immersing in the dream data started with the focusing session on the collected dreams. The focusing session developed into a journey with my body as the main touchstone for the arising stages. Three body parts became alternately apparent that were each connected to dream sequences and bodily sensations.

Throughout, the stages of the body became more and more clear. Firstly, there was dizziness in my head, which felt like a mental struggle of having to make decisions accompanied by corresponding dream images.

The tension then moved to my heart where a dream sequence was sparked. The dream sequence told the story of a girl feeling mentally off-track and then experiencing an encounter with a protective surrounding. This released the tension and expanded my heart and the focus went down to my stomach, which felt heavy like after a big meal. The heaviness pulled me down towards the earth with the longing to release everything I could not digest into the ground.

Directly after the session I captured the experience in a sketch, as shown in Figure 36 (left image). When examining my sketch after the focusing session, the illustrated heaviness in my stomach sparked a memory in me.

I remembered the point of time when I asked participants about their dreams, which was in the interview phase during the last two days of the Butterfly programme. Almost every interviewee stated at some point that they feel "so full" of everything so that it seems almost impossible to put everything that happened to them into words yet. Phrases as "time to digest" and feeling "full" were used.

It occurred to me that the focusing experience might represent a snapshot of the participants' general state of heart and mind accessed through immersing in the dreams that came from that time. Indeed, interviews revealed that participants had to face emotional challenges during the programme as well as reports of gradually opening up their hearts and feeling fully alive. This simultaneously caused mental stimulation and confusion in them, which in the interviews brought about reflections regarding their everyday life back home and questions of how to integrate what has been experienced.

Contemplating this discovery I re-read my field notes from the Butterfly programme. In doing this, I came across a drawing I copied into my research journal during the evaluation session that team members facilitated during the last days of the Butterfly programme (see Figure 36, right image).

What struck me was the fact that the same body parts were chosen as an instrument of evaluation and that participants actually had been using the metaphor of the figure with the three body parts to reflect on their experiences. Essentially, it appeared as though the dreams created an interface between me, the focuser, and participants' actual evaluations and reports from that time.

Nonetheless, I strongly felt that there was another pattern of interconnections underlying the data, which had to do with the nature of the dream itself. But, like an object hidden under fabric, I could sense it but could not see it. However, an image kept flaring up which seemed to capture it all: a snake biting its tail. At the time, it made intuitively sense to me but did not reveal meaning in an explicit, intellectual way.

After sharing this with my co-researcher we decided that it was time to set the data aside in order to allow for incubation to take place. This was a critical moment as it, indeed, felt difficult to let go of the data at that point in time. There was the urge to continue the search and also fear of loosing track. Reflecting on this seems important as it demonstrates Key's and Kerr's (2011) case for intersubjectivity in heuristic research. Not only was the co-researcher helpful to allow myself to dwell in my contemplation of

Figure 36. Sketch of my experiences in the focusing session (left) and of the figure used as an evaluation tool for participants at the end of the Butterfly programme (right).

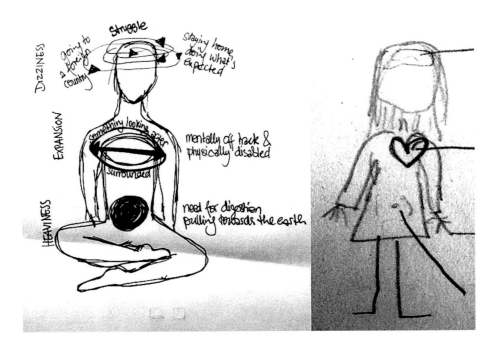

the focusing session it was also decisive for me to know that someone else was holding the space while I could let go of the data.

During the phase of incubation I seized the opportunity to spend time outdoors as a way to release, to open my mind to the wider ecological context and to reaffirm my intention in the work. I also experienced my yoga practice as beneficial to this process of relaxing and releasing.

Nevertheless, a somewhat unusual aspect in the phase of incubation was my decision to start working on the introduction for the present study, reviewing experimental dream research, scientific insight on sleeping and cognition, and literature on the philosophy on science. This constitutes one of the above-mentioned adjustments to the method as the subject of enquiry is usually entirely put to rest. However, this did not feel like interference as it clearly activated the intellectual and analytical mind in me. It rather created a sense of returning to the more familiar terrain of academic work and kept my mind from wandering back to what I experienced in the phase of immersion.

After all, it was this occupation that eventually led to a decisive clue, which in turn gave rise to my moment of illumination.

While working on the introduction for the present study I came across the term "depersonalised dream" by Joseph Campbell (2008). This sparked my interest, as the term intuitively felt like it captured my subject of enquiry and as Campbell's outline of the depersonalised dream or Hero's Journey[54] is a well-known metaphor of adventure

---

54 The term "Hero" is used to refer to both male and female.

Figure 37. Illustrations of the phases immanent in rites of passage (left) and Kerr and Key's (2011) adaptation of Jahn and Dunne's (2001) model of mind-matter interactions (right).

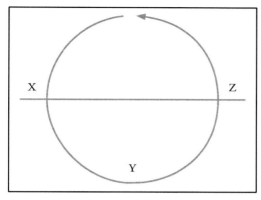
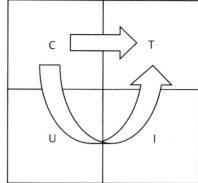

and transformation that is often used in relation to the Solo time ritual. Thus, the term led me deeper into Campbell's work *The Hero with a Thousand Faces*. Here, I stumbled upon a figure[55] (see Figure 37, left side), which captivated me. The figure represented the three phases immanent in rites of passage: separation (x), initiation (y) and return (z). The phases also constitute the foundation for the standard path of the mythological adventure of the hero as outlined by Campbell. Yet, initially my fascination was not sparked by the content but by the shape and movement of the illustration. I had seen a similar figure before in a different context and allocated the figure (see Figure 37, right side) in an article on the ontology of connectedness in ecopsychology research by Kerr and Key (2011). The two pictures are presented in Figure 37.

Studying the figures I had two realisations. Firstly, there is a strong resemblance in the process of the Hero's Journey and Jahn and Dunne's model of mind-matter interactions (see chapter 5.1) and secondly, the stages of the Hero's Journey seemed to resonate with the content of the dreams.

As elaborated in chapter 5.1 dreams, if remembered, are indeed experiences that spring from the quadrants below the x-axis and emerge back into consciousness, as captured by the bent arrow in Jahn and Dunne's model of mind matter-interactions. Seen from this perspective Jahn and Dunne's model represents the process of dreaming and the movement through different states of consciousness. The x-axis in his model divides consciousness into the conscious and the unconscious mind. It is in the nature of dreaming that we start our journey in a waking state of mind and then continue to venture into the unconscious, making fresh experiences in the dream world and eventually advancing back into wakefulness. Furthermore, the moment a dream is recalled an opportunity presents itself to extract meaning for everyday life.

Concurrently, the horizontal in the Hero's Journey also divides the world into two realms. Above the horizontal is the realm of the known, the world of common day. Underneath the horizontal is the realm of the unknown, the region of supernatural wonder (Campbell, 2008). The hero starts his journey in the ordinary world. He then crosses the threshold from the known into the unknown (x), where he faces

---

55   Copyright © Joseph Campbell Foundation (jcf.org). Used with permission.

challenges and temptations and experiences mysterious adventures with transformative power (y). Eventually, after having lived through the adventure the hero crosses the threshold again into the ordinary world (z). However, the journey remains meaningless unless the hero is able to extract fresh knowledge and understanding to bring back to his community.

Led by this insight I started to review the collected dreams against the background of the key story elements that Campbell (2008) identified on the metaphorical path to personal transformation. Along this process I felt more and more that the vast majority of dreams each captured one of the key elements as proposed by Campbell (2008). Even though this was an intriguing discovery, I was aware of the danger of having entered a state of biased perception and over-interpretation.

To avoid this pitfall I consulted my co-researcher again presenting her with my emerged understanding. In this phase we encountered what Key and Kerr (2011) called "creative tension". While I felt tempted to assign the dreams to the eight key elements as proposed by Campbell, my co-researcher drew attention to potentially incongruous aspects inherent in some of the key elements such as cultural slant. This way I was able to recover a more differentiated view, and what initially might have felt like a throwback then helped to form a more neutral framework for the dream data.

After another phase of incubation I re-analysed the dreams in respect to the more general phases of the Hero's Journey, leaving aside further elaborations of Joseph Campbell's eight key story elements.

In the following I will tell the Hero's Journey, weaving in eight of the eleven dreams in accordance to the elements they resonated with (see also Figure 38[56]).

5.4.1.2 The dreams in the mirror of the Hero's Journey

The story of the Hero's Journey first manifested itself in the ancient myths but is still widely present in contemporary literature and film. The reason for this timelessness is that the Journey reflects the pattern of human experiences when facing challenge or change in life. This process is sometimes painful and confusing but it is a journey of self-discovery, which enables re-evaluation of thinking, behaviour and perspective and ultimately facilitates the maintenance of balance in life (Apolinario, 2008)[57].

For the Journey to begin the hero must receive the call to adventure, which sparks the hero's awareness of a world beyond the one he knows. This may be set off by an experience that prompts the hero to rethink what he knows.

> *It* [the dream] *was about my girlfriend. Because she is completely different from me. And maybe she would never enjoy something like this* [the Butterfly programme]. *Not because she doesn't like it. Because she enjoys more something else. And I dreamt about her that she comes here and says, "Wow, how amazing is this!" She enjoyed playing guitar, she is a guitar player, around the fire, she was

---

[56] The image of the Hero's Journey has been released into the public domain/ Wikimedia Commons. The Joseph Campbell Foundation makes no claim to the rights of this illustration.
[57] The following summary of the Hero's Journey is based on an outline provided by Apolinario (2008).

singing with all of us. And she was doing practical jobs as all of us. [...] And that was a dream that really caught my attention because–I'm laughing because we are completely different and this really impressed me (Dream I).[58]

The call to adventure can also gradually make its way into everyday life. It initially might be perceived as a vague sense of discontent, imbalance or incongruity in life, which then stirs the wish to uncover what is missing.

I dreamt of E [another participant] *that she took a lot of pills. Yes, and somehow she was sick but she takes so many pills and antibiotics and I just saw her with this mushroom. And that was somehow very strange. And there is not much more present. But I was in this position- I wanted to show her a different path. That she doesn't need to take this mushroom. And it was very strange when I woke up* (Dream II).

On a psychological level the call might be an awareness of a shift of the emotional point of balance as previously adapted roles or known surroundings feel outgrown.

So I came back [from Findhorn] *and I was supposed to fly immediately to Japan for this voluntary job and my mother told me, "Oh, but it's not good, you have to work and you leave AGAIN and you have to earn MONEY and why do you leave AGAIN?" And I had also the part like, Oh, yeah, I should WORK, I'm already back from two weeks in FINDHORN and now I want to do another voluntary job and I have some obligation with this responsibility that I LOVE [...] and there is this thing in Japan and should I really go or not? And it was like a big struggle in my mind like, Do I go or don't? And then, finally, I went because I was like, I have already paid the flight* (Dream III).

In order to start the adventure the hero must cross the threshold from the known to the unknown, which is a world full of challenges and dangers. At the threshold the hero might be confronted with situations that reflect his greatest fear, the catalyst for the journey, which is equally threatening and daring the hero to take up the battle. But there is not only challenge. At the threshold, the hero might also encounter a helper. The most important of the helpers is the mentor or guide, who gives stability and a psychological foundation in times when great danger is experienced.

And when I dreamt, I dreamt that I was out in the wilderness cold and afraid. And there was something there. As though something was watching me. So I turned to this other thing. And it was a figure or something. I went to the figure and suddenly I was warm lying next to the sea, [...] which was keeping me cool. In the sun. And I just felt safe and absolutely unreal (Dream IV).

---

58   According to Jung encountering others in dreams may be interpreted as encountering a part of oneself. In this dream for instance the girlfriend may be interpreted as a part of the dreamer himself.

Generally, helpers can appear throughout the journey, fortunately often at the most apt moments. Once the threshold is crossed, the adventure into the unknown begins. The journey can be an external one into a physical unknown or an internal one into a psychological unknown. Regardless, the adventure is always risky, physically and emotionally, and as the Hero's Journey progresses the challenges become increasingly difficult. The challenges along the journey reflect the hero's fears, and needs for a direct confrontation with personal weaknesses is needed in order to turn the hero's "demons" to "gods".

> *A group of people, including me, is trying to escape this huge King Kong-like gorilla which is raging, in the process of destroying the city. We gather and hide in a skyscraper and have to watch the gorilla through the huge glass window front coming closer and closer. Then, he reaches our building and turns towards us. We fearfully await the attack* (Dream V).

The next stage of the journey is the abyss. The abyss represents the greatest challenge of the Hero's Journey as it reflects the hero's greatest fear. Here, complete surrender to the adventure is required as it is only through conquering the abyss and overcoming the greatest fear that the transformation becomes complete. However, there is always the risk that the challenge beats the hero.

> *Together with the other Butterfly participants I am standing on a small planet, which is hovering in space. The planet is slowly falling apart. Huge pieces break off, fall down and pull people down to their death. The planet pieces fall on some kind of ground, which seems to exist underneath the planet. In the split seconds before the planet pieces hit ground there is this decisive moment of life-and-death. As there are people on the falling pieces it is crucial which side of the piece hits the ground. Depending on that the people either survive or crush and die* (Dream VI).

The final step in this process is a moment of death and rebirth, representing a part of the hero that dies so that a new part can come to life.

> *In one* [dream] *I'm in a caravan high up on a cliff, which I had been able to look at from Culbin forest. I was inside of it, my Dad drove it and we turned around on the cliff and then we fell down. And I died. And then I wasn't dead after all but disabled.* [...] *And something, which surrounded me, took care of me there.* [...] *I think I was somehow mentally off track. And then there was some kind of surrounding which looked after me* (Dream VII).

The transformation process is marked by a revelation, which might occur suddenly and radically changes the way of thinking and the perspective on life. After the transformation the hero advances into atonement, which refers to the incorporation of the changes caused by the journey and allows for the hero to be fully reborn.

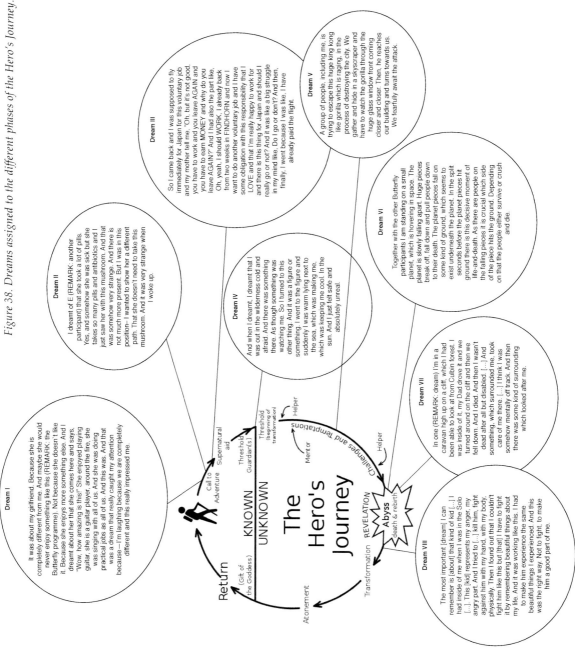

Figure 38. Dreams assigned to the different phases of the Hero's Journey.

5 INTUITIVE DREAM ENQUIRY

> *The most important* [dream] *I can remember is* [about] *that kind of kid* [...] *I had inside of me when I was in the Solo* [...]. *This* [kid] *represents my anger, my angry part. And I tried to* [...] *kill him, fight against him with my hand, with my body, physically. Then I found out that I couldn't fight him like this but* [that] *I have to fight it by remembering beautiful things about my life. And it was working like this. I had to make him experience the same beautiful things I experienced. And this was the right way. Not to fight, to make him a good part of me* (Dream VIII).

Now, the initial imbalance that has sent the hero on his quest has been corrected. After transformation and atonement the final stage of the journey begins: the return to everyday life. On his journey back the hero discovers his gift, which has been given as a result of the hero's new skills and awareness. As the hero crosses the threshold into the common world he faces the risk of putting himself back into the same situation he came from and thereby losing his newly gained understanding. On return the hero must resolve two worlds: divine and human, known and unknown. Another essential part of his return, though, is to begin contributing to his community by means of sharing his discoveries with others. While the hero encounters many people incapable of understanding beyond their physical world, he inevitably eventually meets another who hears the message, and arises as the next hero.

5.4.1.3 Explication

The intention for applying the intersubjective-heuristic method was to attend to the second leading question for the analysis of the dream data. This question is concerned with the more subtle layers of information that the dream data potentially reveal. This includes the question of how the shared experience of the programme unfolds on a more subtle level and whether there is an immanent depersonalised dream in the dream data.

In the present study dreams have been utilised as research data in order to study the participants' experience of the Solo as the core of the Butterfly programme. Conventionally, research data are retrieved by methods that are based on the assumptions of linearity and causality as apparent when conducting an interview: the interviewer asks a concrete question and usually receives a direct answer by the interviewee. In this study, however, neither the experience of interconnectedness as an integral part of immersive experiences in wild nature (see chapter 6.1.1), nor dreams as data necessarily follow these principles. Pertinently, instead of illuminating the subject of enquiry in this conventional manner, dreams reveal intriguing interconnections and reflections and already thereby seem to mirror the topic of enquiry itself. In this way, it can be argued that the dream incorporates and reflects simultaneously the knower and the known, or the observer and the subject of observation.

It appears that dreams in their dual role, their character as a data source and their content, contribute to understanding the experience under investigation in manifold ways.

Firstly, it seems as though the Hero's Journey, as the universal pattern of the human experience of transformation, and the dream world follow a similar process. This was elaborated earlier when comparing the figure of the Hero's Journey with Jahn and Dunne's model of mind-matter interactions. Both "realms" offer the opportunity for self-discovery and can be reached by crossing a threshold into an extraordinary other world, involving both the conscious and unconscious mind. This resemblance may be a clue pointing towards an important offer both spaces make to the dreamer or voyager.

The dream world provides a gateway to the unconscious and thereby to a space free of social desirability, duties and self-censorship. Similarly, embarking on the transformative journey of self-discovery leads into a space where the voyager aims to free herself or himself from restraints in life. These restraints may include beliefs and assumptions about our own abilities as well as approaches to life that might have been imposed by the social environment. In that, both dreamer and voyager penetrate to the core of their genuineness.

Joseph Campbell depicts this process as facing "the inner dragon" and according to Campbell the way to slay this dragon is to find and follow one's bliss in life. In Campbell's view finding this bliss is strongly related to the importance of finding work in the world, which is enjoyable to the individual. So instead of setting the initial intention to save the world, he argues, real transformation takes place through people who feel fully alive and by that vitalise the world and save it after all (Campbell, 1988).

Thus, the journey space may support orienting towards this bliss just like Jung believed that dreams, as an expression of the unconscious, help the individual to orient towards her or his wholeness.

Indeed, interview outcomes from the Butterfly sample seem to confirm at least parts of this process. The gain of authenticity, unravelling one's personal contribution to the world and especially aligning one's life with the personal discoveries made throughout the programme were reported as integral outcomes of the participants' overall experience.

An additional contribution of applying intersubjective-heuristic enquiry may be seen in the way interconnectedness presented itself in this study.

It seems as though interconnections inherently became apparent as soon as I, the researcher, offered myself as an additional tool to retrieve knowledge as intended in heuristic enquiry. Along the research process interconnections revealed themselves through the experiences in the focusing session, when my own perceptions and emotions appeared to reflect the participants' state of mind and heart at the final phase of the programme. Moreover, by following my intuitions and the emerged images, I discovered a framework that allowed for the dreams to be woven together into one greater story.

The greater story, in this study, is reflected in the depersonalised dream or universal myth of the Hero's Journey and thereby mirrors part of the enacted and shared experience of the participants. In the programme, the Journey was enacted in the form of the implemented Solo ritual but also in the programme's general nature of facilitating personal growth and self-discovery.

An additional contribution can be retrieved from the process of working with dreams through the above-mentioned aspect of "dream weaving". Each individual dream told its own story but seen by itself was unable to solve the puzzle of the experience under investigation. However, when putting the dreams together interconnections became apparent, and a greater story emerged. This act of weaving appears to embody an important revelation participants reported as a result of the programme. In essence, participants described the empowering effect of experiencing interconnectedness, which entailed an immanent understanding of being part of a larger whole or a greater story, just as the dream weaving confirmed.

In this way the dream seems to act like a koan[59]. The dream becomes the question it wants to answer and by doing this sparks intuitive revelations about essential features of the topic of enquiry.

In a strikingly intelligent way, the dreams demonstrate the interconnectedness of the research topic, the researcher and the community of people that were researched. Thus, the dreams together initiate the whole.

5.4.1.4 Creative synthesis

It is a well-known phenomenon that in the split seconds of waking the dream still lingers on, simultaneously felt and known by the dreamer. In the process of reaching out for it, however, it often slips away, sometimes never to be remembered again.

This phenomenon well reflects my experience of distilling the very essence of this study. Many layers have been peeled off, yet there is a deeply rooted one that continues to escape my intellectual understanding. What remains, after all, is the image of the snake biting its own tail, the Ouroboros, which seemed to have followed me throughout the entire research process:

It initially appeared during the first phase of immersion and it surprised me again with its presence in Kekulé's dream, which I came across when reviewing the research literature for this study during the phase of incubation. And finally, in my mind, it insistently queued up with the picture sequence I studied during the second phase of immersion, just like the root tone in a triad and eventually impossible for me to ignore (see Figure 39).

Words like cyclicality, self-reflexivity, unity and constant re-creation came to mind.

Having accepted its place I continued working on other parts of this study. Along the way, I stumbled across an excerpt of an essay by Schopenhauer, which seemed to address the heart of my intuitive understanding of the Ouroboros in this study. Later on, again another unexpected connection arose when I discovered that Campbell, too, drew on this very excerpt in an interview on the power of myth (Campbell, Moyers, & Flowers, 1991).

In the following, and deliberately without further elaboration, I depict the excerpt from Schopenhauer's essay (Schopenhauer, 1974). By merging the surfaced interconnections with the symbol of the Ouroboros and Schopenhauer's tale of the great dream of life, I wish to offer the reader, too, an offbeat synthesis or impression of the present study.

Figure 39. Illustrations depicting Kerr and Key's (2011) adaptation of Jahn and Dunne's (2001) model of mind-matter interactions (left), the phases of rites of passage (middle) and the Ouroboros snake (right).

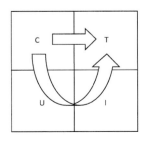 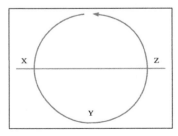 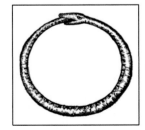

---

59   In Zen Buddhism, a paradox to be meditated upon that is used to abandon ultimate dependence on reason and thereby facilitates sudden intuitive insight.

> *The external operation of circumstances had to assist one another in the course of a man's life in such a way that, at the end thereof when it had been run through, they made it appear like a well-finished and perfected work of art, although previously, when it was still in the making, it had, as in the case of any planned work of art, the appearance of being often without any plan or purpose. But whoever came along after its completion and closely considered it, would inevitably gaze in astonishment at such a course of life as the work of the most deliberate foresight, wisdom and persistence* (p. 207).

> [If we acknowledge the similarity of the individual life to a dream, we should] *note the difference that in the mere dream the relation is one-sided… only one ego actually wills and feels, whereas the rest are nothing but phantoms. In the great dream of life, on the other hand, a mutual relation occurs, since not only does the one figure in the dream of the other exactly as is necessary, but also that other figures in his dream. Thus by virtue of a real harmonia praestabilita, everyone dreams only what is appropriate to him… and all the dreams of life are so ingeniously interwoven that everyone gets to know what is beneficial to him and at the same time does for others what is necessary… It is the great dream that is dreamed by that one entity, but in such a way that all its persons dream it together* (pp. 219-220).

5.4.2 Results of the applied thematic analysis

The first leading question for the analysis of the dream data was to analyse the dreams for shared themes across individuals. In regard to this question I performed a thematic analysis of the dream data after the intersubjective-heuristic enquiry. I executed the analysis based on the principles of applied thematic analysis (APA) as described in chapter 4.3.6.4 using Dedoose, a software for qualitative, quantitative and mixed methods research.

5.4.2.1 Common themes

The thematic analysis revealed three main themes that were widely shared among dreamers.

Sense of danger

Seven of the eleven dreams incorporated a sense of danger. This is represented through dream contents such as physically fighting, being afraid and alone in the wilderness, falling off the edge of a cliff, standing on a rupturing planet, escaping from a big monster or just sensing a strong underlying dangerous atmosphere in the dream.

Another considerable commonality that stuck out within this domain were images of different kinds of dwellings that seemed to be endangered, destroyed or disappeared, for example, sitting in a caravan that falls off a cliff, standing on a planet which is falling apart, seeking refuge in a skyscraper and discovering that the personal tent has been stolen.

Imbalance

Eight of the eleven dreams contained an element of mental and/or physical imbalance either experienced from a first person narrative or observed by the dreamer in another dream figure. Mental imbalance is represented by dream reports of facing one's own inner anger, feeling afraid, being caught up in one's struggling mind or feeling mentally "off track".

The physical imbalance is reflected in dream images as planet pieces that are breaking off and pulling people down to their death, discovering a large bruise on one's body, being physically sick or disabled.

Drastic turn/ potentiality

In the course of seven of the eleven dreams, pairs of opposites emerged. In the story line of those dreams the pairs either represent a drastic turn of events that has taken place or demonstrate a decisive moment which yields to a range of diverging possible outcomes. Table 46 illustrates these pairs of opposites with each line representing another dream.

In this way, these opposites simultaneously reflect drastic change and potentiality, which reflects the vastness of different, even opposing, outcomes immanent in a given situation.

The following dream vividly illustrates a sudden and drastic turn of events.

> *I think that [...] the most rewarding dream I ever had was actually during my Solo. I had just watched the sun and the sea for a few hours each. And when I dreamt, I dreamt that I was out in the wilderness cold and afraid. And there was something there. As though something was watching me. So I turned to this other thing. And it was a figure or something. I went to the figure and suddenly I was warm lying next to the sea, which [...] was keeping me cool. In the sun. And I just felt safe and absolutely unreal. I woke up and I was, "Ahhh!" (SIGHS RELIEVED).*
>
> (B1, 2011, line 114-121)

Table 46

Emergent pairs of opposites in the dream contents

Pairs of opposites	
From cold and afraid	To warm and safe
From fighting anger physically	To fighting by remembering beautiful memories
From dying	To continuing to live after death
From a girlfriend with differing lifestyle and interests in life	To a girlfriend that shares the dreamer's interests and lifestyle
Observing someone taking pills to cure	Being aware of and wanting to point out a different path to cure
From staying home to earn money	To flying to a foreign country to volunteer
Potentially being crushed to death	Or potentially surviving

The next dream on the other hand exemplifies a decisive moment, which holds the potential for a drastic turn of events:

> *Together with the other Butterfly participants I am standing on a small planet, which is hovering in space. The planet is slowly falling apart. Huge planet pieces break off, fall down and pull people down to their death. The planet pieces fall on some kind of ground, which seems to exist underneath the planet. In the split seconds before the pieces hit ground there is this decisive moment of life-and-death. As there are people on the falling pieces it is crucial which side of the piece hits the ground. Depending on that the people either survive or crush and die.*
>
> (D1, 2011, line 7-13)

5.4.2.2 Pattern of dream themes

Analysing the interconnectedness of dream themes within the story lines of the dreams a pattern emerged as shown in Figure 40.

The themes are presented in bold rectangles with the numbers in brackets indicating occurrence contrasted by the total number of dreams. Rectangles attached to the themes represent subthemes with the bracketed numbers indicating their relative frequency.

All of those dreams, which included the theme "drastic turn/ potentiality" also contained the theme "imbalance" as indicated by the bold line connecting the two themes. As would be expected, there was also a high degree of co-occurrence between the themes "sense of danger" and "mental and physical imbalance" as again indicated by the bold line in Figure 40.

Figure 40. Emergent pattern of dream themes.

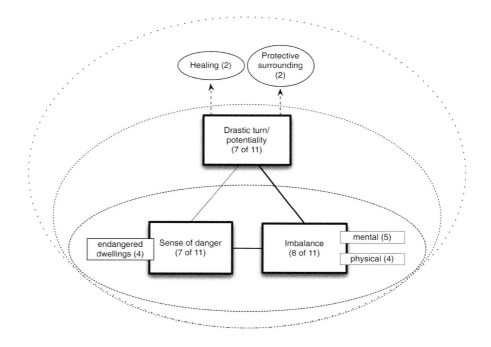

Moreover, the occurrence of themes appears to reflect a movement of expansion as intuitively emergent when studying the chart from the core to the outer layer. However, this reading direction should not be confused with the order of appearance of the themes in the dreams. The dreams merely seem to vary in the degree to which they continued to include additional themes. While 27 percent of the dreams exclusively circle around the themes "imbalance" and "sense of danger" 55 percent of the dreams additionally involve the theme "drastic turn/potentiality". Furthermore, four out of the seven dreams that contain the theme "drastic turn/potentiality" proceeded to include a healing event or an environment where dreamers suddenly felt protected and well looked after as though someone or something was surrounding them.

The following dream serves as an example of a story line that expands through all the layers of the chart and was retrieved as part of the interviews conducted at the Butterfly programme.

> *Interviewee: In one* [dream] *I'm in a caravan high up on a cliff, which I had been able to look at from Culbin forest. I was inside of it, my Dad drove it, and we turned around on the cliff and then we fell down. And I died. And then, however, I wasn't dead but disabled.* [...] *Something, which surrounded me, took care of me there.*
>
> *Interviewer: When you were disabled?*
>
> *Interviewee: Yes. I think I was somehow mentally off track. And then there was some kind of surrounding which looked after me.*
>
> (B8, 2011, line 385-393)

5.4.2.3 Summary
Summarised, the collective imprint of the eleven dreams appears to be reflected in the dream experience of physical or mental imbalance often associated with a sense of danger. This in turn was strongly coupled with a drastic turn of events or the confrontation with the potentiality of a situation, which in some dream cases then further included a dissolution of prior experienced difficulties or was soothed by the presence of a protective surrounding.

5.5 Discussion
After the leading questions have been addressed by means of the two methods of analysis this chapter will primarily concentrate on the overarching aims of this study.

5.5.1 *The interface between results*
One of the overarching aims of this study was to complement the information as retrieved from other data sources and methods of analysis such as the Butterfly interview data or the outcomes of the thematic analysis of the dream data. Hereby, I aspired to gain deeper insight into the phenomenon as a whole.

When comparing the results of the thematic analysis of the dream data with the findings of the intersubjective-heuristic method it becomes clear that, veritably, parallels do exist. This is not surprising as the results spring from the same data set. Nevertheless, findings of the two analyses differ and indeed seem to complement each other.

The results from the thematic analysis inform about shared themes that are mainly elaborated isolated from one another. This, however, leaves the question open of how to draw the themes into a greater contextual meaning. As yet sense of danger, imbalance and potentiality remain detached from the experience under investigation and give way to a vast space of free interpretation. However, when merging the dream themes with the process of personal transformation as exemplified in the Hero's Journey the themes seem to fall into place. In doing this, sense of danger can be understood as an immanent part of venturing into the unknown and embarking on an adventure, just as imbalance can be viewed as an inseparable part of increasing awareness along the process of personal transformation. Seen from this perspective, the potentiality immanent in any given situation and drastic turns in life represent prerequisites for and the teachings of true change in life. It appears as though outcomes of the intersubjective-heuristic method, in this context, provide a map that serves as a guideline and framework for interpretation. Thus, through complementing the information a process is added to the themes, which may represent part of the personal journey participants experienced throughout the programme.

As Mazzarello (2000) concluded results from dream research suggest that dreaming can be related to a learning situation. Experiences during wakefulness that convey new concepts are during dreaming better expressed and processed and finally enter consciousness as a retained dream. Participants of the Butterfly programme indeed reported that the Butterfly experience expanded their horizon by introducing to them new perspectives on life. In the thematic analysis of the interviews this aspect is reflected in the participants' reports of an altered approach to life. Furthermore, the aspect of expansion can be found in my bodily experience of expansion during the focusing session, in the dream theme "potentiality/drastic turn" and in the overall pattern of themes, which seemed to reflect expansion through gradually including additional themes (see chapter 5.4.2.2). Summarised, expansion in the context of the Butterfly experience may be represented by an increase of freedom gained through an expanded horizon and consequently, an expanded awareness for the range of possibilities in life.

Nevertheless, encountering new concepts and perspectives may also entail critical reflections on life, which could result in increased awareness of imbalances in the world or in the personal experience of imbalance. Going back to the focusing session this may be simultaneously reflected in the experience of dizziness in my head and heaviness my the stomach. Both bodily sensations were strongly associated with interview sequences where participants reported "not yet being able to make sense of the experience" as well as "feeling full" and "needing time to let it rest", which may indicating the above mentioned aspect of imbalance.

Another striking facet of the dream data lies in the noticeably strong presence of negatively connoted dream themes such as sense of danger and imbalance. As reports of threat or a sense of danger were absent in the interview data this is an intriguing finding. However, this may be explained by turning to the analytical psychologist

C. G. Jung, one of the best-known contributors to dream analysis. In his opinion dreams spring from the Self, which embraces the totality of all psychological functions and bears an imprint of the individual's wholeness. In Jung's view the unconscious or Self advances the development of an individual towards wholeness, which Jung called the process of individuation. Jung believed that each dream potentially holds information for the individual on how to orient towards this wholeness. Thus, with regard to consciousness the unconscious works in a compensatory and corrective manner. This means that the more one-sided the conscious attitude of a person is the more likely it is that dreams will reveal contrasting content, as an expression of the individual's strive for wholeness and balance (Roesler, 2010). Seen from this perspective, the contrast between the negatively connoted dream material and the participants' largely positive self-reports may be the result of a bias, immanent in the programme or group, towards primarily concentrating on positive emotions and empowerment during wakefulness. This way the more painful and challenging aspects inherent in change, broadening of awareness and embarking on a journey of personal transformation would remain rather unattended. In the interviews this may be indicated by a noticeable underrepresentation of negative or critical reports on the programme and by strongly positive programme characterisations such as terms like "bubble of love".

These "shadow aspects", however, are present within the dream data and find their authorisation within the framework of the Hero's Journey, which may explain why the dreams seem to resonate with it in such a consistent way.

5.5.2 Dreams as data and methodological considerations

The second overarching aim of the dream enquiry was to explore dreams as a data source and the associated methodology.

In order to understand a phenomenon fully, research aims to illuminate as many immanent facets as possible. However, when examining an experience and what it means to the individual, numbers and interviews can only capture a limited fraction of the phenomenon as a whole. It is in the nature of commonly used methods that study participants are biased to inform primarily about those aspects of their experience that correspond to the questionnaire items or interview questions. This in turn automatically leaves out other aspects of the experience that might be of importance. Undoubtedly, an experience can never be fully assessed, as there is always a part of an experience that escapes language. However, there may be aspects of a phenomenon that the individual is not entirely aware of yet but which are, in principle, accessible as for instance through dreams.

Dreams spring from the unconscious, which undeniably operates differently than the conscious mind. Therefore, the emergent dream data are constituted in a different manner than ordinary research data. Dreams exceed rational explications through their power of transmitting images, symbols and impressions that combine emotions, memories and personal processes in a condensed and creative way. This feature of dreams seems to simultaneously attract and confront with a challenge, as it is a difficult exercise to find means of translating the dream's particular imagery into expedient information. This points towards two issues worthy of discussion. One refers to the appropriate method of translation and the other is concerned with the usefulness of the dream imagery as research data.

Regarding the latter, the brief summary of research findings on the nature of dreams already made a case for the expressiveness of dreams due to their strong correlation with daytime experiences. Furthermore, dreams prove to be useful to the individual in the areas of emotional coping, memory consolidation, creative problem-solving and personal insight.

However, there are a few aspects of dreaming that should be brought to awareness when considering dreams as research data.

Firstly, dreams represent a rather unpredictable data type, as not everyone is able to remember her or his dream. Thus, it will remain uncertain how many dreams will show up during data collection or if there will be any at all. Furthermore, the researcher entirely depends on the dreamer's ability of self-observation, as the dreamer is the only one who has direct access to her or his internal dream world. This, however, is also true for any kind of research that involves self-reports, such as questionnaires and interviews.

Secondly, only those dreams can be reported that are well remembered. This might imply a selective bias in the collection process of the dreams, which may particularly favour the emotional salient dreams. Nevertheless, this potential bias does not negatively affect the outcomes or interpretation of the dreams in this study. On the contrary, in this study the collection of dream data was intentionally selective, as participants were specifically asked to report a remarkable night dream. Thus, in this context, the possible bias rather serves as an explanation for the collection of the noticeably rich and meaningful dream imagery than representing a potential pitfall.

Neuropsychologist and dream researcher Patrick MacNamara states in an interview for a BBC documentary (Colville, 2009) that there is a particular meaning immanent in someone telling a dream. In his opinion, sharing a dream appears especially valuable and reliable because the dreamer discloses information that is not faked and therefore reveals something very personal and interesting about the dreamer. Here, MacNamara refers to the peculiarity of the dream's content independent of the dreamer's conscious control. As other types of self-reports are always subject to self-censorship and social desirability, one could argue that the lack of control over the dream's theme enhances the dream's validity as research data. Naturally, dreams also carry the risk that uncomfortable sequences are edited out. Nevertheless, it seems much more unlikely to make the effort of changing the whole story of a dream rather than simply drawing on the excuse of being unable to remember the dream.

As stated earlier, the other essential issue of discussion refers to the appropriate method of translating the dreams. This appears especially relevant when reviewing the numerous transformations that are immanent in the development from the actual experience to meaningful data.

As a first step, daytime experiences are translated into dream imagery. The dreamer then translates the dream content into words when reporting it. In intersubjective-heuristic enquiry this process is even taken a step further, when the researcher attempts to retrieve meaning from the gathered dream data by means of generating her or his own imagery and intuitions in response to the dreams and thereby again translates it.

The several stages of translation pose a challenge, as the process seems to create further distance to the standard scientific aspiration of objectivity. However, there is still considerable value in using dreams and applying methods like intersubjective-heuristic enquiry to dream data.

Undeniably, different data types require different methods of analysis. The constitution of the data virtually informs the researcher about how to accommodate to it in the methodically most appropriate way. Just as numbers cannot be deciphered using thematic analysis, dreams need to be met on their own terms, too. Consequently, it seems sensible when widening the field of data to dreams to concurrently widen the methods of working with the data.

It appears as though intersubjective-heuristic enquiry permits the researcher to remain in the same sphere of language as the dream. This is reflected in the act of translating the dream material into images and intuitions of the researcher and in the inclusion of practices that enable the researcher to enter an altered state of consciousness as shown in the focusing session.

Undoubtedly, deliberately including subjectivity enhances the risk of the researcher acting as a "chaotic attractor" within the research process as Key and Kerr (2011) pointed out. The "chaotic attractor", in this context, refers to the researcher's potential bias of interpreting the data according to her or his unresolved issues and experiences. However, in order to limit this risk, Key and Kerr (2011) suggested a modification of the heuristic method by including a co-researcher as a supervising entity, which was attended to in this study.

As elaborated earlier, leaving the conventional tracks of empiricism in order to tap into novel facets of the studied phenomenon is an integral intention of the present study. Working with dreams in this way, and especially using the outcomes to complement the information retrieved by means of conventional methods, constitutes the explorative character of this study and its methodological contribution to innovative research.

Nonetheless, it seems important to reflect on the status of subjective approaches to data, as they appear to activate a deeply rooted understanding and value system regarding the criteria for valuable research.

One of the most popular and generally accepted benchmarks for thorough research is objectivity, the counterpart of subjectivity. It is this aspect that calls for balance, as even in the most rigorous experimental research design objectivity, even though strived for, is never completely achieved. By her or his mere presence the researcher always takes part in and thereby influences the study one way or the other, a phenomenon known as the "experimenter effect"[60]. Nevertheless, this is not to devalue scientific enquiry, as objectivity serves as a goal and guideline instead of a premise. However, even though commonly observed the immanent issue of subjectivity is rather treated as given and therefore largely neglected in conventional research reports. This circumstance bears the danger of communicating a misleading picture of the reality of science and its objects instead of embracing its systemic nature. Clearly, research, too, is embedded within a complex system of interactions. It is against this background that it appears valuable to specifically bring back the attention to subjectivity and its exploration in regard to potential benefits, rather than treating it solely as a confounding variable. As long as this is not mistaken for a permission to interpret unrestrainedly but practiced within a thorough methodical framework,

---

60 The influence of the experimenter's behaviour, personality traits, or expectancies on the results of his or her own research.

one could argue that this contributes to validity. For instead of ignoring the issue of subjectivity it is closely monitored, open to transparency and incorporated as an immanent part of the research process.

To conclude this chapter, it seems valuable to regain a bird's eye view and reflect on the more general contributions that can be drawn from the explorative dream enquiry. The dream study clearly adds novel and unusual aspects to the commonly known mixed methods approach as touched on in the previous sections. But seen within the wider context of the overall research project there is a further layer that emerges. This has to do with another implication that lies within the remit of subjectivity, as it is not only thoroughness that demands the systematic inclusion of the researcher.

The word "research" originates from the French word "rechercher", which means "to go about seeking". Therein lies a journey one has to embark on when entering the research process as well as an immanent initial question or mystery that is calling the researcher. Even though deeply rooted in the word, it seems as though only little recognition and appreciation for this facet of research has survived until today (see also Romanyshyn, 2007; Braud & Anderson, 1998). The dream synthesis honours those dimensions of experiencing that are largely ignored within conventional research, but which have the power to elevate the fascinating and mysterious aspects of research and life. In the present study this is realised through the researcher's entitlement to give way to self-reflexivity and intuitive insight as an equally valid part of the research process and through the dream itself, which represents an aspect of the human psyche that is an unsolved mystery and brings about wonder and excitement. Thereby, research and the role of the researcher are revitalised and movement, exploration and connection are re-introduced into the process. In the context of this study this appears almost mandatory, as an essential feature of the topic of enquiry appears to be interconnectedness, which in itself expresses the vibrancy of the fundamental architecture of life. The integration not only provides a meaningful context for the subject of enquiry but also the potential of transformation for the researcher. The transformation of the researcher gets right to the heart of an essential contribution of this study to the research discipline for, as C.G. Jung's stated (Jung, 1970), "the capacity for inner dialogue is a touchstone for outer objectivity" (§ 187).

6

Overall discussion

6.1 Summary and integration of survey, interview and dream data

As outlined in the methods chapter, on a broader level the present research aimed to tackle and extend the limitations of common research methodology by probing new methods, approaches and instruments. This was realised via the implementation of the mixed methods approach, which allowed for the assessment and integration of different types of data. Therefore, an overarching research question was how the different types of data are interconnected and what can be learned from integrating them. The present chapter will respond to these questions by providing a visual and written summary and simultaneous merging of the results across all data types that is quantitative, qualitative and intuitive-qualitative.

Notably, as a consequence of the triangulation process, the following section resumes information from the previous results section. Thus, the novelty and gain lies in the first-time presentation and merging of the main findings against the background of congruencies and differences across the different data types.

An in-depth discussion of selected aspects of these findings will be provided in further following sections.

6.1.1 Phenomenology of immersive experiences in wild nature

One of the main objectives of the present work was to explore the phenomenology of immersive experiences in wild nature. An additional intention was to illuminate features that facilitate such experiences as well as to explore the content of consciousness during the Solo time. In order to investigate the latter, for the first time the Phenomenology of Consciousness Inventory (PCI) was applied to the context of the Solo.

Furthermore, the Solo was researched in the context of two distinct programmes. While the time span of the Butterfly programme was approximately twice the length of the Solo-only programme, it also included additional ways of encountering nature, for instance via outdoor living, as well as an additional focus on community living for instance via sharing personal stories in council. Therefore, I constantly scanned the results of the Butterfly sample for common or distinct features between both programmes.

A visual summary of the results across data sources is presented in Figure 41.

6.1.1.1 Perceptual state and attitude in nature

It has been shown that the perceptual state and attitude of participants was different when in nature. Interviewees reported that this was additionally influenced by the intention they set for their Solo time as well as by fasting during that time span. The altered perceptual state and attitude in nature shows across the different data sources. In Figure 41, qualitative and quantitative results that seem to mirror similar aspects are presented together in one box. Correspondingly, the interviewees' reported enhanced sensual perception in nature was reflected in several enhanced PCI (sub-) dimensions as altered awareness, altered perception of time, altered perception of surrounding objects and particularly pronounced imagery. The interview data further illuminated that the participants also interpreted their altered awareness in nature as an effect of the overall Solo ritual, which framed the Solo experience. An altered perception of time, on the other hand, was also perceived as an effect of fasting.

Many interviewees furthermore indicated that being in nature gave rise to a switch from being in the head to being in the present moment. This is supported by the quantitative PCI data that revealed less volitional control over thoughts during the Solo as well as less rational thinking. The latter was, in the interviews, again also mentioned as an effect of fasting. The PCI results additionally revealed slightly more silent talking during the Solo time and slightly more negative emotions than under ordinary conditions. Notably, negative emotions as part of the Solo experience were underrepresented in the interview data. Therefore, it is all the more interesting that this aspect appeared quite strongly in the dream study. The majority of the reported dream contents contained a sense of danger and some kind of physical or mental imbalance, possibly revealing the challenging, rather concealed effect of encountering new concepts and perspectives and opening up to a process of self-enquiry.

6.1.1.2 The experience of interconnectedness with nature

The second overarching theme in the phenomenology of immersive experiences in nature was the participants' experience of interconnectedness with nature. Additionally, interconnectedness emerged on several levels in the dream study, which will be explicated later on (see in chapter 6.1.4). In the interview data the experience of interconnectedness with nature was reported on a variety of levels namely the transpersonal, the practical, the physical, the emotional and the psychological (for further detail go back to chapter 4.4.1.1). To recap, the transpersonal dimension was reflected in reports of immersive experiences in nature that dissolved or extended the participants' boundaries of their sense of self. This experience was often coupled with strong emotions such as deep feelings of awe, sadness and/or connection as well as with moments of personal insight. Equally, this showed in the PCI data via strongly pronounced dimensions such as altered experience, which includes the experience of the body extending the boundaries of the skin and a sense of unity, awe and wonder. Additionally, the PCI revealed strong feelings of love and joy during the Solo time, which also supports the qualitative findings.

Figure 41. Summary of the phenomenology of immersive experiences in wild nature across data sources.

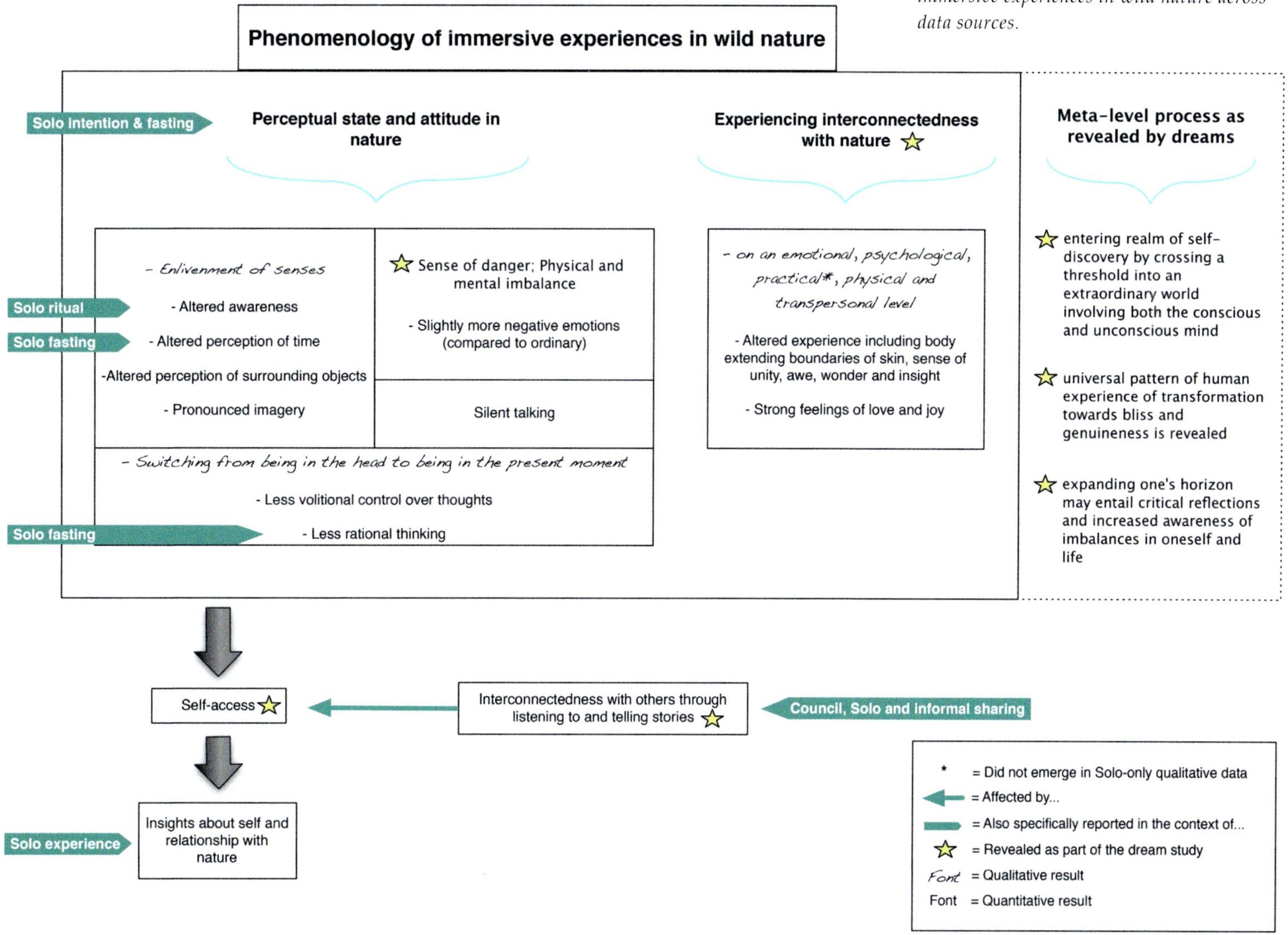

Phenomenology of immersive experiences in wild nature

Perceptual state and attitude in nature

☆ Sense of danger; Physical and mental imbalance
- Slightly more negative emotions (compared to ordinary)

Silent talking

- *Enlivenment of senses*
- Altered awareness
- Altered perception of time
- Altered perception of surrounding objects
- Pronounced imagery

- *Switching from being in the head to being in the present moment*
- Less volitional control over thoughts
- Less rational thinking

Solo intention & fasting
Solo ritual
Solo fasting
Solo fasting

Experiencing interconnectedness with nature ☆

- *on an emotional, psychological, practical*, physical and transpersonal level*
- Altered experience including body extending boundaries of skin, sense of unity, awe, wonder and insight
- Strong feelings of love and joy

Meta-level process as revealed by dreams

☆ entering realm of self-discovery by crossing a threshold into an extraordinary world involving both the conscious and unconscious mind

☆ universal pattern of human experience of transformation towards bliss and genuineness is revealed

☆ expanding one's horizon may entail critical reflections and increased awareness of imbalances in oneself and life

Council, Solo and informal sharing

Interconnectedness with others through listening to and telling stories ☆

Self-access ☆

Insights about self and relationship with nature

Solo experience

* = Did not emerge in Solo-only qualitative data
↓ = Affected by...
▮ = Also specifically reported in the context of...
☆ = Revealed as part of the dream study
Font = Qualitative result
Font = Quantitative result

6 OVERALL DISCUSSION | 211

6.1.1.3 Meta-level process as revealed by the dream study

Against the background of these quantitative and qualitative outcomes, the dream study seems to contribute a meta-level process underlying the extracted phenomenology. This meta-level process, as revealed by the dream study, reflects the universal pattern of human experience of transformation as outlined by Campbell (2008; see chapter 3.3.1), which can serve as a guideline and framework for interpretation of the data. In this way, the dream study adds a specific process to the themes, which may represent part of the personal journey participants experienced throughout the programmes but particularly during their Solo time as the designated space for self-discovery. The suggested process of transformation includes entering a particular realm of self-discovery by crossing a threshold into an extraordinary world, which involves both the conscious and unconscious mind. Generally, on the journey to personal authenticity and bliss, inner and outer challenges have to be met. Interpreting the participants' dreams against this background *sense of danger*[61], as part of the dream contents, can be understood as an immanent part of venturing into the unknown and embarking on an adventure just as *imbalance* can be viewed as an inseparable part of increasing awareness along the process of personal transformation. Seen from this perspective, the *potentiality* immanent in any given situation and *drastic turns* in life may represent prerequisites for and the teachings of true change in life. In some dream cases this then led to dissolution of prior experienced difficulties or was soothed by the presence of a protective surrounding, which may be found in the participants' reported sense of home in nature or in their sense of community in the Butterfly group.

The participants' entrance into a realm of self-discovery is also confirmed by the qualitative interview data, which revealed the high-level theme "self-access" as an essential part of the participants' Solo experience. Interviewees described that the altered perceptual state they experienced in nature, such as enhanced sensual perception and arrival in the present moment, along with their experience of emotional and psychological interconnectedness with nature, facilitated self-access. The descriptions in the interviews suggest that self-access is part of a personal process participants experienced in nature, which inevitably led to the gain of personal insights about self and their relationship with nature. This experience was mostly specifically mentioned in the context of the participants' Solo time. However, even though not entirely part of the nature experience as such, self-access was also gained through the participants' experience of interconnectedness with others via listening to and telling stories to each other. This route to self-access was mainly brought up in the context of the storytelling after the Solo, which constitutes part of the Solo ritual, but also in the context of other group councils and as part of informal sharing with others. This is intriguing as it highlights that similar effects and processes are initiated, both via the experience of interconnectedness with others as well as via the experience of interconnectedness with nature.

---

61   Terms in italics in this section represent, via thematic analysis extracted, dream themes.

6.1.1.4 Characteristic common features of the Solo time

Another research question was whether there is a common pattern for content of consciousness during the Solo time as assessed via the PCI. It showed that the Butterfly and Solo-only sample did not differ significantly in their means of the assessed dimensions of consciousness. Thus, aspects of the Solo experience appear to be shared among the Solo-only participants and the Butterfly participants, regardless of differences between both groups such as differences in location and context.

However, there was part of the phenomenology of the interviewees' nature experience, which differed between the Butterfly and Solo-only group. It turned out that Solo-only participants did not report the practical dimension of interconnectedness with nature. This seems only logical as the practical dimension of interconnectedness with nature describes the participants' experience of a reciprocal and practical dependency between humans and nature, which was primarily experienced in the context of running an outdoor camp during the Butterfly programme. Thus, consistently, this dimension was not part of the Solo-only participants' nature experience.

6.1.2 Short- and long-term programme evaluation outcomes

The second main area of interest in the present research was to evaluate immersive experiences in nature as a potential facilitator for personal development and behaviour change. Therefore, the research focus was placed on the immediate and long-term effects of the Butterfly programme in the areas of: activism, nature-related changes, changes related to self, changes related to others and world and life-related changes.

A visual summary of the results across data sources is presented in Figure 42 and Figure 43. All qualitative results represent reports, which were still valid one and a half years after the Butterfly programme ended while the quantitative results are distinguished in immediate (pre/ post test) and long-term results.

6.1.2.1 Nature-related changes

In the area of nature-related changes interviewees described having realised their own ability to adapt to a simpler lifestyle. This was due to their experience during the Solo time as well as to their experience of living outdoors for two weeks, and often entailed a contemplation of their assumed needs. Another notable feature of the follow-up interviews as well as of the Solo-only interview data was the frequent personification of nature in the interviewees' accounts. Interviewees repeatedly utilised the process of making friends with other people as a metaphor to explain how their relationship with nature has changed due to their nature experiences during the programmes. Additionally, interviewees described noting an altered awareness and a more sensual perception when in nature, which was sustained one and a half years after the Butterfly programme. Moreover, the follow-up interviews revealed that Butterfly participants perceived a greater attraction to natural places since the programme. Concurrently, this might be reflected in the noted decrease of statistical variance for the item "current contact with nature" which indicates that even though participants, on average, might not go out more often less participants go out "very little" one and a half years after the programme (for further elaboration go back to section 4.4.5.4).

Figure 42. Summary of the short- and long-term evaluation outcomes across data sources.

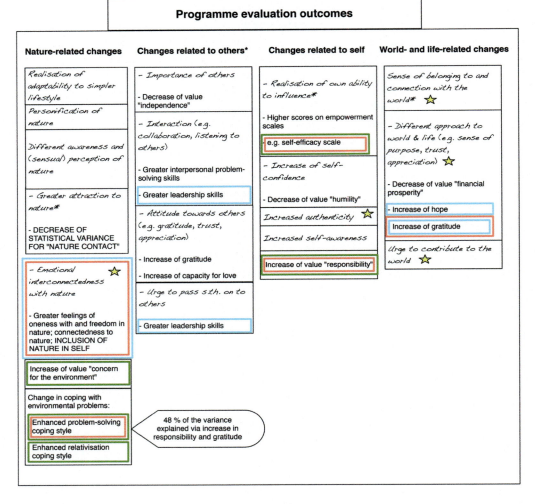

A further nature-related change immanent in the interview data was the prevailing perceived emotional interconnectedness with nature. Higher scores on several nature connectedness measures immediately after the programme support this qualitative long-term result, along with enhanced inclusion of nature in self one and a half years after the Butterfly. The pretest/ posttest increase in measures of connectedness to nature furthermore correlated significantly with the participants' increased hope, their reported sense of community in the Butterfly group as well as with an increased concern for the environment. Additionally, the quantitative data analysis revealed a change in the participants' style of coping with environmental problems immediately after the programme. Butterfly participants reported an enhanced problem solving coping style, which is described as a problem-focused and action-centered coping style and is, in the literature, associated with proenvironmental behaviour. The increase of this coping style correlated significantly with the participants' increase of hope and increase of connectedness to nature. Forty-eight percent of the variance (adjusted R^2) of the coping style Problem Solving was explained both via the increase of the participants' sense of responsibility as a behaviour guiding value as well as via their increase of gratitude for others and life. Apart from Problem Solving participants also reported an enhanced deproblematisation-focused coping style, Relativization, which represents the individual's belief that solutions will manifest despite discrepancies between the actual and target state and, in the literature, is found to correlate negatively with stress (Homburg *et al.*, 2007). In the present study, the increase of Relativization correlated significantly with the participants' increase of connectedness to nature.

Altogether, this highlights an interesting pattern. While participants felt increasingly connected to nature, they also felt increasingly concerned for it. Furthermore, it is not environmental concern but nature connectedness, which was significantly related to action-centered coping with environmental problems. Also, while nature connectedness was positively related to environmental concern, it was simultaneously positively related to hope and relativization. This may suggest that hope and environmental concern are not mutually exclusive but can instead co-exist when feeling connected with nature.

6.1.2.2 Changes related to others

In the area of changes related to others, follow-up interviewees reported a heightened awareness of their interconnectedness with others and of the importance of community and other people in their lives due to their Butterfly experience. This seems to be in accordance with the quantitative decrease of the value Independence, which represents the principle "It is important to make my own decisions and make things my way", possibly indicating a switch from independence to interdependence.

Interviewees also reported an altered interaction with others, which included an increased willingness to collaborate and share with other people, to interact with other people in more considerate ways and, as a key learning, participants reported having learned to truly listen to other people. Correspondingly, the quantitative data showed greater interpersonal problem-solving skills and greater leadership skills in participants right after the programme. The increase of leadership skills, in turn, correlated significantly with the participants' sense of community in the Butterfly group, potentially hinting at the importance of feeling part of something in order to evoke responsibility and action.

As a result of the Butterfly, interviewees furthermore reported changes in their attitude towards other people. Accounts included trusting other people more, carrying a more positive attitude towards and feelings of gratitude for others as well as being more open. In accordance, pretest/posttest survey data revealed an increase of the participants' gratitude for life including others as well as an increase in the participants' reported capacity for love. Capacity for love, as assessed in the present study, represents generally valuing relationships especially those, which include reciprocally sharing and caring for each other.

Lastly, follow-up interviewees described to now bear the inner wish to pass on their experiences and share what they experienced or learned with other people. This may be reflected in the reported increase of leadership skills right after the programme, which represents the participants' self-ascribed leadership ability and effectiveness in that role.

6.1.2.3 Changes related to self

Regarding the changes related to self, Butterfly interviewees revealed that they had realised their own strength and ability to make a difference. This also seems to show in the quantitative data, specifically in higher scores on the empowerment scales. For instance, participants indicated an increase of self-efficacy, which correlated significantly with the participants' increase of hope and connectedness to nature. Interviewees, furthermore, frequently reported a gain of self-confidence. This may also be reflected in the statistically detected decrease of the value humility, which represents the belief that it is important to be humble and modest about one's own accomplishments.

According to the interviewees, a further outcome of the Butterfly was an increase in personal authenticity. Interviewees described having freed themselves from what other people think and from the pressure they sense in society to be someone else. They not only reported being able to accept their own weaknesses and coping with them better but also meeting their inner strength with more awareness and appreciation. As touched upon in the previous section this seems to support the process of human transformation towards genuineness and bliss as suggested by Campbell (1988) and the dream study.

Another theme that repeatedly emerged in the interview data was heightened self-awareness, which manifested in participants' reports of greater understanding, clarity or awareness of their inner workings.

Lastly, the quantitative data additionally revealed an increase of the behaviour guiding value Responsibility, which represents the perceived importance of being dependable and trustworthy. Interestingly, this increase correlated significantly with increased hope and increased connectedness to nature.

6.1.2.4 World and life-related changes

In the area of world and life-related changes Butterfly participants explained that they felt more connected with the world and to their lives. Interviewees reported having experienced that they are part of a larger whole, an insight which stayed with the interviewees until one and a half years later and which facilitated a sense of place and belonging on earth.

Furthermore, interviewees also reported still approaching life and the world differently, one and a half years later. This change encompasses a variety of aspects such as engaging with life or work more passionately, having readjusted life objectives, being able to perceive more depth, purpose or quality in life, having incorporated a more caring, trusting, open-minded, mindful and appreciative attitude towards their lives as well as a broader awareness for world affairs. Correspondingly, after the Butterfly, survey data indicated a decrease in Financial Prosperity as a value guiding behaviour, which mirrors the belief that it is important to be successful at making money or buying property. Also participants reported an increase in hope and gratitude for life, both of which correlated significantly with their sense of community.

One and a half years later, interviewees also reported that the Butterfly programme had evoked in them the urge to contribute something to the world, reflected in the arising wish to be useful and serve a purpose in the world in very general terms. They repeatedly described that they were able to gain a clearer vision of the type of contribution they wanted to offer the world. Concretely, participants elaborated that the Butterfly experience activated in them the need to realign their career-related paths with the sense of self and the world that they had gained. Therefore, unsurprisingly, in the interview data, the urge to contribute to the world also co-occurred with a reported increase in authenticity.

Notably, all of the boxes or thematic areas grouped under world and life-related changes seem to be mirrored in the dream study.

Firstly, the process of "dream weaving" itself showed that only through weaving the individuals' dreams together did interconnections become apparent, and a greater story emerges. This act of weaving therefore appears to embody an important revelation participants reported as a result of the programme. In essence, participants described the empowering effect of experiencing interconnectedness, which entailed an immanent understanding of being part of a larger whole or a greater story, just as the dream weaving confirmed.

Furthermore, the reported changes in approaching life and the world as well as the arising urge to contribute meaningfully to the world and associated adjustments in the participants' lives are reflected, again, in the dream study. This suggests that the space of self-discovery may support orienting towards genuineness and bliss as Campbell (1988) indicated. According to Campbell (1988) an individual's bliss is furthermore strongly related to the importance of finding enjoyable work in the world. So instead of setting the initial intention to save the world, Campbell (1988) argues, real transformation takes place through people who feel fully alive and, thereby, vitalise the world and save it after all. Feeling more alive and aligning one's career choices with personal passions is, indeed, also immanent in the interview data presented above.

6.1.2.5 Comparison between Butterfly and Solo-only sample

When comparing the emergent interview themes between the Butterfly and Solo-only interviewees it needs to be highlighted again that changes reported by the Solo-only interviewees only refer to anticipated changes, as opposed to the Butterfly follow-up interview data which depict actual self-reported changes in the participants' lives one and a half years after the Butterfly programme. Nevertheless, Solo-only interviewees anticipated a surprisingly high number of changes, which, in the follow-up study, Butterfly interviewees reported to have implemented. However, with regard to nature-related changes, Solo-only interviewees did not mention foreseeing a greater attraction to nature after the programme. Furthermore, only the Butterfly interviewees revealed that they had realised their own strength and ability to make a difference in the world as well as a greater sense of belonging to and connection with the world. Unsurprisingly, changes in the relationship with others also constituted a missing aspect in the reports of the Solo-only sample which may indicate that the interactional level of the Solo-only programme mainly focused on the relationship with oneself and nature as opposed to equally providing a learning environment for the exploration of group dynamics and interrelations with others that expand the social aspects of the Solo ritual. Notably, the encounter with other Butterfly participants, the facilitation team and Findhorn as role models, as well as the growing urge to pass their experiences on to other people, were essential triggers for taking action as evident in Figure 43. This circumstance possibly makes a case for the importance of integrating interconnectedness in its fullness by acknowledging that the sense of interconnectedness between humans and nature and the sense of interconnectedness among humans are mutually reinforcing and, indeed, inseparable.

6.1.3 Activism as part of the long-term results

As already indicated, another central research interest was to find out whether the Butterfly participants' experiences led to actual behaviour change up to one and a half years after the programme. For this reason I screened actual environmental behaviour and practical engagement, qualitatively and quantitatively. Moreover, in the context of reported behaviour change, I asked participants in the interviews to explain what triggered such change in their understanding.

A visual summary of the results across data sources is presented in Figure 43.

First of all, the great majority of interviewees reported changes in environmental behaviour and practical engagement one and a half years after the Butterfly programme. Practical engagement that interviewees attributed to their Butterfly experience encompassed: implemented career changes such as pursuing a career path in line with personal values and visions, initiating own Youth in Action programmes, attending trainings and programmes which deepened their own skills, or voluntarily supporting new projects dealing with global social change. Notably, a lot of these actions were connected with nature awareness work or sustainability matters, which is why both types of activism in the qualitative data actually cannot be separated fully as the dotted line in Figure 43 illustrates. Consistently, the participants' proenvironmental behaviour, one and a half years after the programme, significantly correlated with how much they engaged in their local communities two months after the programme. Notably, only practical engagement was supported quantitatively via a significant increase in scores on the community participation scale. Proenvironmental behaviour, as assessed via the Proenvironmental Behaviour (PEB) scale, did not change significantly over three measurement points. It is possible that the increase could not manifest in the quantitative data due to a ceiling effect as participants, from the start, already scored high compared to averages reported in the literature (see Schultz *et al.*, 2005). Furthermore, in the interviews Butterfly participants also reported an increase in their care for animals and plants as part of newly adopted proenvironmental behaviours, which may indicate that the PEB might not have addressed all of the relevant environmental behaviours for the present sample. Forty percent of the variance of the participants' proenvironmental behaviour one and a half years after the programme was explained via the participants' increase of the Inclusion of Nature in Self (INS) scale and their leadership skills as reported right after the programme.

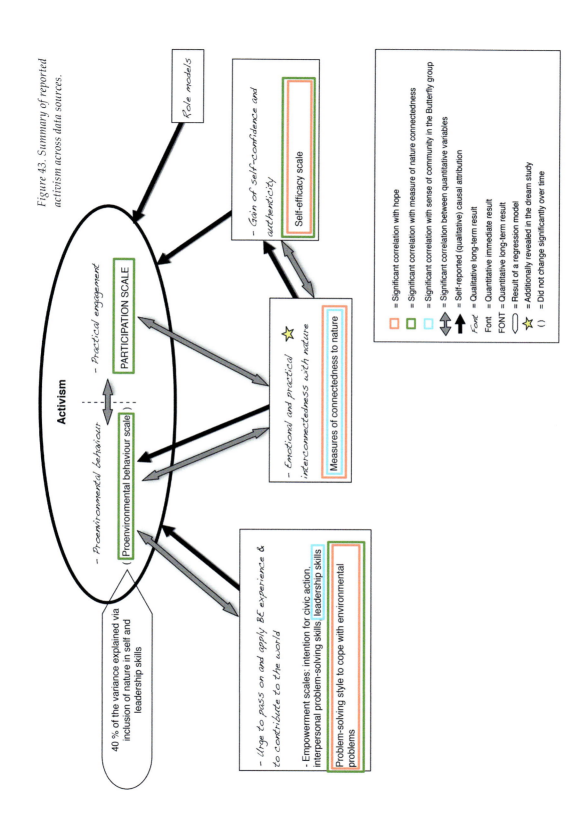

Figure 43. Summary of reported activism across data sources.

Interviewees named their urge to pass on and apply their Butterfly experience as a prime mover for their generally increased activism, which is mirrored in the quantitative increase of scores of the empowerment scales such as the leadership scale as well as in the enhancement of the problem-solving coping style.

Interviewees explained their changes in proenvironmental behaviour additionally by their emotional interconnectedness with nature and by their experience of practical interconnectedness with nature while living and working outdoors. Equally, measures of connectedness to nature correlated significantly with PEB. However, interestingly, they also correlated significantly with the participants' reported increase of community participation pointing towards a possible mutual reinforcement of the sense of interconnectedness between humans and nature, and the sense of interconnectedness among humans as a prerequisite to feel involved and empowered enough to truly take action. One possible link between the two types of interconnectedness may be found in the participants' reported gain of self-confidence and authenticity. Interviewees explained that they had gained self-confidence through their nature experiences and that it was largely that gain in self-confidence which empowered them to engage on a community level after the Butterfly programme (see section 4.4.3.5). This is equally supported by the significant correlation between the participants' increased feeling of oneness with nature and increased self-efficacy.

Furthermore, what appeared to have greatly impacted the interviewees' activism was their encounter with role models. For the interviewees' role models, as other participants, the Butterfly team and Findhorn as a model for ecological community living, acted as real-life evidence for the practicability of change.

6.1.4 Interconnectedness and separateness as meta-level outcomes

Throughout the whole thesis there was a particular dichotomy which emerged again and again: interconnectedness and separateness.

In the introduction I briefly outlined how the present environmental situation and associated human behaviour points towards a societal issue, which prevents us from "connecting the dots" and from living a lifestyle in service of collective welfare instead of self-interest. I explained how the notion of separateness from nature appears to dominate the human mind and behaviour, despite the fact that we are deeply embedded in the world through countless physical and psychological interdependencies.

In this way, separateness can be seen as the antithesis of interconnectedness and thus, both notions, in their own way, speak to the same zeitgeist. While separateness reflects the current way of human thinking and operating in the world, interconnectedness highlights this societal fallacy by representing the antidote to the problem or the opposing alternative reality.

Interconnectedness as a theme emerged in the qualitative interview data as the participants' lived experience of interconnectedness with nature, particularly during the Solo time, and as their experience of interconnectedness with other people in the group. And it re-emerged as a core finding of the dream study.

In the dream study, interconnectedness surfaced in four ways (see Figure 44). It was immanent in my experiences during the focusing session, when my own perceptions and emotions appeared to reflect the participants' state of mind and heart at the final phase of the Butterfly programme. Thereby, interconnectedness between me, as the researcher, and the research participants was revealed.

Also interconnectedness emerged in the process of working with dreams through "dream weaving". It turned out that only when putting the participants' dreams together did interconnections become apparent, and a greater story, the universal myth of the Hero's Journey, emerged. In that, the interconnectedness of dreams became apparent.

On a broader level, the dream study allowed for the emergence of interconnectedness between me, the researcher, and a fundamental part of the phenomenology of the research object. Through the intersubjective-heuristic method and the associated researcher's entitlement to give way to self-reflexivity and intuitive insight as an equally valid part of the research process, research and the role of the researcher were revitalised and movement, exploration and connection were reintroduced into the process. These reintroduced aspects, in turn, seem to mirror crucial features of interconnectedness itself. In this way, I encountered interconnectedness between my own experience of the research process and one of the core findings of the present work: interconnectedness.

Similarly, interconnectedness as a fundamental part of the phenomenology of the research object seemed to be reflected in the character of dreams, which reveal intriguing interconnections between dream content and day-time lived experience.

Altogether, the dream study provided a unique space for the multiple facets of interconnectedness to emerge, which may have been difficult to assess via methods that work within the paradigm of claimed objectivity and separateness. The incorporation of dreams, as the counterpart of our daytime consciousness, thereby almost seemed to reconcile the separateness, which like interconnectedness emerged as an overarching theme throughout various sections of this dissertation.

Markedly, the theme of separateness emerged more subtly than interconnectedness, in danger of being overlooked, as it was not revealed *in* the data as such. As outlined in the literature review, separateness showed up in the contemporary worldview as the human habit to perceive and understand the world in isolated pieces. Particularly relevant in this thesis, this is also reflected in the man-made divide between human

Figure 44. Interconnectedness and separateness as emergent throughout the thesis.

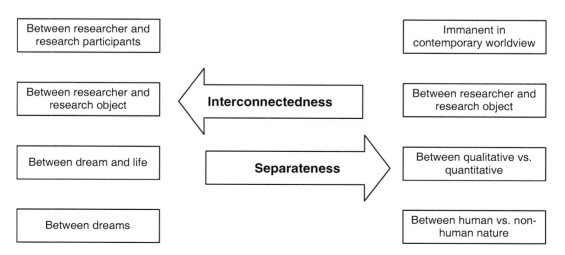

and non-human nature. And on a very basic epistemological level this is mirrored in the prevailing research paradigm which intentionally separates researcher and research object and is clearly subdivided into qualitative and quantitative research approaches with the latter being the more acknowledged one.

All in all, the meta-level outcomes, particularly interconnectedness in this work's manifestation, invalidate the commonly accepted epistemological assumption of a possible separation between object and subject as well as between researcher and research object. Ultimately, phenomena such as interconnectedness are hard to assess, let alone explain, within our contemporary worldview and clearly call for a more complementary approach to understanding the world as demonstrated via the dream study.

6.2 Further elaborations of selected outcomes

6.2.1 Nature experience

As outlined in the literature section of this work, an often neglected aspect in the study of significant life experiences has been the investigation of the "internal environment" of individuals, which may be essential in the process of attributing significance to external events (Chawla, 1998). In that sense, an essential contribution of the present work is the illumination of shared individual inner experiences of the outer environment.

As Payne (1999) pointed out, these simultaneously encompass the body as well as the mind. Reflected in the participants' reports of their experience of an expansion of bodily boundaries but, more commonly, also in reports of their enhanced sensual perception in nature the importance of including physicality as part of human interaction with nature is clearly highlighted in this study. In line with the findings of Snell and Simmonds (2012), participants, once in nature, switched from an analysing and thinking mode to a rather reflective, sensual and contemplative mode, leading to profound personal changes and insights. Snell and Simmonds extracted these features in the context of investigating spiritual experiences in nature, and their sample included individuals who self-identified as having had significant experiences in nature. Interestingly, participants in the present study reported this mode of mind as part of their general nature experience, regardless of the retrospective significance they assigned to it. A plausible explanation for this might be that the Solo ritual itself already represents a strong framework, which invites spiritual significance from the start (see 4.4.1.4).

Study participants also associated their enhanced sensual perception in nature with feeling free from distractions when in nature and with their arrival in the present moment. This reminds of the notion of mindfulness which has been shown to enhance the experience of nature and nature connectedness (Howell *et al.*, 2011).

One of the links between mindfulness and the participants' nature experience may be found in their reports of enhanced awareness when in nature. After all, in Howell *et al.*'s study (2013) it was the awareness scales of the mindfulness measures, thus awareness of experiences in nature, which correlated with nature connectedness, rather than the acceptance scores. Similarly, in the present study, enhanced presence and sensual perception in nature brought about the feeling and realisation of emotional interconnectedness with nature. This altered way of being in and encountering nature persisted long after the programme ended. It seems as though, through the programmes, especially the Solo, participants learned to perceive nature differently and to be more aware of and "in" nature. Importantly, moreover, Butterfly participants seemed to have been able to transfer this way of being and perceiving into their casual, non-facilitated way of being in nature later on. Just as Hinds (2011) suggested that a diary-based account of engaging with nature can lead to mindful awareness, the Solo ritual may be another way or practice to promote such a state of mind. However, it cannot be ruled out that mindfulness generally arises when being in natural surroundings regardless of the framework for the nature experience.

As mindfulness today is mainly associated with meditation practices, it would be interesting to expand this emphasis to different contexts and practices in order to illuminate potentially different pathways to and features of mindfulness.

At least one distinction seems quite apparent when comparing the phenomenology of mindfulness in nature to mindfulness in the meditation context. While the long-term meditation practitioner knows how to calm down thoughts, "empty the mind", go inwards and concentrate on the breath, nature experiences as researched in the present work simultaneously lead in *and* outwards. In the present work, the enlivenment of the senses and associated arrival in the present moment helped participants to immerse themselves in their surroundings, in symbols, images and meaning, and to start a deep process of reflection on their personal lives. Future research should track the different shapes and effects of mindfulness depending on the context it arises in. The seemingly contradictory nature of both "mindfulness practices", however, dissolves in the light of Eastern, especially Buddhist, philosophy, as "emptiness" and "fullness" are understood as two sides of reality.

Another aspect of enlivenment of all senses was the immersion in countless "micro universes" in nature as evident in the following interviewee quote:

> *Because I was not distracted, because I had the time to observe my surroundings with a loving eye. Especially the flies, all the insects and all the- well, I was able to make use of all my senses in order to allow nature to permeate through me* (B8).

This touches on what Braud and Anderson (1998) outlined as "compassionate knowing". In their book, they refer to the experience of a scientist researching corn fungus under a microscope. In the process of observing the microscopic reality of the fungi the researcher described how she began to immerse in their world and how she started to feel more and more akin to them. Braud & Anderson (1998) suggest that "to know persons, we must love them first and look at the world from their perspective. To know any thing, we must love it and become its friend" (p. 80-81). They continue to explain that only through deeply and lovingly engaging with an experience one starts to perceive it from the inside and begins to see what is actually there.

Compassionate knowing seems to tap into those phenomena, which I categorised under the transpersonal dimension of interconnectedness with nature. Here, interviewees reported immersive experiences in nature that dissolved or extended their boundaries of their sense of self. For instance, some interviewees reported experiences such as taking over nature's perspective. Moreover, the experience of the transpersonal dimension was often accompanied with strong feelings of love, awe, and connection, and commonly entailed profound insights. The transpersonal dimension of the participants' experience of interconnectedness with nature also seems to relate to a concept, which William James (1958) introduced as the "noetic quality" of a mystical experience. James explains that "although so similar to states of feeling, mystical states seem to those who experience them to be also states of knowledge (p.293)."

Indeed, it seems as though participants describe events where a strong emotional bond with nature and the cognitive component of insight are experienced at once, potentially reflecting an "emotional state of knowing" or as suggested by Braud and Anderson (1998) "compassionate knowing". However, whether this is what participants indicated by using expressions like "it went under my skin at a different level" or "I realised 'everything is connected' at another level" remains a matter of further research.

Furthermore, interviewees jointly reported an experience of emotional interconnectedness with nature, an instantly arising emotional reaction, which was frequently expressed as feeling at home, at peace, connected or hopeful when being in nature. As shown this had nothing to do with the participants' actual familiarity with the place (see results section 4.4.1.1).

Weber (2003) suggests that the emotions which natural places evoke in us root in feeling the balance of complementarities, which nature enacts "through the unknowing wisdom of communing among myriad feeling bodies, plants and organsims" (p.). Possibly, we step back into this perpetual communing when immersing ourselves in nature and maybe it is reconnecting with these roots which brings about these feelings of being home and at peace.

An additional frequently reported experience in this work has been the interviewees' experience of psychological interconnectedness with nature. Here, participants seemed to experience nature as a mirror through an on-going dynamic interplay between their own psyche and the natural world. Interviewees reported having recognised their personal stories, intentions, issues, or thoughts as real-life metaphors in natural landscapes or objects. These reflections, in turn, often had an impact on participants' initial experience of the subject and stimulated an inner psychological process leading to the acquisition of additional self-knowledge.

While this mirroring process is clearly something that was introduced as part of the preparation for the Solo time (see description of threshold walks in section 4.3.3.1), the interview data provided such a rich and vast amount of accounts of this phenomenon that it seems as though there was an innate readiness to engage with nature in such a way. Inevitably, the question arises why this phenomenon occurs so readily and what its potential use may be.

In the literature, identification with nature is at times regarded very critically. Indeed, there is an ambiguity at play, which Chawla (1998) points out by providing two definitions of empathy. According to Webster's Encyclopedic Unabridged Dictionary (1989) empathy is described as the "identification with or vicarious experiencing of the feelings, thoughts, or attitudes of another", but it is also summarised as the "imaginative ascribing to an object of feelings or attitudes present in oneself". In this light, it seems questionable whether the participants' experience is pure projection or something more reciprocal[62] that goes beyond that. Chawla (1998) warns that imposing one's emotions or needs on nature supports "a Cartesian philosophy of

---

62 As suggested in the present work by using the code name "psychological interconnectedness".

nature, in which ecosystems are seen as mechanisms without intrinsic feeling" (p. 12). Correspondingly, Gusetti (2014) denounces that it would be an anthropocentric fallacy to find nature only worthy of protection once it is personified.

While these critiques are certainly valid, projections may be more than solely human ignorance of nature's intrinsic value. Possibly, identifying and highlighting similarities, and in that sense maybe even an initial self-centeredness, is merely part of the human process of making sense of ourselves, others and the world. After all, indications of a human mirror neuron system suggest that we are wired to mirror each other (Rizzolatti & Sinigaglia, 2010) and that this process bears far-reaching social implications (see 2.1.3). It is known that if we believe we are mirrored by another affiliation, empathy (Lakin & Chartrand, 2003) and connectedness (van Baaren *et al.*, 2009) is built between interaction partners. Therefore, recognising oneself in nature may be a natural part of the process of building affiliation and connectedness, which may apply to the human-human and the human-nature relationship alike.

Considerations like these are not novel and are found in several research approaches. For instance, Schultz (2002) developed the Inclusion of Nature in Self (INS) measure based on research on interpersonal relationships. Referring to Aron *et al.*'s research (Aron, Aron, Tudor, & Nelson, 1991; Aron *et al.*, 1992; Aron & Fraley, 1999) Schultz (2002) summarises "that in close [human] relationships, the cognitive representations of self and other become integrated. That is, the schematic representation of self and other overlaps with many shared qualities. Taken to the extreme, self and other become one" (p. 68). Accordingly, intimacy is build through a process of self-disclosure, which is exactly what happens when Solo participants enter nature with an intention and engage in highly personal processes. Moreover, Tam *et al.*'s (2013) studies revealed that connectedness to nature mediated the link between anthropomorphism and proenvironmental behaviour. Intriguingly, personification of nature has been equally found in the qualitative data of the present work and, indeed, several interviewees independently utilised the process of making friends with other people as a metaphor to explain how their relationship with nature had changed due to their nature experiences during the programmes (see chapter 4.4.3.1). Possibly, this also explains why, in the qualitative data, similar themes and processes have been found for the human-human and human-nature relationship. For both areas, others and nature, emotional and psychological interconnectedness emerged as crucial facilitators for self-access and the acquisition of self-knowledge. It is conceivable that the way "the other" affects us follows a consistent route no matter whether the other is represented by other people or nature.

According to Romanyshyn (2007) it is the cultivation of metaphoric sensibility, which enables true dialogue with an "other". Romanyshyn (2007) elaborates:

> *A metaphoric sensibility may open one to the necessity of dialogue with an other, but it is the inner work with one's shadow other that makes the dialogue possible. […] To the degree that one does not admit the validity of the "other" within oneself, he or she denies the other person the right to exist. [..] it is essential to understand the coupling between the other out there and the "other" within.* (p. 341)

Elements of the process described above are also reflected in interviewees' accounts of psychological interconnectedness with others as exemplified in the following quote:

> *Because when I am looking at the negative side* [of people] *and I am judging people I am usually doing that because I am doing that to myself. And I am not being as happy with myself. So I am looking out to other people and I have learned to look at the good in people and see the good in people and to look at their qualities because when I look at their qualities and I look at the good in them I can see that in myself* (B5).

However, generally, metaphoric sensibility and the associated inner work described by Romanyshyn (2007) seems to be particularly present in participants' experiences of psychological interconnectedness with nature. And possibly, this indicates that participants had an experience of a larger (ecological) self, which according to Bragg (1996) is marked by perceiving analogies and relatedness to other natural elements.

"Meeting the other within" also reminds of Weber's (2013) case for our need of nature. As Weber (2013) explains we need this "«living inside», this otherness, that stands in front of us" (p.34) because it discloses our blind spots of self-understanding. Notably, psychological interconnectedness with nature in the present study was not only expressed in recognising similarities but also in the recognition of differences, which served as personal inspirations. As shown in the associated results section (4.4.1.1), accounts of psychological interconnectedness also included personal insights, which were evoked through the confrontation with unexpected situations or unknown elements in nature. This implies an immanent expansion of one's horizon through "the other" and contradicts the argument of mere navel-gazing.

As an explanation for the amount of self-reflection and insight found in this work, one hypothesis might be that nature triggers restoration processes and thereby provides a suitable context for reflection. Adhemar (2008) proposes that this might be the reason why nature seems to evoke greater levels of meaning and coherence for humans.

The notion that nature facilitates self-reflection and insight not only occurred in this study but also has been found in other research studies (see Mayer *et al.*, 2009). However, in Mayer *et al.*'s study participants had been asked to only think of minor life issues during their time in nature due to the limited amount of time they were given, which is why the authors restrict the benefits of spending time outdoors to minor life issues. This has been different in the present study where participants had 24-hours and plenty of extra time in nature, which explains why participants also started to deal with major life issues. Thus, the present work supports the beneficial effects of nature, claimed in the literature, for self-reflection and the ability to deal with life issues, and moreover suggests that this may also apply to a wider range of life issues provided that a proportional timeframe is given.

Many of the insights that participants gained in nature dealt with their experience of the human-nature relationship, which changed as a result of the programmes. Possibly, as neuroscience suggests, this was the case because they were able to physically experience and thereby internalise what they cognitively might have known before already. After all, survey data revealed that participants were fairly environmentally conscious from the start and nevertheless the level of activism and the relationship with and perception of nature seemed to have changed after the programme.

Possibly, the crucial point is not necessarily the development of environmental awareness but rather of environmental-self-awareness. This might explain why the practice of Solo time in nature proved to be as powerful as shown in the present work, for it integrates awareness for the natural surroundings with self-awareness by enabling the soloist to experience her or himself in the mirror of nature. In that, immersive experiences in nature may be one way of complementing the empirical way of understanding the world by disclosing it through inner experience, as called for by Walach (2014).

Generally, it seems as though the participants' nature experiences initiated what has been described as reenchantment in the literature. As Barlett (2008) explains:

> *Reenchantment begins with moments of sensory and aesthetic expansion, the experience of being outside oneself or caught up in wonder, and a positive mental or physical effect described as peacefulness, serenity, or joy. These experiences offer a different context for the self, an identity as a part of a web of living things. […] Such relationships are often expressed in a deepened ethic of care for the earth and caretaking of particular locales. These dimensions of reenchantment are for some people a sequence– from experience to action–and for others nested or only partly articulated.* (p. 1089)

Regarding the relationship with nature the data furthermore revealed two, at first glance, surprising findings. Firstly, unlike often suggested in the literature, there was no significant correlation between the participants' reported nature-related changes and their amount of childhood experiences in nature. Secondly, there was no significant increase of the participants' contact with nature after the Butterfly programme. However, as already touched upon in the results section, the latter finding may be explained via the following plausible circumstance: as Cervinka, Zeidler, Karlegger and Hefler (2009) found out, it is quite common for people to spend time outdoors in summertime and therefore contact with nature in summertime does not necessarily reflect the level of connectedness to nature. However, spending time in nature during wintertime, when most of the socialising takes place indoors, seems to be a meaningful indicator of connectedness to nature. As the follow-up measurement took place in wintertime, it is quite a remarkable finding that the amount of contact with nature did not change significantly (compared to summertime), which might speak for a greater level of connectedness after the programme. Nevertheless, this would need to be investigated in comparison with a control group in order to draw a direct conclusion.

Regarding the lack of correlation between nature-related changes and the participants' childhood experiences, a valuable explanation may be found in Brixler and Morris' study (1997). Brixler and Morris (1997) compared recreation seekers' and non-recreation seekers' childhood experiences in nature. They found no significant difference regarding the amount of play experiences in nature during childhood. However, recreation seekers did have more childhood and adolescent experiences of wild areas under the mentorship of meaningful others. Thus, as elaborated in the literature section 2.2.3, the more influential factor seems to be nature "experiences that socialize [the children] into interpreting nature in positive or meaningful ways" (Chawla, 1998, p. 17). This highlights the crucial role of meaning-making and the importance of other people in the process of affiliating with nature, which leads to the next subject of discussion.

6.2.2 The social dimension of nature experiences

An intriguing result of the analysis of the quantitative data has been the significant correlation between the Butterfly participants' increase in community participation and their increase in connectedness to nature. This points towards a potentially intertwined relationship between affiliation with nature and the social dimension of engaging with the world. Notably, connectedness to nature was also significantly associated with the participants' reported sense of community in the Butterfly group. Possibly, this reflects what Chawla (2007) described as the "process of joint attention" where the social and physical plane work hand in hand to sustainably influence a child's experience of nature. Joint attention, according to Chawla (2007), underlines the importance of the quality of attention displayed by others, that is, at best, others who engage with nature in an appreciative way in combination with a physical experience of nature. Perhaps, the emerged pattern between sense of community, connectedness to nature and community engagement can be at least partly explained via a similar group process of joint attention.

After all, such a pattern has been repeatedly reported in the literature as well, for instance in Fraser, Clayton, Sickler and Taylor's study (2009) on zoo volunteers. Volunteers were asked about their motives for volunteering, their benefits from the experience and their relationship to the other volunteers. Commonly, as an initial motivation, volunteer described their love for animals. However, as the primary reason for continuing their work they named their relationship with the other volunteers. Partly, this was due to their shared love of animals but, as it turned out, volunteers had also incorporated "being a zoo volunteer" into their social identities[63]. Thus, volunteers had found a social niche which provided them with a sense of belonging in the world (Harré, 2011). Possibly, Butterfly participants experienced something similar, which may be why their increase in environmental concern was not only associated with the participants' sense of connectedness to nature but also with their ascribed importance of belonging to a group and with the increased importance of personal reliability, thus responsibility, as a behaviour guiding value.

However, the social facet of experiencing nature seems to work in several ways. For instance, Zhang *et al.* (2014) were able to show that the mere exposure to beautiful nature in a laboratory setting increased the study participants' prosocial behaviour.

Furthermore, natural environments are known to influence group dynamics uniquely, as they tend to diminish role barriers and formality which, in turn, facilitates the establishment of group identity, trust, more open communication and sharing of personal thoughts and decisions among group members (Driver & Peterson, 1986). Therefore, Roggenbuck and Driver (2000) propose that a "lived experience" of nature also encompasses the group dynamics within these facilitated experiences. Over and above, they suggest that the group dynamics can crucially determine whether the benefits of organised nature group experiences described in the literature manifest or not.

Again this highlights that the sense of interconnectedness between humans and nature, and the sense of interconnectedness among humans, are mutually reinforcing and should therefore, as emphasised before, be equally consolidated in programmes in order to empower individuals to truly engage with the world and take action.

---

63 Assessed via a "collective self-esteem scale" measuring whether volunteers were valued as a member of the volunteer group, whether they themselves valued their role, whether their role was publicly valued and whether they conceived their role as important.

Notably, in the qualitative data, the encounter with other participants, the facilitation team and Findhorn as role models, as well as the growing urge to pass their experiences on to other people, were essential triggers for taking action. A potential explanation why role models and the witnessing of other people's changes during programme time was so powerful for interviewees may be found in contemporary knowledge on neuronal mirroring, imitation behaviour and social norms. As summarised in chapter 2.1.3, human minds are to a certain degree interconnected. Especially if expedient, we are wired to automatically and sometimes even unconsciously assimilate other people's behaviours. What might have been especially effective in the Butterfly programme is the actual demonstration of behaviour to encourage change. Thus, the Butterfly provided the valuable combination of knowing and saying one thing and simultaneously putting this into action. For instance, an often mentioned aspect in the interviews was the fact that the facilitation team appeared highly authentic as they facilitated the camp free of charge simply because they believed in the importance of the work. Also, no fear of nature was demonstrated by the team and all the programme components and facilities were implemented and set up outdoors, which gave participants the empowering experience of the feasibility of living sustainably in close contact with nature. Importantly, living sustainably was not implemented in a bleak and restrictive kind of way but realised by integrating aesthetics, tasty food, care and fun.

Moreover, humans are highly receptive to a person's behaviour and the social rewards they attract. This was reinforced via Findhorn as a famous large-scale role model for the feasibility of living in communion with others and nature, but also via the appreciative tone and atmosphere that was set by the team and picked up immediately by the participants. This explains well why for some participants it was very inspiring to watch others change. In line with Bandura's approach, Harré (2011) believes that it is much more important to have "people on the ground" as role models than to apply more distant forms of modeling via, for instance, media campaigns. Through one-on-one contact a multiplier effect is much more likely to occur especially if a group is diverse which was the case in the Butterfly group.

After all, one and a half years after the programme, interviewees reported to have adopted a similar philosophy of "seeding", which they described as silently transmitting to others what they have learned by acting as a role model instead of pointing things out directly.

6.2.3 Meaning-making

6.2.3.1 Meaning-making and the power of stories
One aspect in the literature which appeared repeatedly in different research contexts was the importance of meaning (-making).

As revealed in the chapter on imitation, people do not pick up behaviour randomly – they also seek its meaning. Moreover, significant life experiences (SLE) research showed that childhood experiences in nature seem to have a more sustainable impact if accompanied by meaningful others. Also, it has been found that the meaning-making component of spirituality significantly mediated the association between nature exposure and psychological well-being, as well as between connectedness to nature and psychological well-being (Kamitsis & Francis, 2013). Consequently, Kamitsis *et al.* (2013) concluded that spirituality and its innate "meaning-making" might function as a source, which facilitates the benefits of nature experiences.

The bottom line seems to be that we need meaning in order to feel good and in order to effectively initiate behaviour. However, as criticised by many (e.g. see Weber, 2013), our fragmented perception of the world today seems to lack exactly this – meaning.

It is in this context, that it seems important to look at one of the emergent qualitative results more closely; namely, the power of stories. In the present work, stories, as shared after returning from the Solo, functioned as meaning-makers for the participants' Solo experience, but participants also extracted meaning for their lives from listening to other people's stories, which were told either as part of other participants' Solo experiences or as part of further Councils that took place in other contexts. Specifically, stories turned out to be the medium through which emotional and psychological interconnectedness with others was experienced, and which facilitated self-access and personal insights also regarding the participants' nature experiences.

Oral stories bear such power because they can be intersubjective, participatory and physical and therefore emotionally affect the listener more than written stories (Sandlos, 1998; Sanger, 1997). Moreover, oral stories entail active participation of the listener as she or he automatically starts to visualise the story, which, for instance, exceeds the passive absorption of information through television. Even more so, if the story is told close to where it took place, as was the case for the Solo stories, the listener can be inspired to travel to that place imaginatively. Thus, the listener, the storyteller and the place conjoin (Mander, 1991). This is in line with Basso's (1996) research into the language and landscape of a native American tribe. Basso found out that for this tribe the shared stories literally "took place", in the sense that stories actually created lasting bonds between the listener and the features of the landscape.

Consistently, interviewees revealed that the Solo stories deepened their own experiences and even inspired self-reflection on thus far novel aspects of themselves and of their experiences. All in all, as Lutts (1985) recognised, stories seem to "join together the pieces of our experiences and the experiences of others in a way that gives order, significance, and meaning to the chaos around us" (p. 39).

6.2.3.2 Meaning-making and hope

Meaning furthermore can be related to hope. For instance, Vaclav Havel (1990) theorised that hope is reflected in the faith that things are meaningful.

It is conceivable that hope and meaning naturally arise when an individual engages in a meaningful action. As Ojala (2012) observed, "when people start to do something concrete it seems as if hope is evoked by the actions themselves. Hope, in a sense, becomes embodied" (Ojala, 2012, p. 13). This may be mirrored in the significant correlation between the increase of hope and self-efficacy as well as the action-centred coping style problem-solving, which potentially reflects the Butterfly participants' experience of the power of a small act during programme time. This would also support Zimmerman's (1990) theory of learned hopefulness (see chapter 2.1.2).

Referring to Folkman's (2008) research, Ojala (2012) furthermore argues that positive emotions such as hope may facilitate activism in the face of climate change by providing people with a necessary respite from the difficult situation and thereby with the strength needed to take action (Folkman, 2008).

Notably, in the present study, hope also seems to bear a social dimension, as revealed by the significant correlation between the Butterfly participants' increase of hope and their sense of community in the group as well as by their increase of their capacity for love (for others). Love for other people and the inspiration that participants got out of other participants as role models was also confirmed in the qualitative data. Possibly, participants felt more hopeful the more they felt connected to other people because this increased their trust in other people's abilities. This effect of "everyone pulling together" is in line with Ojala's (2012) research showing that another constructive source of hope is trust in other actors, which is also positively related to proenvironmental behaviour. Indeed, it is theorised that experiences which promote interaction and mutual help are more empowering (Zimmerman, 1990).

However, generally, there is only little known about the kind of interventions that can actually effectively influence people's level of hope (Alarcon, Bowling, & Khazon, 2013). Against this background, this study's findings regarding hope and its various associations seem all the more interesting, as they provide concrete clues as to what kind of components should be considered as part of an effective programme.

Summarised, the literature suggests that meaning influences human well-being and behaviour as well as the formation of significant experiences. Meaning-making of the Butterfly participants' nature and community experiences seems to have been facilitated particularly through sharing oral stories about these experiences. Moreover, meaning may be closely related to hope which, in the present study, may be traced back to the participants' experience of collective strength and of the power of a small act.

6.3 Methodological considerations

The endeavour to research organised wilderness group programmes poses a number of challenges to the researcher, which have been thoroughly outlined by Ewert and McAvoy (2000). Such programmes require field studies, which, in contrast to laboratory research, need to be conducted in the natural setting of the programme itself. Thus, the difficulty lies in conducting valid and reliable research, which, at the same time, is not intrusive to the participants.

Often in Solo programmes group sizes are kept small to facilitate positive group dynamics and in order to keep the necessary level of concentration for the group sharings. Small sample sizes therefore require the investigation of several groups spread over time. This was also the case in the present work that investigated two different programmes, which contained the Solo as a core component. Thereby, internal validity threats may come into play such as the effect of "history" that is unexpected situational influences and events like weather conditions during both programmes, which could have distorted the outcomes. However, the diversity in both programmes simultaneously contributes to the external validity of the present work as the studies investigated the phenomenology and impact of immersive experiences in nature under varying conditions such as country, type of landscape, group composition and number, facilitation team and selection processes of participants. As I consistently compared themes in the qualitative data as well as PCI dimensions in the quantitative data, I was able to detect potentially consistent features of immersive experiences in nature as evoked through a Solo across both samples. However, the reported findings only apply to young adults as age did not differ considerably among groups.

Another point of criticism may be found in the selection process of the participants. Naturally, in programmes which challenge personal boundaries, participation needs to be voluntary. One could argue that this poses a threat to the study's internal validity as the selection process for the two programmes might have attracted specific kinds of people. This is in line with Borstelman's (1977) finding who investigated beneficial effects from Outward Bound outdoor and wilderness programs. Borstelman (1977) revealed that participants of such outdoor programmes were often ready to change to begin with, a phenomenon which he called the "readiness to change syndrome". As a result, the question arose whether self-reported changes actually rooted in the nature experience or merely depicted pre-existing differences in the individual's motivation for participation. This is, also in the context of the present studies, a valid point even though it should be considered that the formal frame of the programmes might have weakened the bias in the selection process. Notably, the Butterfly Effect programme was funded and promoted by the European Youth-in-Action-Programme, which limited the individual's effort and financial contribution to a bare minimum and thereby might have also attracted people who did not specifically look for a Solo experience[64]. Similarly, the Solo-only programme was offered as a part of a one-year programme so that no active seeking out of such an experience was necessary. After all, a few of the Butterfly interviewees stated that they had never even slept in a tent before participating in the Butterfly programme which underlines that some participants were completely new to such experiences.

However, most importantly, due to the lack of a control group, I never conducted the present research with the intention to compare groups and make generalisable, universal statements about the impact of immersive experiences in nature, but with the intention to conduct basic research.

Furthermore, in the light of this study, the characteristic "readiness for change syndrome" does not belittle the power of Solos, as Solos are traditionally facilitated as a rite of passage and readiness for change means that change has not taken place yet. Thus, self-reported changes after the programmes suggest that the Solo, as intended, actually functioned as a rite of passage for desired change.

Moreover, the present work constitutes exploratory research, which means that I preliminarily assumed no pattern or process as potential facilitators of the assessed changes. Even though the present research intentionally focused on immersive experiences in wild nature, the data revealed that the self-reported changes were, indeed, a product of mutually reinforcing nature and community experiences. This outcome neither diminishes nor idolises immersive experiences in nature but underlines the importance and interconnectedness of the human-human and the human-nature relationship.

As Ewert and McAvoy (2000) aptly pointed out, another difficulty in researching wilderness programmes are their logistics and schedules. Participants often come from various places and in the case of the Butterfly programme even from various countries, which complicates the data collection prior to the programme. Also due to the logistics of living outdoors, the Solo itself, the tight schedules of such programmes and the prospect of leaving the intact group and returning to everyday life, leave very little time and energy on

---

64 Notably, even though the Solo was listed as part of the programme it was not further explained in the official call for participants.

the participants' side for posttest data collection. Fortunately, I was able to find a feasible solution regarding the pretest for the Butterfly programme (see 4.3.4.1) which allowed for testing in the participants' home countries before the programme started. However, the participants' time and energy dropped noticeably at posttest when I asked participants to fill out the extensive surveys shortly before leaving. This might have caused minor distortions of the self-reports and should be kept in mind when reading the results.

Nevertheless, I ensured that the qualitative data for the present studies were collected in a relaxed atmosphere and in an open time slot.

However, these aspects touch on an important point, which is the general dilemma of conducting research in the field without distracting the process of the group and the individuals' experiences. As Ewert and McAvoy (2000) elaborated, on the one hand, the researcher needs to be integrated enough to collect valid data and, on the other hand, she or he has to be careful not to influence the group. After all, participants came to take part in an outdoor experience and not to give interviews or fill out surveys. Also programmes, which work with group dynamics and facilitate individual self-discovery, often generate intensified emotions in the group. Against this background, participants may feel that research attempts impair the quality of their highly personal experiences (Ewert & McAvoy, 2000). Thus, especially regarding the qualitative data collection, it is of great importance that there is a trusting relationship between the researcher and research participants so that they can "reveal the true depth of their experience to an outsider" (Ewert & McAvoy, 2000, p. 15). One strength of the present study is that I considered this potential threat to validity by including a survey item at posttest I, which assessed whether participants felt that the evaluation was disturbing their personal process during programme time. The item was answered on a four-point Likert scale ranging from 1 (not at all disturbing) to 4 (disturbed a great deal) and the statistical analysis revealed a mean of 1.4 with a standard deviation of .58, which means that the average answer to this question was positioned in between "not at all" and "not very much". Moreover, interview participants frequently stated how they enjoyed revisiting their experience through the interview, which suggests that the relationship between me, the interviewer, and the interviewees allowed for the necessary depth and intimacy.

Nevertheless, some experiences, especially novel and exceptional ones, are very difficult to put into words, and this became evident from time to time when interviewees tried to describe parts of their immersive experiences in nature. This depicts a perpetual common tension between experiencing and the conceptualisation of an experience. Furthermore, it is possible that the interview itself influenced the participants' perception of their experience as it, at the very least, stimulated additional reflection on the experience. However, especially the stories about the participants' Solo times had been told before in the group and, as Bartlett (1932) first noted, the account of an experience is exceptionally persistent in memory. Importantly, whether this causes a threat to validity depends on the research intention. As Neisser (1988) pointed out, by merely focusing on the veracity of memory its most substantial function may be missed which, according to Neisser, is utility. Neisser argues (1988) that "as we proceed through our lives, what matters most is not the actual past but how we understand and use the past in meeting the present and future" (Chawla, 1999, p. 16). Therefore, meaning-making, is welcomed in the present research as valuable research data instead of attempting to diminish it as a potential bias. This is also the reason why I collected the PCI data after the storytelling and mirroring which followed the actual Solo time (see description of the Phenomenology of Conciousness Inventory in chapter 4.3.5.1).

With regard to the quantitative data, a potential issue is that some of the instruments might have been not sensitive enough to measure the Butterfly groups' changes, as some mean scores were close to the maximum value at pretest already. This was especially evident for the quantitatively assessed proenvironmental behaviour as this contradicted the qualitative outcomes, which indicated an increase in proenvironmental behaviour. However, I avoided the potential pitfall of drawing premature conclusions by triangulating the data. This way I was able to understand that the qualitative data indicated an increase in proenvironmental behaviours that were simply not scanned quantitatively. Nevertheless, generally, the accuracy of self-reported environmentally responsible behaviour is still uncertain and data should be interpreted with caution as some studies revealed a response bias (e.g. see Hamilton, 1985). For this reason, I assessed and analysed social desirability as a control variable in the present study. Statistical results suggested that social desirability had not been significantly associated with any of the relevant variables (see 4.4.7). Thus, it does not appear as though participants' self-reports were distorted by this potential fallacy.

All in all, it should be noted that I only applied non-parametric statistics, which means that, especially with regard to the lack of control group, I handled the data as conservatively as possible. Furthermore, statistics were almost completely based on change scores and I included a number of potentially confounding variables in the analysis. Additionally, I always checked and displayed the non-parametric test results visually by means of boxplots.

Summarised, due to the nature of the investigated programmes it would have been inexpedient to conduct the present research through an experimental design such as a randomised controlled trial. This, in turn, limits the internal validity of the studies and has to be taken into account when interpreting the results. Thus, the quantitative results should be understood as a tendency, which only applies to the larger Butterfly group. However, the validity of the findings is strengthened through the triangulation of the different types of data. Additionally, I reinforced external validity through the investigation of immersive experiences in nature under differing conditions in terms of the setting, programme duration, facilitation team and the degree of cultural diversity in the group.

Markedly, despite voluntary participation in the programmes and randomisation of the interview partners, Solo participants still represent a particular sample as touched on earlier. However, within the scope of the present research, the intention to firstly explore the phenomenological content of the experience, and thus conduct basic research, and at the same time to extract (statistical) trends towards change in the Butterfly group enhances the informational value of the results.

After all, as Gergen (2001) aptly pointed out, "psychology amasses methods to generate predictions: but what utility does that have for the culture outside the laboratory?" (p. 6). In line with Gergen (2001) Polkinghorne (1992) suggested that "the criterion for acceptability of knowledge claim is the fruitfulness of its implementation" (p. 162).

Against the backdrop that the present work is based on applied research of already existing, intact programmes, this aspect seems to be met. Possibly, engaging with the natural world in the investigated manner is not everybody's choice. But for those who are open to the idea these programmes may hold fruitful novel pathways to facilitating lasting changes in the way individuals engage with the world including self, others and nature.

Obviously, the way I worked with the data, several shifts in perspective, paradigm and philosophical assumption took place throughout the thesis. I allowed for these shifts in order to avoid overlooking important dimensions of social experience due to the limits set by the methodological tradition (Mason, 2006). As each research tradition also represents the epistemology that lies behind a study, in the present research, I aimed to shed light on this by explicating epistemological debates, controversies and assumptions such as the qualitative versus quantitative debate, dreams as a data source and expanded views on validity. It seems important to be aware that all the knowledge acquired in traditional research, whatever the methodology, is based on assumptions. This realisation, at best, leads to open-mindedness in research across traditions and speaks for the necessity of mixing methods and worldviews. After all, mixing methods merely represents what is actually taking place in the wider world of research. As every discipline and individual choses and uses their own approach the world consists of a large variety of worldviews and approaches. Mixing them in a research project means to piece them together in a kaleidoscopic manner, which, in the end, might even bring about a more accurate representation of the world. As physicist Niels Bohr's pointed out "the opposite of a profound truth may well be another profound truth" (as cited in Heisenberg, 1971, p. 102). Quantitative and qualitative approaches, thus, provide complementary ways to elucidate how various experiences and their interactions can be perceived in a "more 'continuous' or 'unifying' light" (Payne, 1999, p. 374). As the initiatory summary section of the discussion chapter shows this seems to have been accomplished in the present research and constitutes one of the salient strengths of this work.

Another asset of the present work lies in the integration of an often avoided but essential part of psychology as a discipline. After all, which research field if not psychology can tap into the emotional, soulful, spiritual and psychological aspects of the human-nature relationship and its effects on human behaviour?

Intriguingly, those words, which bear most meaning to humans, are the most condemned in science, or rather a certain brand of science that is still very much inspired by its positivist past. These are words such as love, wisdom, intuition and "I" as a representation of the first-person narrative and potential subjectivity. Paradoxically, even though deeply rooted in human nature, spirituality seems to be a stigmatised, deterring term in science. This is especially remarkable in a research field like psychology whose etymology is rooted in the Greek word for "soul". As Gergen (2001) excellently elaborated in his article:

> *Language is world constituting; it assists in generating and/or sustaining certain forms of cultural practice. In this sense, to do science is not to hold a mirror to nature, but to participate actively in the interpretive conventions and practices of a particular culture. The major question that must be asked of scientific accounts, then, is not whether they are "true to nature," but what do these accounts (and*

> *the practices in which they are embedded) offer to the culture more generally. The local truths of scientific cultures are essential to sustaining their traditions, but to presume the local to be universal is not only arrogant; it sets the stage for conflict and a deathly silencing.* (p. 806)

In the present work, I consciously intended and tried to extend some of the interpretive conventions and practices of postmodern science and to deliberately include "extended language" into my research.

Ultimately, all of these above mentioned "silenced aspects" such as love, intuition and spirituality seem to be present in individuals' reports of immersive experiences in nature and, I would suggest, reflect an important dimension of the human-nature relationship, which needs to be included when aiming to understand how to facilitate change in the world.

Nevertheless, "research with soul in mind" as proposed by Romanyshyn (2007) still constitutes a curiosity in the scientific community, be it as a research object or as the subjective, experiential dimension of the researcher her or himself. Thus, the present work also contributes to an extension of validity by consciously including the subjective experience of the researcher in the various stages of the research process.

One could argue that the self-reflexive preface and in-between passages of self-reflexivity should, if anything, be assorted to the discussion. However, every individual, hence every researcher, sees things through tinted glasses. Thus, this tint can be found in any academic paper throughout each section however structured and objective it aims or seems to be. To consciously depict the researcher's process and the research process that preceded or influenced the constitution and writing up of a section makes this tint strongly visible. Firstly, that way I intend to help the reader to get to know and identify the researcher's perspective and to thereby gain more freedom in and ability of critically reflecting on the work. And secondly, this serves as a recurrent reminder of the subjective dimension of experiencing the world as a valid and inseparable plane of human experience.

6.4 Self-reflection on the research process

As is probably often the case, writing the first words of my dissertation was one of the most challenging steps I had to take along the research process. I felt like I had collected truly valuable information, which called me to piece it together into a comprehensive mosaic. And simultaneously I felt a strong sense of responsibility to do it justice. When approaching my research subject I still assumed that I would accomplish this by following the conventional guidelines.

However, initially perhaps rather intuitively than rationally, I also decided to collect dream data. I did this without knowing why I should and how I could possibly integrate such data with the rest of my research data. And when it was time to start the writing and analysis process of my work I found myself lost among the numbers from the survey data and the words from the interviews, which both were, as a matter of fact, evidently easier to transform into straightforward outcomes than the dream data. Nevertheless, it was through initially working with the dream data that I found my way into the heart of my research topic and into the writing process. I think this was the case because the still "unformed gestalt" of my dissertation and dreams shared an important parallel — making use of an expression by poet Brendan Kennelly (1998), possibly a dream is an "absence longing to be a presence" (p. 9) and that was exactly what my dissertation was at the time. Thus, somehow, the only way to start manifesting the thesis was by integrating dreams, a particular night-time experience, which can never be captured fully nor understood completely. By giving the dream data a rightful place and working with it on many levels, from intuitive to intellectual, it seems to me that I subconsciously decided that this range and the intangible dimension of dreams was to be an essential part of my research and the data behind it. Retrospectively, it felt like saying "I know that I cannot write down the soul (of things) and something of the soul is always left behind" (Romanyshyn, 2007, p. 30). And that ultimately gave me the freedom and courage to start.

Along the way in the writing process, as outlined in earlier self-reflective passages, I realised that the methodology or common practices of modern psychological science as well as the underlying worldview were unfit for research subjects which touch on topics like interconnectedness. Simply, common methodology did not enable me as the researcher to approach the research topic appropriately because I had to pretend not to be part of it. In this way, the subject of enquiry pushed me more and more to the edges of common practice and towards an explicit expansion of the worldview or, to put it differently, towards an interconnected way of researching. Through the process of synthesising the data, I can now see more clearly something that initially only "felt right", namely — the empirical value and contribution to research that this way of researching brings about. That is, the immanent broadening of the range of explorable phenomena and the different view on reality associated with it.

My experience and the understanding derived from it, is visualised in Figure 45. Essentially, it points to the conclusion that conventional research methods reflect a certain worldview and can therefore only produce knowledge which conforms to this worldview (left column).

Moreover this worldview is mostly only subtly present to us, and even in the academic realm it is mostly not explicated, hence the dotted box in the left column. However, when choosing to research a topic which may require an expansion of the conventional worldview, such as immersive experiences in wild nature, then using conventional methods will only capture those aspects of the experience that are in accordance with the worldview underlying them (middle column). As a result, the derived knowledge may be arguable in the sense that it might fail to depict the true gestalt of the phenomenon.

Therefore, possible incongruences between worldview, research topic and methods need to be brought to awareness in the first place. And consequently, when aiming to understand a phenomenon that is rooted in an extended worldview, extended research methods are in need in order to produce novel knowledge (right column). If the phenomenon under investigation has interconnectedness at its core, but the only research methods applied are those, which are designed to assess the world in isolated pieces then interconnectedness will be captured inadequately or not at all.

It was a moment of epiphany for me to realise that the conventional philosophy of science seems to perfectly reflect the separateness that characterises the contemporary human-nature relationship as well as the global situation that we face today.

Generally, it was a challenging process to truly widen the worldview I grew up with. Even though I thought I already held a rather wide worldview I did not notice how much the conventional scientific one was simultaneously ingrained in me as "the right way". Once again, this shows the difference between holding certain beliefs and actually practicing them. Thus, it was not easy to formally allow intuition to play a role in my research process and, over and above, to even document this in writing.

On many occasions I felt confused as to what was the right thing to do.

For instance, as part of the reading for my research I once came across a report of someone's experience with a blackbird. I realised then that I had difficulty imagining the situation, as I did not know what the blackbird sounded like. So I went online and dwelled in recordings of the blackbird's song for quite some time. Before allowing myself to do so, though, I doubted myself. I momentarily wondered whether this

Figure 45. My epistemological understanding derived from my experience of the present research process.

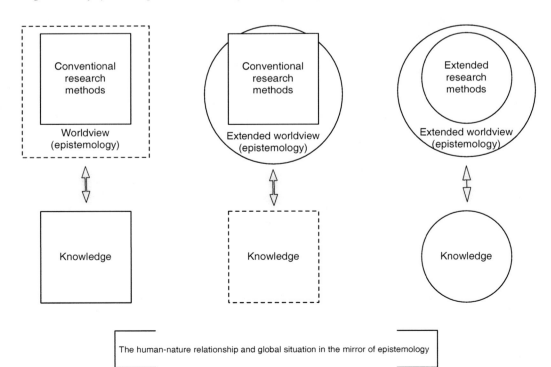

was one of the typical examples I was warned against in books on scientific writing: whether this was something I only wanted to do to distract myself or whether I simply got lost in detail. I asked myself, is this "productive"?

However, as in the case of the blackbird, I found out that immersing myself in something seemingly "research unrelated" which triggered my attention often led me to important insights and often facilitated a truly fruitful creative process. Surely, there needs to be a certain degree of trust in one's own intuition to go down that road and, if lucky, experience moments of flow and, of course, one also needs practice to distinguish between yielding to distraction and yielding to intuition. Engaging with something, which initially seems irrelevant to the research work does not seem to be a commonly recommended practice. But it was in moments like these that I frequently gained the clarity I was looking for.

Another example of meeting my own conditioning was when I chose to put the female form first (e.g. "when the researcher decided that she or he"). This seemingly tiny detail felt immensely strange to me the first few times I implemented it.

Also, as one of my supervisors pointed out to me, I, initially, repeatedly switched between passive and active voice in my self-reflective preface. This happened even though I consciously declared that particular passage as a subjective, self-reflexive passage. Nevertheless, I constantly slipped back into the suggested invisibility of the researcher, which showed me just how far reaching my conditioning was.

What this additionally reflects is something Gergen (2001) aptly cautions in his sharp article "Psychological Science in a Postmodern Context":

> In the postmodern intellectual context the distinction between fact and value becomes blurred. While one may carry out research from a value neutral standpoint, theory, research findings, and methods of inquiry may all enter cultural life as "authoritative intelligibilities." Thus the theoretical distinctions we make (e.g. between rapid as opposed to slow information processing), the findings we report (e.g. that the aged are inferior in information processing), and the research methods we favor (e.g. where manipulation and control are keys to "proper understanding"), all enter society as guiding intelligibilities with the capacity to alter cultural life for good or ill – according to some standard. To avoid these issues is not only myopic but irresponsible. If our intelligibilities favor certain ways of life while possibly destroying others, then it is essential that we develop a robust program of reflection – ethical, political and conceptual. (p. 808-809)

As cultural slant is immanent in most facets of research, transparent self-reflection is not only necessary in order to reintegrate subjectivity as valuable information but also because we need to take responsibility for and respect the influence research has on our culture. Interestingly, this kind of self-reflection resembles "deep questioning" as proposed by Arne Naess (1986). Devall and Sessions (1985, p. 8-9) described deep ecology as "a process of deeper questioning of ourselves, the assumptions of the dominant worldview in our culture, and the meaning of truth in our reality." They further elaborated that "we cannot change consciousness by only listening to others, we must involve ourselves."

It is for these reasons that I chose to integrate self-reflexivity or the inner dimension of living as part of my research methodology. I am aware that this dance between "conventional" and "extended" research may feel unfamiliar or even bumpy at times but I see my endeavour as an attempt and truly exciting possibility to transform research into something more integral and alive. For me, taking on this challenge means to fuel the vital and enlivening aspect that research can bear for the researcher. But, most importantly, I believe that an interconnected way of researching facilitates the depth and understanding of the topic of enquiry as well. In this way, research subject and researcher enter a relationship of circularity and mutual enrichment, which generates continuity and coherence as, to me, reflected in the Ouroboros symbol.

7

Conclusion

In the introductory problem statement I ended with two questions that are deeply seated in the present research: what is our place in nature and what is nature's place in us[64]?

What my research shows is that there are striking parallels between the human-nature relationship and the relationship between humans – and that they are in fact intertwined and mutually reinforcing:

In the qualitative data *both* the experience of interconnectedness with nature as well as the experience of interconnectedness with others motivated the study participants to take action in the world. Consistently, the participants' connectedness with nature correlated positively *both* with their proenvironmental behaviour as well as with their community engagement.

Moreover, some interviewees described their deepened relationship with nature by drawing upon the process of making (human) friends.

Additionally, past research showed that the way significant others introduce us to nature impacts how we experience nature and relate to it throughout life (e.g. Brixler & Morris, 1997). Similarly, it is assumed that group dynamics do determine whether the benefits of an organised nature group experience manifest or not (Roggenbuck & Driver, 2000).

But most strikingly the qualitative data of the present work revealed that the experience of interconnectedness with others and nature *alike* enabled the interviewees to open up to deep self-enquiry and produced for them a precious amount of personal insights.

The outcomes of this work highlight that we in fact *need* to experience interconnectedness in general in order to make sense of ourselves and engage with the world. And consequently, in our striving for self-understanding and wholeness, we need to encounter and incorporate all facets of nature, human and non-human alike.

All this ultimately proves that the separation between human and non-human nature is illusory and that we are undeniably a part of it. We are clearly affected by each other no matter whether "the other" is other people or the non-human natural world.

As the results of the Inclusion of Nature in Self scale intriguingly indicated, Butterfly participants, already from the start, regarded themselves as part of nature to a large extent. This raises the question why their experience of interconnectedness still influenced their lives so dramatically on various levels.

---

64   as posed by Clayton and Myers (2011, p.4)

As Vining *et al.* (2008) found out, people who see themselves as part of nature do not necessarily include humans in their definition of nature. Some participants in Vining *et al.*'s study even explicitly elaborated that they felt separate from nature even though they simultaneously saw themselves as a part of it.

What may be learned from this is that we need to be aware of the depth and extent of the inner and outer separateness that we face today. There may be a huge gap that exists between our mental conceptualisations and worldviews and the actual embodiment of them. This may even mean that we think ourselves as part of nature, yet have not truly and fully assimilated this reality.

The present research suggests that it is most likely the actual experience of interconnectedness which is needed in order to embody the intellectual understanding that we are, indeed, part of nature.

With regard to environmental protection and awareness this may mean that people do not necessarily need to be convinced of their connectedness as such, but most importantly need to be provided with an experience of it. After all, participants in Vining *et al.*'s study explained their ambiguity of feeling part of and simultaneously separate from nature with a lack of contact with nature and a lack of everyday closeness.

7.1 Practical implications

Thus, on a practical level, both dimensions, social and natural, should be taken into account when crafting a programme for young adults, which aims to deepen the human-nature relationship and to empower change agents in the world.

The benefits of actually being in contact with nature clearly call for an environmental education that goes beyond the schoolroom, at best, as outlined in the literature, in the form of long-term or repeated experiences (see Schultz & Tabanico, 2007) or, as shown in the present research, in the form of intensive programmes which at least offer to participants links and networks which transcend programme time. As the United Nations (2014) predicts that 66 percent of the world's population will live in cities by 2050, free encounters and contact with the natural world already are and will be more and more difficult to access. Therefore, opportunities for connection should be made accessible on a broader scale, for instance, through the educational curriculum. As the present research showed, an educational effect may not only be reached by transmitting factual knowledge on sustainability matters but moreover by offering a first-hand experience of the interconnectedness of all of life.

The present research furthermore clearly speaks to the popular question of how significance of experience is socially constructed.

Participants not only created meaning in their lives through self-reflection in nature but also through contact with other people involved in the programme who acted as role models through their actions but also through their shared stories. Thus, meaning-making of the participants' community and nature experience was enhanced through verbally sharing their Solo experiences in the circle of the group as well as through additionally facilitated councils. Therefore, future programmes should consider incorporating storytelling as an effective medium and tool for reflection and meaning-making.

7.2 Closing words

In conclusion, the underlying key feature of the programmes might have been what Weber (2013) called "enlivenment". According to Weber (2013, p. 62), "opening up oneself to the other's aliveness makes possible the experience of 'embodied interbeing'". He further elaborates:

> […] *Enlivening processes can truly transform society and one's own consciousness. This notion brings us from the idea of First-person-ecology to the broader practice of what we might call «First-person-sustainability.» If a new individual practice is going to enhance sustainability, it must also enhance life. It must increase the generativity and the felt authenticity of the agents involved.* (p. 61)

Therefore, the crucial step towards change may not be about systematically changing behaviour and values but to find out what, sustainably, makes humans feel more alive. The Solo embedded in a group experience, like in the Butterfly programme, may be an example of such a practice of first-person-sustainability, which potentially explains why the experience seems to have influenced so many diverse areas in the participants' lives (e.g. relationships with nature, others, self, the world, career choices and new forms of activism).

The bottom line may be that the appropriate question is not "how can we change human behaviour in order to save the world?" but rather, to start with, "how can we re-explore what it means to be alive and human in this world?"- trusting that as a consequence a different kind of relationship with and treatment of the planet and all its human and non-human inhabitants will emerge naturally from this exploration.

The approach presented in this work therefore differs from interventions that aim to create behaviour change. The approach proposed here simply offers a conscious experience of a reality seemingly forgotten, namely one of the interconnectedness of all living things: with humans and with the non-human, with oneself and with the planet. It is possibly the conscious encounter and exploration as well as sharing and reflection of the experiences via storytelling that creates meaning, or in the words of the interviewees, a sense of purpose and belonging in the world. Through this process aspects of the world are highlighted which might not be perceived in everyday life and alone, thereby, may bear the potential to facilitate change.

As William James (1890) rightly put it: "My experience is what I agree to attend to. Only those items which I notice shape my mind" (p. 403).

References

Abram, D. (1997). *The spell of the sensuous: Perception and language in a more-than-human world*. New York: Vintage Books.

Abramson, L. Y., Seligman, M. E., & Teasdale, J. D. (1978). Learned helplessness in humans: Critique and reformulation. *Journal of Abnormal Psychology, 87*(1), 49-74.

Ajzen, I. (1991). The theory of planned behavior. *Organizational Behavior and Human Decision Processes, 50*, 179-211.

Alarcon, G. M., Bowling, N. A., & Khazon, S. (2013). Great expectations: A meta-analytic examination of optimism and hope. *Personality and Individual Differences, 54*(7), 821-827.

Algoe, S. B., & Haidt, J. (2009). Witnessing excellence in action: The "other-praising" emotions of elevation, gratitude, and admiration. *The Journal of Positive Psychology, 4*(2), 105-127.

Apolinario, P. (2008). *The Hero's Journey*. Retrieved from www.alemany.org/ourpages/auto/2008/5/15/.../The%20Hero.pdf.

Aron, A., & Fraley, B. (1999). Relationship closeness as Including other in the self: Cognitive underpinnings and measures. *Social Cognition, 17*(2), 140-160.

Aron, A., Aron, E. N., & Smollan, D. (1992). Inclusion of Other in the Self Scale and the structure of interpersonal closeness. *Journal of Personality and Social Psychology, 63*(4), 596-612.

Aron, A., Aron, E. N., Tudor, M., & Nelson, G. (1991). Close relationships as including other in the self. *Journal of Personality and Social Psychology, 60*(2), 241-253.

Bandura, A. (1965). Influence of models' reinforcement contingencies on the acquisition of imitative responses. *Journal of Personality and Social Psychology, 1*(6), 589.

Bandura, A. (1982). The psychology of chance encounters and life paths. *American Psychologist, 37*(7), 747.

Bandura, A., Ross, D., & Ross, S. A. (1961). Transmission of aggression through imitation of aggressive models. *The Journal of Abnormal and Social Psychology, 63*(3), 575-582.

Barlett, P. F. (2008). Reason and reenchantment in cultural change: Sustainability in higher education. *Current Anthropology, 49*(6), 1077-1098.

Barrett, D. (2001). *The committee of sleep: How artists, scientists, and athletes use dreams for creative problem-solving – and how you can too*. New York: Crown House Publishing Limited.

Bartlett, F. C. (1932). *Remembering*. Cambridge, UK: Cambridge University Press.

Basso, K. (1996). *Wisdom sits in places: Landscape and language among the Western Apache*. Albuquerque: University of New Mexico Press.

Baumeister, R. F., & Leary, M. R. (1995). The need to belong: Desire for interpersonal attachments as a fundamental human motivation. *Psychological Bulletin, 117*(3), 497.

Bless, H., Bohner, G., Schwarz, N., & Strack, F. (1990). Mood and persuasion: A cognitive response analysis. *Personality and Social Psychology Bulletin, 16*(2), 331-345.

Bobilya, A., McAvoy, L. H., & Kalisch, K. R. (2005). Lessons from the field: Participants perceptions of a multi-day wilderness solo. In C. Knapp & T. Smith, *Exploring the power of solo, silence, and solitude* (pp. 103-120). Boulder, CO: Association for Experiential Education.

Bodenhausen, G., Kramer, G., & Süsser, K. (1994). Happiness and sterotypic thinking in social judgement. *Journal of Personality and Social Psychology, 66*(4), 621-632.

Bodkin, M., & Sartor, L. (2005). The rites of passage vision quest. In C. Knapp & T. Smith, *Exploring the power of solo, silence, and solitude* (pp. 31-48). Boulder, CO: Association for Experiential Education.

Bögeholz, S. (1999). *Qualitäten primärer Naturerfahrung und ihr Zusammenhang mit Umweltwissen und Umwelthandeln* [Qualities of primary nature experience and its association with environmental knowledge and environmental behavior]. Wiesbaden: VS Verlag für Sozialwissenschaften.

Borden, R.J. (1985). Personality and ecological concern. In D. Gray with R. Borden & R. Weigel, *Ecological beliefs and behaviors: Assessment and change* (pp.87-122). Westport, CT: Greenwood Press.

Borstelman, L.J. (1977). *Psychological readiness for and change associated with the Outward Bound program*. Unpublished paper presented to North Carolina Outward Bound School, Morgantown, North Carolina.

Boyd, R., & Richerson, P. J. (2009). Culture and the evolution of human cooperation. *Philosophical Transactions of the Royal Society B: Biological Sciences, 364*(1533), 3281-3288.

Bragg, E. A. (1996). Towards ecological self: Deep ecology meets constructionist self-theory. *Journal of Environmental Psychology, 16*(2), 93-108.

Bratman, G. N., Hamilton, J. P., & Daily, G. C. (2012). The impacts of nature experience on human cognitive function and mental health. *Annals of the New York Academy of Sciences, 1249*(1), 118-136.

Braud, W., & Anderson, R. (1998). *Transpersonal research methods for the social sciences : honoring human experience*. Thousand Oaks, Calif.: Sage Publications.

Brixler, R., & Morris, B. (1997). The role of "Outdoor Capital" in the socialization of wildland recreationists. In H. Vogelson, *Proceedings of the 1997 Northeastern Recreation Research Symposium* (pp. 237-242). Bolton, NY: Northeastern Forest Experiment Station.

Brown, D., & Crace, K. (1996). *Life Values Inventory*. Chapel Hill, NC: Life Values Resources.

Brügger, A., Kaiser, F. G., & Roczen, N. (2011). One for All? *European Psychologist, 16*(4), 324-333.

Buchholz, E. (1997). *The call of solitude: Alonetime in a world of attachment*. New York: Simon & Schuster.

Byrne, R. W. (2005). Social cognition: Imitation, imitation, imitation. *Current Biology, 15*(13), R498 – R500.

Campbell, J. (1988). Interview by B. D. Moyers. *The power of myth, Episode one* [Television broadcast]. Arlington: PBS.

Campbell, J. (2008). *The hero with a thousand faces* (3rd ed.). Novato, California: New World Library.

Campbell, J., Moyers, B. D., & Flowers, B. S. (1991). *The power of myth*. New York, NY: Anchor Books.

Cantrill, J. G. (1998). The environmental self and sense of place: Communication foundations for regional ecosystem management. *Journal of Applied Communication Research, 26*, 301-318.

Capra, F. (1997). *The web of life: A new synthesis of mind and matter*. London: Flamingo.

Carver, C. S. (2003). Pleasure as a sign you can attend to something else: Placing positive feelings within a general model of affect. *Cognition & Emotion, 17*(2), 241-261.

Cervinka, R., Roderer, K., & Hefler, E. (2012). Are nature lovers happy? On various indicators of well-being and connectedness with nature. *Journal of Health Psychology, 17*(3), 379-388.

Cervinka, R., Zeidler, D., Karlegger, A., & Hefler, E. (2009). Connectedness with nature, well-being and time spent in nature. In H. Gutscher, H.-J. Mosler, B. Meyer, S. Mischke & M. Soland (Eds.), *8th Biennial Conference on Environmental Psychology*. Lengerich: Pabst Science Publishers.

Chartrand, T. L., & Bargh, J. A. (1999). The chameleon effect: The perception-behavior link and social interaction. *Journal of Personality and Social Psychology, 76*(6), 893-910.

Chartrand, T. L., & Lakin, J. L. (2013). The antecedents and consequences of human behavioral mimicry. *Annual Review of Psychology, 64*(1), 285-308.

Chartrand, T. L., & van Baaren, R. (2009). Human Mimicry. *Advances in Experimental Social Psychology, 41*, 219-274.

Chavis, D. M., Hogge, J. H., McMillan, D. W., Wandersman, A. (1986). Sense of community through Brunswik's lens: A first look. *Journal of Community Psychology, 4(1)*, 24-40.

Chavis, D. M., Lee, K. S., & Acosta, J. D. (2008). *The Sense of Community Index 2 (SCI-2) revised: The reliability and validity of the SCI-2*. Presented at the 2nd International Community Psychology Conference, Lisboa, Portugal.

Chawla, L. (1986). The ecology of environmental memory. *Children's Environments Quarterly, 3*(4), 34-42.

Chawla, L. (1998). Significant life experiences revisited: A review of research on sources of environmental sensitivity. *Journal of Environmental Education, 29*(3), 11-21.

Chawla, L. (1999). Life paths into effective environmental action. *Journal of Environmental Education, 31*(1), 15-26.

Chawla, L. (2001). Significant life experiences revisited once again: Response to vol. 5 (4) "Five critical commentaries on significant life experience research in environmental education." *Environmental Education Research, 7*(4), 451-461.

Chawla, L. (2007). Childhood experiences associated with care for the natural world: A theoretical framework for empirical results. *Children, Youth and Environments, 7*(4), 451-461.

Cialdini, R. B., Brown, S. L., Lewis, B. P., Luce, C., & Neuberg, S. L. (1997). Reinterpreting the empathy-altruism relationship: When one into one equals oneness. *Journal of Personality and Social Psychology, 73*(3), 481-494.

Cialdini, R.B., Reno, R.R., & Kallgren, C.A. (1990). A focus theory of normative conduct: Recycling the concept of norms to reduce littering in public places. *Journal of Personality and Social Psychology, 58* (6), 1015-1026.

Clayton, S. (2003). Environmental identity: A conceptual and an operational definition. In S. Clayton & S. S. Opotow, *Identity and the natural environment: The psychological significance of nature* (pp. 45-65). Cambridge, MA: MIT Press.

Clayton, S., & Myers, G. (2011). *Conservation psychology: Understanding and promoting human care for nature.* Chichester, UK: Wiley-Blackwell.

Clayton, S., & Opotow, S. (2003). Justice and identity: Changing perspectives on what is fair. *Personality and Social Psychology Review, 7*(4), 298-310.

Cohen, J. (1988). *Statistical power analysis for the behvioral sciences.* Hillsdale, NJ: Erlbaum.

Colville, C. (Director & Producer). (2009). Why do we dream? [Television series episode]. In Van der Pool, J. (Series producer), *BBC Horizon.* United Kingdom: BBC Two.

Costa, P. T., & McCrae, R. R. (1992). *Revised NEO Personality Inventory (NEO PI-R) and NEO Five-Factor Inventory (NEO-FFI) professional manual.* Odessa, FL: Psychological Assessment Resources.

Courville, S., & Piper, N. (2004). Harnessing hope through NGO activism. *The Annals of the American Academy of Political and Social Science, 592*(1), 39-61.

Creswell, J. W., & Plano Clark, V. L. (2007). *Designing and conducting mixed methods research* (2nd ed.). Thousand Oaks, CA: Sage.

Crowne, D. P., & Marlowe, D. (1960). A new scale of social desirability independent of psychopathology. *Journal of Consulting Psychology, 24*(4), 349-354.

Csutora, M. (2012). One more awareness gap? The behaviour – impact gap problem. *Journal of Consumer Policy, 35*(1), 145-163.

Daniel, B. (2005). The life significance of a wilderness solo experience. In C. Knapp & T. Smith, *Exploring the power of solo, silence, and solitude* (pp. 85-102). Boulder, CO: Association for Experiential Education.

De Lisle, J. (2011). The benefits and challenges of mixing methods and methodologies. *Caribbean Curriculum, 18,* 87-120.

DeCremer, D., & Van Vugt, M. (1999). Social identification effects in social dilemmas: A transformation of motives. *European Journal of Social Psychology, 29,* 871-893.

Devall, B. (1988). *Simple in means, rich in ends: Practicing deep ecology.* Salt Lake City, UT: Gibbs Smith.

Devall, B., & Sessions, G. (1985). *Deep ecology: Living as if nature mattered.* Salt Lake City,UT: Peregrine Smith.

Diehm, C. (2006). Gestalt-Ontologie und Identifikation mit der Natur: Über Arne Naess und die Philosophie der Deep Ecology [Gestalt-ontology and identification with nature: On Arne Naess and the philosophy of deep ecology]. *Natur und Kultur, 7*(2), 3-23.

Diessner, R., Solom, R. D., Frost, N. K., Parsons, L., & Davidson, J. (2008). Engagement with beauty: Appreciating natural, artistic, and moral beauty. *The Journal of Psychology, 142,* 303-332.

Dimberg, U., Thunberg, M., & Elmehed, K. (2000). Unconscious facial reactions to emotional facial expressions. *Psychological Science, 11*(1), 86-89.

Drach-Zahavy, A., & Somech, A. (2002). Coping with health problems: The distinctive relationships of Hope sub-scales with constructive thinking and resource allocation. *Personality and Individual Differences, 33*(1), 103-117.

Driver, B.L., & Peterson, G.L. (1986). Benefits of outdoor recreation: an integrating overview. In: *A literature review – President's Commission on Americans Outdoors* (pp. v-1 – v-10). Washington, D.C.: Government Printing Office.

Drury, M., & Van Swal, L. M. (2006). *The effects of shared opinions on nonverbal mimicry.* Presented at the International Communication Association Annual Conference, Dresden, Germany.

Dutcher, D. D., Finley, J. C., Luloff, A. E., & Johnson, J. B. (2007). Connectivity with nature as a measure of environmental values. *Environment and Behavior, 39*(4), 474-493.

Eckersley, R. (1999). Dreams and expectations: Young people's expected and preferred futures and their significance for education. *Futures, 31*(1), 73-90.

Eigner, S. (2001). The relationship between "protecting the environment" as a dominant life goal and subjective well-being. In P. Schmuck & K. M. Sheldon, *Life goals and well-being: Towards a positive psychology of human striving* (pp. 182-201). Göttingen, Germany: Hogrefe and Huber.

Epley, N., Akalis, S., Waytz, A., & Cacioppo, J. T. (2008). Creating social connection through inferential reproduction: Loneliness and perceived agency in gadgets, gods, and greyhounds. *Psychological Science, 19*(2), 114-120.

Epley, N., Waytz, A., & Cacioppo, J. T. (2007). On seeing human: A three-factor theory of anthropomorphism. *Psychological Review, 114*(4), 864-886.

Ernst, J., & Theimer, S. (2011). Evaluating the effects of environmental education programming on connectedness to nature. *Environmental Education Research, 17*(5), 577-598.

European Commission (2009). *Europeans' attitudes towards climate change.* Retrieved from http://ec.europa.eu/public_opinion/archives/ebs/ebs_322_en.pdf.

Evans, G. W., & McCoy, J. M. (1998). When buildings don't work: The role of architecture in human health. *Journal of Environmental Psychology, 18*(1), 85-94.

Ewert, A., & McAvoy, L. H. (2000). The effects of wilderness settings on organized groups: A state-of-knowledge paper. In S. McCool, D. Cole, W. Borrie, & J. O'Loughlin, *Wilderness Science in a Time of Change Conference–Volume 3: Wilderness as a place for scientific inquiry* (pp. 13-26). Ogden, UT: U.S. Department of Agriculture, Forest Service, Rocky Mountain Research Station.

Fajersztaijn, L., Veras, M., Barrozo, L. V., & Saldiva, P. (2013). Air pollution. *Nature Reviews Cancer,* (13), 674-678.

Fogassi, L., Ferrari, P. F., Gesierich, B., Rozzi, S., Chersi, F., & Rizzolatti, G. (2005). Parietal lobe: From action organization to intention understanding. *Science, 308*(5722), 662-667.

Folkman, S. (2008). The case for positive emotions in the stress process. *Anxiety, Stress & Coping, 21*(1), 3-14.

Foster, S. E., & Little, M. R. (1999). *The four shields: The initiatory seasons of human nature.* Big Pine, CA: Lost Borders Press.

Foster, S., & Little, M. (1996). *Wilderness vision questing and the four shields of human nature.* Moscow: University of Idaho Wilderness Research Center.

Fox, W. (1990). *Toward a transpersonal ecology: Developing new foundations for environmentalism.* Boston: Shambhala.

Frantz, C. M., & Mayer, F. S. (2014). The importance of connection to nature in assessing environmental education programs. *Studies in Educational Evaluation, 41*, 85-89.

Frantz, C. M., Mayer, F. S., & Sallee, C. (2013). *A children's version of the Connectedness to Nature Scale Revised* (under revision).

Frantz, C. M., Mayer, F. S., Gordon, H., & Handley, G. (2010). *Venture outdoors report: Oberlin subsample analysis.* Internal report.

Fredrickson, B. L. (2013). Positive emotions broaden and build. *Advances in Experimental Social Psychology, 47*, 1-53.

Fredrickson, B. L., & Branigan, C. (2005). Positive emotions broaden the scope of attention and thought-action repertoires. *Cognition & Emotion, 19*(3), 313-332.

Fredrickson, B. L., & Losada, M. F. (2005). Positive affect and the complex dynamics of human flourishing. *American Psychologist, 60*(7), 678-686.

Fredrickson, L. M., & Anderson, D. H. (1999). A qualitative exploration of the wilderness experience as a source of spiritual. *Journal of Environmental Psychology, 19*(1), 21-39.

Gatersleben, B., Murtagh, N., & Abrahamse, W. (2012). Values, identity and pro-environmental behaviour. *Contemporary Social Science: Journal of the Academy of Social Sciences, 9*(4), 374-392.

Gatto, N., Henderson, V., Hodis, H., John, J., Lurmann, F., Chen, J.-C., & Mack, W. (2014). Components of air pollution and cognitive function in middle-aged and older adults in Los Angeles. *NeuroToxicology, 40*, 1-7.

Gendlin, E. T. (1978). *Focusing.* New York: Bantam Books.

Gergen, K. J. (2001). Psychological science in a postmodern context. *American Psychologist, 56*(10), 803-813.

Gergen, K. J. (2013). Qualitative inquiry and the challenge of scientific status. In N. K. Denzin & M. D. Giardina, *Global dimensions of qualitative inquiry.* Left Coast Press.

Glassman, S. (1995). The experience of women discovering wilderness as *psychologically healing.* The Union Institute, Vermont.

Goldberg, L. R. (1999). A broad-bandwidth, public domain, personality inventory measuring the lower-level facets of several five-factor models. *Personality Psychology in Europe*, *7*, 7-28.

Goldin-Meadow, S., & Alibali, M. W. (2013). Gesture's role in speaking, learning, and creating language. *Annual Review of Psychology*, *64*(1), 257-283.

Goldstein, N. J., Cialdini, R. B., & Griskevicius, V. (2008). A room with a viewpoint: Using social norms to motivate environmental conservation in hotels. *Journal of Consumer Research*, *35*(3), 472-482.

Gordon, H., Frantz, C. M., & Mayer, F. S. (2012). *The relationship between ego- and eco-motivation, environmental attitudes, and environmentally responsible behavior*. Poster Presented at the Annual Meeting of Society for Personality and Social Psychology, San Diego, CA, USA.

Gray, H. M., Gray, K., & Wegner, D. M. (2007). Dimensions of mind perception. *Science*, *315*(5812), 619.

Griffin, D. R. (Ed.). (1988). *The reenchantment of science*. Albany: State University of New York Press.

Grønhøj, A., & Thøgersen, J. (2009). Like father, like son? Intergenerational transmission of values, attitudes, and behaviours in the environmental domain. *Journal of Environmental Psychology*, *29*(4), 414-421.

Grønhøj, A., & Thøgersen, J. (2012). Action speaks louder than words: The effect of personal attitudes and family norms on adolescents' pro-environmental behaviour. *Journal of Economic Psychology*, *33*(1), 292-302.

Guest, G., MacQueen, K. M., & Namey, E. E. (2012). *Applied thematic analysis*. SAGE Publications.

Gusetti, A. (2014). *Kopfüber in die Natur* [Headfirst into nature]. Hannover, Germany: Der blaue Reiter.

Hamilton, L. (1985). Self-reported and actual savings in a water conservation campaign. *Environment and Behavior*, 17, 315-326.

Harré, N. (2011). *Psychology for a better world*. Aukland: University of Aukland.

Hartmann, E. (1996). Outline for a theory on the nature and functions of dreaming. *Dreaming*, *6*(2), 147-170.

Hawk, S. T., Fischer, A. H., & Van Kleef, G. A. (2011). Taking your place or matching your face: Two paths to empathic embarrassment. *Emotion*, *11*(3), 502-513.

Hedlund-de Witt, A. (2013). Pathways to environmental responsibility: A qualitative exploration of the spiritual dimension of nature experience. *Journal for the Study of Religion, Nature and Culture*, *7*(2), 154-186.

Hegarty, J. R. (2010). Out of the consulting room and into the woods? Experiences of nature- connectedness and self-healing. *European Journal of Ecopsychology*, *1*, 64-84.

Heisenberg, W. (1971). *Physics and beyond*. New York: Harber & Row.

Helliwell, J. F., & Putnam, R. D. (2004). The social context of well-being. *Philosophical Transactions of the Royal Society B: Biological Sciences*, *359*(1449), 1435-1446.

Helt, M. S., Eigsti, I.-M., Snyder, P. J., & Fein, D. A. (2010). Contagious yawning in autistic and typical development. *Child Development*, *81*(5), 1620-1631.

Hendee, J. C., & Brown, M. H. (1988). How wilderness experience programs facilitate personal growth: The Hendee/Brown model. *Renewable Resources Journal, 6*(2), 9-16.

Herrmann, A., Rossberg, N., Huber, F., Landwehr, J. R., & Henkel, S. (2011). The impact of mimicry on sales – Evidence from field and lab experiments. *Journal of Economic Psychology, 32*(3), 502-514.

Herzog, T. R., Black, A. M., Fountaine, K. A., & Knotts, D. J. (1997). Reflection and attentional recovery as distinctive benefits of restorative environments. *Journal of Environmental Psychology, 17*(2), 165-170.

Hicks, D. (1996). A lesson for the future. *Futures, 28*(1), 1-13.

Hicks, D., & Holden, C. (2007). Remembering the future: What do children think? *Environmental Education Research, 13*(4), 501-512.

Hill, C. E., Diemer, R., Hess, S., Hillyer, A., & Seeman, R. (1993). Are the effects of dream interpretation on session quality, insight, and emotions due to the dream itself, to projection, or to the interpretation process? *Dreaming, 3*(4), 269-280.

Hillman, J., & Ventura, M. (1999). *We've had a hundred years of psychotherapy and the world is getting worse*. New York: Harper Collins.

Hills, A. M. (1995). Empathy and belief in the mental experience of animals. *Anthrozoos: a Multidisciplinary Journal of the Interactions of People & Animals, 8*(3), 132-142.

Hinds, J., & Sparks, P. (2008). Engaging with the natural environment: The role of affective connection and identity. *Journal of Environmental Psychology, 28*(2), 109-120.

Hinds, J., & Sparks, P. (2011). The affective quality of human-natural environment relationships. *Evolutionary Psychology, 9*(3), 451-469.

Hobson, J. A. (1994). *The chemistry of conscious states: Toward a unified model of the brain and the mind*. Boston: Little & Brown.

Holloway, J. (1991). *Roles for professional psychology in environmental action: Reframing the dominant social paradigm through ecofeminism and deep ecology* (Unpublished doctoral dissertation). California School of Professional Psychology, Los Angeles.

Homburg, A., Stolberg, A., & Wagner, U. (2007). Coping with global environmental problems: Development and first validation of scales. *Environment and Behavior, 39*(6), 754-778.

Hood, R. W. (1975). The construction and preliminary validation of a measure of reported mystical experience. *Journal for the Scientific Study of Religion, 14*, 29-41.

Howe, K. R. (1988). Against the quantitative-qualitative incompatibility thesis or dogmas die hard. *Educational Researcher, 17*(8), 10-16.

Howell, A. J., Dopko, R. L., Passmore, H.-A., & Buro, K. (2011). Nature connectedness: Associations with well-being and mindfulness. *Personality and Individual Differences, 51*(2), 166-171.

Howell, A. J., Passmore, H.-A., & Buro, K. (2013). Meaning in nature: Meaning in life as a mediator of the relationship between nature connectedness and well-being. *Journal of Happiness Studies, 14*(6), 1681-1696.

Howell, D. C. (1997). *Statistical methods for psychology* (4 ed.). Belmont, CA: Duxbury.

Hughes, J. D. (2000). Dream interpretation in ancient civilizations. *Dreaming, 10*(1), 7-18.

Iacoboni, M. (2009). Imitation, empathy, and mirror neurons. *Annual Review of Psychology*, *60*(1), 653-670.

Ingulli, K., & Lindbloom, G. (2013). Connection to nature and psychological resilience. *Ecopsychology*, *5*(1), 52-55.

Intergovernmental Panel on Climate Change. (2014). *Climate change 2014 – Synthesis report*. Retrieved from https://www.ipcc.ch/news_and_events/docs/ar5/ar5_syr_headlines_en.pdf.

Jahn, R. G., & Dunne, B. J. (2001). A modular model of mind/matter manifestations (M5). *Journal of Scientific Exploration*, *15*(3), 299-329.

Jakes, S., & Shannon, L. (2002). *The community assets survey*. Retrieved from http://ag.arizona.edu/sfcs/cyfernet/nowg/Scale.PDF.

James, W. (1890). *The principles of psychology*. New York: Henry Holt.

James, W. (1911). *Some problems of philosophy: A beginning of an introduction to philosophy*. New York: Longmans, Green.

James, W. (1958). *The varieties of religious experiences*. New York: New American Library.

Jones, S. L., Nation, J. R., & Massad, P. (1977). Immunization against learned helplessness in man. *Journal of Abnormal Psychology*, *86*(1), 75-83.

Jung, C. G. (1970). The transcendent function. In *The structure and dynamics of the psyche, The collected works of C. G. Jung* (Vol. 8). Princeton, NJ: Princeton University Press.

Kalisch, K. R., Bobilya, A. J., & Daniel, B. (2011). The outward bound solo: A study of participants' perceptions. *Journal of Experiential Education*, *34*(1), 1-18.

Kals, E., Schumacher, D., & Montada, L. (1999). Emotional affinity toward nature as a motivational basis to protect nature. *Environment and Behavior*, *31*(2), 178-202.

Kamitsis, I., & Francis, A. J. P. (2013). Spirituality mediates the relationship between engagement with nature and psychological wellbeing. *Journal of Environmental Psychology*, *36*, 136-143.

Kaplan, R., & Kaplan, S. (1989). *The experience of nature: A psychological perspective*. Ann Arbor, MI: Ulrich's Bookstore.

Kaplan, S. (1990). *Beeing needed, adaptive muddling and human-environment relationships*. Presented at the Conference of the Environmental Design Research Association, Champaign-Urbana, IL.

Kaplan, S., & Talbot, J. F. (1983). Psychological benefits of a wilderness experience. *Human Behavior & Environment: Advances in Theory & Research*, *6*, 163-203.

Kasmel, A., & Tanggaard, P. (2011). Evaluation of changes in individual community-related empowerment in community health promotion interventions in estonia. *International Journal of Environmental Research and Public Health*, *8*(12), 1772-1791.

Kennelly, B. (1998). *The man made of rain*. Newcastle: Bloodaxe Books Ltd.

Kenny, G. (2012). An introduction to Moustakas's heuristic method. *Nurse Researcher*, *19*(3), 6-11.

Kerr, M. (2008, March). *Sense of self among mindfulness teachers* (Unpublished doctoral dissertation). The Open University, Milton Keynes, UK.

Kerr, M., & Key, D. (2011). The Ouroborous (Part I): Towards an ontology of connectedness in ecopsychology research. *European Journal of Ecopsychology*, *2*(1), 48-60.

Knapp, C. (2005). *The mountains can't always speak for themselves: Briefing and debriefing the solo experience*. In C. Knapp & T. Smith, *Exploring the power of solo, silence, and solitude* (pp. 19-30). Boulder, CO: Association for Experiential Education.

Knapp, C., & Smith, T. (Eds.). (2005). *Exploring the power of solo, silence, and solitude*. Boulder, CO: Association for Experiential Education.

Korpela, K. M. (1989). Place-identity as a product of environmental self-regulation. *Journal of Environmental Psychology, 9*(3), 241-256.

Korpela, K. M. (1992). Adolescents' favourite places and environmental self-regulation. *Journal of Environmental Psychology, 12*(3), 249-258.

Korpela, K. M., Hartig, T., Kaiser, F. G., & Fuhrer, U. (2001). Restorative experience and self-regulation in favorite places. *Environment and Behavior, 33*(4), 572-589.

Kouzakova, M., van Baaren, R., & van Knippenberg, A. (2010). Lack of behavioral imitation in human interactions enhances salivary cortisol levels. *Hormones and Behavior, 57*(4-5), 421-426.

Lakin, J. L., & Chartrand, T. L. (2003). Using nonconscious behavioral mimicry to create affiliation and rapport. *Psychological Science, 14*(4), 334-339.

Larson, R. W. (1997). The emergence of solitude as a constructive domain of experience in early adolescence. *Child Development, 68*(1), 80-93.

Lawshe, C. H. (1975). A quantitative approach to content validity. *Personnel Psychology, 28*(4), 563-575.

Lazarus, R. S. (1966). *Psychological stress and the coping process*. New York: McGraw-Hill.

Lazarus, R. S. (1994). *Emotion and adaptation*. Oxford University Press.

Lee, K. N. (1994). *Compass and gyroscope: Integrating science and politics for the environment*. Washington, DC: Island Press.

Legewie, H. & Paetzold-Teske, E. (1996). *Transkriptionsempfehlungen und Formatierungsangaben* [Recommendations for transcription and formatting specifications]. Retrieved from http://web.qualitative-forschung.de/publikationen/post-partale-depressionen/Transkription.pdf.

Leopold, A. (1966). *A Sand County almanac*. New York: Ballantine Books.

Long, C. R., Seburn, M., Averill, J. R., & More, T. A. (2003). Solitude experiences: Varieties, settings, and individual differences. *Personality and Social Psychology Bulletin, 29*(5), 578-583.

Lutts, R. H. (1985). Place, home, and story in environmental education. *The Journal of Environmental Education, 17*(1), 37-41.

MacDonald, D. A., Friedman, H. L., & Kuentzel, J. G. (1999). A survey of measures of spiritual and transpersonal constructs: Part one-research update. *Journal of Transpersonal Psychology, 31*(2), 137-154.

Mackie, D. M., & Worth, L. T. (1991). Feeling good, but not thinking straight: The impact of positive mood on persuasion. In J. P. Forgas, *Emotion and social judgements. International series in experimental social psychology* (pp. 201-219). Elmsford, NY: Pergamon Press.

Macy, J., & Brown, M. Y. (1998). *Coming back to life: Practices to reconnect our lives, our world*. Stony Creek, CT: New Society Publishers.

Mander, J. (1991). *In the absence of the sacred*. San Francisco: Sierra Club.

Mason, J. (2006). Mixing methods in a qualitatively driven way. *Qualitative Research, 6*(1), 9-25.

Maxted, J. (2005). Coming home: Adolescents and the nature-based solo. In C. Knapp & T. Smith, *Exploring the power of solo, silence, and solitude* (pp. 121-136). Boulder, CO: Association for Experiential Education.

Mayer, F. S., & Frantz, C. M. (2004). The connectedness to nature scale: A measure of individuals' feeling in community with nature. *Journal of Environmental Psychology, 24*(4), 503-515.

Mayer, F. S., Frantz, C. M., Bruehlman-Senecal, E., & Dolliver, K. (2009). Why is nature beneficial? The role of connectedness to nature. *Environment and Behavior, 41*(5), 607-643.

McDonald, M. G., Wearing, S., & Ponting, J. (2009). The nature of peak experience in wilderness. *The Humanistic Psychologist, 37*(4), 370-385.

McGeer, V. (2004). The art of good hope. *Annals of the American Academy of Political and Social Science*, (1), 100-127.

McIntosh, D. N. (2006). Spontaneous facial mimicry, liking and emotional contagion. *Polish Psychological Bulletin, 37*(1), 31-42.

McMillan, D. W., & Chavis, D. M. (1986). Sense of community: A definition and theory. *Journal of Community Psychology, 14*(1), 6-23.

Meltzoff, A. N., & Moore, M. K. (1983). Newborn infants imitate adult facial gestures. *Child Development, 54*(3), 702-709.

Merkl, K. (1995). Ecopsychology: Exploring psychological aspects of our relationship to nature. *Dissertation Abstracts International, Section B. Sciences and Engeneering, 56*, 3455.

Metalsky, G. I., Abramson, L. Y., Seligman, M. E. P., Semmel, A., & Peterson, C. (1982). Attributional styles and life events in the classroom: Vulnerability and invulnerability to depressive mood reactions. *Journal of Personality and Social Psychology, 43*(3), 612-617.

Miller, J. F., & Powers, M. J. (1988). Development of an instrument to measure hope. *Nursing Research, 37*(1), 1-6.

Moely, B. E., Mercer, S. H., Ilustre, V., Miron, D., & McFarland, M. (2002). Psychometric properties and correlates of the civic attitudes and skills questionnaire (CASQ). *Michigan Journal of Community Service Learning, 2*, 1-12.

Morewedge, C. K., & Norton, M. I. (2009). When dreaming is believing: The (motivated) interpretation of dreams. *Journal of Personality and Social Psychology, 96*(2), 249-264.

Moustakas, C. (1990). *Heuristic research: Design, methodology, and applications.* Newbury Park, CA: SAGE Publications.

Myers, G. (1997). *Significant life experiences and choice of major among undergraduate minorities and nonminority students majoring in environmental studies and other disciplines.* Presented at the Annual Conference of the North American Association for Environmental Education, Vancouver, British Columbia.

Naess, A. (1973). The shallow and the deep, long-range ecology movement. A summary. *Inquiry, 16*(1-4), 95-100.

Naess, A. (1985). Identification as a source of deep ecological attitudes. In M. Tobias, *Deep ecology* (pp. 256-270). San Diego: Avant Books.

Naess, A. (1986). The Deep Ecology movement: Some philosophical aspects. *Philosophical Inquiry, 8*, 10-31.

Naess, A. (1988). Self realization: An ecological approach to being in the world. In J. Seed, J. Macy, P. Fleming, & A. Naess, *Thinking like a mountain: Towards a council of all beings* (pp. 19-30). Philadelphia, PA: New Society Publishers.

Naess, A. (1989). *Ecology, community and lifestyle*. Cambridge: Cambridge University Press.

Naess, A. (2005). Self-realization: An ecological approach to being in the world. In A. Drengson, *The Selected Works of Arne Naess* (pp. 2781-2797). Dordrecht: Springer Netherlands.

Naval, C. C., & Repáraz, C. C. (2008). Spanish children's concerns for the future. *Citizenship Teaching and Learning, 4*(2), 31-42.

Neisser, U. (1988). Time present and time past. In M. M. Gruneberg, P. E. Morris, & R. N. Sykes, *Practical aspects of memory* (Vol. 2, pp. 545-560). New York: Wiley.

Nicholls, V. (2009). *Quiet time: A sense of solitude*. Presented at the Fourth International Outdoor Education Research Conference, Victoria, Australia.

Nicholsen, S. W. (2002). *The Love of Nature and the End of the World: The Unspoken Dimension of Environmental Concern*. Cambridge, MA: MIT Press.

Nolan, J. M., Schultz, P. W., Cialdini, R. B., Goldstein, N. J., & Griskevicius, V. (2008). Normative social influence is underdetected. *Personality and Social Psychology Bulletin, 34*(7), 913-923.

Obermiller, C. (1995). The baby is sick/the baby is well: A test of environmental communication appeals. *Journal of Advertising, 24*(2), 55-70.

Ojala, M. (2007). *Hope and worry: Exploring young people's values, emotions, and behavior regarding global environmental problems* (Doctoral dissertation), Örebro Studies in Psychology 11. Örebro University, Sweden.

Ojala, M. (2008). Recycling and ambivalence: Quantitative and qualitative analyses of household recycling among young adults. *Environment and Behavior, 40*(6), 777-797.

Ojala, M. (2012a). Hope and climate change: The importance of hope for environmental engagement among young people. *Environmental Education Research, 18*(5), 625-642.

Ojala, M. (2012b). Regulating worry, promoting hope: How do children, adolescents, and young adults cope with climate change? *International Journal of Environmental and Science Education, 7*(4), 537-561.

Ojala, M. (2013). Coping with climate change among adolescents: Implications for subjective well-being and environmental engagement. *Sustainability, 5*, 2191-2209.

Oskamp, S. (2000). A sustainable future for humanity. *American Psychologist, 55*, 496-508.

Palmer, J. A., Suggate, J., Bajd, B., Hart, P.K., Ho, R. K., Ofwono-Orecho, J. K. W., … van Staden, C. (1998). An overview of significant influences and formative experiences on the development of adults' environmental awareness in nine countries. *Environmental Education Research, 4*(4), 445-464.

Patterson, M. E., Williams, D. R., Watson, A. E., & Roggenbuck, J. W. (1998). An hermeneutic approach to studying the nature of wilderness experiences. *Journal of Leisure Research, 3*(4), 423-452.

Payne, P. (1999). The significance of experience in SLE Research. *Environmental Education Research, 5*(4), 365-381.

Pekala, R. J. (1991). *Quantifying consciousness- An empirical approach*. New York: Springer.

Pekala, R. J., Steinberg, J., & Kumar, V. K. (1986). Measurement of phenomenological experience: Phenomenology of consciousness inventory. *Perceptual and Motor Skills, 63*(2), 983-989.

Perrin, J. L., & Benassi, V. A. (2009). The connectedness to nature scale: A measure of emotional connection to nature? *Journal of Environmental Psychology, 29*(4), 434-440.

Peterson, C. (2000). The future of optimism. *American Psychologist, 55*(1), 44-55.

Peterson, C., & Seligman, M. E. P. (2004). *Character strengths and virtues: A handbook and classification*. Oxford, UK: Oxford University Press.

Plous, S. (1993). Psychological mechanisms in the human use of animals. *Journal of Social Issues, 49*(1), 11-52.

Quirin, M. & Kuhl, J. (2015). Selbstzugang [Self-access]. In M. A. Wirtz (Eds.), *Dorsch – Lexikon der Psychologie*. Retrieved from https://portal.hogrefe.com/dorsch/selbstzugang.

Popper, K. R. (1959). *The logic of scientific discovery*. London: Hutchinson.

Pretty, G. M. H. (1990). Relating psychological sense of community to social climate characteristics. *Journal of Community Psychology, 18*(1), 60-65.

Rader, S. S. (2009). *Ecopsychology revealed: An empirical look at the benefits of nature experience for human beings and the world*. Alliant International University, Los Angeles.

Reed, M. B., & Aspinwall, L. G. (1998). Self-affirmation reduces biased processing of health-risk information. *Motivation and Emotion, 22*(2), 99-132.

Rego, A., Sousa, F., Marques, C., & Cunha, M. P. E. (2012). Retail employees' self-efficacy and hope predicting their positive affect and creativity. *European Journal of Work and Organizational Psychology, 21*(6), 923-945.

Reininger, B., Evans, A. E., Griffin, S. F., Valois, R. F., Vincent, M. L., Parra Medina, D., … Zullig, K.J. (2003). Development of a youth survey to measure risk behaviors, attitudes and assets: Examining multiple influences. *Health Education Research, 18*(4), 461-476.

Rickinson, M. (2001). Learners and learning in environmental education: A critical review of the evidence. *Environmental Education Research, 7*(3), 207-320.

Rizzolatti, G., & Sinigaglia, C. (2010). The functional role of the parieto-frontal mirror circuit: Interpretations and misinterpretations. *Nature Reviews Neuroscience, 11*(4), 264-274.

Roesler, C. (2010). *Analytische Psychologie heute*. Freiburg: Karger Publishers.

Roggenbuck, J. W., & Driver, B. L. (2000). Benefits of non-facilitated uses of wilderness. In S. McCool, D. Cole, W. Borrie, & J. O'Loughlin, *Wilderness Science in a Time of Change Conference–Volume 3: Wilderness as a place for scientific inquiry* (pp. 33-49). Ogden, UT: U.S. Department of Agriculture, Forest Service, Rocky Mountain Research Station.

Romanyshyn, R. D. (2007). *The wounded researcher*. Spring Journal Books.

Rorty, R. (1999). *Philosophy and social hope*. Penguin Books Limited.

Roszak, T. (1979). *Person/Planet: The creative disintegration of industrial society*. New York: Doubleday.

Roszak, T. (1992). *The voice of the earth*. New York: Simon & Schuster.

Russell, B. (2007). *The Analysis of Matter*. Nottingham, UK: Spokesman Books.

Russell, R., Guerry, A. D., Balvanera, P., Gould, R. K., Basurto, X., Chan, K. M. A., ... Tam, J. (2013). Humans and nature: How knowing and experiencing nature affect well-being. *Annual Review of Environment and Resources, 38*(1), 473-502.

Rux, M. (2002). *Erprobung der deutschen Übersetzung des Phenomenology of Consciousness Inventory von Pekala: Normwerte, Gütekriterien, Änderungsvorschläge* [Testing the German version of the Phenomenology of Consciousness Inventory by Pekala]. Justus-Liebig-Universität Gießen, Gießen.

Sadalla, E., & Krull, J. (1995). Self-presentational barriers to resource conservation. *Environment and Behavior, 27,* 328-353.

Sandlos, J. (1998). The storied curriculum: Oral narrative, ethics, and environmental education. *The Journal of Environmental Education, 30*(1), 5-9.

Sanger, M. (1997). Sense of place and education. *The Journal of Environmental Education, 29*(1), 4-8.

Scherl, L. M. (1989). Self in wilderness: Understanding the psychological benefits of individual-wilderness interaction through self-control. *Leisure Sciences, 11*(2), 123-135.

Schopenhauer, A. (1974). Transcendent speculation on the apparent deliberateness in the fate of the individual. In E. F. J. Payne, *Parerga and paralipomena: Short philosophical essays* (Vol. 1, pp. 201-223). Oxford, UK: Clarendon: Clarendon Press.

Schredl, M. (2000). The effect of dreams on waking life. *Sleep and Hypnosis, 2*(3), 120-124.

Schultz, G. (1890). Feier der Deutschen Chemischen Gesellschaft zu Ehren August Kekulé's [Ceremony of the German Chemical Society in honour of August Kekulé]. *Berichte Der Deutschen Chemischen Gesellschaft, 23*(1), 1265-1321.

Schultz, P. W. (2002). Inclusion with nature: Psychology of human-nature relations. In P. Schmuck & P. W. Schultz, *Psychology of sustainable development* (pp. 61-78). Boston: Kluwer Academic Publishers.

Schultz, P. W. Gouveia, V.V., Cameron, L.D., Tankha, G., Schmuck, P. and Franek, M. (2005). Values and their relationship to environmental concern and conservation behavior. *Journal of Cross-Cultural Psychology, 36*(4), 457-475.

Schultz, P. W., & Tabanico, J. (2007). Self, identity, and the natural environment: Exploring implicit connections with nature. *Journal of Applied Social Psychology, 37*(6), 1219-1247.

Schultz, P. W., Nolan, J. M., Cialdini, R. B., Goldstein, N. J., & Griskevicius, V. (2007). The constructive, destructive, and reconstructive power of social norms. *Psychological Science, 18*(5), 429-434.

Schultz, P. W., Tabanico, J., & Rendón, T. (2008). Normative beliefs as agents of influence: Basic processes and real-world applications. In W. D. Crano & R. Prislin, *Attitudes and Attitude Change* (pp. 385-409). Psychology Press.

Seligman, M. E. (1975). *Helplessness: On depression, development and death*. San Francisco: W. H. Freeman.

Shapiro, S. L. (2009). The integration of mindfulness and psychology. *Journal of Clinical Psychology, 65*(6), 555-560.

Smith, T. (2005). Going outside to go inside: Frameworks for the solo experience. In C. Knapp & T. Smith, *Exploring the power of solo, silence, and solitude* (pp. 3-18). Boulder, CO: Association for Experiential Education.

Snell, T. L., & Simmonds, J. G. (2012). "Being in that environment can be very therapeutic": Spiritual experiences in nature. *Ecopsychology, 4*(4), 326-335.

Snyder, C. R. (2000). Genesis: The birth and growth of hope. In C. R. Snyder, *Handbook of hope* (pp. 25-38). San Diego: Academic Press.

Snyder, C. R., Rand, K. L., & Sigmon, D. R. (2002). Hope theory: A member of the positive psychology family. In C. R. Snyder & S. J. Lopez, *Handbook of positive psychology* (pp. 257-276). Nex York, NY: Oxford University Press.

Sparks, P., & Shepherd, R. (1992). Self-identity and the theory of planned behavior: Assessing the role of identification with "Green Consumerism," Social Psychology Quarterly, 55(4), 388-399. *Social Psychology Quarterly, 55*(4), 388-399.

Steg, L., & Vlek, C. A. J. (2009). Encouraging pro-environmental behaviour: An integrative review and research agenda. *Journal of Environmental Psychology, 29*, 309-317.

Stel, M., van Baaren, R. B., Blascovich, J., van Dijk, E., McCall, C., Pollmann, M. M. H., *et al.* (2010). Effects of a priori liking on the elicitation of mimicry. *Experimental Psychology, 57*(6), 412-418.

Stickgold, R., Hobson, J. A., Fosse, R., & Fosse, M. (2001). Sleep, learning, and dreams: Off-line memory reprocessing. *Science, 294*(5544), 1052-1057.

Stöber, J. (2001). The Social Desirability Scale-17 (SDS-17). *European Journal of Psychological Assessment, 17*(3), 222-232.

Strauch, I., & Meier, B. (1996). *In search of dreams: Results of experimental dream research*. Albany, NY: State University of New York Press.

Strauss, K., Niven, K., R McClelland, C., & Cheung, B. K. T. (2014). Hope and optimism in the face of change: Contributions to task adaptivity. *Journal of Business and Psychology*.

Stukas, A. A., Clary, E. G., & Snyder, M. (1999). Service learning: Who benefits and why? *Social Policy Report: Society for Research in Child Development*, 13, 1-19.

Sward, L. L. (1999). Significant life experiences affecting the environmental sensitivity of El Salvadoran environmental professionals. *Environmental Education Research, 5*(2), 201-206.

Talbot, J. F., & Kaplan, S. (1986). Perspectives on wilderness: Re-examining the value of extended wilderness experiences. *Journal of Environmental Psychology, 6*(3), 177-188.

Tam, K.-P. (2013). Concepts and measures related to connection to nature: Similarities and differences. *Journal of Environmental Psychology, 34*, 64-78.

Tam, K.-P., Lee, S.-L., & Chao, M. M. (2013). Saving Mr. Nature: Anthropomorphism enhances connectedness to and protectiveness toward nature. *Journal of Experimental Social Psychology, 49*(3), 514-521.

Tanner, T. (1980). Significant life experiences: A new research area in environmental education. *The Journal of Environmental Education, 11*(4), 20-24.

Tashakkori, A., & Teddlie, C. (1998). *Mixed methodology: Combining qualitative and quantitative approaches*. Thousand Oaks, CA: SAGE.

Tashakkori, A., & Teddlie, C. (2003). *Handbook of mixed methods in social and behavioral research*. Thousand Oaks, CA: SAGE Publications.

Teddlie, C., & Tashakkori, A. (2009). *Foundations of mixed methods research: Integrating quantitative and qualitative approaches in the social and behavioral sciences*. Thousand Oaks, CA: SAGE Publications.

Terhaar, T. L. (2009). Evolutionary advantages of intense spiritual experience in nature. *Journal for the Study of Religion, Nature and Culture, 3*(3), 303-339.

Thomashow, M. (1995). *Ecological identity: Becoming a reflective environmentalist*. Cambridge, MA: MIT Press.

Threadgold, S. (2012). "I reckon my life will be easy, but my kids will be buggered": Ambivalence in young people's positive perceptions of individual futures and their visions of environmental collapse. *Journal of Youth Studies, 15*(1), 17-32.

Ulrich, R. S. (1984). View through a window may influence revovery from surgery. *Science, 224*(4647), 420-421.

United Nations Department of Economic and Social Affairs. (2014). *World urbanization prospects: The 2014 revision*. Retrieved from http://esa.un.org/unpd/wup/Highlights/WUP2014-Highlights.pdf.

Valli, K., Revonsuo, A., Pälkäs, O., Ismail, K. H., Ali, K. J., & Punamäki, R.-L. (2005). The threat simulation theory of the evolutionary function of dreaming: Evidence from dreams of traumatized children. *Consciousness and Cognition, 14*(1), 188-218.

Van Baaren, R., Janssen, L., Chartrand, T. L., & Dijksterhuis, A. (2009). Where is the love? The social aspects of mimicry. *Philosophical Transactions of the Royal Society B: Biological Sciences, 364*(1528), 2381-2389.

Van Genepp, A. (1960). *The rites of passage*. Chicago: University of Chicago Press.

Vining, J., Merrick, M. S., & Price, E. A. (2008). The distinction between humans and nature: Human perceptions of connectedness to nature and elements of the natural and unnatural. *Human Ecology Review, 15*(1), 1.

Wagner, U., Gais, S., Haider, H., Verleger, R., & Born, J. (2004). Sleep inspires insight. *Nature, 427*(6972), 352-355.

Walach, H. (2014). *Secular spirituality: The next step towards enlightenment*. Springer International Publishing.

Walach, H., & Stillfried, von, N. (2011). Generalised quantum theory—Basic idea and general intuition: A background story and overview. *Axiomathes, 21*(2), 185-209.

Webb, O. J., Eves, F. F., & Smith, L. (2011). Investigating behavioural mimicry in the context of stair/escalator choice. *British Journal of Health Psychology, 16*(2), 373-385.

Weber, A. (2013). *Enlivenment- Towards a fundamental shift in the concepts of nature, culture and politics*. Berlin, Germany: Heinrich Böll Foundation.

Weigert, A. J. (1997). *Self, interaction, and natural environment*. Albany: State University of New York Press.

Weinstein, N., Przybylski, A. K., & Ryan, R. M. (2009). Can nature make us more caring? Effects of immersion in nature on intrinsic aspirations and generosity. *Personality and Social Psychology Bulletin, 35*(10), 1315-1329.

Wells, N. M., & Lekies, K. S. (2006). Nature and the life course: Pathways from childhood nature experiences to adult environmentalism. *Children, Youth and Environments, 16*(1), 1-24.

Wheeldon, J., & Ahlberg, M. K. (2011). Mapping mixed-methods research: Theories, models, and measures. In *Visualizing social science research: Maps, methods, and meaning*. Thousand Oaks, CA: Sage Publications.

White, M. P., Alcock, I., Wheeler, B. W., & Depledge, M. H. (2013). Would you be happier living in a greener urban area? A fixed-effects analysis of panel data. *Psychological Science, 24*(6), 920-928.

Whitmarsh, L., & O'Neill, S. (2010). Green identity, green living? The role of pro-environmental self-identity in determining consistency across diverse pro- environmental behaviours. *Journal of Environmental Psychology, 30*(3), 305-314.

Wildman, W.J. & McNamara, P. (2010). Evaluating reliance on narratives in the psychological study of religious experiences. *International Journal for the Psychology of Religion, 20(4)*, 223-254.

Williams, K., & Harvey, D. (2001). Transcendent experience in forest environments. *Journal of Environmental Psychology, 21*(3), 249-260.

Wilson, E. O. (1984). *Biophilia*. Cambridge, MA: Harvard University Press.

Winter, D. D. N., & Koger, S. M. (2004). *The psychology of environmental problems* (2nd ed.). Mahwah, NJ: Lawrence Erlbaum Associates.

World Health Organization (2012). *Depression: A Global Crisis, World Mental Health Day, October 10, 2012*, Retrieved from http://www.who.int/mental_health/management/depression/wfmh_paper_depression_wmhd_2012.pdf.

Zavestoski, S. (2003). Constructing and maintaining ecological identities: The strategies of deep ecologists. In S. Clayton & S. Opotow, *Identity and the natural environment* (pp. 297-315). Cambridge, MA: MIT Press.

Zelenski, J. M., & Nisbet, E. K. (2014). Happiness and feeling connected: The distinct role of nature relatedness. *Environment and Behavior, 46*(1), 3-23.

Zelezny, L. C. (1999). Educational interventions that improve environmental behaviors: A meta-analysis. *The Journal of Environmental Education, 31*(1), 5-14.

Zhang, J. W., Howell, R. T., & Iyer, R. (2014). Engagement with natural beauty moderates the positive relation between connectedness with nature and psychological well-being. *Journal of Environmental Psychology, 38*, 55-63.

Zhang, J. W., Piff, P. K., Iyer, R., Koleva, S., & Keltner, D. (2014). An occasion for unselfing: Beautiful nature leads to prosociality. *Journal of Environmental Psychology, 37*, 61-72.

Zimmerman, J. M., & Coyle, V. (1996). *The way of council*. Las Vegas, NV: Bramble Books.

Zimmerman, M. A. (1990). Toward a theory of learned hopefulness: A structural model analysis of participation and empowerment. *Journal of Research in Personality, 24*, 71-86.

Zimmerman, M. A. (2000). Empowerment theory: Psychological, organizational and community levels of analysis. In J. Rappaport & E. Seidman (Eds.), *Handbook of community psychology* (pp.43-63). New York, NY: Kluwer.

Appendices

Appendix A
Rules of transcription

Theme	Representation in transcript	Explanation
Anonymisation	BF1	Capital abbreviation of sample and consecutive numbering as synonyms for interviewees' names
Accentuation	VERY	Word in capital letters
Prolongation	nooo	Several vowels in a row
Para-linguistic actions and events	(LAUGHTER) (SIGHS)	Description in capital letters in brackets
Pauses	* ** *3*	Short pause Longer pause Duration in seconds
Incomprehensible text segment	(INCOMP.: 12:36)	Time specification (minutes:seconds) on audio recording
Speakers interrupt each other	Interviewee: I wanted// Interviewer: How do you feel now?	Double slash (//)
False starts, incomplete sentences	Then we went–Originally, the idea was to go home.	EM-dash
Upper and lower case	We checked the Internet.	Conventional use
Specification of references in excerpts	"Here (REMARK: Butterfly camp) I did not think about it."	Unclear references (in speech) that solely result from the process of extracting interview excerpts are specified in brackets labelled with "REMARK".
Punctuation	:;.,!?	Conventional use

Excluded from transcription: feedback words and sounds within a sentence

Appendix B

Man-Whitney test significance values for differences between the Butterfly and Solo-only sample regarding the PCI dimensions.

Null hypothesis for the PCI dimensions	Significance value	Decision
The distribution of the „altered experience dimension" is the same for both groups.	,711[1]	Null hypothesis is not rejected.
The distribution for „body image" is the same for both groups.	,967[1]	Null hypothesis is not rejected.
The distribution for „time sense" is the same for both groups.	,592[1]	Null hypothesis is not rejected.
The distribution for „perception" is the same for both groups.	,483[1]	Null hypothesis is not rejected.
The distribution for „unusual meanings" is the same for both groups.	,923[1]	Null hypothesis is not rejected.
The distribution for „positive affect" is the same for both groups.	,500[1]	Null hypothesis is not rejected.
The distribution for „joy" is the same for both groups.	,328[1]	Null hypothesis is not rejected.
The distribution for „sexual excitement" is the same for both groups.	,386[1]	Null hypothesis is not rejected.
The distribution for „love" is the same for both groups.	,858[1]	Null hypothesis is not rejected.
The distribution for „negative affect" is the same for both groups.	,631[1]	Null hypothesis is not rejected.
The distribution for „anger" is the same for both groups.	,711[1]	Null hypothesis is not rejected.
The distribution for „sadness" is the same for both groups.	,731[1]	Null hypothesis is not rejected.
The distribution for „fear" is the same for both groups.	,815[1]	Null hypothesis is not rejected.
The distribution for „attention" is the same for both groups.	,815[1]	Null hypothesis is not rejected.
The distribution for „direction of attention" is the same for both groups.	,573[1]	Null hypothesis is not rejected.
The distribution for „absorbtion" is the same for both groups.	,650[1]	Null hypothesis is not rejected.
The distribution for „imagery" is the same for both groups.	,098[1]	Null hypothesis is not rejected.
The distribution for „imagery amount" is the same for both groups.	,092[1]	Null hypothesis is not rejected.
The distribution for „imagery vividness" is the same for both groups.	,314[1]	Null hypothesis is not rejected.
The distribution for „self-awareness" is the same for both groups.	,902[1]	Null hypothesis is not rejected.
The distribution for „altered state of awareness" is the same for both groups.	,945[1]	Null hypothesis is not rejected.
The distribution for „arousal" is the same for both groups.	,417[1]	Null hypothesis is not rejected.
The distribution for „rationality" is the same for both groups.	,731[1]	Null hypothesis is not rejected.
The distribution for „volitional control" is the same for both groups.	,752[1]	Null hypothesis is not rejected.
The distribution for „memory" is the same for both groups.	,837[1]	Null hypothesis is not rejected.
The distribution for „internal dialogue" is the same for both groups.	,082[1]	Null hypothesis is not rejected.

Appendix C
Daily Butterfly Programme

Day 1, 13.8.

Theme of the day: Travel to Findhorn

Overall aim: To have all participants at the camp

	Activity	Method	Learning
AM	Travel		
PM	Travel, setting up camp	Finding own space, putting up tents	Pitching tent, basics of camp life
Evening	Dinner and welcome activities	Open evening, non-structured activities for those who arrive	First contact and names

Day 2, 14.8.

Theme of the day: Group building, Introduction

Overall aim: To know all names and countries, to become familiar with the place, to understand context of the project.

	Activity	Method	Learning
AM	Group building activities	Name games, icebreakers	People know the names, countries and feel OK in the group, have basic confidence
	Programme intro - context, aims, methods, times. - practical info, service groups and structure	Presentation	Understanding the aims of the exchange, clarity about the structure of service groups.
PM	**Expectations + previous experience of participants**	Work in pairs and small group work, sharing	People summarise their expectations, share the main ones.
	Learning + Youthpass intro	Simulation, presentation - main learning styles, comfort – stretch – panic zone. Preparing personal learning diary	Understanding learning preferences. Awareness about Youthpass as a tool for reflection and evaluation.
	YiA context and info	Puzzle in small groups + short presentation, collecting experience of participants.	Knowing about YiA main priorities, objectives and basic structure. Place of our project in YiA
Evening	**Diversity evening** - personal	Sharing stories connected with a personal object.	Openness towards the group, confidence, learning more about the others.

Day 3, 15.8.

Theme of the day: First taste

Overall aim: To learn more about the place, to taste the flavours of the group and group work

	Activity	Method	Learning
AM	**Morning check-in** (daily in following days)	Council type of activity, (with a new theme each day)	Focus on the programme, hear personal needs, summarise personal goals
	Service (daily in following days)	Managing the campsite	Practical skills for camping and light-weight lifestyle, responsibility for self and group
	Findhorn ecovillage tour	Guided tour	Orientation in the village, history, main activities, rules…
	Connect with the place and community	Dynamic group game, debriefing	More about the place and the people. Contact with the locals. Fun, movement, familiarity with the place.
PM	**Council intro and practice**	Council as a method – explanation and practice of different types of council.	Listening, speaking the essence, group as a tool for self-reflection.
	Group reflection intro and practice	Dividing into groups and explaining the system of group reflection. Later daily a new tool for creative reflection will be offered.	Sharing the outcomes of the day in a small group, group as a support tool, collecting personal needs and wishes, responsibility.
	Preparation for the evening	Country group preparation	Check in with Country group, cultural expression, efficiency, creativity, improvisation.
Evening	**Diversity evening**	Common evening. Each group presents their local products, preferably organic, with the context and story.	Compare the situation in organic and local food usage in each country. Cultural diversity.

Day 4, 16.8.

Theme of the day: Our environment

Overall aim: To explore the resources, to experience nature-based methodology especially deep ecology

	Activity	Method	Learning
AM	**Resources and energies** - water, wood, fire, electricity, rubbish, cleaning systems…	Treasure hunt, group work, presentation, discussion.	How the energies and resources work in the community, what are their sources and stories.
PM	**Gaia and deep ecology** - intro and practice	Introduction, simulation exercise, presentation, individual reflection, discussion	Gaia theory, Deep ecology background, experience of the connection with nature.
	Evening group reflection (as set up on the day before, daily in following days)	Small group work with creative tools.	Sharing the outcomes of the day in a small group, group as a support tool, collecting personal needs and wishes, responsibility for self and others
Evening	**Movie night**	Movie with a related theme, eg. "The Eleventh Hour"	Impulse for thinking and discussions, inspiration

Day 5, 17.8.

Theme of the day: Our community

Overall aim: Understanding what community is and can be

	Activity	Method	Learning
AM	**Community life models incl. Findhorn example** - roles, structure, money, decision making, activities..	World café with local representatives, small group work, presentation, discussion, sharing.	What are possible scenarios for community life, decision making, monetary structures. What is the local system in Findhorn, pros/ cons.
PM	**Work for the place**	Practical help on different places in the eco-village with the explanation of reason and context.	Practical skills, knowledge about gardening, foresting, permaculture.
	Free afternoon slot	Free time	Relax, self-reflection.
Evening	**Free, bonfire..**	Bonfire	Songs, games.

Day 6, 18.8.

Theme of the day: Outdoor life

Overall aim: Setting up a camp, learning about camping.

	Activity	Method	Learning
AM	**Packing, leaving the camp, crossing the bay to Culbin**	Walk and crossing the bay by taxi boat to the Culbin Sands.	Efficient packing for walking trip.
PM	**Setting up the camp in Culbin Outdoor life practical workshops I**	Practical workshops in small groups about ropes, knots, tents, making fire, cooking outside, storing things, managing water.	Skills and knowledge for camping with limited equipment and resources, teamwork.
Evening	**Sharing stories and songs about and from life outdoors**	Discussion around fire	Inspiration, communication skills.

Day 7, 19.8.

Theme of the day: Life in the nature

Overall aim: Preparing for 24h solo time.

	Activity	Method	Learning
AM	**Threshold practice and the mirror of nature**	Explanation of Threshold practice, experience, sharing in small groups.	Learning about Threshold as a method, individually define the reason for going out for the 24h solo
PM	**Going through the solo area**	Walk around the limits of the solo area, marking it clearly.	Where are the borders, personal health and safety in the outdoors, concept of "challenge by choice"
	Find your spot	Individual time for finding the right spot.	Connection with nature, self-reflection.
	Practical workshops II	Small groups.	Learning to set up a tarp, how to live and behave during the 24 hours solo time.
Evening	**The Four Shields , Songs for the Solo**	Presentation and discussion at the camp fire	The psychological model of The Four Shields, learning songs that might support the solo experience

Day 8, 20.8.

Theme of the day: Solo

Overall aim: Being with oneself: personal reflection and growth

	Activity	Method	Learning
AM PM Evening	24h solo	Packing, Participants are leaving for their places. Setting up the personal space, enjoying the solo.	Being alone, self-reflection, setting up a place for oneself, deep contact with nature and the place. Reflection on personal themes.

Day 9, 21.8.

Theme of the day: Return

Overall aim: Closing the solo experience, returning to the group, going back to the main camp.

	Activity	Method	Learning
AM	Return from the solo to the base camp, sharing stories and mirroring	Small group discussion and mirroring the stories – interpretation, explanation.	Meanings of personal stories, more possible explanations, learning from each other, inspiration, openness.
PM	Return to the Findhorn camp	Packing the camp in Culbin, walk and taxi boat back to Findhorn camp.	How to leave the campsite clean and with as little impact as possible.
Evening	Free, optional activities	Hot tub, drumming, bonfire … Experience of group and its dynamics after solitary time	

Day 10, 22.8.

Theme of the day: Nature, creativity and art

Overall aim: Expression using creative expression in a natural environment

	Activity	Method	Learning
AM	Mid-term evaluation Free morning	Creative evaluation in pairs, small groups and Council in the whole group.	Summary of achieved knowledge and skills, looking back at the expectations, setting up new personal goals to be reached until the end of the exchange.
PM	Creativity and art in nature	Introduction, short input as inspiration, collecting proposals, small project group work	To understand nature and environment in context, awareness of the connections, expressing it in a creative way.
Evening	5 rhythms dance	Joining the regular activity of community.	Expression through movement, body awareness.

Day 11, 23.8.

Theme of the day: Open space

Overall aim: Giving the space for sharing, personal interests and needs.

	Activity	Method	Learning
AM	Plants, animals and humans	Part I. – Introduction, small group work – exploring, sharing. Part II – practical workshops with explanation.	Role of plants and animals in the community, understanding interconnectivity, basic practical skills and experience with animals
PM	Open space I	Open space technology to respond to personal learning needs of participants and to offer space for sharing the richness of the group.	According to the attendance and theme on the slots.
Evening	Open space II		

Day 12, 24.8.

Theme of the day: Practice

Overall aim: Local impact, present the results

	Activity	Method	Learning
AM	Project for the community II	Groups design a small project to contribute something to the community using the knowledge and skills gained in previous days.	Practice sustainable life; develop sensitivity for the place, group communication and cooperation.
PM	Presentation of the projects, reflection.	Groups present the outcomes and the process of making the project.	Variability, creativity.
	Country groups input, sharing realities and possibilities	Country groups prepare a small reflection based on the experience of the exchange compared to their local conditions and reality. They point out connections and areas of possible change.	Reality in other countries, diversity, areas of possible future activities
Evening	Presentation for the community	Open evening at the campsite for the community of Findhorn; pax present outcomes of the project.	Presentation skills, creativity.

Day 13, 25.8.

Theme of the day: Transfer, closure.

Overall aim: Design ideas for follow-up projects, evaluate, close the exchange.

	Activity	Method	Learning
AM	**YiA II – more practical info**	World cafe style session with different themes of YiA (actions, project cycle, non-formal learning)	YiA basics according to individual interests.
	Future planning, Transfer	Introduction, individual proposals, groups based on the proposals, small group work.	Cooperation, transfer into practice.
	Learning II + Youthpass	Making individual learning summary based on the learning diary.	Learning summary possibly used later for Youthpass, self-reflection.
PM	**Check-out council**	Last closing council session	Listening to the group, sharing overall experience.
	Evaluation	Variety of activities to evaluate different aspects of the project – written, expressive, painted. Last small group reflection.	Summarising all the different aspects of the project (programme, group, practicalities…), realizing the outcomes, being creative.
	De-connection	Short expressive activity to disconnect from the place and people.	Being aware that everything ends, prevent feelings of unfinished business.
Evening	**Final evening**	Party prepared by participants.	Creativity, improvisation in given conditions.

Day 14, 26.8.

Theme of the day: Departure

Overall aim:

	Activity	Method	Learning
AM	Break camp, clean up, Goodbye, departure	Groups work	Cleaning up and leaving things in order is an important part of project work

Acknowledgements

It seems almost impossible to come up with an exhaustive list of everyone and everything I want to give thanks to.

If I were to go in chronological order my deepest gratitude goes to the wild places I visited, inside and out. My experiences in, with and as nature widened my perspective on life to an immeasurable degree. Without these experiences I would not have had the curiosity, courage and foundation to initiate the present research.

On that note, I would like to express my gratitude for the beautiful shady oak tree in Ojai under whose branches I talked about the present research endeavour for the first time. I am also thankful to my friend Yvan who was with me then and who asked the right questions.

I am aware of and grateful for both of their support and presence, which back then enabled me to dream my ideas out loud.

I would like to thank my supervisor Harald for selflessly encouraging me to follow my research idea. His open-mindedness towards new ideas and approaches impresses and inspires me over and over again. The things I have learned from him are beyond words.

I am also grateful to my second supervisor Mags who appeared at the right time and place and agreed to accompany me on this journey just because she believed in it. Mags challenged me to go deeper and become more adventurous and authentic. With her I discovered yet another side to research and female leadership.

I am thankful to have experienced with both my supervisors that professionalism, guidance and friendship are not mutually exclusive.

On a very fundamental level, I found the greatest support in those people who believed in me even when I had trouble to do so. These include my partner Andi and my dear and faithful friends Heike, Paula and Anna who helped me through recurrent lean periods.

I would also like to thank my parents who seeded my connection with nature and my way of experiencing the world by taking me out as a child and filling me with countless rich and colourful stories.

The essence of my research, though, are the participants and people who allowed me to take part in their programmes. I am genuinely grateful to the study participants who shared their rich, wise and beautiful stories with me. I learned a lot from each one of them and it truly felt like a gift to have been trusted in this way.

Lastly, I want to say thank you to Andi who has always supported, encouraged and believed in me one-hundred percent. I know for sure that the last year of writing up would not have been possible without him. I am so very grateful for the incalculable source of strength that Andi along with my son Mio brought to my life and this work.

In the spirit of the butterfly effect, it is my intention to pass on the countless gifts I received throughout my research journey whenever possible.